STROLL

Psychogeographic Walking Tours of T...

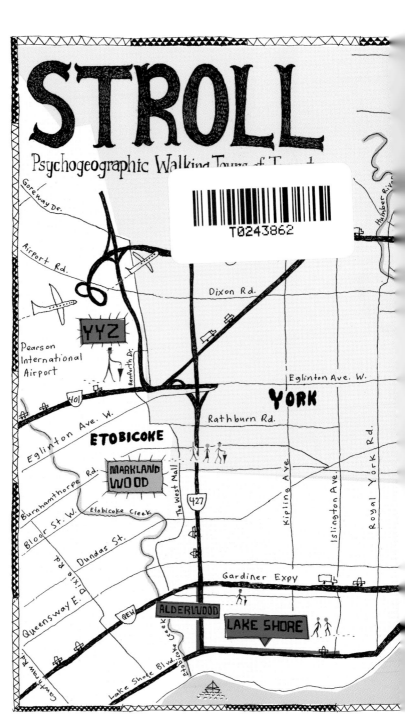

T0243862

Finch Ave. E.

Sheppard Ave E.

48

ROUGE PARK

McCowan Rd.

Altona Rd.

SCARBOROUGH CITY CENTRE

smere Rd.

SCARBOROUGH

BENDALE

Lawrence Ave E.

Markham Rd.

Highland Park

Morningside Ave.

Port Union Rd.

Lower Highland Park

Brimley Rd.

Midland Ave.

KINGSTON GALLOWAY

ngston Rd.

STROLL LEGEND

- Alderwood/Lake Shore Blvd 118
- Bathurst Street 139
- The Beach 306
- Castle Frank/Brick Works 294
- CNE/Western Waterfront 128
- CN Tower 64
- Danforth/Crescent Town 264
- Dorset Park 243
- Downtown East Side 271
- Dundas Street 96
- Dupont Street 154

- Eglinton/Borough of York 186
- Finch Hydro Corridor 214
- Gerrard Street 299
- Harbourfront 57
- Kingston-Galloway/ Guildwood Village/ The Bluffs 223
- Markland Wood 115
- NPS/Sheraton Ctr/ PATH 68
- Pearson Airport 109
- Port Lands/Leslie Spit 310

- Rouge Park 218
- Scarborough City Centre/Bendale/ Meadoway 231
- Sheppard Line 205
- Spadina 162
- St. Clair Ave 177
- Thorncliffe/ Flemingdon Park/ Don Mills 251
- Toronto Islands 51
- University Ave 79
- Yonge Street 18
- Yorkdale/Lawrence Heights 195
- Yorkville 88

* This map is not to scale.

© marlena zuber

NORTH

N

NE

E

STROLL

STROLL

PSYCHOGEOGRAPHIC WALKING
TOURS OF TORONTO

UPDATED EDITION

SHAWN MICALLEF

ILLUSTRATIONS BY MARLENA ZUBER

COACH HOUSE BOOKS, TORONTO

Second Edition

 Canada Council   Conseil des Arts Canadä
for the Arts   du Canada

 ONTARIO ARTS COUNCIL
CONSEIL DES ARTS DE L'ONTARIO   **Ontario** 🏵
an Ontario government agency
un organisme du gouvernement de l'Ontario

Published with the generous assistance of the Canada Council for the Arts and the
Ontario Arts Council. Coach House Books also acknowledges the support of the
Government of Canada through the Canada Book Fund.

LIBRARY AND ARCHIVES CANADA CATALOGUING IN PUBLICATION

Title: Stroll : psychogeographic walking tours of Toronto / by Shawn Micallef; illustrations by Marlena Zuber.
Names: Micallef, Shawn, author. | Zuber, Marlena, illustrator.
Description: Updated edition. | Includes index.
Identifiers: Canadiana (print) 20240283767 | Canadiana (ebook) 20240283813 | ISBN
9781552454800 (softcover) | ISBN 9781770568075 (EPUB) | ISBN 9781770568082 (PDF)
Subjects: LCSH: Walking—Ontario—Toronto—Guidebooks. | LCSH: Toronto (Ont.)—
Description and travel. | LCGFT: Guidebooks.
Classification: LCC FC3097.3 .S87 2024 | DDC 971.3/541—dc23

Stroll: Pyschogeographic Walking Tours of Toronto is available as an ebook: ISBN 978 1 77056
807 5 (EPUB), ISBN 978 1 77056 808 2 (PDF)

Table of Contents

Foreword

A new, cool style of engaging and enjoying metropolitan realities has recently emerged in Toronto among certain young writers, artists, architects, and persons without portfolio. These people can be recognized by their careful gaze at things most others ignore: places off the tourist map of Toronto's notable sights, the clutter of sidewalk signage and graffiti, the grain inscribed on the urban surface by the drift of populations and the cuts of fashion.

Their typical tactic is the stroll. The typical product of strolling is knowledge that cannot be acquired merely by studying maps, guidebooks, and statistics. Rather, it is a matter of the body, knowing the city by pacing off its streets and neighbourhoods, recovering the deep, enduring traces of our inhabitation by encountering directly the fabric of buildings and the legends we have built here during the last two centuries. Some of these strollers, including Shawn Micallef, have joined forces to make *Spacing* magazine. But Shawn has done more than that. He has recorded his strolls in EYE WEEKLY, and these meditations, in turn, have provided the raw material for the present book. The result you have in your hands is a new introduction to Toronto as it reveals itself to the patient walker, and an invitation to walk abroad on our own errands of discovery, uncovering the memories, codes, and messages hidden in the text that is the city.

Foreword from first edition, Toronto, 2010
John Bentley Mays, 1941–2016

His writing, especially his book *Emerald City: Toronto Visited*, was an inspiration for *Stroll*.

A Flâneur Manifesto

With each step, the walk takes on greater momentum; ever weaker grow the temptations of shops, of bistros, of smiling women, ever more irresistible the magnetism of the next streetcorner, of a distant mass of foliage, of a street name.

— Walter Benjamin, *The Arcades Project*

In a quarter century of walking around Toronto, it has never become boring to me. The city routinely has the capacity to reveal heretofore hidden details, sometimes in plain sight, in neighbourhoods I thought I knew: a side street I hadn't noticed, a plaza unvisited, or a ravine reach I've not yet wandered. Again and again. It's the sign of a good city.

Writing this, I feel like I'm paying homage to Samuel Johnson's famous quote from 1777, when he was trying to convince James Boswell that London would never become a bore if he moved there from Scotland, that it would elicit the same excitement as it did during his visits. 'Why, Sir, you find no man, at all intellectual, who is willing to leave London. No, Sir, when a man is tired of London, he is tired of life; for there is in London all that life can afford.' Intellectual or not, Toronto remains a compelling place to explore.

Even if Toronto had remained static since 2010, when this book was first published – a city-as-museum as some famous places become – I'd wager it would remain compelling for a long time, so vast and layered it is. But it never stopped changing. Toronto almost endlessly reinvents itself, even if many of its residents complain that it's too much, too fast. If your job is to pay attention to Toronto, as mine sort of has been, the speed of its change can surprise and even shock: *Where did* that *come from?*

Undertaking an update of this book nearly fifteen years after it was 'finished' was supposed to be an easy job, but as I started to walk up Yonge Street, the book's first chapter, I realized within a block that this was going to be a major effort. Every detail, every observation needed to be checked again – to see if it was still the same or, even, if it still existed. Every walk needed to be rewalked with a copy of the original book in one hand and a pen in the other, to cross things out and add in marginalia, a new city replacing the recent one. Usually, we register change one building or storefront at a time, every now and then; considering nearly fifteen years of changes all at once impressed on me the magnitude of Toronto's transformation. And yet, much remained of that not-so-old city too. The process of revisiting it all reminded me that I very much love this place, even if it can be extremely frustrating sometimes. All great cities can evoke these extremes in emotion.

When I was growing up in Windsor and occasionally visiting Toronto, it seemed like a spaceport city, made up of places like the Eaton Centre, Ontario Place, and the CN Tower. It had subways that ran underneath the city like an electric bloodstream and streetcars that rumbled above, street ships promising total freedom and complete mobility that could be hopped onto and off of at will. An acquaintance described the streets, seen from the Gardiner Expressway, as like a microchip firing away. It seemed endless and exciting. That postwar *Clockwork Orange*–style modernism caught my eye first, a result of the city's incredible midcentury boom, yet through the gaps I'd catch glimpses of row houses, ravines, and streets like Dundas or Davenport that weren't space age at all. These places seemed like a kind of remixed British colonial landscape, and I didn't know how they fit with the Toronto I thought I knew. The city was asking to be explored.

When I moved here in 2000, my internal Toronto map had big blank spots. I knew the landmarks, and streets like Yonge or Queen that must be walked during visits to the city, but once I got here I was struck by how big the place was and how much of it I didn't know. Not knowing where the streets ended, where College Street went after it curved in Little Italy or why the Queen streetcars said 'Long Branch' on them, made me nervous, as I knew the city I came from inside out (or so I thought). So I started walking. I walked out to the Beach and the Kingsway, negotiated the PATH system, tried to make it across Rosedale without ending up where I started, forgetting about food and water as the city distracted me. In short, I turned into a flâneur, someone who wanders the city with the sole purpose of paying attention to it.

The first edition of *Stroll* was made up of observations compiled during the first ten years I lived in Toronto. It was a process of joyful discovery, and I consider it a kind of informal thesis project after a period of long study. In the beginning, I wrote down what I saw on my walks and emailed these thoughts in dispatches to a list of friends. Some asked to be taken off my list, but I kept walking and writing while trying to figure out how this city works, who's here, how it's all put together, what's a street or two over, where strangely named neighbourhoods lie, and, ultimately, what Toronto means. I'll likely never completely figure out that last point, so I'll keep walking.

Later, I poured those observations into my *Psychogeography* column in the late, great EYE *Weekly* newspaper, and into my *Flâneur* column at *Spacing* magazine, which continues to this day. Those columns, greatly expanded, became the core of the original *Stroll*. Since 2012, I've been writing a weekly column in the *Toronto Star* that is a blend of exploration and commentary on politics and urban life. That, and other city writing, contributed to this updated edition, replacing outdated text or expanding existing chapters. As the process of updating became overwhelming when the magnitude of civic change was apparent, I decided to expand rather than create new walks. Yet, even with over 100,000 words dedicated to exploring, I look at the map at the back of this book indicating where I walked, and it feels like I barely touched the city. I filled in more areas with my 2017 book, *Frontier City: Toronto on the Verge of Greatness*, but there is an awful lot more for other people to explore and write about. Toronto needs more people writing about it.

It's an odd place. Over and over, we're told that Toronto is not Paris, New York, London, or Tokyo. There's a built-in comparison to other cities, perhaps a colonial hangover. The sentiment that Toronto is no good often comes from within: nobody will run down Toronto quicker than a Torontonian, something that doesn't happen in, say, Montreal. We've been trained to be underwhelmed, and our attention is directed elsewhere. There are references all over the city that remind us that this place started out as a provincial city in a distant part of the British Empire, with streets named after places and people in the colonial mothership, often people who never visited here, all reminders of how Brit-focused Toronto was during the sliver of time Europeans were here, but few names to represent the more than ten thousand years of human history here.

Toronto was not designed to be a great city. Its nicknames were 'Muddy York' and 'Hogtown,' after all. Since Toronto seems to exist without design or reason, we don't expect to turn the corner and see beauty or be amazed. Canadians from coast to coast are taught to hate Toronto, even if they can't always articulate why. But when you really talk to Torontonians about their city, after they've run through the perfunctory down-on-Toronto spiel to assuage their guilty feelings about the matter, many people are genuinely amazed about being Torontonian. People need permission, a nudge even, to reveal they like, maybe even love, Toronto. Going for a walk can expedite that.

Any Toronto flâneur knows that exploring this city causes the burden of civic self-deprecation to disappear. And anybody can be a Toronto flâneur.

More people should take the opportunity because this city is more than the sum of its parts, but those parts can be found only on foot. As American essayist Rebecca Solnit writes in her book *Wanderlust: A History of Walking*, to walk a place, city or otherwise, is to travel at a speed where one can notice things and be able to make sense of them. 'I like walking because it is slow, and I suspect that the mind, like the feet, works at about three miles an hour,' she writes. 'If this is so, then modern life is moving faster than the speed of thought or thoughtfulness.' In a city where the speed of change is intense, a walk is even more important.

A flâneur is anyone who wanders, and watches, the city. The nineteenth-century French poet Charles Baudelaire called the flâneur a 'perfect idler' and a 'passionate observer.' Baudelaire was a flâneur himself, and when he wasn't writing poems and spending his trust fund on dandy outfits and opium, he drifted through the streets of Paris. Later, philosopher Walter Benjamin collected a chunk of thoughts on the idea of the flâneur in his epic volume of notes on Paris, *The Arcades Project*. The flâneur wanders the city, slightly invisible, just on the outside of everything – observing from an anonymous perspective.

That invisibility can disappear, however, if you're not a man, or your skin colour is just a shade or two away from white. What I've done in this book – walk largely unnoticed – may not be possible for everybody. I have some unearned luck: I fit the traditional mould of a flâneur more easily than many others. The notion of the flâneur will be different for whoever engages in this activity, even in a diverse metropolis like Toronto. But that doesn't mean that other flâneurs can't carve out ways to navigate the city comfortably, recording their own insights and noticing the ways their own particular bodies and histories interact with the cityscape. Over the last decade there's been something of a renaissance in *flâneurie* and the notion is being expanded to more and more people. For instance, in her 2017 book *Flâneuse: Women Walk the City in Paris, New York, Tokyo, Venice, and London*, author Lauren Elkin looks at how women writers have inhabited the persona and method of the flâneur, overtly or not, in order to explore and write about the city around them.

Around the same time I began walking in my new city, I started to find other people who were deeply excited about Toronto. Back then, people tended to keep that kind of feeling in the closet. One night, in Suspect Video, a tiny indie movie and culture shop that was buried in the side of the now-razed Honest Ed's department store along Markham Street, I picked a zine called

Infiltration off the magazine rack and paged through it. Published by the late Jeff Chapman, who went by the name Ninjalicious, *Infiltration* was legendary in urban exploration circles – Chapman even coined the movement's name – for taking readers to the behind-the-scenes places where Toronto's pipes, boilers, and exhaust fans do their business. It was an epiphany: other people thought about the city the same way I did; others saw it as a seemingly infinite and mysterious place waiting to be explored and discovered.

Chapman's first issue of *Infiltration* chronicled his adventures in the Royal York Hotel, a place he loved, and where he later spent his honeymoon, shortly before he died of cancer in 2005. Subsequent issues detailed places like Union Station, City Hall, a drain under St. Clair Avenue, and St. Mike's Hospital, where he wandered the halls with his IV pole during his illness. Chapman's dedication inspired us all to uncover and listen to our own fascination with the layers of Toronto you see when you're on foot. Even more explorers started to appear.

At a party sometime during my first year in Toronto, the hostess introduced me to Todd Irvine, who, she said, 'liked to walk' too. We were thrust into a corner, and after some initial awkwardness, we were soon comparing the worn-out soles of our shoes. We figured a walking date was appropriate, so we met the following Thursday at his house on De Grassi Street. We walked west. We were nervous, not knowing each other, and sometimes we would bump into each other because our eyes were on the buildings. We were on something like a date. We crossed the empty West Don Lands – now a completely changed landscape with the Canary and Distillery Districts – and eventually ended up at a bar. It was fun, friendly, and I saw parts of Toronto I hadn't yet seen.

We walked again the next week with Marlena Zuber, who filled the book you're holding with psychogeographic illustrations and maps, and who has also updated those maps, another task that was much bigger and more complex than expected. On subsequent Thursdays, more people joined us. Walks became our weekly thing, our mobile salon, and I named us the 'Toronto Psychogeography Society,' though some people thought it sounded pretentious, and it probably was, but an over-the-top name seemed somewhat fitting.

Our practice was simple: we picked a meeting spot and started walking. A street corner. A subway station. An art opening. Usually on a Thursday night, a.k.a. 'Little Friday,' the kind of night made for a leisurely walk. Sometimes there were two people, sometimes twenty-five, and we drifted through the city, each corner or fork in the road presenting a choice, and whoever was in front led the group in whatever direction looked most interesting. We still walk like this, years later. If you have the urge to walk but think you don't have anybody to walk with, put out a call to friends and acquaintances for a random walk and I bet you'll quickly have your own walking group. People just need a nudge.

Toronto is big – the fourth-biggest municipality in North America by population – and that can be a daunting thing when you start exploring. The best way to start is just to walk. As Glinda the Good Witch of the South says in *The Wizard of Oz*, 'It's always best to start at the beginning – and all you do is follow the Yellow Brick Road.' Though there is no beginning to Toronto (and no Yellow Brick Road, for that matter), you can follow any of the thirty-one walks in this book, veering off whenever you want, in whatever direction you like, or you can put this book down now and start out on your own, in any direction, to find Toronto. While there are general routes described in each chapter, my notes are really just starting points for your own walks through the city. Fill in your own marginalia. If things go right, you'll even get lost sometimes. That's good. You'll eventually find your way back to someplace that looks familiar, or you'll find a bus to take you to a subway station. Toronto is a grid and you'll always hit a big arterial road and a TTC route.

This kind of walking is also called *psychogeography*, a term invented by Guy Debord and the Situationists in 1950s and 1960s Paris. They were an avant-garde group of artists, writers, and intellectuals, concerned, in part, with the effects of geography on human emotions and behaviour. They did absurd things like walk around Paris using a map of London. They got lost, and we tried to do the same – by breaking out of our usual routes and habits, by following our fancy rather than our logic, by going to places we wouldn't normally choose to go because they aren't on our mental map of the city.

One of the Situationist methods we employed the most was the *dérive*, or the drift Where the Situationists were trying to strike a blow against capitalism and society, we took a lighter view of psychogeography, best expressed by Christina Ray, the founder of New York's former Glow Lab gallery, when she described it as 'simply getting excited about a place.' Everything leads from there. Despite a lighter touch (this manifesto is barely a manifesto), there is much criticism in this book, of architecture and politics, policy and design, and many of the people who came on our walks used the explorations in their own advocacy and activism in making the city a better place for everyone. But it's still a celebration of Toronto.

My approach to writing about Toronto is that people will not fight or agitate for a better city if they don't have a reason to care about it, if they don't like or even love the place. People need a reason to fight, and as I revised this book I was reminded there are many good things here, and many reasons to fight for a better Toronto – that, and it's important to simply know the place better, something I'm often surprised is not a universal Toronto trait. Knowing a place better affords a connection that can lead to deeper civic engagement. If any of this is too earnest, never mind, just go for a walk and see what happens.

Walking like a drifting flâneur makes Toronto seem new, and though I've walked a lot of Toronto, repeatedly, I routinely see it through new eyes. All it takes is a slightly different angle than we're used to, like coming on an intersection we might pass through every day from an alleyway instead of a sidewalk, or even as simple as from a different direction. Most of us really know only a small part of the city well, and the rest we think we know well but just have a few brush-stroke ideas about the place, enough to fill that mental map a bit.

The edges of the 416 are different from the centre; the alleys are different from the streets. When walking through places that don't fit an established mental picture of the city, we create what Bertolt Brecht called a *Verfremdungseffekt*, a distancing effect, taking what's familiar and making it strange. By removing ourselves from our habits and context, and letting some unpredictability seep into the routine, we're better able to see what all the excitement is about. This is why the psychogeographic approach reveals so much.

We all took what we wanted from these walks. We've found parts of the city we didn't know existed, and its public spaces have become personal. Some enjoyed going into dark ravines with the comfort of a group, one way of mitigating the limitations for would-be flâneurs who don't fit the traditional model of who's allowed to walk wherever and whenever they want. Others used it in their own work. Marlena started interpreting our walks in paintings, illustrations and, later, maps. I collected details and they fed my writing on the city. Walking also helped inspire *[murmur]*, a mobile-phone oral history documentary project I co-founded in 2003. During *[murmur]*'s ten-year run, we recorded short stories and anecdotes about specific locations and put a sign in that spot with a phone number that passersby could call to hear that story in the place where it happened. Working on *[murmur]* gave me an excuse to ask people about their memories and experiences of Toronto, and to get underneath the surface of this city a little bit more. Those stories, in turn, helped me write this book by giving me a deeper background on the city, and helped me fall in love with Toronto.

'What does love have to do with it?' asked the late Pier Giorgio Di Cicco in his 2007 book, *Municipal Mind: Manifestos for the Creative City*. He was Toronto's second poet laureate, from 2004 to 2009, and the book is his legacy project from that time. Di Cicco had a passionate, sometimes combustible-seeming connection to Toronto. A practising Catholic priest, he wore black leather jackets and turtlenecks, smoked cigarettes, and spoke with a fantastic gravelly voice. A cool priest even, cooler than I ever knew from thirteen years of Catholic school. 'A town that is not in love with itself is irresponsible, and civically apt for mistakes,' he wrote. 'A citizenry is incited to action by the eros of mutual care, by having a common object of love – their city. A town that is not in love with itself will cut corners; lose sight of the common good.'

Love is also something you would be hard-pressed to find in official city statutes, but ask yourself if you love Toronto or whichever city you live in. Often the answer is no: cities are frustrating, but how can we care about something we don't also love? In a section of *Municipal Mind* called 'Restoring the Soul to the City,' Di Cicco tried to conjure a Toronto that could be – something we could aspire to. 'Developers are generally not known for their philosophical bent, but for their market enthusiasm,' he wrote. 'But it was a developer who told me the truest thing about cities: Speaking of Florence, a place that revitalized a civilization by a standard of civic care and design excellence, my friend remarked, "You know, Florence was already there, before a building ever went up."'

Toronto is certainly not Florence, and those with little imagination will dismiss the poetry about a city as useless, but Di Cicco was encouraging us to dream up an ideal Toronto that could be something to strive for as this place continues to grow and change. It could be about the architecture, but it also could be the sidewalks, more equitable and affordable housing, lusher parks, or ample public washrooms. Is Toronto living up to the city we dream of? From Di Cicco's point of view, these collective ideals and visions are what make Toronto beautiful, rather than the stuff already built. It's possible to dream of a better Toronto even while loving the current one. Perhaps it's the only way to dream.

I undertook many of the walks in this book either alone, with one or two partners for company, or sometimes with the big group. Sometimes I was with Sebastian the poodle, who had his own psychogeographic way of navigating the city, and I always saw something different when I was patient enough to let him lead. Any way you choose to walk the city is fine – you'll see different details with different people, pets, or kids, and when in a group, your conversation will start to bounce off the geography, taking both your body and mind to places you didn't expect. Sometimes I covered similar ground again and saw different things and took other detours. Even if you walk the exact same route, no two walks are the same: things change, new people will be out and about, and you, too, will be different.

Though I've been walking since I moved here, the walks and interviews in this book initially took place between 2004 and late 2009, and though the early texts were revisited and updated for publication in 2010, my words were snapshots in time and some were dated almost immediately, such is the pace of change. This edition is updated as best I can, but it, too, is a momentary snapshot. These essays are just starting points and initial sketches – it's up to you to fill in the spaces between, to update them again, with whatever you find on your own walks.

– Shawn Micallef
Toronto, April 2010, updated May 2024

The Middle

Yonge Street

 day trip

 dress to impress

 scenic views

Connecting walks: Harbourfront, Nathan Phillips Square/PATH, Dundas, St. Clair, Eglinton, Finch Hydro Corridor, Sheppard, Downtown East Side

Toward the end of high school – circa 1992 – four of us from Windsor got into a Dodge Shadow and drove up the 401 to Toronto for our first real road trip. We didn't know much about Toronto other than the tourist places like the CN Tower or Casa Loma – neighbourhood names like the Annex, Rosedale, or even Kensington Market had only a faint ring of familiarity. 'Cabbagetown' sounded ridiculous. But we knew the first place we had to go was the Yonge Street strip. We exited the 401 at Yonge, we drove south, we parked, we walked back and forth, ate a slice of pizza, and eventually we were served drinks at a second-floor bar, staring in awe into the giant rotating neon discs of Sam the Record Man. We were in the promised land.

If you're from a small town or a car-dominated city like Windsor, the initial moments along Yonge are made up of all the big-city clichés: crowds of people like your hometown has never seen, amusements, stores open late into the evening, and pho restaurants near sex-toy shops. And though you can still see wide-eyed tourists taking it all in the way we did that first time – the most euphoric of them ready to throw their hats in the air like Mary Tyler Moore did when she moved to Minneapolis – Yonge Street isn't what it used to be. In fact, it's a little boring, and poking around the history of this stretch might leave you wishing for a return to the days when Toronto presented a big-city show, long before it ever worried about being world-class.

Despite being this city's main street, and though it holds a mythic place in the Canadian psyche, Yonge occupies a strange place in Toronto's imagination. We all know it's important, but we often ignore it. It's not the main shopping street anymore. The seedy bars are seedy in the wrong way. Yonge is simply not cool. Yet when the city needs to come together, it comes here. This is where a million people gather for the annual Pride parade, and it's the only place to go when a sports team wins – if the Leafs ever do win the cup, the street will likely burn to the ground from the heat of all that pent-up fan adrenaline.

But perhaps most telling of its importance to Toronto are events that, nearly thirty years apart, came to symbolize our collective anxiety about being a big city.

Yonge starts right at Lake Ontario. It's an inauspicious beginning for such a mythical street – at least, it is right now, as this part of the waterfront is in flux, and has been for a while. To the west and east are the residential buildings – some new, some old – that Torontonians often complain about.

Once there was a spectacular attraction: Captain John's floating seafood restaurant, which was docked in the harbour at the very foot of Yonge Street. Venturing onto the ship revealed a surf-and-turf cocktail-lounge time warp of tuxedoed waiters and deep-fried foods. The ship itself was a relic from the former Yugoslavia called the *Jadran*, and the restaurant's owner, Captain John Letnik, had sailed the ship to Toronto in 1975 after purchasing it from the Yugoslav government for $1 million. For a time, he had two seafood ships here, but his first, the *Normac*, sank in 1981. In 2009, Letnik tried to sell the *Jadran*, but this floating wonder had fallen out of repair and fashion, and in 2015 it was towed to Port Colborne, where it was scrapped. Today, there is a monument to Captain John at the end of quay with a plaque and the bell and anchor from the *Jadran*.

If you look along the sidewalk at the foot of Yonge, by the docks where the water taxis do brisk business on hot summer days, you'll see a short metal balcony that extends over the water and lists the distances to various Ontario towns on the 'world's longest street' – it reminds me of the directional signs that tourists or expats put up pointing to home. Though Yonge's longest-street claim is challenged, as you stand here, looking north, it's a good way to feel connected to the rest of the province on a street that everybody knows about.

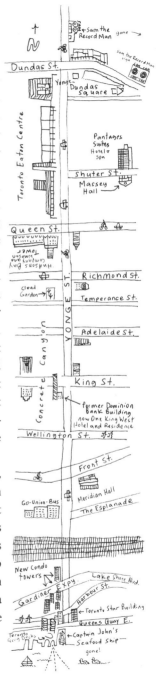

Yonge's first hundred metres are wide and, though the parking lots that languished for years here have mostly been filled in with new buildings, it is still a frumpy start – or end – to a main street. Across the street, on the northwest corner of Yonge and Queens Quay are the 'Residences of the World Trade Centre,' part of the early wave of condos built here in the early 1990s, before the recession paused Toronto's boom for more than half a decade, and one of many weirdly named residential buildings in the city. In front of it is a giant metal artwork by Richard Deacon called *Between the Eyes* that looks rather like two egg beaters fused together. The Gardiner, just to the north, was blamed for cutting off Torontonians from the waterfront but has been consumed by condo towers on both sides, reducing its visual impact considerably here and throughout downtown. The raised expressway isn't exactly disappearing, but it is becoming just another part of this landscape rather than the dominant view. Once underneath the much longer railway underpass, Yonge rises up to the original shoreline of Lake Ontario and crosses what is now Front Street. Here, at the southeast corner, is Meridian Hall (née the Sony Centre, the Hummingbird Centre, and, originally, the O'Keefe Centre), a perfectly modern performance venue designed by the late Toronto architect Peter Dickinson, which now has the Daniel Libeskind–designed 'L Tower' condominium sprouting out of one side. On the west side of Yonge, the second tower of CIBC Square has filled in what was once the GO bus station (now housed in the base of the complex's first tower on the south side of the railway), and the two towers are connected by a new public-private rail deck park.

Between Front and Richmond Streets, Yonge is a concrete canyon. Day trippers returning from the Toronto Islands on the Ward's Island ferry can get a wonderful glimpse of it from the water. While no longer a particularly interesting pedestrian experience – much of the on-street retail and human energy has, as with much of the financial district, disappeared into the underground PATH tunnels – One King West catches the eye as it rises out of the former Dominion Bank Building. The original 1914 structure serves as a plinth for an impossibly razor-thin, fifty-one-storey hotel and condo tower that slices through the downtown sky like a schooner. As impressive as it is, though, it's a subtle part of the skyline. From many angles, it's just a nondescript part of the familiar clump of downtown buildings, so its narrow form can surprise when viewed from the north or south.

A block north of the hotel, at Adelaide, is the Bay Adelaide Centre's east tower, opened in the mid-2010s. Bay Adelaide Centre, a three-building complex, first got its start in the late 1980s but was halted by the early-1990s recession. That resulted in the notorious 'Bay Adelaide Stump,' which stood here for more than ten years, with its unfinished concrete elevator shaft a kind of memorial to the Mulroney era and the hazards of capitalism. An impressive piece by Toronto artist Micah Lexier called *Two Circles* has been installed here. Two twenty-two-feet-in-diameter black-and-white circles are on either side of the elevators. One is solid, one an outline; together they're created out of 1.6 million handmade ceramic sticks, so be sure to take a close look at its details when passing by. The outline circle on the north side, along Temperance Street, pulls the eye down to the labyrinthine PATH corridors below.

At the Temperance corner are two heritage facades of former Holt Renfrew buildings that were previously on the Adelaide corner. They were moved here and complement the refurbished Dineen Building on the north side, creating a kind of heritage intersection. Temperance Street was always short, but now it's tiny and cute, as it was narrowed after the completion of the last Bay Adelaide Tower in the early 2020s and remade with paving bricks. On the north side of Temperance is Cloud Gardens, a park home to the *Monument to Construction Workers*. Artist Margaret Priest collaborated with Baird/Sampson Architects and twenty-seven Ontario trade unions on an eighty-five-foot-long structural steel grid with quilt-like insert panels. Each trade union fabricated a panel representative of their specific materials and expertise, based on Priest's original drawings. For example, copper shingles evoke roofing, pipes for pipefitters, concrete rebar, clusters of wire, and so on. 'Where our banks and financiers have buildings and streets named after them, the construction workers that actually raised the beams of the skyscrapers are celebrated here,' says David Kidd, a CUPE member and labour historian who has led labour-themed walks through Toronto. There's also a conservatory here that, when open, is a lovely, brief refuge from the city, especially in the winter when the humidity inside will immediately fog up spectacles and soothe parched skin.

Despite all the corporate money in the neighbourhood, there's a lot of labour history too (which there is everywhere, even if it isn't always celebrated). Just down the block, at 37 Temperance Street at Bay Street, was Bell Telephone's central exchange. In 1907, hundreds of women telephone operators walked out in response to Bell's plan to cut their wages and increase work hours, a precursor to today's precarious employment struggles. At the time, though, 'William Lyon Mackenzie King, the future prime minister, was assigned to investigate the circumstances leading to the walkout, and due to the women's insistence and organization, they did get improvements to their working conditions and eventually a union,' says Kidd.

The 'Yonge Street Strip' – the part that resonates with Maritimers and Windsorites alike – runs roughly from Richmond Street up to Wellesley Street. In its glory years, it was what the internet is to us today: a place where sex, drugs, and rock 'n' roll are just a step away from all things moral and upright. What made it magnificent is that it all played out in real time, in real space. This *Midnight Cowboy* Toronto included places like Mr. Arnold's, 'Canada's adult entertainment centre,' which boasted uncensored stag movies for two dollars, or one dollar for seniors. In 1971, the *Toronto Star* reported on the Catholic Church's concern that 'sex shops and pornographic bookstores are destroying Toronto the Good.' In fact, it was first- and second-hand knowledge of Yonge Street's tawdry spectacle, the one you can see if you watch the 1970 Canadian cinema classic *Goin' Down the Road*, where two fellas from Cape Breton drive to the big city, that made the notion of 'Toronto the Good' a bit of a mystery to me for years. Yonge Street, and Toronto, really did seem pretty cool.

Toronto's tolerance for this activity ended in July 1977, when twelve-year-old Emanuel Jaques, a Yonge-and-Dundas shoeshine boy, was raped, drowned in a sink full of water, and ultimately dumped onto the roof of 245 Yonge across from the Eaton Centre. The cleanup of the street that followed grew bigger than originally intended, eventually leading to a moral panic and a gay witch hunt that reached its peak with the infamous bathhouse raids of 1981.

Those raids had a galvanizing, Stonewall-like effect on Toronto's gay population, which had long been concentrated along Yonge north of College Street. Many of Toronto's early gay bars were located here, including the St. Charles Tavern at 488 Yonge, a former fire hall with a Victorian clock tower that has now been incorporated into a new residential tower along with a public artwork called *City of Letters* by Micah Lexier in collaboration with writer Derek McCormack. There are hidden messages woven into the artwork's array of stainless-steel letters affixed to the building, including in the alleyway behind (glance up at the rainbow spire atop the fire hall tower too). Equally important was the Parkside Tavern at 530 Yonge (currently a

Japanese restaurant, but previously a Sobeys and a Burger King). It had long been a Toronto tradition for mobs of people to gather by what is now the Courtyard by Marriott hotel to heckle the drag queens as they entered the St. Charles every Halloween night. Many came just to watch and enjoy, as people do on Church Street now, but violence was never far away. In 1968, police found several gasoline bombs behind the St. Charles, and, by 1977, a hundred-officer-strong police square was needed to control spectators who tossed insults, bricks, and eggs.

Yonge was decidedly queerer than the rest of the city, and it was also wetter. This is where Toronto the Good's lapsed Presbyterians and Methodists came to drink, at places like the Silver Rail at Yonge and Shuter Street, which opened in 1947 as one of Toronto's first licensed cocktail lounges. Half a block south, a three-lot strip on Yonge facing the Eaton Centre is strangely derelict, at odds with its ornate and storied past. At 197 Yonge stands the former Canadian Bank of Commerce building, built in 1905, now part of the Massey Tower. Just north, at 205, you'll find the former Bank of Toronto, built in 1905 by E. J. Lennox (of Old City Hall and Casa Loma fame). The Colonial Tavern once stood between the two banks. On the Colonial's stage, jazz greats from Gillespie to Holiday to Brubeck played in surroundings so intimate that people could chat with the performers by the stage after the show. Years later, in a basement space dubbed the Meet Market, notorious Toronto punk pioneers the Viletones further eroded Toronto's morals just as their contemporaries in New York did at CBGB. Many of these musicians and venues are memorialized in tall murals on the side of a residential building between Gerrard and Carlton.

So where have you gone, Yonge Street? Walking along, it's hard to find a drink in reasonable surroundings, and the good bands and DJs don't play much here anymore. The centre of the strip now would appear to be Yonge-Dundas Square, probably the most controversial bit of real estate in the city. Everybody, it seems, has something bad to say about it, and its name and renaming have been controversial. The square is the commercial heart of Toronto, sometimes unfairly called 'Toronto trying to be Times Square.' Many big cities have a square or intersection where the giant neon video billboards seem to be feral, as they seem here. In the 1990s there was a desire to create a new, large public space in downtown Toronto, as Nathan Phillips Square at City Hall was the only real open space. The design competition was won by Brown + Story Architects, the commercial buildings here previously were razed, and the square officially opened in 2002. Look up on the east side of the square to see the Sam the Record Man neon sign atop the Toronto Public Health building, moved here after the famous record store closed on Yonge Street a few blocks north.

The square's creation opened up a new, expansive view of the Eaton Centre, Toronto's downtown mall and office complex that opened in 1977. Created on land owned by the now-defunct Eaton's department store chain, the Eaton Centre was designed by Eberhard Zeidler and modelled after the Galleria Vittorio Emanuele II in Milan, Italy. The design was ultimately required to respect the Church of the Holy Trinity on the west side of the building, as well as Old City Hall. Today it's one of the – if not *the* – most visited attractions in Toronto, and Jane Jacobs, the patron saint of all things urban in Toronto and beyond, even had a hand in creating it.

The famed author and urban thinker, who moved to Toronto from New York City with her family when her sons were Vietnam-draft age, often threw her support behind unexpected places, subverting what people thought she would do – and one of those places was the Eaton Centre itself. As her son Jim Jacobs explained to me, when Eaton's, the once-great Canadian department store empire, and their developer partner Cadillac Fairview planned to put a mall in downtown Toronto in the mid-1970s, the City of Toronto opposed it vehemently. 'They were at complete loggerheads,' recalled Jim in our 2016 interview. To come to a compromise, the city brought in Jane Jacobs to represent their interests, and Cadillac Fairview, partly owned by the Bronfmans (of Seagram company fame), brought in Bronfman heir Phyllis Lambert. 'They had a very good time together,' said Jim. 'They agreed on almost everything. Jane had a lot of knowledge and experience in shopping centre design, as she had worked extensively with Victor Gruen, inventor of the shopping centre. She thought a lot about how those principles of suburban shopping centre design could work in the city.' The two worked out the structure of how it would work and fit into the city, Cadillac Fairview dismissed their original architect and hired Zeidler, and today Toronto urbanists have a building they love to hate that mall-studying Jane Jacobs helped create.

Though Yonge-Dundas Square's beloved/unbeloved status is in flux, as is its name, almost everybody can agree that 10 Dundas East – the building on the northeast corner of the intersection, formerly known as 'Metropolis,' and as 'Toronto Life Square' for a very brief time – isn't inspiring in its architecture or interior design. At one of Toronto's most visible locations, an entirely appropriate place for movie theatres and stores, it seems entirely designed to hold large advertisements. Its saving grace, perhaps, is that it houses some of Toronto Metropolitan University and, in the basement, the wonderful Little Canada, a miniature recreation of the country that should be visited multiple times, each encounter revealing more. North of it is TMU's student centre, a fantastic glass building designed by Norwegian firm Snøhetta that finally gave the university a footprint on Yonge and is just about the only kind of thing that could make the destruction of Sam the Record Man palatable.

At Yonge and Gerrard is Aura, a supertall condo, currently the highest residential building in Canada. Eaton's opened its flagship store at the north end of this block at College Street in 1930, and while still a magnificent example of art moderne architecture, it was just one part of a bigger plan to build the largest office and retail complex in North America that was thwarted by the Great Depression. The downturn nixed plans for a thirty-six-storey Empire State Building–style tower, and the surrounding land was filled with unsympathetic structures and, eventually, parking. If you happen to find yourself in the seventh-floor Carlu – the streamlined reception and concert hall where Lady Eaton lunched and Glenn Gould liked to play – check out the huge architectural model on display and see what could have been. And though some may lament the Winners discount store that has moved into the main shopping hall downstairs, it's closer to the Eatons' mass-retailing, something-for-everybody ethos than anything that has been in this space since Eaton's vacated the site when the Eaton Centre was opened in 1977. Behind it is the park that lends this area the name 'College Park' with the new Barbara Ann Scott Ice Trail.

Though Toronto derives its name from an Iroquois word, *Tkaronto*, which means 'place where trees stand in the water,' examples of Indigenous public art around the city have been rare. One giant exception is found in the atrium of the former Maclean-Hunter building at College and Bay Streets. The plain glass tower's basement houses *The Three Watchmen*, three totem poles (one fifty feet tall, the other two thirty feet) by artist Robert Davidson of the West Coast Haida Nation. Maclean-Hunter may not exist anymore (it was subsumed into the Rogers empire), but Davidson's contemporary totems mark the day in 1984 when a Canadian print media company was mighty enough that it could afford its own skyscraper.

On Grosvenor Street, just west of Yonge, there is a mural painted on the pavement in front of Toronto Fire Station 314 that reads, 'Running the Strip

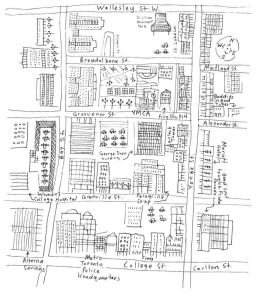

since 1871.' This station replaced the old fire hall (with the now-rainbowed clock tower) around the corner. I read it every time I walk by on my way to the Metro Central YMCA next door. I love the way it celebrates and mythologizes both the fire department and Yonge Street. The YMCA, another mythologized organization, has been a part of this city since the mid-1800s, now with multiple locations, but the Metro Central Y is its heart and, as far as gyms go, a palace. Opened in 1984, the building was designed by Jack Diamond's firm, Diamond and Schmitt Architects, the same folks who also built the Four Seasons Centre for the Performing Arts at University and Queen.

The Y is one of our best public(ish) buildings. Its different geometric shapes wrap around a six-storey grand central staircase called the Athlete's Stairs, designed as a place where people can bump into each other and chat (which they absolutely do). The building is one of the best examples of 1980s postmodern architecture in the city too. When the Y opened, architecture critic Adele Freedman wrote in the *Globe and Mail* that it was 'tall enough to inspire heavenly thought.' The pool room was inspired by the architecture of Roman baths and has a vaulted ceiling full of round skylights that allow beams of sunlight to pierce the water. They look brilliant underwater. The rooftop track is the most dazzling skyscraper-lit space by night, and the green roof is a kind of oasis in the middle of it all.

North to Bloor, Yonge is a jumble of shops and restaurants, some housed in classic Yonge Street Second Empire buildings, others in the new residential towers that have changed the face of Yonge here in recent years. It can't be stated often enough that because so many parts of the city have been off-limits to development – that is, adding new housing – much of it is forced onto main strips like Yonge, putting small shops and restaurants, often independent rather than chains, at most risk. The best illustration of this is the loss of Roy's Square, where the One Bloor skyscraper is now. The 'square' was simply two unpretentious outdoor alleyways – one from Bloor, the other from Yonge – that met by a subway entrance behind a clutch of buildings. What could have been just a place to pass through quickly had numerous tiny shops and restaurants. Cheap plastic patio chairs and tables were often placed there too. It was cozy and useful. The thing about Roy's Square is it was never pretty. It likely didn't appear on any postcards, a memorable place now because it's gone and hard to replicate, but an unremarkable one when it existed. The collection of buildings that One Bloor replaced was a classic hodgepodge of Yonge Street structures, just two or three storeys, often small and narrow. Most prominent was City Optical, with its avalanche of signage, on the Yonge-Bloor corner. There was, to list just a few businesses: a falafel shop, a shoe repair outlet, a psychic, a watch repair service, a Harvey's, a coffee shop, and Thai, Caribbean, and Indian restaurants. It was small, packed in, not fancy but interesting. The small-scale retail, the car-free passage, and the density are all things people travel to enjoy in other places far from Toronto. In Edinburgh, Roy's Square would have been called a *close*, the name for passages that make walking that city seem like a honeycomb adventure. Tokyo, Lisbon, hilltop towns in Sicily, and countless other places seem to effortlessly create small commercial areas; yet, in Toronto, it's so difficult. Yonge and Bloor is absolutely an appropriate place for a tall residential building, of course, but in this bigger context of zoning and city development policies, Toronto's beloved retail strips, where much of our public life happens, are under a lot of pressure, especially on Yonge Street.

For a change, take the Yonge parkland passage, which runs parallel to the street just a few steps east between Bloor and Wellesley stations. A series of pedestrian passageways that include three linear parks sit where structures were cleared away for the Yonge subway line. (Subway nerds will notice that north of College station, the Yonge subway line shifts to the east and runs just adjacent to the street rather than directly under it.) To walk the alternative passage, start at James Canning Gardens, which is at the south end, a block north of Wellesley, and continue north through Norman Jewison Park, named after the late Canadian film director whose dedication to Toronto meant he kept his Yorktown Productions office in a neighbouring yellow building for years. The northern park is named after the late George Hislop, the long-time gay activist who ran as an MPP in 1981 after the Toronto bathhouse raids and was later involved in the class-action lawsuit that saw same-sex pension benefits applied retroactively to 1985, the year the Charter of Rights and Freedoms was amended to include gay and lesbian equality rights. The passage then leads through a parking garage with a colourful 2019 mural by German artist Justus Becker painted on its western facade. It celebrates the relationship between Toronto and sister city Frankfurt. Note the two city skylines reflected in the sunglasses.

With the addition of towers on the southern corner of Yonge and Bloor, the presumptive 'centre of the universe' is now cornered in tall buildings, two from the 1970s and two from the last decade. On the northeast corner of Yonge stands the kind of building that gives concrete a bad name. Perched on what is arguably Toronto's most important corner, the former Hudson's Bay building and store present a wraparound wall of concrete. The adjacent Royal Bank branch, which is raised above street level, even had a 'no sitting' sign on its steps. The money may be safe, and the interior of the store was fine, but what about the people outside? A few holes punched into the facade to give the inside and outside more of a relationship would go a long way. A memorial to late street performer and perennial mayoral candidate Ben Kerr, who stood on this corner playing his guitar and singing for years (it was his audience that prompted those 'No Sitting' signs), would be welcome too.

A walk along Yonge is still not without excitement and charm, but as the not-so-old-timers will say, it isn't like it used to be – but it probably never was, as it's human nature to pine for a nostalgic past, especially if one's youth intersected with that period. Nevertheless, Yonge has had many lives and eras, and, even as many other streets can make a claim to being the (or a) heart of Toronto, Yonge can still grab us by the throat, as it did on Boxing Day in 2005 when fifteen-year-old Jane Creba was killed during a gun battle right near the spot we had those high school drinks back in 1992. There are many reasons this event so deeply affected Torontonians during the so-called 'Year of the Gun,' just as Emanuel Jaques's murder did in '77; one of them, surely, is that both traumatic events played out on the street that is our collective living room, a place everyone can relate to, even if it's one we don't use all that often. Later, the Eaton Centre shooting in 2012 triggered a similar response and public conversation. The mythic main street can still be very real, a lightning rod for Toronto.

Yonge tends not to elicit such high emotional and cultural impact as it passes quietly through some of Toronto's more genteel neighbourhoods north of

Bloor. The first stop along this stretch may just be the smartest place in the city. If this town had a physical brain, the Toronto Reference Library would be it. It's big, it's public, and it's one of the few places where all types can bump into each other. Men in suits read statistics near the guy who waves his arms and reads to himself aloud. At around two or three in the afternoon it's invaded by high school students who need a place to hang out in a city that is often hostile to their kind if they're not actively purchasing something. I often sit on the fourth floor by the north windows, surrounded by students calculating things on laptops while they share tables with retirees reading journal articles, all of us occasionally peering out the windows across the treetops of Rosedale.

Pierre Berton researched many of his novels here, and the inventors of Trivial Pursuit dug up some of their answers in these stacks. The TRL's resources are so deep that most of us can find a bit of ourselves somewhere in it – like an old City of Windsor directory from 1966 that listed my grandfather, then a recent émigré to Canada: 'Micallef, Paul C. Labourer, Chryslers. 816 Dougall Avenue.' Line by line, Toronto's and Canada's stories are told as a matter of fact, with no embellishment needed.

I've found out more about what it means to be a Torontonian (and a Canadian) inside the TRL than anywhere else apart from walking around. When I show people Toronto, I take them here and make them ride the glass elevator to the top of the enormous five-storey atrium. It's like the opening shot of *Metropolis*, all the layers and movements visible at once, or a really nerdy ant farm. An echo of this can be found in another of Raymond Moriyama's buildings, the former Scarborough City Hall (now home to City of Toronto offices and open to the public), which has an equally impressive atrium, as well as his North York Central Library, built a decade after the TRL.

Inside the TRL's front doors lies a cement pond and waterfall, typical of Moriyama's style. Opened in 1977,

some of the TRL's expressiveness has been tempered or removed, like the fabric sculpture called *Lyra* by Japanese-Canadian artist Aiko Suzuki, which used to hang like a jungle over that pond. The sculpture was made of a million feet of fibre, separating the chaos outside from the order inside, but it was removed in the early 2000s due to deterioration. The very 1970s orange-carpeted walls have been subdued and the hanging plants that used to dangle over the edge of each level wax and wane in length over the years. All are vestiges of the (Prime Minister) Pierre Trudeau and (Mayor) David Crombie years and the middle of Toronto's great midcentury era of public city-building. That the library has survived so many lean years intact, and that it is used and loved by all kinds of Torontonians – manufacturing a steady stream of public intellectuals – could be why a civic renaissance is possible even today. When Rob Ford was mayor, and he and his brother Doug wanted to cut funding to the libraries, people rallied outside of the TRL (the Fords backed down largely due to public pressure). And when Abel Tesfaye, the musician better known as the Weeknd, wanted to film a video for his song 'Secrets,' he did it here – as well as at the U of T Scarborough campus, both brutalist homages to his hometown.

Though still a vision of utopian, modern architecture, the half-century-old building was updated by Moriyama's son Ajon as it entered middle age in human years. The changes preserve the space-ageness of the original design and include a new glass entry, an interior expansion, and the addition of the

The Toronto Reference Library's very quiet and very big atrium.

Bram & Bluma Appel Salon on the east side of the building. The Toronto Public Library system is said to be the busiest in the world, and this is its mothership.

Behind the library, the duplex house at 21 and 23 Park Road was the site of the Advanced School of Contemporary Music set up by legendary Canadian jazz musician Oscar Peterson along with fellow jazz stars Ray Brown and Phil Nimmons. Formerly a boarding house, the school opened here in the 1960s after starting out in Peterson's Scarborough basement. Though Toronto did not have a wider reputation as being a hot spot at the time, it was home to quite a few jazz players, some surely helped by their work at the school, and many big jazz acts would stop in the city when touring.

Next door to the former Advanced School location is Asquith Green, a small park that includes a narrative sculpture by artist John McEwan called *Patterns for the Tree of Life*. Installed in 1989, it has three parts. Atop a terrace there is a postmodern frame of an old one-storey Ontario house, an homage to the kind typically found all over the province and relics of the pioneer days. Two howling wolf silhouettes are below on the green, as well as a small deer. Take a close look at the black iron fencing atop a small mound, as it includes two inscriptions that read, 'In the faces of our Children / In the sounds of our voices.'

Across from the library on Yonge are two towers that incorporated an entire block of older, low-rise buildings into their Yonge facades. Along with 18 Yorkville, a narrow point tower, these and other new neighbours serve as glassy distractions from the heavier CIBC and Hudson's Bay towers to the south. Number 18 was designed by Toronto architect Peter Clewes and his firm architects–Alliance; it's an example of the kind of neo-modern style that so many new Toronto buildings have followed. With the construction of 18 Yorkville, Toronto also got Town Hall Square, opened between the Yorkville library branch and the condo building. Named after the former Yorkville town hall that used to be nearby, the park is modelled after a French parterre (a formal garden of paths, plantings, and trimmed hedges) and designed by Toronto landscape architecture firm Janet Rosenberg & Studio. It turns the top of an underground parking garage into a geometric green maze that invites exploration, though Torontonians don't seem to know what to do with it beyond walking their dogs through it. Landscape as art, or something toward art, can be tricky.

Walk east past the Yorkville library branch to the fire hall and look up at the facade to see the original coat of arms that was found on the old Yorkville town hall. The symbols on it – a beer barrel, brick mould, jack plane, anvil, and sheep's head – represent the professions of the councillors at the time. Next door to the fire hall is Mist Garden, a park designed by NAK Design Strategies and the late Claude Cormier. Small shrubs create a rose shape and make for a contemplative short walk. The rose theme continues on the adjacent wall in an artwork by Montreal sculptor Linda Covit that produces mist every ten minutes during the summertime.

On the wedge of land formed at Yonge by Davenport Road and Scollard Street is Frank Stollery Parkette, named for the owner of a landmark menswear store at Yonge and Bloor. Renovated in 2010, it contains a series of plaques explaining how Davenport follows an ancient Indigenous trail just beneath the escarpment, the former shoreline of 13,500-year-old glacial Lake Iroquois that once covered everything south of it.

The building at the northwest corner of Yonge and Davenport seems a bit out of place. It's old and grand in a neighbourhood of taller and shinier buildings. We don't hear much about Freemasons anymore, but they used to build some great public buildings, like their main Toronto Masonic Temple here, opened in 1918. Decades later, as the Rockpile nightclub, it hosted Led Zeppelin's first Toronto appearance in 1969 in front of 1,200 people. It went by other names, including the Concert Hall in the 1980s and 1990s, when it attracted both mainstream and alternative acts, and the Rolling Stones used it as a rehearsal space. Later, it became CTV's studio for *The Mike Bullard Show*, then home to MTV Canada's various music-free chat shows. A new attempt has been made to use the temple as a live music venue, so going to a medium-sized show on Yonge Street may become a thing again.

Called the 'unofficial mayor of Yorkville,' Budd Sugarman is the namesake of the small park along Yonge Street just south of Rosedale subway station. A long-time merchant in the neighbourhood, he was an important figure in preserving the neighbourhood's historic buildings and in establishing the Village of Yorkville Park. This spot affords a good view of Yonge Street as it dips alongside Ramsden Park and the subway station, a subtle trace of buried Castle Frank Brook below. Ramsden Park itself was originally a Victorian brickworks, its yellow clay giving Yorkville buildings and homes their distinctive colour. Speaking of the old days, Yonge Street was named after George Yonge, a friend of Ontario's first lieutenant-governor John Graves Simcoe. Yonge is yet another guy some part of Toronto was named after who never visited. A more appropriate name might be – if naming things after humans remains in vogue – Berczy Street, as William Berczy was an early German pioneer, sometimes considered a co-founder of Toronto, who helped clear what became the settlement of York and built twenty-five kilometres of Yonge Street starting at Eglinton.

Behind the Rosedale subway station is Severn Creek Park. It feels like a secret place, especially when accessed by the staircase leading down from Crescent Road, just east of the subway entrance. The forested staircase leads to a wide expanse of pleasant lawn, with Rosedale mansions perched atop the wooded ravine walls. Down here it's possible to get a sense of the buried creek flowing below and see how Rosedale station – one of the original stations when the subway opened in 1954, designed by Toronto modernist architect John B. Parkin and historically designated – was built elegantly into the ravine walls. It feels leafy and bucolic, like so many of the tube stations in the suburban parts of London that follow the English garden style of development. The hidden creek is now called Castle Frank Brook, but the park's name is an homage to its previous names of Brewery Creek or Severn Creek, named after John Severn, one of the early Village of Yorkville aldermen who operated a brewery in this area, along the stream, beginning in 1835. Walk the park south, following the buried creek toward Rosedale Valley Road, past a coach house that once served the mansion at the top of the ravine, and then by some very fine midcentury apartment buildings. The creek eventually empties into the Don River a few kilometres southeast of here, connecting this valley with Toronto's vast ravine network.

Yonge continues north along the open-air trench of the subway line, flanked by a mix of low- and high-rise buildings. Here, Yonge becomes Rosedale's main street, with high-end home-decorating shops and a block of stores long known as the 'Five Thieves' due to their high prices. At Marlborough, take note of the gargoyles on each windowed archway of the building on the southwest corner. Cast stone sculptures by artist Merle Foster, they were originally part of the ornate showroom built in 1930 for the Pierce-Arrow Motor Car Company, a Buffalo-based luxury automobile manufacturer that went out of business in 1937 (and some of those Foster sculptures are much more automotive than medieval). Before its latest conversion into a mid-rise residential building, it was an inglorious Staples store for a time, perhaps the only big-box store with gargoyles. Long before that incarnation, the showroom was bought by the CBC in 1954 and turned into television studio D/4, which housed iconic Canadian shows like *Mr. Dressup, Front Page*

Challenge, The Tommy Hunter Show, and even a production of Macbeth starring a pre–James Bond Sean Connery. It remained a studio until the CBC consolidated its facilities, once spread across twenty-six buildings, into the massive broadcast centre on Front Street in 1992.

Across the street, midtown's refurbished North Toronto Train Station, built in 1916 at Summerhill by the firm Darling and Pearson (they also did the Dominion Bank building at One King West), houses the world's fanciest liquor store. Restored and retrofitted in 2004, its ornate interior was hidden behind acoustic drop ceilings. Out front is Scrivener Square, the kind of small urban square Toronto needs more of. Designed by Toronto architect Stephen Teeple and named after the late MPP Margaret Scrivener, it includes a 'tipping fountain' by artist Robert Fones and a series of small, angular streams and ponds that are refreshingly free of the unnecessary safety barriers that too often ruin good urban design. Those who want green can walk east between two condo buildings and eventually find a passageway into the Vale of Avoca Ravine and the wonderful Swiss Family Robinson–style trails high on the ravine wall.

As Yonge dips under the set of railway tracks that once served the North Toronto station (and may again one day, as it would not be hard to get those platforms back in working order), it starts moving uphill, climbing the Lake Iroquois escarpment. On the east side, a condo tower called the Ports vaguely resembles the decks of a cruise ship. The name is even more appropriate considering that this was, until 1983, the site of the Ports o' Call, by one account 'a drinkers' Disneyland' of Polynesian-, Western-, and Roman-themed restaurants and lounges. The late Toronto jazzman Ian Bargh played the Polynesian room and once told me Ports o' Call was a hotbed of the Toronto jazz scene in the sixties. How such a weirdo place existed in famously uptight Toronto is a mystery on the surface, but Toronto the Good could be a wonderfully bad place when that Orange and WASPy surface was scratched. That the condo developers saw fit to memorialize this place in the new name should inspire other developers to give their buildings names that actually mean something to Toronto.

Further up the hill was the historic 'CHUM DIAL 1050' sign; though, due to various media buyouts and reorganizations, it has recently been reinstalled at Duncan and Richmond Streets. On May 27, 1957, 1050 CHUM became the first Canadian station to play rock music exclusively. Later, as an oldies station, it reminded baby boomers of their golden youth. CHUM sat on top of Gallows Hill, so named because a fallen tree here once resembled the beam of wood that hangmen found so useful, though it's not so much a hill as just part of the escarpment. When CHUM's tight rotation allowed them to play Bowie's 'Rebel, Rebel,' it would've been easy to pretend it was an homage to William Lyon Mackenzie's rebel forces, whose advance was stopped here in 1837. In front of the residential building that replaced the CHUM building is a large stainless-steel disc sculpture by artist Sue de Beer, installed in 2019 and evoking the old signage and the records that were played here.

Unless you peek down an alley running west off Yonge, just south of St. Clair Avenue, it's easy to miss St. Michael's Cemetery. Opened in 1855 when the area was countryside, it's now tucked in behind buildings. When I lived nineteen floors up, across Yonge Street on Pleasant Boulevard, I used to watch kids igniting fireworks there at night, briefly lighting up the vast darkness, as would the ultra-bright beams of police spotlights panning back and forth between the tombstones soon afterward. Some thirty thousand Catholic Torontonians lie buried behind St. Michael's gates, many of them Irish immigrants who fled the potato famine – their county of origin is often listed on the markers – including John Pickford Hennessey, grandfather of 'America's Sweetheart,' actress Mary Pickford. In the middle of the cemetery sits the octagonal dead house, the mortuary vault where caskets were stored during the winter months. It was designed in 1856 by Joseph Sheard, the only architect ever to become mayor of Toronto (and, incidentally, the guy who thought a civic holiday in August might be nice – another reason Ontario should be kind to Toronto). Tucked in here, too, is the Badminton & Racquet Club of Toronto, its courts, sometimes covered in inflatable roofs, a dramatic contrast with the cemetery.

When I stand at Yonge and St. Clair, I find it striking that the intersection is so unsung. Most mid-size towns across Canada dream of a downtown filled with this much activity. After a year of living there when I first moved to Toronto, it did sometimes feel like I was living at the mall – there was an It Store, a novelty store that was big in 1980s malls, across the street at the time – but it has a certain urban elegance to it.

The night we moved in – my first sleep in my own Toronto home – after hauling our stuff up nineteen floors, I went for an exhausted and overwhelmed walk in the evening's warm May air. To the east, I discovered the huge St.

Clair Viaduct that crosses the Vale of Avoca Ravine and Yellow Creek. Far below, in the darkness, the treetops swayed gently in the wind, alternately sinister and magical. The smell. The sound of it all. I had read of Toronto ravines and seen them from Highway 401, but this was my first real encounter with one. Margaret Atwood's novel *The Blind Assassin* opens on this bridge where, in 1945, a car gets stuck in the streetcar track, flies off course, and plunges off the side. There are no rails on the bridge now, but Atwood was right about the streetcar presence: the buried corpses of those old rails push up and crack the asphalt at the St. Clair and Mount Pleasant intersection, where the loop used to be. The northeast side is now a small park named after sculptors Frances Loring and Florence Wyle, partners in art and life, who had a home and studio in a former church on nearby Glenrose Avenue. On later walks, I discovered a network of trails that extend below the viaduct, good for long runs with no traffic and thick, oxygenated air. Entrances go north up the vale, and you can find a secret back entrance to Mount Pleasant Cemetery, but be careful not to get locked in at closing time.

The area up top is called Deer Park. In 1837, Agnes Heath and her son Charles Heath bought forty acres of land here and raised deer. Local historian Joan C. Kinsella writes in the Toronto Public Library–produced *Historical Walking Tour of Deer Park* that the deer 'roamed through the area as far east as Parliament Street and were quite tame. The deer always knew when it was dinner time at the hotel at St. Clair and Yonge and would gather at the corner to be fed by the guests.' Today there are still deer down in the ravine system, but they tend not to wander into neighbourhoods much.

When I first moved to the area in 2000, the only late-night coffee available was at the original Fran's diner (now divided into two different restaurants at 21 St. Clair East with a slicker renovation). The takeout coffee was dispensed from those irritatingly slow pump jugs, but it gave me time to look at the regulars who hung out there, like the woman who painted on one-inch-thick eyebrows. Glenn Gould used to have his own booth there too. Generations of eccentrics and people who lived their entire lives in apartments: it felt very big-city, exactly the kind of place you want to arrive in from a smaller one.

A little to the north, the subway swings from the east side of Yonge to the west, passing under Lawton Parkette, where it rumbles the earth. Mount Pleasant Cemetery pleasantly disrupts Yonge's urbanity, though it is still a city (of the dead). The cemetery property runs from Yonge's east side over to Bayview, a massive green rectangle that sprawls across midtown Toronto.

Apart from the buried dead, it can be considered one of Toronto's largest and nicest parks. Mount Pleasant makes a point of being open for the living – whether walking, jogging, or biking along the gently curving roads – and also functions as an arboretum, playing host to a wide variety of trees. Here, Canada's not-so-famous are buried next to the famous. Some, like the Eatons and Masseys, lie in massive crypts, while others, like the Blacks, rest in large family plots – and yes, there is enough room to accommodate Conrad one day. Explore Mount Pleasant without a map; after many such trips, I finally found, by chance, former Prime Minister William Lyon Mackenzie King's grave, complete with fresh flowers and a Canadian flag. In 2020, former PM John Turner was buried here too.

Back on Yonge, the street dips where Yellow Creek flowed before it was filled in. It runs under the cemetery, meaning quite a few people are buried in fill over a buried creek: cities are all about layers. On the west side of the street is the Davisville Toronto Transit Commission yard, so this bit of Yonge feels quite open and smells of creosote and feral electricity. The old iron railway bridge that crosses Yonge above the cemetery is part of the Kay Gardner Beltline Trail. Cutting a northwest line through central Toronto, it's the city's thinnest park, named after the local councillor who was instrumental in converting the former railway into a cycling and walking trail. Originally a commuter railway, the Beltline opened in 1892 and ran forty kilometres out from Union Station, up the Don Valley, and through new suburban neighbourhoods in Rosedale, Moore Park, and Forest Hill. It operated for only two years before going bankrupt, but left a right-of-way that today allows for a continuous backyard glimpse into Forest Hill. It's a great place to watch the subways, and sometimes the operators will honk at kids waving on the bridge.

Near the corner of Davisville is the W. C. McBrien Building, the TTC's headquarters. Built after the Yonge subway line opened in 1954, it sits at the beginning of a modern high-rise community that houses a near-secret sculpture garden. It was Abraham 'Al' Green, one of the three founders of Greenwin Construction, whose passion for art resulted in these exceptional bits of modern sculpture placed around his equally modern Toronto developments, beginning long before the practice was de rigueur. Many sculptures can be found on the lawns surrounding the tall white Greenwin buildings, which spread east from Davisville station between Davisville Avenue and Merton Street. On Balliol Street, the Al Green Sculpture Park is home to a dozen sculptures by Canadian public-art giants of the sixties and seventies, such as

Kosso Eloul and Sorel Etrog, as well as some by Green himself. A walk here is a journey from utopian modern buildings to our avant-garde past.

Yonge reverts, as it often does, to a low-rise landscape of two- and three-storey retail and restaurants (this is the default typology of Yonge, interrupted only when new developments have gone up, and there are many here) until a few blocks south of Eglinton, where things get much taller and denser. For quite a long time it functioned and was known as the city's uptown, but since the megacity amalgamation rendered Yonge and Eglinton Toronto's geographical midtown, the idea of uptown has drifted north.

Once referred to as 'Young and Eligible,' the neighbourhood embodies the universal civic dynamic of uptown-downtown; there has always been an awkward relationship between the two. In *How Insensitive*, his 1994 novel about Toronto's cultural scene, Russell Smith wrote of a late-night arrival here:

Ted got off the subway at Eglinton. John had told him to just walk north until he saw the cars. He had never been to this part of town before; it was where John had grown up. John never talked about it. Go-Go had sneeringly said it was white, just white and nothing else. In the dark, Yonge Street seemed deserted and sterile. There seemed to be a disproportionate number of specialty food shops with baguettes and jam jars and italic lettering in the windows, all closed. In between them were dry cleaners, a dark Second Cup, an imitation British pub at the base of a mirrored office building.

That pub is still there, but the neighbourhood demographics have changed in the thirty years since, and its far-flung location doesn't seem so far-flung anymore – even if some of the sidewalk banners still insist on referring to the area as 'Uptown Yonge.'

In an article in the *Toronto World* newspaper from 1907 on the area, then the frontier of Toronto's manifest-destiny surge into rural Ontario, it's clear the neighbourhood was long off everyone else's civic radar: 'A good deal is being heard of this most beautiful of Toronto's suburbs, North Toronto, but few people indeed know where it is situated and when the question is asked "Where is North Toronto?" the answer generally is … altogether wrong.' The article goes on to describe the area in topographic terms that current residents might not object to: 'This high altitude secures the town's inhabitants pure air, as the atmosphere is not contaminated with coal smoke and other foul-smelling, disease-producing and death-dealing odours; and consequently makes it a very desirable spot to live in.'

Yonge and Eglinton still is a desirable place to live and, when the subway opened in 1954, a new pressure was added: developers. Eglinton was the end – or beginning – of Toronto's nascent subway system, and it transformed what was a sleepy streetcar suburb into a hub. The black glass towers of Canada Square – previously called Foundation House – were the first to lead Yonge and Eglinton into the postwar modern age. As it did in the early 1960s, Canada Square embodies an unapologetic big-cityness, with movie theatres and corporate head offices attached to underground trains. TVO even broadcasts from the basement – guests on the current-events program *The Agenda* can feel the subway rumbling a few feet below. Nothing was more modern than TV in the postwar era. Toronto's 1964 'Plan for Eglinton' summed up the spirit of the time: 'To the Torontonian boarding a subway train to the City in the morning, or motoring up Yonge Street in the evening rush hour, the Eglinton District presents the picture of dynamic growth and change. Impressive glass office towers, bustling stores, high-rise apartments and the busy intersection of Yonge Street and Eglinton Avenue all contribute to this new image.'

An even newer image is now in the works as the whole area is slated for redevelopment, filling in the TTC yard to the west. And the Eglinton LRT Crosstown has turned this into another Yonge-Bloor kind of transit nexus. On the northwest corner of the intersection is Yonge Eglinton Centre, which had its own renovation and includes rooftop park space. A POPS (privately owned public space), it represents how new public spaces are sometimes being created in this dense city, though not without concern over how such spaces are surveilled, policed, maintained, and if they are even truly public. The entrance is via an elevator in the glassed-in atrium with a prominent green wall.

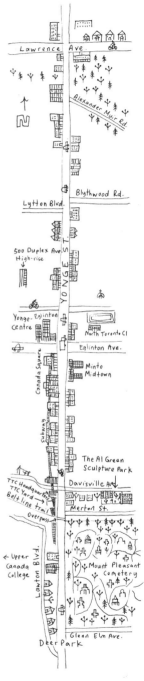

This intersection is still a contentious place, growing taller and denser. The first giant memorials to the two-and-a-half-decade growth spurt are the Minto twin towers – nobody seems to call them by their *James Bond*ish official names, Quantum North and Quantum South, perhaps because even the as-advertised lifestyles of their occupants can't live up to that much fiction. The anti-tower crowd points to them as the neighbourhood killer. In a February 2009 *National Post* article, Councillor Michael Walker called them 'monsters' and added that 'you have to feel for the residents of Yonge-Eglinton' – a strange sentiment given that he represented a lot of folks who seemed quite happy living tall, and, perhaps more importantly, that the area had gone vertical over forty years before. It's a sentiment that continues to evolve over the decades. In recent years, nearby house-owning residents called it 'density creep' – so the resistance to big-cityness continues apace.

During the growth of the 1960s, many residents were all for this vertical expansion. An archival collection of letters to City of Toronto planners in response to the 1964 plan that called for the blocks surrounding the main intersection to be covered in high-density apartments shows that opinions were largely positive. It's strange to read them now, conditioned as we are by decades of consultation where the predominant word is *no*. True, some of the homeowners were likely in favour of the plan because they could sell their property to developers at top price. Today, though, there are only a dozen or so blocks of apartment buildings, which quickly give way to neigh-bourhoods of single-family homes. Growing pains are the story around these parts. Lingering by the fountains in the Anne Johnston Courtyard, sandwiched between the two Minto towers and named after the local city councillor who gave up her political life to defend Toronto's right to skyscrapers, it's easy to forget that there are many storeys above. Done right, tall buildings aren't wastelands at the bottom, and aren't an eyesore on the horizon.

To wander the surrounding blocks today is to travel through a kind of modern wonderland. Low-rise and (very) high-rise buildings with names like the Lord Elgin, the Imperial Manor, the Rosemount, Place de Soleil, and Americana capture the optimistic modern thinking of the era while still being connected to our colonial past. The Berkshire House and the Canter-bury House, two magnificent 1970s concrete buildings found behind the rather austere backside of the Yonge Eglinton Centre, have much in common with brutalist buildings in Britain that have similar traditional 'house' names, yet another trace of Toronto's once-very-strong colonial impulse.

When I'm asked for apartment-hunting advice, which happens often enough in Toronto's inhumane housing market, I often tell people to walk around older apartment neighbourhoods like this and call the number on signs out front. These are generally great buildings, built well, with units that are more spacious than today's standard. They're also run by professional management companies, which means, in theory, tenancy will be stable and for as long as one wants, unlike the more volatile-seeming rental market in condos and houses, where individual owners routinely evict tenants for renovations or other dubious reasons. As the number of rent strikes across the city against large landlords attests, this isn't always the case, but after living in two of these kinds of buildings in my Toronto tenure – one for eight years – I've learned they can be truly good places to live when run properly.

However, the absurdity of Toronto's real estate and rental market, along with its zoning regime, is fully on display here, as quite a few of these rental buildings have development signs out front. Under Toronto's rental-replacement rules, any building with more than six rental units being redeveloped must have those units replaced, so they will be rentals again, but hundreds of lives will be needlessly disrupted (moving is a kind of trauma, especially moving by force), all to preserve those single-family-home neighbourhoods, some not far from here, and others all across the city. The climate implications of tearing down perfectly good buildings are profound here too, as the embodied energy and materials that went into building these will be wasted, and more energy expended to destroy them.

A saved bit of history is Postal Station K at Montgomery Avenue, with its unique and rare King Edward VIII royal cypher (as it was built in 1936, just before his abdication). It's become part of a taller residential development (that local residents and their councillor also protested), and much of the postal station has been transformed into Stock TC, a bar/restaurant/ café/grocery store where the old, weathered, and worn terrazzo was preserved. In front is Montgomery Square, a new public space, and *Montgomery Gates*, a public artwork by Adad Hannah. The name and work evokes the Montgomery Tavern that was located here, where William Lyon Mackenzie's rebels gathered as they began the ill-fated Rebellion of 1837 march south, an attempt to install responsible government and overthrow the Family Compact ruling class. Quoted on the gates are words from Mackenzie's Declaration of Independence of Upper Canada: 'Do you love freedom? / I know you do. / Do you hate oppression? / Who dare deny it?'

Toward Lawrence, Yonge defaults lowish again, another pleasant strip of pleasant stores with some handsome mid-rise pre- and postwar apartment buildings, as well as some newer buildings. Toronto Hydro's Glengrove Substation, from 1930, is called 'The Castle,' so regal is its electric style. In the mid-2000s, *Globe and Mail* columnist John Barber referred to North Toronto, the area around Yonge and Lawrence, as our city's only real ghetto (a rich white one). I worked up here for a while and met some of its nice denizens. They shop at the upscale supermarket Pusateri's, send their kids to Upper Canada College, and, when giving me a ride to the subway, they would point out fancy homes where important wives had left important husbands. As with so many Toronto neighbourhoods, it functions like a small town, where everyone knows everyone and gossip flows through the streets.

Just south of Lawrence and east of Yonge lies the former farm of gentleman farmer John Lawrence. Just before the First World War, this land was subdivided by the Dovercourt Land Building and Savings Company into the Lawrence Park Estates, designed as 'a high-class suburban site.' However, the war and recession resulted in an auction, in 1919, of the many unsold properties at 'any price the public will pay.' Today, people pay multiple millions to live on these leafy streets. Unfortunately, some of the Craftsman houses in this neighbourhood have been torn down to make way for McMansions that must make the old money shudder (unless they're the ones building them).

South of Lawrence Park stretch the ravines that follow Burke Creek, starting with the Alexander Muir Memorial Gardens. These gardens were originally located north of St. Clair, but in 1952 the TTC spent $100,000 to move them to make way for the subway. Muir's massive 1867 Top 40 hit 'The Maple Leaf Forever' isn't sung much anymore, but his park has lovely red crushed-stone paths, a nice change from boring pavement.

Wander deeper into the ravine and you'll find what seem like old-growth forests with a super canopy of white pines that is the natural equivalent of the city's high-rise buildings (those buildings seem far away down here), as the gardens gives way to Blythwood Ravine Park and later Sherwood Park, all the while following Burke Creek. A pitched battle between dog owners and dogless residents took place here during the 1990s, similar to the ones that periodically flare up around the city today; the dog owners won in this case, and dogs now have ample off-leash areas to roam, including a network of fenced-in pathways that keep the sensitive ravine slopes safe from doggy disturbances. There is even a dog drinking fountain dedicated to 'mankind's best friend.' From the plaque: 'We wish them Fun Walks. Happy times. Cool drinks. Willy, thanks for getting us walking in this beautiful park. This clean water is for you and the little fur people ... drink, my loves.'

North of Lawrence, Yonge continues in its default low-rise retail incarnation until it arrives at the end of the old City of Toronto, where it dips deep down into Hoggs Hollow, the western arm of the Don Valley and scourge of north-south cyclists, another place that divides the city. At the southern crest, across from the Loblaws – once the site of the Glen Echo Loop, where a terminal for the Yonge streetcar line was, as well as the car house and freight shed for the Toronto and York Radial Railway that continued north – there is a giant surveyor's compass called 'Toronto's Northern Gateway.' It's a vestige of old Metropolitan Toronto and used to sit on the border between Toronto and North York. As with all borders that don't exist anymore, we cross it without thinking, only occasionally noticing something that reminds us it was there. A little further north, there's an apartment building called 'Top of the Hollow,' which marks an entrance into the community of Hoggs Hollow, a wealthy enclave of big homes and twisting country-like roads. Hoggs Hollow sits at the bottom of a valley, and walking down into it, you can sometimes feel the temperature drop and the humidity go up, a sign that water is near. Some homes even have lawns of ferns, which makes the area feel almost like a North Vancouver neighbourhood.

On the way down into the valley on Yonge, as it enters York Mills Valley Park, there's a TTC escape hatch where the subway below periodically makes itself known through sound, wind, and fragrance. Unlike so many of Toronto's lost streams and rivers, the West Don remains open in places, weaving its way through the park and the big lots in this area. The small bridge that once crossed it here was destroyed by Hurricane Hazel's storm surge in 1954. There is a small plaque on the new bridge that doesn't mention what perhaps many are left wondering: What will happen to all these houses, built on a flood plain, when the next Hazel hits?

On March 17, 1960, five Italian immigrant labourers died while digging a water-main tunnel that passed underneath the Don River in Hoggs Hollow when a fire broke out and the tunnel filled with water and silt. A Royal Commission afterward resulted in new labour safety laws and increased employer accountability for their workers. *Breaking Ground*, a large quilt by fabric artist Laurie Swim honouring the five fallen workers, was installed on

the fiftieth anniversary of the disaster and hangs in the main mezzanine of York Mills subway station today.

Nearby, in the park at the entrance to Hoggs Hollow, there is a monument for artist C. W. Jefferys, whose home and studio still stand on Yonge just north of York Mills. The studio site is surrounded by a cluster of mid-rise glass office buildings that occupy the bottom of the valley. They're tucked into the trees and the Don Valley Golf Course. They're big – one building housed a football-field-sized customer service centre where I temped for a few months after moving to the city – but most Torontonians likely miss both, as many see it from a car speeding by (as Yonge is fast here), while the slower pedestrian view and the details it affords is easy to neglect. On the west side of the street is 4000 Yonge, a handsome midcentury apartment building with some of the most magnificent outdoor fountains in the city.

If you're on foot during the frozen winter, wander onto the golf-course grounds, long a clandestine act but one that became permitted during the WinterTO pandemic program to give people access to outdoor space in the wintertime. The entrance is just before the Highway 401 overpasses, and access to the grounds is easy when the clubs and carts are in storage. All paths lead to a vast, cathedral-like area underneath the quadruple bridges of the 401 high above. One frozen night we ventured down here, with the constant hum of traffic above and light dripping over the sides from the jumbo-sized light towers. On the west side of the river, we scrambled up the banks of the ravine and popped our heads up in the space between the eastbound express and collector lanes. The sound and fury are airport-runway-worthy. The 401 is usually seen from a distance or from within a fast-moving vehicle. Being so close to the flow, with it all coming at us, was like waking up in the middle of a rushing river of steel. We were safe behind the barriers, but close enough to feel the air move as each vehicle passed by.

Yonge itself doesn't pass under the 401 pleasantly, especially when you're on foot. This is the least pedestrian-friendly stretch of the street, and though there are sidewalks, they stop and start, forcing pedestrians to cross the street, and at times it feels like you might be walking on the 401 itself as the on- and off-ramps encourage drivers to go fast. For decades we've heard how the Gardiner is a 'barrier to the lake' when, elevated as it is, it's actually quite porous and relatively easy to cross while walking downtown. The same can't be said about the 401 and some of the other 400-series highways that cut through the city. In any city there should be a hierarchy of concern for vulnerable road users: pedestrians first, then cyclists, then cars (and perhaps a few subcategories within each). Around the 400-series highways, this logic is thrown out, as drivers rule. The main culprit here is the Ontario Ministry of Transportation. Even when City of Toronto staff have all road users in mind and want to do something better, they're often thwarted by the MTO, an institution that may be good at building highways across the province, but is either not skilled at adapting to cities or actively hostile to efforts to make these crossings less hazardous to humans. Even a yield or stop sign is too much at times, and the MTO has often nixed the city's plans and suggestions.

Indoors, in view of the sidewalk that crosses the eastbound 401 on-ramp, is the magnificent Park Lawn Mausoleum, worth the visit to hear your shoes echo on the always-cool marble floors and see the crypts of Sir Henry Pellet, the man who built Casa Loma, and Agnes Hill and Frank Rogers, a couple who drowned when the *Lusitania* sank in 1915. Beyond the on- and off-ramps, North York civilizes somewhat as Yonge approaches Sheppard and the in-transition mix of high-rises and 1950s and sixties low-rise plaza developments clash. North York City Centre, our uptown 'billion-dollar downtown,' is new and will always be compared to the streetscape south of Hoggs Hollow, which was established before the automobile changed the way we do streets. In the middle of all this is one of Toronto's most important public spaces: Mel Lastman Square, named after the long-time mayor of North York who went on to become the first mayor of the amalgamated City of Toronto. This is the uptown-downtown that Lastman built, but this legacy didn't turn out exactly as he planned. In an unguarded moment in the 1990s, Lastman told former mayor John Sewell, who was then writing a column about city politics for NOW magazine, that 'the streetscape turned out like hell. It's awful. It's not what I wanted.' What it's become since is anything but a hell, though the streetscape that is still fast and wide could be fixed.

Places that need to use the word *city* in their name often betray a civic insecurity, but long-time residents have no such anxiety here; some of them still list their address as Willowdale, Ontario, avoiding any reference to Toronto. Right now, it's one of the most interesting places in the city because new and old collide block by block, like two glaciers, complete with archetypal progress scenes where little bungalows cower next to shiny glass towers. Just a generation or two ago, the strip of Yonge between Sheppard and Finch Avenues was a low-rise midcentury streetscape. It still bears those midcentury traces – and even those of the villages that were here before, like Lansing and Newtonbrook – but they are fleeting. In their place is a new, ever-rising skyline and many thousands of people who have moved into this neighbourhood. It's busy twenty-four hours a day, too, with karaoke bars operating at all hours and the sidewalks busy with life otherwise. The subway under Yonge that made all this growth possible reached Finch Station in 1974. And in 1987, North York Centre station was added between Finch and Sheppard stations to accommodate the early wave of development around what was then North York's relatively new city hall, now known as North York Civic Centre.

The growth of Yonge was a key issue in the 1985 North York municipal election. Lastman offered a gung-ho approach, and his opponent, Barbara Greene, pushed for slower 'good development.' Proof of Lastman's over-whelming victory is on record, but also in the air. North York has a real big-city skyline, just like Houston, Calgary, or maybe even a little bit of Hong Kong. It's peppered with unique places, like that former city hall now civic centre, with its dramatic slanted roof done up in the high-tech architectural style that won it a 1982 Governor General's medal in architecture, and next to it, the postmodern building that houses the North York Central Library, built in 1987 and designed by Raymond Moriyama, with his trademark atrium and zigzag staircases. Inside the civic centre, a building that had its political power sucked out of it when the megacity was created, there are happy photo montages of North York declaring 'Dave Winfield Day' in 1993 and 'Wendel Clark Day' in 1994.

Adding to the movie-set strangeness of North York City Centre are the overwrought, nearly baroque condo names: Cosmo, the Monet, the Majestic Phase II, Platinum Towers, Spectrum, and the Ultima at Broadway. How do you invite people over for dinner with a straight face when you live at the Grande Triomphe at Northtown? Even the Vatican has less hubris, though perhaps the same kind of aspirational impulse. The Residences of Dempsey

Park is one of the few buildings with a historical reference in its name. The Dempsey hardware store stood at Yonge and Sheppard, a local landmark since 1860, but moved a few blocks away, to Beecroft Avenue, before construction of the Sheppard subway line began in the nineties. You can now find the store hiding, like the rest of Willowdale – and the Gibson House Museum, in an old pioneer farmhouse – between and behind the new city centre.

The hellish streetscape Lastman spoke of is on the cusp of being tamed – if there's political will. Currently, Yonge is treated like a highway that brings people into and out of the city, never minding or caring that tens of thousands of people live along it now and might need to cross it on occasion. For instance, the distance between the signalled crossings at Park Home Avenue and Churchill Avenue along Yonge is more than half a kilometre. Other crossing points are few and far between, as they are in many of the newer parts of Toronto, so people often run across six or more lanes of traffic just to move around their neighbourhood. The City of Toronto has been slowly moving forward with a 'REimagining Yonge Street' project that would help the streetscape between Sheppard and Finch catch up with the mixed-use and populous neighbourhood the area has become. Part of the plan, created with extensive public consultation, would see new street furniture, trees, public art, better paving material, and improved connections to adjacent parks added to the strip. Cycling infrastructure would be created and, most importantly, pedestrian crossings would be improved. In a dense, highly populated place, frequent and safe crossings are essential. When this happens, it might become Lastman's dream, after all: a downtown behaving like a downtown. It's here, too, that some condo buildings are a model of how they should enhance the city.

The problem with so many new buildings on our main streets, even ones that look nice high up in the air, is they get the first few floors wrong. They're boring. They feel like the mall: overly controlled by one owner. Yet in North York there is an ideal situation, as a few of the towers in this stretch, especially the ones around Northtown Way, have tiny storefronts that have attracted small-scale, independent retail rather than the large corporate concerns like banks and drugstores that usually populate the ground floors of such buildings. It's interesting. It's a city. This is partly the result of something called the 'North York Secondary Plan,' which triggered a finer grain of storefronts and should be emulated everywhere new buildings are gobbling up main strips. On a trip to New York once, I was on the corner of Fifth and 33rd and saw people looking up, so I did too. I hadn't noticed the Empire State Building, among the tallest in the city, was next to me, so interesting was its ground floor. The same effect happens here in Toronto's second, northern Koreatown, with Korean restaurants and shops alongside Persian shops that continue north, plus the usual Toronto mix on top of it.

Hong Kong–style buildings in North York.

It's also here in North York – and in a few other places in the city – that there's a bit of a Hong Kong phenomenon. At the risk of sounding like one of those guys who travels and comes back with an insufferable revelation, a long-awaited first trip to Hong Kong gave me a better understanding of Toronto building podiums, the mostly commercial floors that taller buildings shoot up from. Hong Kong has many kinds of buildings, but there is an incredible number of residential buildings sprouting from large podiums that have restaurants and shops in them – especially in new areas and neighbourhoods outside of the older, established ones. Seeing a common and not particularly appreciated Toronto-style building form working somewhere else helped me understand ours and think about how they might evolve.

The Hong Kong podiums were inevitably interesting. We ate in them, had drinks in upper-floor bars, and found unique, independent shops. When I saw an escalator, I went up to see what was there. These podiums were simply part of the city. Inviting, varied, and endlessly interesting. As Toronto continues to grow, the podium-and-tower is not going away. More are coming. As the city gets increasingly dense, perhaps we'll learn to go up and down, and these places will become part of the city we frequent for all kinds of reasons, enjoying the public verticality that cities in Asia do. In a few places, like Yonge Street in North York, this is already starting to happen. Back down Sheppard, peek into the Emerald Park building. It's one of the green ones that look like Gumby is leaning over a bit. There's a grocery store and LCBO, but also a mix of small independent shops and food stalls up and down, a small warren of retail. Between these buildings and the old stock of low-rise buildings, it's an exciting place. The upper storeys of buildings are sometimes the most interesting, with hidden cafés, karaoke bars, and more quotidian outfits like insurance brokers, muscle clinics, and ESL schools. These buildings contain everything a city needs, layered vertically the way cities do best, so there's always something to discover.

For now, the towers begin to thin out at Finch Avenue, though this, too, is quickly changing, as more spring up along Yonge. Between Finch and the hydro corridor is the North American Centre, two towers connected at the base, and one the last of big office megaprojects (the second tower completed in 1992) before the 1990s recession. On the lower floor, the centre is a self-contained version of the downtown PATH system, with water features that give off a chlorine smell, permeating the air the way indoor pools in big hotels do. The over-the-top name, though derived from the North American Life insurance company, is like a matching bookend to the Residences of the World Trade Centre at the foot of Yonge, as if insisting that this street always means something bigger than it seems to be.

All this is – or was – Newtonbrook, an early-nineteenth-century village. Most traces of this historic village disappeared when the area was subdivided into a huge residential development in the 1950s. Lost, too, was the Methodist manse at the corner of Yonge and Hendon Avenue where Prime Minister Lester B. Pearson was born. His term as prime minister is partly responsible for Newtonbrook's contemporary multiculturalism, as his government started opening Canada's doors to newcomers in a big way. Today, his intersection is home to the Finch subway station's kiss 'n' ride depot (now, sadly, referred to as 'passenger pick-up and drop-off locations,' or PPUDO, as the technocrat acronym goes), housed in a flying-saucer-shaped building and certainly a fitting memorial to the Nobel Prize–winning atomic-age peacemaker.

Standing at the Steeles Avenue curb, where Yonge Street continues into the clutches of the rest of Ontario, we might be tempted to call this place the crossroads of nowhere, but it's as busy as Yonge and Bloor. Buses from York's Rapid Transit service, Viva, and standing-room-only TTC caravans pass by constantly (the buses pouring out of Finch Station will be reduced substantially by the eventual subway extension beyond the city limits). At mid-afternoon, pedestrians are everywhere, crossing all seven lanes of Yonge or Steeles. Some of the pedestrians cross north to Richmond Hill – big-sky country.

At the end – or beginning – of Toronto, any lingering doubts as to this place's importance are cleared up by Centerpoint Mall's self-assured modish logo of four arrows pointing inward. Not midtown. Not uptown. It's the centre. Inside, the standard Toronto second-tier mall mix of rug emporiums, discount electronics, leather goods shops, and other independent stores make it worth a visit or two. There are redevelopment plans with a cluster of mixed-use buildings and high-rises. Like other malls, Centerpoint is sitting on incredibly vast and lucrative real estate.

Centerpoint was originally going to be called Sayvette City when it was planned in 1961, but changed names before opening in 1964. It, like its popular cousin, Yorkdale Shopping Centre, is a bit of a modernist gem, with horizontal windows along the tops of corridors and a food court in a huge round room with a sweeping ceiling that feels like a 1960s airport – though it was altered at some point to increase retail footprints. The scene in the food court is typical of these kinds of malls that have become community centres: people sit and chat, scratch lottery cards, and play backgammon on ornate Armenian-style boards.

Back outside at Yonge and Steeles, Richmond Hill's own growing skyline rises as the remarkable busyness of Toronto strip malls continues here, too, like at the Yonge Centre Plaza, a.k.a. Iranian Plaza, across from and a bit south of Centerpoint. An older cedar-shingled building that houses Iranian butchers, jewellery stores, cafés, and the Tehranto Exchange money transfer service, Yonge Centre Plaza – along with Centerpoint – is a fine welcome to the city. Yonge Street, from top to bottom, can accommodate all sorts of variety, both human and architectural.

It's our main street, after all.

The Toronto Islands

pack a lunch   Connecting walk: Harbourfront

admission

bathing suit recommended

During the summer, at about noon on Fridays, Toronto starts to empty out. You can almost hear the slow middle- and upper-class drain to the north as tens of thousands of Torontonians make for the highways on their way to faraway-sounding places like Wasaga, Bala, Bobcaygeon, and Killbear. Those of us on the wrong side of the cottage gap are left with a quieter city – some Sunday afternoons feel downright apocalyptic in their emptiness. We're left with no choice but to find our adventures in the urban wilderness and, often, on the Toronto Islands.

The islands are to Toronto what the seaside resorts of Brighton and Blackpool were to Britain: a place where working- and middle-class folks could take cheap holidays of their own. Blackpool would heave with factory workers from the north of England, while Brighton, just a short train ride from London, was an escape from the tumult and pollution of the city. The resorts were full of amusements from giant Victorian piers to streets called the 'Golden Mile.' (Our own Golden Mile is in Scarborough, but that's another story.) Until the 1970s, their beaches and promenades were packed with people; there was nowhere else to go.

With the advent of cheap holiday packages and mass tourism, lobster-red Britons now choose to sun themselves on the Mediterranean shores of Ibiza, Majorca, and Malta. The old resorts are seen as melancholy places where the skies are perpetually cloudy and the beaches cold and windswept. Morrissey summed up the sensibility best in 'Everyday Is Like Sunday,' perhaps the most apocalyptic pop song ever written as he calls for nuclear Armageddon.

Though I'd love an excuse to take maudlin trips to the Toronto Islands and sing sad songs to myself, I can't, because there isn't much that's depressing about the place, even if it functions in much the same way as the British resorts did. Today, the islands are as busy as they were in 1813, when an early European settler, D. W. Smith, observing the Indigenous people who boated to the islands, recorded in the *Gazetteer* that 'the long beach or peninsula, which affords a most delightful ride, is considered so healthy by the Indians that they resort to it whenever indisposed.' Certainly Smith paints too rosy a portrait of Indigenous life under British rule, but I, too, like to sneak over when 'indisposed,' or even when I'm disposed; on at least one occasion I've participated in a conference call while lying on the beach there.

The ferry trip to the islands makes the separation between here and there official. In winter, the Toronto Island ferry plies through the harbour like a light-duty icebreaker, keeping a channel open from the mainland to the Ward's Island dock as it goes back and forth. When the harbour does freeze over, the William Lyon Mackenzie fireboat, named after Toronto's first mayor and Rebellion of 1837 leader, will clear the way. The very old-timey but beloved ferries from a century ago are berthed during the winter, so it's the *Ongiara*, the automobile ferry serving Hanlan's Point in the summer, that runs year-round to the Ward's dock. It isn't young either, though, launched from an Owen Sound shipbuilder in 1963. Visiting the islands during winter is a magical thing. There's barely a lineup for the ferry, just some intrepid winter souls and island residents. Outside, on deck, the sound of the ferry pushing through chunks of ice is like a giant cocktail glass swirling. The skyscrapers pump out steam and the city hums, as if it's collectively trying to keep warm.

Visiting one New Year's Day, I saw a group of winter disc golfers playing the island course. When the ice is smooth, look for the islanders skating: they know when and where the ice is good and safe. There are even heated public washrooms on the island open all year and after dark, something mainland Toronto can't seem to manage well. Whether you're skiing, snowshoeing, or walking, the island itself is quiet, and the further away from Ward's, the fewer people there are. Remarkable in a metropolis of millions of people. Those millions do come in the summertime, though, some 1.4 million of them. All of them come by boat: most by ferry, others by the blessed but more expensive fleet of private water taxis that have made the island much more accessible. Still, it's an awful lot of people to move on antique ferries. New electric ferries are on order, but they will still suffer from slow boarding and disembarking, as they are pinched at their ends. The island will remain a trek to get to for some time, one that can drain the romance away at times.

In the summer, visitors to Centre Island are met with some of the softest, greenest grass I've ever seen in a public park and one of the famous Toronto Parks, Forestry, and Recreation signs that invite people to 'Please Walk on the Grass,' part of the legendary public legacy of Toronto Parks commissioner Tommy Thompson. On weekends, these greens are packed with large groups, often new Canadians cooking food and playing games or just going for walks. Many wear dress pants and shirts to the park, even on heat-alert days, just as most men did here sixty years ago. The formality also reminds me of my own Maltese ancestors, who dragged such sartorial traditions into a more casual era.

Near the docks is Centreville, a cute little amusement park. It's more small-town fair than Canada's Wonderland: the theme is quaint and slightly cheesy, and the rides' modest speeds are unlikely to shatter any world records. Yet, even without the fake mountain, the kids (and their adult handlers) seem to love it.

To the south, beyond Centreville, a series of formal gardens with a series of midcentury modern fountains lead to the islands' only pier, which juts out over Lake Ontario. This 'Avenue of the Island' was once Manitou Road, a much more urban main street with a theatre, shops, dance halls, and even a bowling alley; it was the centre of island life. The new, modern landscape was part of the the late-1950s master plan by Macklin Hancock, of Don Mills fame, and his firm Project Planning Associates, Limited. I wasn't around for it, but this replacement of the main drag is what I imagine wandering the modern public spaces at Expo 67 felt like. Modernist pavilions from the same time also dot the island, designed by architect Irving Grossman. The only amusement on the pier is the view, but onshore whole families rent strange-looking quad-cycles to explore the islands, often going wildly off course.

To the west lie the natural and less-populated parts of the islands. The main road leads along a narrow peninsula – prone to flooding, but the road here has been built higher since a 2017 submersion – between Lake Ontario and the interior waterways (rent a kayak on the mainland and paddle over for a completely different view of island life). As the trail curves north toward the Billy Bishop Airport, small signs direct the curious to Hanlan's Point, Toronto's clothing-optional beach.

People wear as much or as little as they want at Hanlan's. The naked coexist happily with people less willing to burn their sensitive parts. On one occasion, I saw someone lounging in what looked like a woollen Victorian bathing costume, while another time, a man in a three-piece suit walked the hot sands. It's Toronto's most liminal of spaces, an in-between place in our civic backyard that somehow feels far from home. Like our

ravines, Hanlan's is one of the places where nature and metropolis collide and, unlike the largely private cottage country to the north, it's home to a very public beach culture that allows Toronto's urban mix to express itself even more than it does on Queen Street or in Kensington Market. It's easy to forget the city, but then the occasional glimpse of someone's painful-looking genital piercing reminds me that we're still safely surrounded by Toronto's urbanity. It can be an uneasy mix – you'll sometimes hear grumblings from the committed nudists, who complain about the people who don't get completely naked, and sometimes there are creeps, harassers, and homophobes – but this beach is the ultimate manifestation of the kind of freedom Toronto represents: everybody can simply be how they like. Over the last decade, as Hanlan's has become more popular, beachgoers have become much more diverse too, reflecting Toronto's population the way Centre Island has for much longer.

Wander south, away from the crowds, and you'll find secret coves and water so clear it seems downright Bahamian, while the long walk north, into the 'clothed' area, passes through a wonderful dune-and-grass scrubland that continues until a hundred or so metres from the airport runway. During the airshow, this is the best seat in Toronto: the planes fly so low overhead that the pilots' heads are visible and the water vibrates from the sound. Torontonians have been taught to think that we're surrounded by a toxic soup, fit only for three-eyed fish (as people in some places have claimed to have seen), but Lake Ontario is just fine to swim in – in some places, it's even cleaner than some of the world's more celebrated beaches. In fact, numerous Toronto beaches regularly fly a Blue Flag, the internationally recognized eco-label awarded to beaches that meet a list of criteria related to water quality, environmental education, management, safety, and services. Other unflagged beaches are often fine to swim in as well.

Habitués of Hanlan's Point Beach know that for years this precious place has been quickly eroding. Though it was a vast expanse of sand just fifteen years ago, the lake has made its way up to the trees for a long stretch, causing one after another to fall into the lake. It's been heartbreaking to watch, but just as hopeful was seeing the Toronto and Region Conservation Authority and City do something about it. A long time in the making, the Gibraltar Point Erosion Control Project is finally seeing results in the form of a brand-new beach where recently there was just water. Beachgoers watched as barges created groynes, underwater structures that protect the shoreline and encourage sand accumulation, as well as nearshore reefs – both of which were made up of thousands of tons of rocky aggregate. Today, the groynes are marked by short yellow towers sticking out of the water, and new sand has been deposited by the truckful. It's like walking on newly formed volcanic land in Iceland or Hawaii, but in Toronto. The beach is back. Some of it, anyway.

Watching Hanlan's erode has been especially tough for Toronto's LGBTQ community, who have long found a safe refuge here as a somewhat-remote site, away from hostile gazes and worse. That Toronto's first Pride Picnic was here in 1971 is no coincidence. Quite a bit of the clothing-optional area has disappeared into the lake, but the City has extended this libertine designation to the 'new' beach, and the whole thing is rather wonderfully queer.

Where Torontonians can swim and how their bodies and clothing are policed has a long history. A 2021 book by historian Dale Barbour called *Undressed Toronto: From the Swimming Hole to Sunnyside, How a City Learned to Love the Beach, 1850–1935* chronicles how swimming in Toronto was always contested, and always a class and gender issue. Barbour shows how males could swim – or *bathe*, as it was called – naked in the Don River, along the waterfront, and at the eastern and western ends of Toronto Island with a remarkable degree of tolerance for a rather uptight Victorian city. As the industrial waterfront developed, and middle-class social mores expanded, working-class males swam nude in clandestine spots along wharves and shoreline warehouses. Women had far fewer opportunities to swim. Hanlan's, then, is a kind of revival and expansion of a somewhat elusive Toronto tradition.

East of the centre pier lies the residential side of the Islands, where two communities were saved from demolition in 1980, when then-Premier Bill Davis prevented the razing of dozens of cottages. During the 1970s, the Metro Toronto government was intent on making the island 100 per cent parkland, and removing the small resortish main street and adjacent houses was part of that progress. While much of it was removed, two clusters of cute streets with even cuter cottage-style homes on Algonquin Island (which can be reached by a short bridge) and at the end of Ward's Island (near where the island was once attached to the mainland) were preserved. Many people resent the islanders' presence and still wish the bulldozers had completed their work and cleared the islands completely of homes. This is always curious to me, as I like that people live here. I don't feel jealous because I can't think of a worse place to live. It isn't easy, bringing everything you need over by ferry in bike trailers, competing with the crowds in the summer, and enduring no ferry service at times, especially in the frozen winter. Yet, looking over from the mainland, it's comforting to know there are people there, watching over it and populating the place. In recent years, residents have advocated for better ferry service and improved dock experience, something that benefits all visitors. During summer days it's a crowded place, but at night and when the colder winds blow, the islands empty out. The city has more than enough empty green space, and the islands' residents are something unique to Toronto (though at times they can be cranky, and their in-fighting is legendary). Perhaps even a return to that resort 'main street' with a few more bars and hotels might be all right too.

Like anybody, I'd happily take a weekend at the cottage when one is offered. But the islands and their Disney-like perfection are a good substitute – and the ferry ride back at the end of the day beats the Highway 400 crawl back into town.

Harbourfront

neighbourhood jaunt

bathing suit optional

offspring friendly

Connecting walks: Yonge, Toronto Islands, Bathurst, Spadina, CNE/Western Waterfront

In late 2022, its *Toronto Star* sign freshly removed, One Yonge Street was surrounded by a cluster of buildings, some newer than others, and was just another building in a dense urban quarter of the city. It wasn't always thus, though. When the *Toronto Star* moved into the exposed aggregate beast of a building at the foot of Yonge in 1971, Queens Quay was lined with dying industry and railroad tracks. The *Star* was a redevelopment pioneer and, as early as 1963, stories in the *Star* waxed poetic about the future of the waterfront: 'On stage is a panorama of rails, rust and rot ... waiting in the wings are magnificent plans to transform it into office, motor hotels, a marine park, a heliport and ferry terminal extraordinaire.' The decline of the newspaper industry and the *Star*'s move to a smaller suite of offices on Spadina aside, the paper's departure from this building was a kind of bookend for Queens Quay from the start of one era to its near completion. Queens Quay is a proper urban neighbourhood now.

Heliports were hot in the sixties and all the best buildings had them, but the jet age didn't make it to the waterfront as quickly as the *Star* predicted, and the rot continued to rot. Fast-forward forty years and the *Star* was still on the eastern frontier of Toronto's waterfront development. Queens Quay became unfit for its royal name; its semi-industrial scrubland remained relatively contiguous all the way to Ashbridges Bay, near the Beach neighbourhood.

Redpath Sugar shows no sign of leaving the area, and has even reinvested in the site, which is a good thing. Freighters are often docked next to the building, unloading unrefined sugar from the Caribbean, giving Sugar Beach its name and often affording the air a sugary sparkle. The plant employs a lot of people who make physical product (a novel thing in the 'creative city'), but it's also a reminder of Toronto's industrial heritage and of our once-working waterfront. The area beyond, for years a refuge of odd industries, including a golf dome, is being filled in with new residential, commercial, and educational buildings.

There were always things happening along the waterfront, east of Yonge: a big supermarket, the old LCBO headquarters (the facade now part of a new development), legendary megaclubs like RPM, the Guvernment, and the Warehouse. But it wasn't the kind of place that people paid attention to in a 'wow, the city is changing' kind of way. Nothing changed here for so long that even when things were really happening on the waterfront, Torontonians didn't believe it, or were easily bamboozled into thinking otherwise. During Toronto's brief fling with Google's Sidewalk Labs, the 'Smart City' project proposed for some of the remaining post-industrial land east of Queens Quay, there were some bad faith revivals of this trope.

For a few years, Toronto had a very public debate about whether or not to give over prime waterfront land to a big civic experiment. There was a lot to like about the proposal, but a lot to be wary of. The oddest part, one that made Toronto seem like a small, desperate town, was when respected and established urban thinkers wrote variations of 'nothing has happened on Toronto's waterfront' or 'this is our only chance to do something good there' while endorsing Sidewalk. It was simply not true. It's been a slow process,

but democracy is slow, and it's messy, and it can be frustrating. Waterfront Toronto, the agency formed through a partnership of all three levels of government to oversee that change, was established in 2001 and began a series of extensive public consultations before coming up with master plans and getting on with the building and rebuilding of our waterfront. Visually, on the street, it was a slow start, but there was lots going on behind the scenes. Consider this: one of the first major defeats the Rob Ford mayoralty faced was when then–shadow mayor Doug Ford proposed a mall and Ferris wheel in the Port Lands. While a big wheel on its own isn't a bad idea, his new plan was at odds with plans many people had already bought into. It was no wonder that a grassroots opposition to Ford's plan rose quickly and was strong enough to get him to back down. Waterfront Toronto, with their years of consultation, had created a waterfront constituency that defended it when it was threatened.

It's unfortunate that Waterfront Toronto fumbled the initial relationship with Sidewalk, but the agency has absolutely transformed a big part of Toronto and is one of the best governmental initiatives here. If we could zap back to 2000, we wouldn't recognize the lakefront: parcels of empty land developed into buildings like Corus Quay and a George Brown campus, and public spaces like Sherbourne Common and Sugar Beach, with grand promenades at the water's edge. The high quality of these public spaces is unlike what we're used to in Toronto, and more are in the works. Not all of the buildings on Queens Quay are great, built when the waterfront was still a jumbled mess, but the notion that they cut the city off from the lake is also false: save for a handful of locations, including the ferry docks and Redpath sugar factory, it's possible to walk the lake edge from Sherbourne to the HMCS York naval building, west of Bathurst Street, through continuous and excellent public spaces. Waterfront Toronto also undertook three years of construction to transform Queens Quay into a European-style promenade. There's a place for everybody now: there are separate lanes for cars, streetcars, cyclists, and pedestrians. A 'complete street,' as the urban planners say. Despite all this, motorists routinely drive into the streetcar tunnel at Bay Street, requiring painstaking extraction. The City has installed deep grooves in the roadway and bright plastic bollards to deter them, but never underestimate a Toronto motorist's ability to spectacularly screw up. At least here it isn't deadly.

Excitement and anticipation around Toronto's waterfront is nothing new, but neither is disappointment – the *Star* itself inadvertently started the now infamous waterfront 'wall' of 1970s concrete so reviled in our city. The 'wall' is just more city, though, while the real 'barriers' were the Gardiner Expressway and rail corridor. In 1964, Bauhaus school founder Walter Gropius, then a professor at Harvard, saw the plans for new developments as very exciting, and said, 'Toronto is fortunate that its cross-town expressway was built north of the reclaimed land' – observing that, though Torontonians hate it so, the Gardiner could have been much worse, as waterfront freeways are in many other cities.

The main culprits behind the post-Gardiner barrier to the water are the Westin Harbour Castle Hotel and the neighbouring residential towers of Harbour Square, built in the 1970s by Robert Campeau, the later deposed, now deceased, king of Canadian development, who was an eventual victim of 1980s excess. If you walk by at street level, the buildings have all the charm and romance of the fan entrance to a football stadium where only losing teams play. The hotel's gaping mouth contains the most elaborate and well-lit parking ramp in the city, and is often filled with oversized pickup trucks and suvs that can't fit in the parking garage, a phenomenon at many downtown hotels. Figuring out how to walk into the hotel is a challenge, and guests dodge tourists and vehicles with every step. Like the *Star* building, these were all pioneers in a harsh landscape: there was nothing anybody wanted to see on Queens Quay so the buildings turned their back on it.

Harbour Square is redeemed by its lakeside public spaces. There are wooden docks with stairs that lead down to the water and lots of green mixed in with the concrete, and these spaces are populated and well-used. From the ferry, the building looks beautiful and utopic, like a futuristic *Star Trek* city rising out of blue and green nature. Up close, a giant concrete public-art sphere, part of a 1995 installation called *Sundial Folly* by John Fung and Paul Figueiredo, allows passersby to climb around and inside; it seems to float with the lily pads in a fountain. The ball is hollow, with a suspended walkway and an observatory-like view of the islands from inside. This is concrete used for good not evil, and though the south side of the complex is awful, the lakeside of Harbour Square is a fine and unsung pedestrian promenade.

People don't move down here for the sidewalks, though – these towers would be empty if they did. It's the view from the top that counts. In the early 2000s, on one of those summer nights when the city takes over and seems to make plans for you as you walk along through random encounters (this was in the days before I had a cellphone), I ended up at a party thrown by someone I didn't know on the thirtieth floor of Number One York Quay, one of the blue-and-beige towers next to Harbour Square. There was a tub full of beer, a grand piano, torch songs, and a stunning view from the balcony. The Gardiner and the city sparkled into the humidity and smog, magically disappearing, an anonymous view high above a street that's undergoing constant improvements and may one day match that view.

At York Street, the lakeside concrete canyon starts to lighten up with the Queen's Quay Terminal, a giant old warehouse with a glass condo sprouting out of the top. In 1983, Zeidler Partnership Architects turned the 1927 Terminal Warehouse – the first poured-concrete building in Canada, and known as a 'fisherman's dream' for all the products it housed – into offices and luxury condos that eventually became the home of former Ontario premier Mike Harris. Out front is the landscaped and literary Toronto 'walk of fame' with the names of book award winners. The southeast corner is hollowed out four floors high (as if Lake Ontario storms had worn it down to its skeleton over time), with restaurants, some retail, and a theatre inside.

The most promising development in the area has been the addition of a grocery store in the Queen's Quay Terminal. People who don't live near a major grocery store often say it's their neighbourhood's missing ingredient. The terminal building is part of the four hectares overseen by Harbourfront Centre, a federal crown corporation – and now a charitable organization – established in 1972 to revitalize Toronto's waterfront. Though it runs the risk of becoming a tourist trap – it's one of those places where people come in from elsewhere to see 'the city' – it's a good place and it works. On warm nights, it's teeming with people from downtown, uptown, and beyond, and there's opportunity for nice cultural collisions when a band is playing on the open-air stage and folks who might not normally listen to a particular kind of music, let alone attend a show, get to participate. This is how cities should work.

On one summer trip here, I came across a group of Bible-camp teens in the little pocket of grassy knolls by the Power Plant gallery. They were sitting in a circle, asking each other, 'What would Jesus do?' while, a few trees over, a guy in acid-washed jeans dry-humped his date behind a shrub. For a more subtle display, look at the tiny cubes of light scattered in the pathways that change colour over time. It's little details and moments like this, the things you don't see at first but might discover on your seventh visit, that make this place special – like the gardens that were planted in 1996 along the western wall of the Power Plant by Gene Threndyle, an artist and gardener (he also placed the 'ruined' bits of architecture in gardens at Dufferin Grove Park). Included among the flora are chunks of a Shaw Street sidewalk, which make the connection between the waterfront and the city it's attached to. It all mixes just fine in the shadow of the Power Plant gallery, our miniature version of London's Tate Modern, which is housed in another (much larger) former power plant on the banks of the Thames.

The sometimes open, sometimes in disrepair metal-and-wood pedestrian footbridge that crosses the marina to the west of the Harbourfront stage was my preferred route around the area until Waterfront Toronto opened the third of their innovative wave decks at Simcoe Quay in 2009. The undulating wooden sidewalks are dreamlike, as if what we know about urbanity has suddenly become an absurd cartoon. In officious Toronto, the wave decks are an audacious addition to the streetscape and, perhaps predictably, within months of opening were already the subject of one lawsuit from a man who hurt himself while trying to walk them and wanted to blame somebody for his fall. Now there are a guardrail and warning signs.

The bustle of Harbourfront quiets down beyond the Radisson Hotel, a rather regrettable mirror of a building on an otherwise decent stretch of waterfront made even better by H_TO Park just to the west. Designed by Toronto landscape-architecture firm Janet Rosenberg & Studio and Montreal's Claude Cormier, who also did Sugar Beach, Love Park, and Berczy Park (also known as the dog fountain park), the $10.5-million park stretches over 4.3 acres and includes rolling, grassy mounds of earth, trees, Muskoka chairs, sand, and a terraced cement beach, all reminiscent of the Paris Plages, where the banks of the grey Seine are turned into a sandy beach each summer. It's the kind of natural-but-not landscape that we expect from great cities, where humans invent environments that put them in touch with the natural world – Lake Ontario in this case – but without the terror of actual wilderness. Though many beaches in Toronto are perfectly fine for swimming, signs here prohibit such activity, and this is the only ingredient missing in a place that attempts, more so than any other place along this part of the waterfront, to get us as close to the lake as possible.

Just as good as H_TO Park is the naturalized area at the foot of Spadina, beyond the Spadina WaveDeck, where plaques describe the flora and fauna as well as how the shoreline has shifted and expanded over the decades. Even more fun are the secret paths through reeds where your feet squish in the muck, and where you can stand in the place where the lake and land mix together in soft and dirty ways. Nearby, during summer months, tall(ish) ships rock in the swell. Across from here, at 401 Queens Quay, is Harbour Terrace, a 1987 building by Li Architects that won a Governor General's Award for architecture and is a late-modernist beauty that looks straight out of the original *Miami Vice* series.

Bach interpreted: Bring your headphones to the Music Garden.

These wetlands lead to the high and dry Toronto Music Garden, inspired by Bach's *Suites for Unaccompanied Cello*. In the mid-nineties, landscape designer Julie Moir Messervy worked with cellist Yo-Yo Ma to interpret the piece in flora based on its six dance movements – as described on the City's website, Bach's 'Prelude' became 'an undulating river-scape with curves and bends' while his 'Sarabande' became 'a conifer grove in the shape of an arc.' However, on an overcast day, I found Prince's 'Purple Rain' worked well with the space too, which means they did a good job on the park. The garden's trails weave in and out like a song, and there are secret spots and spiral paths between bushes that lead up to an iron maypole. There is even an underutilized amphitheatre on a grassy slope, waiting for somebody to stage a Fringe Festival play or perhaps some other kind of gentle guerrilla theatre. Across the way, Arthur Erickson's King's Landing condo looks, with its terraced floors, like a white cruise ship ready to set sail into Lake Ontario.

The stretch ends with a nice mix of condos and co-ops, complete with a community school where you'll find the most urban-looking basketball courts – in the *Sesame Street* sense – in the city. It's a real waterfront neighbourhood that's socially and economically diverse. The Billy Bishop Airport proponents who often claim this is just the wealthy elite area complaining about the airport's existence have probably only ever seen the neighbourhood from the air. It's not exclusive, and though that rhetoric flares up from time to time, just crank the Bach or Prince and go for a waterfront walk and you won't hear anything about that.

The CN Tower

 neighbourhood jaunt

 dress to impress

admission

Connecting walks: Nathan Phillips Square/
PATH, Spadina

Every time I walk south on Ossington Avenue, a block north of Bloor, I register the CN Tower in my peripheral vision, but when I turn to look at it, I'm surprised each time because what I'm seeing isn't the tower, but rather the dome of the Ukrainian Catholic Church of the Holy Protection of the Mother of God on Leeds Street. Houses along this part of Ossington block the view of the actual tower, but it's the landmark that calibrates my mental map of Toronto, so my brain replaces what's actually there with the CN Tower. Wherever we are in Toronto, we can either see or sort of feel the tower's position and proximity to us. It's the compass that lets us know where we are.

The CN Tower has so penetrated our civic consciousness that it hardly matters that after over three decades as the world's tallest free-standing structure, it was surpassed in 2009 by the Burj Khalifa in the United Arab Emirates. When our tower was built, its world's-best status was a matter of civic and national pride, transcending regionalism the way Expo 67 and Wayne Gretzky and the rest of the 1980s Edmonton Oilers did. The CN Tower gave all Canadians bragging rights.

Planning for the tower began in the early 1970s, when Canadian National and FM radio signals that originated downtown began to be blocked by Toronto's growing skyline. The SkyPod was added during the planning process, as builders realized they had a tourist attraction on their hands, 'a goldmine in the sky selling rides to the top at $2 to $3 each,' according to a 1975 *Toronto Star* article. A few extra feet were added when builders realized it could beat Moscow's Ostankino Tower. When the tower finally opened in 1976, the *Star* reported that people in cottage country had discovered new programs on radio and TV, prompting the mayor of Bracebridge to ask, 'You can't get us some American channels, can you?'

Strangely, though it stayed on top of the world for all those years, that record alone was never enough. The CN Tower always tried to outdo itself, as if our confidence as a world city (municipally) or as a middle power (nationally) was so deeply insecure it required constant maintenance.

In the late 1970s, Jimmy Conklin, the 'Carny King' who ran games and rides at the Canadian National Exhibition, set up Undercurrent, installing $750,000 worth of arcade amusements in the basement of the tower, hosted by costumed attendants Glitch and Short Circuit, creating an 'unsleazy' arcade that newspaper reports said 'appeals to the whole family.' In the 1980s, Citytv's Moses Znaimer produced the Tour of the Universe space simulation ride that he hoped to turn into a North American franchise. In 1997, legendary drug-taking British band Spiritualized played a stunt show in the pod, an attempt at world record status, billed as the 'highest show on earth' (in both senses). In recent decades, a glass floor was added to the pod, its strength measured by the weight of hippos (fourteen of them), followed by a long-overdue LED lighting scheme in 2007. It's as if the comparative height never really mattered at all, so why would it matter now that we are no longer on top?

Though it's a local icon that we share with the rest of the country, the CN Tower is unmistakably Toronto, and it will continue to mean a great deal to this city. Returning to Toronto, even by plane, I experience that special moment as the tower finally comes into a view, when the relieved feeling of being home sets in: I'm safe again and that which lies beyond our city's walls has not managed to destroy me.

We've all got our favourite view of our tower. It's said that tower architect John Andrews's favourite place to view it was from the northeast corner of Bay and King, framed perfectly by the austere black towers of the TD Centre. From there, the SpacePod seems as oversized as the moon does in the posters for the movie E.T., but the tower itself seems almost short and stubby. From the west, around Liberty Village or Fort York, it's suddenly standing alone, far from the downtown cluster, its spectacular size even bigger than you might remember.

Though it looks different depending on the perspective, the tower dominates the skyline from anywhere in the city. When it opened in 1976, the late alderman, journalist, and architect Colin Vaughan wrote that 'some people [complain] that you can't go anywhere in Toronto without having the CN Tower come along too. Turn a corner on a street, look out a window and the tower seems to be there, always present whether you want it or not.' But after nearly two generations of it hanging around every day, losing it would feel like having a civic limb removed.

Imagine a Toronto without the CN Tower. Darren O'Donnell did in his 2004 novel *Your Secrets Sleep with Me*, in which he wrote of a tornado toppling it into

Lake Ontario, forever placing his book into the local dystopia section at the Toronto Public Library. The publisher of this book, Coach House, even produced a poster around the tower's opening, illustrating the crash radius should it fall. We would be just as lost and freaked out without our concrete compass as New Yorkers were when the World Trade Center catastrophically disappeared from their lives, leaving that city's citizens guessing at where the tip of Manhattan was and, consequently, where they were, both physically and existentially.

Amy Lavender Harris, whose book *Imagining Toronto* comprises the most complete collection of Toronto-based literature in the city, outlined literary representations of the tower. In it, she finds the tower irreplaceable: 'Even when we turn our backs upon it, the CN Tower remains a sly presence in our photographs and narratives. Its shadow glides ceaselessly across our memories of the city like the second hand of time. The tower is always there in the corner of our gaze, a visible totem to the ways we inhabit and imagine the city.'

Opinions on the tower have always varied wildly. There are those, like Harris, who love it but find it kind of awkward, and those who take cheap shots at it by dragging out the tired old 'phallus in the sky' criticism, which says more about what's on their minds than about what the tower does for us. I've always thought it was the sleekest thing around, like the skinny architectural version of an Airstream trailer: that long, perfect curve to the ground, the SpacePod looking like a glass-and-steel pill I wish I could ingest. The CN Tower is weird-looking, which is why we haven't been able to stop looking at it all these years.

Airborne concrete: the CN Tower's space-age pod under construction in 1974.

Much of the public record of the CN Tower's rise was captured by photographers such as the *Toronto Star*'s own Boris Spremo, who snapped it as it grew from a concrete stump to when 'Olga,' the Sikorsky helicopter crane, lifted the final piece of the antenna into place. The CN Tower story is usually about its superlatives – 'tallest free-standing' and all that – but there are many more lesser-known stories behind it, including those of the people who built it. One of Spremo's most famous photographs is of two ironworkers sitting on a beam without a harness. Also doing this dangerous work were a large contingent of Iroquois ironworkers who helped build the tower, as they did skyscrapers and bridges across North America.

One man has made it his life's work to compile more of the stories of the 1,537 people who built the tower, from the bean counters to the guys pouring cement at one thousand feet. 'The engineering history of the CN Tower has been overlooked, unlike London's Tower Bridge, the Eiffel Tower, or the World Trade Center,' said Robert Lansdale when I spoke to him on the occasion of the tower's fortieth anniversary in 2016. 'As for the people who built it, their history has been swept under the rug.' A self-proclaimed 'CN Tower kid' who was 'always down there watching it go up' in the early 1970s, Lansdale said he has spent five to six thousand hours compiling and recreating a visual history of the tower's design and construction, scouring public and private archives and collecting many stories along the way. 'This is really about people, not the tower,' he said. 'That's just concrete.'

One of those stories is about crane operator Winston Young, who formed a Toronto folk-singing duo with his wife Mary Jane in the late 1960s before arriving at his perch at the top of the tower. In 1974, Young helped an ironworker daredevil called Sweet William climb to the end of the crane and parachute off. Mary Jane even wrote a song called 'The Ballad of Sweet William' about the event; its animated video can still be found online. Another of Lansdale's stories includes a quote from Franz Knoll, the tower's structural engineer. 'It was built using slide rules, human drafting, no computers, no precedents,' said Knoll to Lansdale.

Being on top didn't cure our insecurity, and though it gave us the chance to boast a little when visitors from abroad were around, it hardly matters that the CN Tower is no longer the tallest free-standing structure in the world. Its usefulness to us has gone well beyond a world record, so Dubai can have that record. From the looks of it, they're even more insecure than Toronto is.

Nathan Phillips Square, the Sheraton Centre, and the PATH System

neighbourhood jaunt

dress to impress

scenic views

Connecting walks: Yonge, Harbourfront, CN Tower, University, Dundas, Downtown East Side

One night in the mid-2000s, a small group of people active in City circles – architects, writers, councillors, urban planners, and even an activist or two – gathered in a room at Grano restaurant on Yonge Street, a few blocks north of Davisville. Roberto Martella, Grano's owner, had turned his (now much-missed) restaurant into a kind of civic salon, hosting talks and dinners about what it means to be a city. On this deep-January night, Project for Public Spaces (PPS), a non-profit organization from New York 'dedicated to creating and sustaining public places that build communities,' talked about their efforts to make Mississauga's public places walkable, people-friendly, and inviting. They also said something that caused an audible gasp in the room: 'Nathan Phillips Square, on a scale of one to a hundred, ranks zero.'

They might have been playing the role of American dilettantes, trying to shock us out of our provincial complacency, but that gasp turned into a collective hiss because, as everybody in Toronto knows, the square works. The folks from PPS were suffering from a condition we can call modern-hate, a knee-jerk orthodoxy that says that any big concrete space is automatically a wasteland and a dystopia of bad planning and execution. That's not the case in Toronto. Nathan Phillips Square is a sacred civic space, perhaps the finest concrete manifestation of peace, order, and good government in Canada. During the day, it's enjoyed by seemingly everybody: scores of office people, wayward hippies with backpacks twice as big as they are, lobbyists on cellphones, married couples just eloped in City Hall, people taking a million photos an hour of the Toronto sign, some homeless folks on the periphery, and a constant stream of people crossing the square on their way to City Hall. Crossing the square is a ceremonial march: you're forced to regard City Hall from afar and approach it on foot – it's huge, but you can walk right in. When Old City Hall opened in 1899, the mayor John Shaw said, 'Great buildings symbolize a people's deeds and aspirations.' He could have easily been speaking at the opening sixty-six years later of New City Hall, a place that has become Toronto's agora.

In ancient Greek city-states, the agora, or 'place of assembly,' was the centre of civic and democratic life, the place where citizens would gather to discuss politics or listen to public speeches, and to run into other citizens. Sometimes the square would also host a market, but generally, it was just a large outdoor space surrounded by public buildings. The agora in Athens included fountains, trees, and temples for various gods like Hephaestus, Zeus, and Apollo. The agora provided space for citizens to meet and a home for institutions that represented the Athenian state – all the elements of a formal public space that became a civic living room.

The square has been undergoing a long renovation, initially planned in the late 2000s. It had acquired some additions over the years that didn't always work, but more importantly, it had become rundown and needed an update – a gentle one, as the original design is beloved and has largely worked. Like Queen's Park, it's a hodgepodge landscape of civic monuments, some more quirky than others, fitting of the cauldron of ideas and people who pass through City Hall and city politics on any given day. At the base of the middle 'Freedom Arch,' which spans the reflecting pool and ice rink, is Toronto's very own chunk of the Berlin Wall. This piece of the wall was purchased by Markus Hess, an engineer from Kitchener, and flown over by the German Consulate in 1991, one of many pieces of the wall that made their way around the world. Today, it's beginning to deteriorate, perhaps a symptom of communist concrete's lack of fortitude or people picking at it for their own personal Cold War souvenir, but most officiously Torontonian is the sign adjacent to this monument to freedom that intones not to climb the Freedom Arch, itself near the sign that tells people not to enter the reflecting pool. Toronto loves signs telling people what they can't do, so it's appropriate they're here at City Hall too, the sign-dictating mothership.

On the west side, by a daycare playground, is a cluster of monuments that includes a granite column from Rome that was given to the city in 1957, as well as a glowering statue of Sir Winston Churchill, moved from a position closer to Queen Street, a kind of landscape demotion that angered the local Churchill Society. Surrounding him are exposed aggregate benches, part of the square's original design, and they are glorious specimens from the midcentury era. The final part of the square's renovation was the addition of the Spirit Garden in the southwest corner, also known as the Indian Residential

School Survivors Restoration of Identity Project. Initiated by Toronto Council Fire, the garden was designed by Gow Hastings Architects and includes a two-metre-tall turtle sculpture by Anishinaabe artist Solomon King and identifies the names of Ontario's seventeen residential schools.

Nathan Phillips Square is located in what was once a dense neighbourhood known as the Ward. Sometimes called Toronto's first immigrant neighbourhood, it was where Toronto's original downtown Chinatown began, centred at Elizabeth Street and Dundas. In the late 1950s, when the area was cleared for the New City Hall project, there was no large open downtown space in Toronto, and a grand civic project, typical of the time, was concocted to create that space at the expense of this diverse and lower-income immigrant community. As a result, the city got a modernist expanse of concrete, the welcome mat to the two crescent-shaped buildings that surround the spaceship-like Council Chamber.

The small collection of Chinese shops and restaurants on Dundas Street between Bay and University is just about all that remains of Toronto's first Chinatown. It migrated west along Dundas when the Ward was cleared out, eventually establishing a new community at Spadina Avenue. Two plaques in the northwest corner of Nathan Phillips Square – part of Heritage Toronto's plaques program – commemorate one of this city's earliest ethnic areas, lost to the march of a particularly forceful era of progress.

Also on the west side of the square is the Peace Garden, a deconstructed postmodern pavilion added in 1984 in a more central location but moved here, to the periphery, during renovations. The well-intentioned pavilion was a design mistake that was added to the square in 1984, one that messed up Finnish architect Viljo Revell's original clean design. Among the lesser consequences of the escalation of the Cold War in the 1980s was the desperate need for peace gardens. But good intentions can run amok, even when you get Pierre Trudeau to turn the sod, the Pope to light the flame with an ember from Hiroshima, and the Queen to christen the whole thing. This story was certainly a cautionary tale for those involved in the 2007 design competition to 'revitalize' the square with a gentle touch.

The plan to revitalize the square with green roofs and improved facilities was a delicate endeavour: How do you fix up a sacred space? The Project for Public Space style encourages programmed human activity in public spaces and sees a modernist expanse like Nathan Phillips Square as empty and maybe even totalitarian in vibe. But we don't always need designed distractions

↑
sod

↑
flame

↑
christen

when in public. What's most noticeable about Nathan Phillips Square is the lack of physical 'stuff.' Apart from the Peace Garden, the skating rink with its three Freedom Arches, and the *Three Way Piece No. 2: Archer* sculpture by Henry Moore in front of the City Hall doors, the square is respectful of the robust democracy it represents (that 'peace, order, and good government' thing). It allows for large groups of people to gather without barrier, even if they're angry with the government of the day. It respects the right and need of citizens to gather. Where else would you want to welcome a Canadian hero like Terry Fox as he triumphantly runs into the city, as he did during his Marathon of Hope in 1980? Thousands cheered as he was given the key to the city in the place that best represents the city. Tens of thousands of people gathered here to protest the Gulf War, or Trump during the inauguration Women's March, or the provincial government's amalgamation of the city. It also became a living memorial for Jack Layton when he passed away, with thousands of temporary chalked tributes.

The flyer distributed to guests invited to the opening-day celebrations in 1965 included the statement of guidance that accompanied the launch of the worldwide design competition for New City Hall initiated in 1957. The statement asked architects to 'find a building that will proudly express its function as the centre of civic government.' Revell, whose design ultimately won the competition over the 520 others submitted, called the square and City Hall 'the eye of government' (the 'spaceship' or 'clamshell' has been called the eyeball and the two towers the eyelids). In that respect, the square is the place where Torontonians can either step back and observe the centre of civic power or walk right up to the front door unencumbered and continue inside, though in recent years layers of security have made access much less smooth or easy.

The square and City Hall instantly came to represent Toronto's bright future and signalled the beginning of its shift from Canada's second city to its cultural and business capital. Though the CN Tower provides some stiff competition, Nathan Phillips Square and City Hall is the iconic image of Toronto, a symbol it was meant to become from the beginning. (A stylized outline of the two buildings, which meet to form a T, can be seen on Toronto's flag and in the front-door handles of City Hall.) That opening-day flyer also included a quote from architecture critic Sigfried Giedion: 'It is the first civic centre of this century worthy of the name.' The winning redesign by Plant Architect and Shore Tilbe Irwin and Partners added more greenery, a cleaned-up and reorganized peace garden, and, in the architect's words, made an 'explicit attempt to bring out the square's role as an agora but also as a civic theatre of focused gathering.' There's a permanent stage to replace the temporary ones and a green roof with public access created on top of the building's podium, a place long off limits but now one to eat lunch in or from which to watch the square itself. The elevated walkway around the square provides a similar experience.

Take a moment to compare the midcentury era of civic-square building to one a few decades later. The busy Peace Garden in Nathan Phillips Square has much in common with Mel Lastman Square, located in front of what was North York City Hall prior to amalgamation. Completed in 1987, nearly ten years after North York's City Hall opened (unlike Nathan Phillips Square, it wasn't one cohesive design but rather two separate initiatives), it was named after the very much alive and in-office mayor of North York, Mel Lastman. Stand on Yonge Street and look west into the square, and your path to the front doors of North York's former City Hall (now the North York Civic Centre) is blocked by a number of obstacles. There's a seven-hundred-seat amphitheatre, a stream that flows over a waterfall, a wedding chamber, and, as in Nathan Phillips Square, a reflecting pool that doubles as a skating rink in the winter months. The square is also multi-level, with staircases leading up and down to areas of different height, a jagged foothill-like topography laid out before the sharp and severe slant of the mountain range that is the civic building. The actual entrance to the building is obscured in a sunken area well below street level. Wherever your eye lands, there's something new to look at. It's the architectural equivalent of MTV-style television editing: no long takes, designed for short attention spans.

Back downtown, the Sheraton Centre Hotel, located across from City Hall, is for many people everything that's both right and wrong with modernism. Walking along all three sides of the hotel is unpleasant, as it offers little for the pedestrian. To enter the hotel on foot is to dodge suvs and taxis in the massive pick-up and drop-off zone, and along Queen there's a ramp half a block long leading into City Hall's underground garage, a product of its era. Its sterile nature is echoed by three sides of the Four Seasons Centre for the Performing Arts to the west.

Catch a glimpse of the Sheraton Centre from a few blocks to the west or east and it seems impossibly thin, cutting through the skyline like a knife. Seen from the front, its thinness gives way to wideness, as the facade is an impossible expanse of concrete and glass, at night appearing like a space-age analog control panel with individual rooms randomly lit up. They don't build them like this anymore. Really, they don't, save for a few exceptions in these parts. New hotels tend to be smaller, more boutique, and, if they're part of a big building, often combined with a residential component like the Four Seasons and Shangri-La hotels are.

The Sheraton Centre is an old-school mothership that goes deep into the earth and high in the sky, with over 1,300 rooms and 12,000 square metres of event space. 'It has a scale that is profoundly metropolitan,' wrote architect Michael McClelland in *Concrete Toronto*, the 2007 guidebook to the city's concrete architecture built between the 1950s and 1970s. 'It was built on the idea that Toronto was a place for phenomenal growth and bold new urban enterprises.' McClelland points out that the Sheraton was meant as a companion to New City Hall, and even has a bar overlooking the square. The City of Toronto expropriated the land in order to have a suitably impressive modern building framing in the south side of Nathan Phillips Square, and it still owns the land and leases it to the hotel.

The view from City Hall to the Sheraton is nearly the same as it was in 1972, when the hotel was completed, but the space behind the civic towers has been filled in. This is a genuine, modernist, midcentury-period view. City Hall connections run even deeper, as Seppo Valjus, a member of its Finnish architectural team led by Viljo Revell, also consulted on the Sheraton with John B. Parkin Associates, the local firm that worked on both buildings. It's a cohesive landscape. Whenever there's an event or rally in the square, I look over to the tower and there are inevitably people in hotel rooms looking down on us. What a civic view they get to behold.

Still, like any building over fifty, it could use additional updates. It is, of course, anti-urban at the ground floor. The sheer size of the motor court reveals the size of the hotel podium, often obscured by the tower's visual domination. Filled with meeting spaces and ballrooms above and below ground, there's even an indoor-outdoor pool atop it, a secret, if decadent, tree-filled elevated oasis downtown. Inside the hotel is another oasis, the courtyard with a terraced garden and waterfalls, a duck pond, and beehives designed by landscape architect J. Austin Floyd with rooms that open onto it motel-style, making it all feel like a retreat in a place far from the city. It's to Toronto what the roof garden and pools of the brutalist Hotel Bonaventure are to Montreal.

Like City Hall, the bowels of the Sheraton are connected to Toronto's PATH system, the thirty-kilometre-long network of underground passages and tunnels that connects over seventy-five downtown buildings. You can start exploring the PATH here in the heart of the city or from any of the connected buildings in the financial district. The PATH has no beginning or end, but for a good suggested starting point, walk north on Bay Street from City Hall to the Atrium on Bay building at Dundas, currently the northernmost point of the PATH. Along the way, you'll find Larry Sefton Park tucked directly behind City Hall. It's a cozy neo-modernist pocket park that was commissioned by the United Steel Workers of America in 1977 in memory of Sefton, a long-time union leader. With steel I-beams bursting dramatically out of the concrete, this quiet place feels like Superman's Fortress of Solitude.

During pre-COVID times, the PATH saw over 100,000 commuters pass through each day. Though the stats show that downtown has not recovered since the work-from-home revolution, and though there are vacancies throughout the PATH, it still feels busy on working weekdays. Those with a good sense of direction can meander down to Queens Quay without ever stepping outside, though it's a challenge to navigate as familiar landmarks disappear and one's sense of direction, even if excellent, becomes easily flipped around.

The PATH is Toronto's version of Paris's arcades, 'a world in miniature' where philosopher Walter Benjamin wandered in the 1920s when trying to understand that city. At first glance, the PATH is a fairly generic shopping mall, but the impressive sum of its parts and the people who populate it make it remarkable. As you walk along, the stores start to repeat like the background in a cartoon chase scene. It's architectural déjà vu, a dream world where the parts are the same, just arranged differently.

In the 1990s, the City of Toronto installed a way-finding system to aid movement between sections, but it's intentionally subtle: each section of the

PATH is privately owned, and as with window- and clock-free casinos, the owners don't want to provide you and your money with an easy escape. The Toronto-Dominion Centre was long an exception to the generic look of much of the path. Architect Mies van der Rohe laid out a mausoleum of a mall down there, a place of order, clean lines, and polished travertine marble. Even the store signs were uniform: white letters on a black background using a font Mies designed specifically for the TD Centre.

This is perhaps the most special part of the PATH. Fifty years ago, when the Toronto-Dominion Centre's first black slab tower appeared on the city's skyline, it preceded Stanley Kubrick's *2001: A Space Odyssey* by a year. In the Kubrick film, an impenetrable rectangular black 'monolith' lands on prehistoric Earth from some alien civilization, causing momentous things to happen. Archival pictures of the TD Centre rising above Toronto in the mid-sixties have the same kind of resonance: a low-scaled provincial city with an assortment of buildings in various classic and colonial styles surrounding an austere black tower that seems like it landed from another planet.

The spaceship that is New City Hall had already opened a few blocks north, but the TD Centre was much taller and dominated a skyline that was once the dominion of the Royal York Hotel, Commerce Court, and various church steeples. That it was one of the last projects by Mies (as all the cool kids call him), a continuation of the International Style themes he made famous with his 1958 Seagram Building in New York and others that followed, added to its gravitas. Mies's original plan was for two towers and the banking pavilion at the corner of Bay and King Streets, but in the decades after his 1969 death, four more towers were added. Purists say the towers diluted his rather pure vision, but most people passing by or through the complex wouldn't notice unless they looked closely, save for the final Ernst & Young tower that was built slightly differently and over the old Toronto Stock Exchange.

As the TD Centre approached its fiftieth birthday it needed some rehab, so Cadillac Fairview embarked on a multi-year, $250-million rehabilitation of all six buildings and exterior plazas. 'It takes six years to repaint the tower,' said Dora Yeoh, senior manager of tenant projects for Cadillac Fairview when we spoke in 2017, glancing up at the workers dangling on rigs suspended on the side of the original and tallest tower. 'Hopefully this will last twenty-five years.' An architect, Yeoh had been with Cadillac Fairview for six years and before that was with b+h Architects, the firm that was contracted to work on the TD Centre and, when they were known as Bregman + Hamann, one of the Toronto firms Mies collaborated with on the original plan; they also designed the subsequent towers on the site. Mies famously said, 'God is in the details,' and Yeoh was the guardian and caretaker of his Toronto details.

'The challenge of this complex is it's steeped in architectural history,' she said. 'Sometimes we have to remind people of that.' On a tour of the buildings, I asked her if, after all these years caring for these buildings, she has Mies dreams. 'Yes,' she chuckled. The buildings are austere monoliths only from a distance, and walking around the complex, Yeoh referred to the many details that she and her team worked on, such as the tower directories. The directory and lobby in the original tower remain as they were in 1967, with each occupant listed on a backlit panel, a detail that is part of the building's heritage designation. Yeoh pointed out that if one tenant takes up multiple floors, it leaves an awful lot of blank space on the old-style directory. The other lobbies have had touch screens fitted into the original directory frames, and LED lights have been added in another building lobby. It's about 'tweaking' the original design while respecting it, said Yeoh. Other tweaks include a lush green roof over the banking pavilion, white rather than black-grey rooftops to keep them cooler, and reglazed windows, all things that have contributed to the TD Centre's LEED Platinum certification, the highest environmental efficiency ranking possible.

The TD Centre remains a unique aesthetic experience to walk through today, distinct from the heterogeneous jumble of much of downtown. 'The way the towers are set in urban space with all this open and green space is outstanding,' said Yeoh. 'It set a precedent that very few developers have been able to match.' Down in the PATH, you used to be able to always tell when you were in the TD Centre. It was calming, clean, and uniform, distinct from the visual clutter and noise in much of the rest of the PATH. However, that rigorous attention to detail changed in the 2000s, when the uniform white-on-black typeface Mies designed himself for the underground shops was largely scrapped, and each store was allowed to install their own individual vernacular signage, as Cadillac Fairview, wholly owned by the Ontario Teachers' Pension Plan, looked to increase that fund by letting stores entice more shoppers as they wished. Perhaps only those who care about these things will notice the Miesian bits that are gone and those that are still there, but it remains a shame: Toronto had a mall designed by Mies van der Rohe, and there was even a Miesian cinema down there. Now it has become more of the same.

The Mies legacy is much better preserved above ground at the TD Centre and was quite safe in the hands of Yeoh and her team. That renovation was a lesson in the importance of maintenance, being true to good design and reinvesting in the buildings already built. As so many midcentury towers and structures reach a time in their lives when they need some renewal, the attention to detail and mostly gentle tweaks the TD Centre receives should be, as it was in 1967, trendsetting.

From the TD Centre zig and zag south to the basement of the Royal York Hotel on Front Street, where the oldest passageway on the PATH system connected that hotel to Union Station. Even after the pandemic, at rush hour, the flow of commuters close to Union is an unstoppable force – just try to swim upstream – as people make their way to the GO trains and all points 905. When it's hockey or basketball night in Canada, the wide passage beyond the trains leads thousands of fans into the Scotiabank Arena, located in what used to be the Canada Post Delivery Building, and past the spectacle of sports paraphernalia and virtual games that soak up whatever remaining money fans may have after breaking the bank on excessively expensive tickets. The art deco walls left over from the building's first incarnation are an example of successful facadism, having been integrated into what is now the one of the busiest arenas in North America. South of the tracks, the PATH is elevated, Calgary-style, and crosses over and under roadways to the buildings on Queens Quay.

In *Emerald City*, John Bentley Mays's collection of essays on Toronto, the architecture critic writes of his concern that our submerged mall will have us forget that the word *underground* once had sinister connotations: 'Moving through those immaculate and almost shadowless corridors, one finds none of those characters typically associated with the undergrounds in legend and story – sexual desperados, outlaws, mad hermits, wild boys who rule whole terrifying tracks of the dark world.' Though the PATH cowboys and girls with phones strapped to their hips like six-shooters may be the terror of the mutual-fund crowd, both groups appear benign in the late afternoon, the latter tired, with shirttails and suit jackets wrinkled from sitting at desks all day. The Toronto underground, it would seem, is rather well-heeled and sometimes even impeccably tailored, and escapes as soon as the five o'clock whistle blows. Do visit during the day, at high noon, to see the human show, but go after dark as well, when the halls are empty and the shops and fast-food outlets have rolled down their gates and closed their doors. The piped-in muzak echoes more and competes with the hum of the cleaning machines that polish the marble floors. It's then that the PATH still holds mystery and suspicion – when any of those furtive characters in the next corridor or rounding a corner could be the desperado you were looking for.

University Avenue

 neighbourhood jaunt

dress to impress

offspring friendly

Connecting walks: Harbourfront, Nathan Phillips Square/PATH, Yorkville, Dundas

University Avenue is Toronto's grandest street, but it's not made for walking – the scale is too big, designed more for Santa Claus parades and triumphant runs into the city by Terry Fox than for intimate strolling. Cities need big roads like this. Imagine Paris without Haussmann's wide boulevards cutting through the tight and dense arrondissements like air ducts, letting people breathe and affording some longer vistas. Of course, the Paris we know today came at tremendous cost, destroying neighbourhoods and lives for glorious avenues. University didn't require that kind of destruction. Some argue the boulevards are more for cars than for people, but Haussmann designed before the car, and if cars one day disappear, we'll still require a road like University to be a kind of parade ground and linear public space.

University runs from Front Street up to College Street, where it becomes Queen's Park Crescent for the stretch around and above the provincial legislature building, then it's simply and briefly called Queens Park (without the apostrophe) for two short blocks to Bloor before continuing north as Avenue Road, a sort of extension of University, carrying traffic to and from the wealthy North Toronto neighbourhoods. This street changes names so much it thinks it's European. The character and proportion of the street are different on either side of Bloor: the street is largely residential to the north, but bears an institutional, corporate, and governmental identity south of Bloor.

Once you've been in Toronto awhile, the weirdness of 'Avenue Road' wears off. I don't mean the road itself, but its name. Imagine it was called 'Road Avenue.' That's probably as weird as it sounds to fresh ears. The road isn't given much thought beyond that, as it's essentially a six-lane highway, continuing the Queen's Park speedway north of Bloor. In fact, on maps older than 1997 you'll see Avenue Road marked as Highway 11A, as it was an alternative to what was historically Highway 11, Yonge Street. Its current highway-like nature is ironic, considering it was once an elegant, tree-lined road and how, it's said, it got the name Avenue. Whatever trees manage to exist on it now are squeezed onto some of Toronto's narrowest sidewalks, where two people can

barely pass without one being nudged into traffic. It's the rough, beastly edge of fancy, gentle Yorkville.

At Bloor, the Park Hyatt Hotel underwent a renovation, making the sidewalk a bit more friendly. Across the street, the old, wonderfully brutalist Four Seasons Hotel tower has been converted to residences and gained a second, higher glass residential tower where the hotel's Giller Prize–hosting banquet halls once were. The sidewalk here is also better than before, but the fast, wide road sets the tone.

At 66 Avenue Road is a mid-rise residential and commercial building that, completed in 1984, is old enough to be considered nearly heritage now. It's the kind of building we should have hundreds more of today, a half-dozen terraced storeys with unique sunrooms that jut out at odd intervals. It's Yorkville-adjacent, so numerous plastic surgeons have hung their shingles out front, advertising the possibility of personal architectural change on Avenue Road too. North, along the west side of Avenue, is a stretch of mostly Victorian houses converted from residential to retail. Here, Boswell Avenue ends at the Boswell Parkette, a pocket of landscaped green space. Created in 1973, then with just three planters, it was part of the 'traffic maze' phenomenon of the 1970s that tried to insulate residential neighbourhoods from traffic.

Just before 'Av and Dav,' the Avenue and Davenport Roads intersection, the beloved row of florists is a tiny Toronto version of a European flower market. Across the street, a new residential building called Avenue 151, designed by Teeple Architects, should please those who have glass-box fatigue. Its ten storeys include white precast concrete panels that have a retro-futuristic look harkening back to the 1960s and 1970s plastic-looking sci-fi shuttles and space stations. A taming of Avenue, too, will make all of this much more pleasant, and there are people agitating for change.

Back at Bloor, the Royal Ontario Museum (ROM) begins the march south. The former Lillian Massey Department of Household Science, on the southeast corner across from the ROM, once served the University of Toronto as the female equivalent of the all-male Hart House almost a kilometre south, complete with a gymnasium and swimming pool (which is now hidden under a false floor). According to John Wilcox, owner of Vitreous Glassworks, a Toronto-based stained-glass restoration and design company, you can find stained-glass windows inside by British artist and designer Henry Holiday in the Pre-Raphaelite style, depicting Egyptian women 'in diaphanous gowns' performing household tasks, and naked and near-naked men hunting and harvesting, antiquated gender roles forever frozen in glass.

The ROM's crystal addition is subtle when viewed from Avenue Road. It pokes over the top of the roof and juts off the north side but leaves the classical east side of the building intact. More than twenty years after it was designed, the addition is still both liked and loathed, but perhaps most telling is the focus put back on the main, old entrance on Queens Park without as much fanfare. On the south end of the ROM sits the round hump of the former McLaughlin Planetarium, which crouches like a neglected child. Beloved by some and met with indifference by others (it's described as a 'slightly phony temple' to the stars by a character in Alice Munro's short story 'The Moons of Jupiter'), the building was sold to U of T in 2009, its future in flux since.

Wedged in between the old Lillian Massey building and the university's Emmanuel and Victoria College buildings of similar age and pedigree stands the very contemporary Gardiner Museum of Ceramic Art, which underwent a major expansion in 2006 by Toronto's KPMB architecture firm. Its concrete and glass boxes seem to float – as all good concrete should – in orbit of each other. It is yet another example of how very contemporary buildings can exist among their older ancestors, a family that doesn't banish the children when the grandparents are around. Just south of here, inside Victoria College's midcentury modern E.J. Pratt Library, cubicles with views of the Queens Park traffic are excellent places to procrastinate while studying.

Queen's Park, the grounds around the Legislative Assembly, is a place that serves dual roles. Home to arguably the most important building in the province, the people's house, it ceremonially represents more than 15 million people, but it's also a public park for the people who live in and visit Toronto. One of the first city parks in Canada, it was opened in 1860 by Queen Victoria's son, the Prince of Wales, who later became King Edward VII. He's the fellow on the horse on the north side of the Legislative Assembly, a statue brought to Canada in 1969 from Delhi, where it was unwanted during India's postwar purge of colonial monuments. Queen's Park is also the original site of King's College, precursor to the University of Toronto. The university moved a few hundred metres west and the city leased the land from it in 1859 for 999 years. With its lease set to expire in 2858, there's no need to think about renewal just yet. When the province parcelled off the southern half of the park and opened the Legislative Assembly in 1893, University Avenue and Queen's Park Crescent were not the four-lane highways they are today, and the road ran only along the east side of the building and park.

The grounds on the south, provincial, side are a hodgepodge of monuments of varying size with no fewer than three rose gardens opened by Queen Elizabeth II; a big sculpture for William Lyon Mackenzie, who led the Rebellion of 1837; a tree dedicated to victims of the 1985 Air India disaster; a large veterans' memorial; and even a rock from Gandesa, Spain, to commemorate the Mackenzie-Papineau Battalion, Canadians who volunteered to fight the Fascists during the Spanish Civil War. It's a landscape of important commemoration, but with pathways that lead to busy roads, often without proper crossings, a variety of incongruent paving surfaces, and a general shabbiness to the landscaping and layout, it doesn't honour it in all the ways it could. Large hedges also make gatherings awkward, though perhaps that's the point. An ugly, half-used parking lot also sprawls in front of the Legislature, a blight on this magnificent building. While a drop-off loop for ceremonial motorcades would be appropriate, parking should be hidden from this postcard view. In the summer the flowers are quite nice.

It's here, on the front lawn, that many protests against not only provincial policies but federal and even international struggles take place. During Premier Mike Harris's reign in the 1990s, this lawn was often a battleground between the not-very-Progressive Conservative government and a long list of other groups. In June of 2000, during a regular stop at the provincial human resources department across the street to look for a job as I fashioned myself a would-be civil servant upon finishing grad school, the visit coincided with the Ontario Coalition Against Poverty's march and demonstration, which resulted in a pitched, hour-long battle between people and police. It was as if the air and rules changed in Toronto that afternoon. I remember only a few vivid scenes of it now: a mom with a stroller running into bushes to avoid police horses; an old man stumbling into traffic, bleeding from the head, banging on the windows of a passing minivan and asking for help; a brick flying over my head and smashing into an officer's helmet, tipping him over so he hit the ground like a tin soldier. Ten years later, similar scenes occurred during the G20. It's scorched psychological earth in the middle of Toronto.

Contrast the front yard, managed by the province, to the north side, the Legislative Assembly's 'backyard' and part of the City of Toronto's jurisdiction. It, too, became shabby over the years, but a multi-year rehabilitation undertaken by the parks, forestry, and recreation department improved the experience of how it was already being used. Paths that were prone to flooding in wet weather and during the spring thaw have been completely redone with handsome paving stones, and the plaza around King Eddy is worthy of whatever honour you wish to afford him or his horse. There's also new seating, with many dozens of rather nice metal-and-wood benches lining the pathways now, along with wheelchair-accessible picnic tables, new tree plantings, and improved landscaping. The statue of poet Al Purdy looks on with contentment. The amount of seating in Queen's Park north should be a model for all other parks in Toronto, a city quite miserly when it comes to places to sit. The benches, along with new pavers, make the north side seem downright European. Royal, even. Access has been improved on the south side over the years, with six crossings that have either signals or stop signs regulating traffic. Still, Queen's Park sits in the middle of a campus of more than sixty thousand students, many of whom traverse it between classes, crossing roads where drivers routinely speed and blow red lights, a Toronto plague that will inevitably take more innocent victims.

Follow Queen's Park Crescent East to the northeast corner of College Street and you'll find the Leslie Dan Faculty of Pharmacy building, which British architect Sir Norman Foster designed for U of T. Foster's classroom-sized balls dangle inside the building's massive glass atrium. These massive orbs are suspended by steel arms and contain intimate lecture theatres and open-air study lounges on top. From the outside they look like white eggs stuffed into the building; they're the suspended complement to OCAD University's box-in-the-sky building a few blocks away on McCaul. Foster's indoor and outdoor concrete pillars are somewhat bare, but they match those that support 700 University (formerly Ontario Power Building, Hydro Place, Ontario Hydro Building, Ontario Power Generation Building) across the street. Opened in 1975, the building was heralded for being energy efficient, and for its multi-layered, two-acre plaza. 'It won't be the usual windswept plaza, but

One of the Pharmacy Building's big hanging balls.

a place where you can sit down, relax, and read your newspaper,' said landscape designer Keith Spratley in 1973. I have a soft spot for this beast because of those days when it reflects the clouds and sky perfectly, how its curves match those of Queen's Park and the government building that sits kitty-corner to it, and how at night the fluorescent lights on each floor are aligned in a radial starburst.

I once went into the lobby of the building, resumé in hand, and asked for human resources – always a good excuse to explore a building. I was told to leave it at the front desk and that somebody would contact me. They haven't called me yet. It's just as well: you can't see the glass waterfall from the inside of the building itself.

The 1935 art-deco Ontario Hydro Building (now the Campbell Family Building) a little to the south may just be the nicest building in Toronto. It's part of Princess Margaret Hospital now, but notice the waterfalls carved in stone out front, a reminder that Ontario's power was once supplied exclusively by Niagara Falls. For those lucky enough not to have a specific reason to visit Princess Margaret, it's worth going in through the front doors and finding the huge postmodern atrium in the rear addition to the hospital, a heavy and dark building that hangs over Murray Street (a variance bylaw was made for this specific addition so the Hydro building could be built) and that, unless viewed from the west, seems to disappear among the other University Avenue hospital buildings. With its mountains of hospitals – Toronto General, Sick-Kids, Princess Margaret, Mount Sinai, and Toronto Rehab – University Avenue is a virtual canyon of sickness, recovery, and death, where the happiest and saddest dramas play out daily above the sidewalks, and where the names of the donors seem to be the only things that change on the buildings.

The MaRS Discovery District, which spans College Street between Elizabeth Street and University, is one of those places in which the employees likely have a hard time explaining to their parents exactly what they do. The acronym MaRS is derived from the term 'Medical and Related Sciences,' which means to connect science and technology to business. However, most of us civilians think of it as the restoration of the former Toronto General Hospital, the site of Banting and Best's insulin discovery in 1922. The most dramatic changes in the building are inside, where a vast public atrium, complete with an underground passage to the present-day hospital, marks the transition between new and old. Across College, on the northeast corner of University, is the new Schwartz Reisman Innovation Campus, a unique-for-Toronto building that resembles a squat version of San Francisco's Transamerica Pyramid building.

Oddly, the best walk on University is down the green space in the centre of the boulevard – it's Toronto's narrowest park, and it affords the best views of our attempts at civic grandeur. Walk the length of it and you'll pass a mural depicting Terry Fox's run, subway exhaust tunnels, and various memorials, including the one for the Boer Wars (the size of the statue suggests we won). This is where a plan called 'University Park' can be most easily envisioned: one that would turn 9.5 acres of city-owned asphalt (one side of University) into parkland, with pedestrian walkways, bike paths, and more art that would connect the green spaces of Queen's Park and the Waterfront – still with room for four lanes of traffic. It would tame our beast of an avenue and bring it closer to the kind of place it was when created.

University Avenue was created in the 1820s and was a private road for over fifty years, with wooden gates and a gatehouse at Queen Street to prevent public carriages from entering (they were torn down in 1882). Horse chestnut trees were specially imported to line the street, and a boulevard of grass was laid in the middle of the street to provide promenades for the general public when the gates were open. When Charles Dickens visited North America in the 1840s, before the Legislature was built, the plans for it and University Avenue were one of the few Toronto sights he mentioned in his *American*

Notes: 'It will be a handsome, spacious edifice, approached by a long avenue which is already planted and made available as a public walk.' Today, in front of SickKids hospital, there's a bust of Mary Pickford, the early Hollywood star who was born in a house on University Avenue in 1892, another relic of a different era in the avenue's history.

Osgoode Hall sits on the northeast corner of University and Queen, a colonial wedding cake behind a heavy iron fence and ornate gates. It's an interesting island in a district marked by much more modern buildings. For many, Osgoode is one of Toronto's architectural gems, but I've never been particularly interested in it. It seems so overtly non-Torontonian and colonial. That is, it's of a style and grandeur that makes it seem like it was plucked from someplace else and set down here. Certainly, much of Toronto is made up of non-local-style mash-ups, so perhaps it's just the fence that makes the place seem like a museum piece or movie set (which it often is). A recent sign of Osgoode's beloved status was the public uproar when the Ontario Line subway station was planned for the southwest corner of the grounds. Behind Osgoode Hall sits a more modern Ontario court building, which seems more in line with the spirit of Toronto. I recognize that my opinion is unpopular, especially considering the magnificent armoury building that was demolished in the 1960s to make way for the newer court building, but the near-abstract wing that hangs over what could be a pleasant public space – if it were cared for properly – has utopic ambitions that are hard to ignore. Osgoode faces one of the plain sides of the Four Seasons Centre for the Performing Arts across Queen Street, where much of its budget and design savvy were saved for the interior and its lantern-like front facade. Across University is the Canada Life building with its weather-predicting beacon, and north of it the U.S. Consulate, which, even during the deepest days of conservative politics south of the border, unfurls a huge Pride flag in June.

Just south of Queen, in the middle of University, is the monument to Sir Adam Beck, the German-Canadian politician and early advocate for public hydroelectricity in Ontario. If you look around the base of the monument, the locations of Ontario's hydroelectric generating stations are listed. The sculpture was designed by German-Canadian sculptor Emanuel Hahn, perhaps most famous for his *Bluenose* design on the ten-cent coin. University's wide median peters out at Adelaide, where it's just a foot across. If you walk down this narrow garden, you're left exposed in the middle of traffic, protected only by an aluminum 'veer right' sign.

Further south, through a canyon of mirrored glass, the Shangri-La on the west side is fairly typical of the kind of buildings that have gone up in Toronto over the last few decades. Wrapping around the front facade is *Peace Pigeons*, a sculpture by artist Zhang Huan, who says he wants 'mankind and nature [to] live in harmony.'

University ends after a short jog east at Union Station and the Royal York Hotel. Here, it joins York Street for the short hike under the railway tracks to the cluster of glass-point towers in and around Maple Leaf Square. Located in front of the Scotiabank Arena, the square is one of Toronto's most surprising public spaces and can accommodate up to five thousand people. During the Raptors' recent playoff runs, 'Jurassic Park,' as the cluster of towers became known, was the place to be. A little further on, York slips under the Gardiner Expressway and ends at the harbour, but not before one last moment of grandeur.

In the summer of 2023, Love Park opened here, where the York-Bay-Yonge eastbound Gardiner off-ramp once spiralled its way from the elevated expressway to the ground. The 8,000 square metres the ramp's removal freed up is a striking example of how much valuable space car infrastructure occupies. Long a forgotten and dirty block, Love Park was designed by Montreal's late Claude Cormier and his firm (the people behind the redesign of Berczy Park, with its beloved dog fountain), along with Toronto's gh3*. The centrepiece of the park is a heart-shaped pond ringed by a red-tiled edge – also good for sitting – with an island that includes a mature tree that miraculously grew inside the off-ramp for years. Once obscured, it's now the star of the show. There's a cute area for dogs, grassy berms, flower gardens, and a few more mature trees that were saved. There is also a collection of animal sculptures, including a raccoon, beaver, and rabbit, echoes of Cormier's dog sculptures at Berczy. The whole thing is cute. It's already an Instagram machine, doing yeoman's work of advertising Toronto as a tourist destination far and wide, and a fitting new end to Toronto's glorious ceremonial avenue.

Yorkville

neighbourhood jaunt

dress to impress

offspring friendly

Connecting walks: Yonge, University, Dupont

When the subway pulls into Bay station, the fine print underneath the word 'Bay' says 'Yorkville,' a reminder that Yorkville is an important enough location to warrant mention, an honour the TTC hasn't given to any other Toronto neighbourhood. Yorkville is a mythic place for Torontonians. It's where things happened, where Canadian cultural history was made in the 1960s – the place the baby-boomer nostalgia machine can't stop talking about. Today, things still happen in Yorkville, but it's not the epicentre of culture, low or high, that it once was.

Today, Yorkville is known mainly as a place to shop for high-end goods, but just a decade ago the Rolling Stones would stay at the Yorkville Four Seasons when in town, and during the Toronto International Film Festival it was the centre of the universe, though that's all shifted to King Street now. Yet even as Yorkville is now all about fashion and retail, it still plays a big role in supporting Toronto's myth and ontology. So perhaps there's some style below that fashion, something deeply Torontonian that endures – something a little rebellious. If there is, it's best found on foot, as Yorkville's secrets are often down little passageways, meant to be stumbled upon randomly.

In your search of Yorkville's deepest counterculture roots, head over to Yonge, just south of the Reference Library, where the Red Lion Inn once stood. Though it was a breeding ground for the Upper Canada Rebellion of 1837, there is little indication of the inn or mention of the rebellion now, just a sign marking where Albert Britnell's bookstore also used to be, near the inn's original site. Here, in an early example of Toronto standing up for itself, William Lyon Mackenzie, Toronto's first mayor, tried to overthrow the Family Compact, Upper Canada's tight-knit ruling class. Toronto ought to send Christmas cards bearing pictures of Mackenzie to Queen's Park and Ottawa to remind them of what we're capable of when we're upset, though today an uprising would be over something like public-transit or housing funding rather than undemocratic powers.

Just south of here, at the corner of Yonge and Bloor, hulks 2 Bloor East (formerly the Hudson's Bay Centre), the kind of place that gives concrete a bad name because of the lack of windows and the uninteresting sidewalk interaction. With the actual Hudson's Bay sadly gone, there's potential for a new, more permeable life for the building. This complex and the buildings several blocks west are connected by a smaller PATH-like underground mall system, with a vintage 1970s disco tunnel under Yonge featuring smoky mirrors and brass accents. From Yonge/Bloor subway station, the outdoor-phobic can walk west to Bay Station and even south into the Manulife Centre without coming up for air. The first underground stop from Yonge and Bloor is the Cumberland Terrace mall, a vintage curiosity and product of the 1970s inclination to build downtown malls. Cumberland is a clunky, smaller, and less successful version of the Eaton Centre, running a full block along Cumberland Street, behind the CIBC building and Holt Renfrew, with a glass wall that runs most of its length and gives a sort of indoor-outdoor experience at street level.

Slated for imminent demolition for nearly a decade and a half now, it's one of the few rebuild projects in Toronto that seems to take its time, perhaps complicated by its location over the Bloor subway line. In fashionable Yorkville, Cumberland remains wonderfully out of fashion. Cumberland Terrace has never been fully renovated, so it remains an amazing museum dedicated to 1974, the year it opened, its Quaalude-cool tiles, with geometric patterns in green, blue, yellow, orange, and brown, are nearly the last stand of an earth-toned, Fleetwood Mac soft-rock style. Most curious are the clusters of operational pay phones, found in groups of four or even six. It's reminiscent of phone banks in courthouses and other public buildings in the 1940s and 1950s, when members of the press would all rush into phone booths at once to dictate their breaking stories to their editors.

Despite Cumberland Terrace being on death's door for so long, the hardest-working Christmas tree in Toronto was always here. Every year, the stubby, artificial tree came out from storage and was set up with care on the brown tiles, decorated with white and gold ornaments. As corporate Christmas trees go, it was understated, without a star or angel, just an electric cord running out of the top. There was a certain nobility to it, among surroundings that are no longer in style. It failed to appear as Christmas 2023 approached, so the end of Cumberland Terrace is likely close at hand. I like to think it was a memorial tree for Potter's Field Cemetery that used to be here, Yorkville's non-sectarian cemetery for the poor. Though closed in 1855, after which the 6,685 bodies were moved to the Toronto Necropolis and Mount Pleasant Cemetery, this was their first resting spot and these unnamed, dispossessed early Torontonians deserve a nice tree of their own.

Back out at Yonge, near the 1837 Rebellion site, you'll find yourself standing on ground that played host to a protest more fitting with contemporary Yorkville values. In 1868, Yorkville's town council voted to move the Yonge and Bloor tollgate to the northern limit of the village because, as was reported in the town records, 'its present position in the heart of this village is an eyesore to the inhabitants and a great injury to them in a pecuniary point of view.' Nearly a century later, residents again resisted new developments when Ian Richard Wookey, deemed a 'folk hero to the chic set' by the *Toronto Star* in 1974, assembled the properties that would become Hazelton Lanes, now called Yorkville Village, the mall that currently houses Whole Foods and other higher-end shops. Ursula Foster, who had lived in the same Victorian house at 30 Hazelton Avenue for fifty years, successfully fought to save her sunlight, forcing the Hazelton condos to angle backward away from her house. This kind of setback became a trend – later taken to extremes – and, eventually, official City policy. Though it, recently and thankfully, has been much limited, the policy known as the 'angular plane' led to a generation of ziggurat-like buildings across the city, limiting the amount of new housing built and increasing costs. Her house is still there, though it has been sandblasted and turned into offices, and Hazelton's streetscape is largely intact.

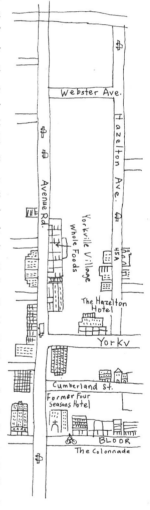

With the addition of Hazelton Lanes and other commercial infill developments, Yorkville began losing the cultural venues that made it Canada's Haight-Ashbury in the 1960s. But Yorkville was a cultural hotspot even when those hippies were still teens. From the mid-1940s to 1963, Clement Hambourg ran Yorkville's House of Hambourg.

Billed as 'Three Stories of Jazz,' the fourteen-room house on Cumberland hosted folks like Cannonball Adderley, Miles Davis, and Louis Armstrong. In the sixties, as jazz went downtown, the folk and rock scenes took over. Dozens of coffee houses lined Cumberland and Yorkville avenues, among them the Purple Onion, Café Anglais, Penny Farthing, Mynah Bird, El Matador, and Sammy's. The Riverboat, at 134 Yorkville, was where musicians like Gordon Lightfoot, Joni Mitchell, Steppenwolf, Neil Young, and Rick James played before they went south. The Riverboat site is now the Hazelton, an

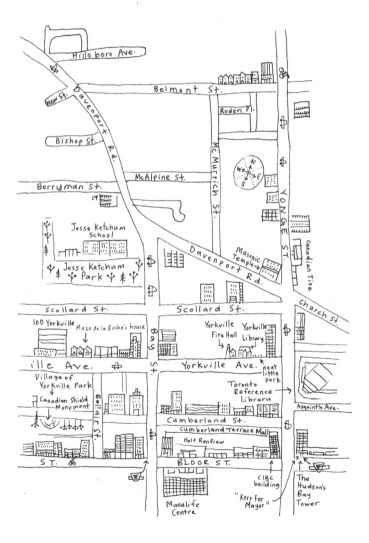

upscale hotel and condo. In 1969, a proposed twenty-two-storey apartment hotel was refused on the same lot, deemed at the time to be 'clearly at variance with the spirit' of Yorkville.

Older Torontonians remember the parking lot that once ran along Cumberland, in the heart of Yorkville, and that languished for over thirty years (one of many that blighted Yorkville), while even older residents recall the Victorian row houses that were there before. The houses were cleared to make way for the subway in the 1960s, and, in 1991, an overdue design competition chose a bid by Oleson Worland Architects that imagined a linear park marking the ghosts of those row houses with distinct Canadian environments, including a pine forest, a marsh, and an orchard. Though controversial at the time because of the cost of transportation and installation, the giant rock shipped in from the Canadian Shield that sits in the middle of that park has become a favourite meeting spot in Toronto. Next to the rock, the entrance to the Bay subway station matches the contemporary look of some of the newer buildings in the area and hints at the infrastructure that lies below the park. The University Theatre, which sat between the park and Bloor Street and for many years played host to countless film festival gala screenings, was shuttered in 1986 and eventually replaced by a condo building nearly fifteen years later. The theatre's facade lives on as retail space. Next door to it is a subtle passage known as the 'Festival Walkway,' with Reinhard Reitzenstein's 2003 grapevine artwork arching above.

Across the street from the old theatre, there's the Colonnade. It provides Gucci-encrusted 'Mink Mile' shoppers a small public square in the shape of an elegant half-oval. The building was completed in 1963 and was Toronto's first combined residential, commercial, and retail development. After disappearing during a recent renovation, the plaque on the unique zigzag staircase has returned. It proclaims that this one-and-a-half-turn spiral was 'the only one ever built without a central support,' adding that 'the Colonnade is a totally Canadian project' – certainly things to be proud of in the 1960s, when provincial Toronto was emerging from the shadow of the Empire.

Back up in the heart of Yorkville, located at 86 Yorkville Avenue, an old house has been converted to retail space. In the twenties and thirties, author Mazo de la Roche lived here, and it's where she wrote the first of her sixteen *Jalna* novels. She isn't well-known in Canada anymore, but her books have sold at least 9 million copies around the world, making her one of Yorkville's first cultural exports.

Yorkville really began to change by the early seventies, when Wookey and others started building and the hippies got older. Anybody who has watched *The Big Chill* knows how this story plays out: the hippie kids grow up, give up the ponchos and the protests, switch from pot to cocktails, and go shopping for Halston sheets. Though the Riverboat lasted until 1978, Yorkville denizens mark the beginning of the end as early as 1968 and 1969, when a hepatitis scare put a chill on all the free love. In 1971, the Four Seasons built their hotel at Avenue and Cumberland, establishing a beachhead for fifty years of condo and office-tower development. By the mid-1980s, Yorkville was primarily a high-end shopping district galvanized, in part, by the Holt Renfrew Centre on Bloor, which opened in 1979. The coffee houses became boutiques, salons, and bars whose dress codes were a little more *Dallas* or *Real Housewives* and a lot less *Easy Rider*.

A few doors down from de la Roche's old place, at 100 Yorkville, what was once Toronto's first Jewish general hospital, Mount Sinai, is now the aptly (if obviously) named 100 Yorkville at Bellair, a condo development that incorporated the hospital's facade into its design, now housing a Chanel store (the luxury empire founded by a notoriously anti-Semitic fashionista), and filled in the parking lot that was behind the hospital. Many of these new developments and infill constructions replaced old surface parking lots. If you look at aerial photos of Yorkville at the height of its hippie days in the late sixties, the amount of land given over to parking is staggering. If we could be teleported back to those days, we'd likely be in shock at how open the neighbourhood was compared to how dense it is now.

Around the corner at 39 Hazelton, just up the street from Ursula Foster's former house, there's a forbidding-looking building. While trying to peek in once, I met an angry security guard who refused to appreciate that the building used to be the Nimbus 9 recording studios. Producer Jack Richardson opened the studios in the late sixties and a who's who of classic rock royalty, including Alice Cooper, the Guess Who, Dr. John, Peter Gabriel, KISS, and Bob Seger, made pilgrimages to Nimbus 9 to work with Richardson and his young employee, Bob Ezrin. (Ezrin went on to produce part of Pink Floyd's *The Wall* there too.)

Further up Hazelton Avenue, hang a right on Berryman Street and walk up to number 19. In the early seventies, Toronto architect Barton Myers turned this former warehouse into a house-cum-showcase for his design ideas. (He also did the 1978 addition to the rear of the Yorkville Library, which still exists.) It's one of the few pieces of cool post–Expo 67 mod design in Toronto and is the residential articulation of the change Yorkville saw in the seventies when the Victorians were either replaced by modern buildings, renovated, or incorporated into other buildings. Slip down the alley next to number 19 and walk around Jesse Ketchum Junior and Senior Public School. On the south side of the school, there's a huge playing field that seems too vast for Yorkville and affords a great secret backdoor view of the Bloor skyline. Walk right up to the back windows of Nimbus 9 – all traces of its storied past are gone, plastered over, renovated. Like the rest of Yorkville, this building has been given a facelift that makes its history unrecognizable. Yet if you continue to wander northeast, to Davenport and then over to Belmont and back down to Yonge, you'll find bits of Yorkville's past tucked in between the swaths of its future: an old house, the original fire hall, the roof of a house peeking over a store, or even the strip of townhouses along Belmont just before Yonge that were some of the first in the area to be renovated in the 1960s – all remnants of somebody's historic Yorkville and pieces of somebody else's current one.

Westish

Dundas Street

 day trip
 dress to impress
 scenic views

Connecting walks: Yonge, Nathan Phillips Square/
PATH, University, Bathurst, Dupont, St. Clair,
Downtown East Side, the Beach

Dundas is a street that snakes through many neighbourhoods, adopting local flavour like a chameleon – a street for Torontonians, not for tourist brochures. In the east, it gets rolling as a residential street that doubles as quick route downtown for cars and bikes. This first bit, from Kingston Road, where Dundas begins, to Broadview Avenue, by the Don River, was a postwar creation. Look at prewar maps of the city and you'll find only an amalgam of short and non-contiguous roads that were eventually joined to form the street we now know. Dundas Street, as it passes through central Toronto, hasn't always been known as Dundas Street. It barely has, really. A country road that runs through parts of southwest Ontario, it is named after a Scottish guy who never set foot here and was involved in the slave trade. Calls to change the name have been met with resistance in some quarters, and accusations of erasing history, but 'history' here is quite recent. Dundas, the country road, once meandered east toward Toronto through Ontario, until it curved south along what is now Ossington Avenue, terminating at Queen Street, then the edge of the city. Later, as the city grew more dense and needed another east-west route, Dundas was created – invented, really – by linking together fifteen different streets east of Ossington, all the way to where Dundas now meets Kingston Road. All of these streets lost their names too, pity their history, but this is why Dundas is such a funky, zigzaggy street, meandering as it does, and why lots sometimes flank it at awkward angles and houses are sometimes too close to

the road. Entire blocks west of Jones are all garages, as if Dundas was a really wide alley. At Broadview, it picks up its steel backbone of streetcar rails and crosses the Don Valley. It's a cobbled-together creation. Most of Dundas's invention was within the last century, and the eastern portion as late as the 1950s.

Once past the Don River and the Mercedes dealership where director David Cronenberg filmed scenes for *Crash*, Dundas is changing fast. The rebuilding of Regent Park that began in 2009 has altered the streetscape dramatically: residential glass buildings that meet the sidewalk have replaced the old brick Regent Park blocks that were set back behind neglected landscaping. Surrounded by podiums and townhomes, the new towers meet the street, and there are retail-style units that give the sidewalk more activity. The great gamble of Regent Park is that by offering a mix of affordable and market housing, city planners hope to keep this new-but-old neighbourhood balanced and vibrant while still being affordable and welcoming.

West of Parliament Street, Dundas runs through the downtown east side along the top of what was once the Moss Park estate, a space that's now home to a housing project of the same name that stretches out along Queen Street, with towers that make an M when viewed from above. This area is also slated for additional housing and a renovation, though not on the same scale as Regent Park. Dundas curves around the exceptional neon of Filmores Gentlemen's Club, the kind of building whose quirky shape and size should be more common in Toronto. Dundas has many quick and sharp curves like this one, curves that awkwardly toss streetcars in a new direction, sending their tails swinging around trying to catch up. Here, too, Dundas is an amalgamation of a number of streets that were eventually joined together. It breaks up Toronto's usual grid and makes for interesting intersections shrouded in the mystery that's created when you can't see the end of the street ahead of you.

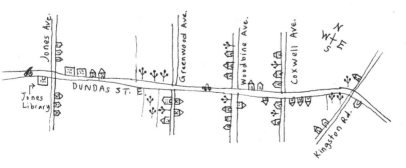

Torontonians get upset when people compare the city to New York (as it has become a bit of a cliché), but Dundas does serve as our Broadway, floating loosely across the grid. Across from Filmores sit some fine but worn-out old Victorian piles (about as rough-looking as old Toronto gets), holdouts next to their tall new neighbours – the first of many as Dundas travels into the heart of downtown.

If you're west of Jarvis Street at night, the glow from Yonge-Dundas Square is like an electric cloud, especially when it's humid, snowing, or raining. For some people, this is the crossroads of the city, but the first block of Dundas West, just past Yonge, is perhaps the city at its most boring. Here, it is dominated by the Atrium on Bay on the north side and the Eaton Centre and Toronto Metropolitan University's Ted Rogers School of Management on the south side. Canadian Tire, a company whose store designs commit some of the most grievous assaults against urbanity, does try to be somewhat urban here, with windows that are almost like those seen on a traditional retail strip, though they're often cluttered or covered in adverts. Still, it's clear the inner big-box is trying to come out of the closet, as there's only one entrance and lots of dead space along the sidewalk.

Located kitty-corner to the Canadian Tire, 600 Bay is about as film noir as Toronto gets, the kind of place where you might expect Sam Spade to have an office on one of the upper floors, his name written on the window in arched lettering. This is another type of building that should be more common in the city; dusty, wide-gauge venetian blinds still hang in some windows, suggesting the sensibility of the office behind them is retro without the chic. Behind the building, a narrow alley runs off Bay and leads to a dirt courtyard and the rear doors of other Dundas buildings, a reminder of what the area

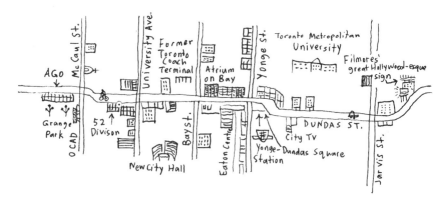

was like when it was known as the Ward, the neighbourhood that was cleared out when New City Hall was built.

The destruction of the Ward also pushed out Toronto's original Chinatown, but traces of it remain between Bay and University (a handful of restaurants and old buildings that seem out of place today). One City Hall Place, a fifteen-storey condo located on Elizabeth Street, just behind the back of the real City Hall, looks like a giant that's hunched over concentrating on something when viewed from Dundas. Its design invites us to walk around it and look down a narrow passageway, where an artwork by Ken Lum called *Across Time and Space, Two Children of Toronto Meet* evokes immigrant children and the old Ward. The condo, by Toronto firm Hariri Pontarini Architects, bucks the trend of all-glass towers for a low-rise building with horizontal glass and concrete lines rather than vertical ones. It's a contrast to City Hall – likely one of the landmarks it's most difficult to build next to in Toronto – but it works, and One City Hall breathes life (and the sure sign of a real neighbourhood, a supermarket) into the old Ward, a neighbourhood that has evolved in the middle of our most institutional of areas. On the north side of Dundas at Chestnut is Masjid Toronto. Located in a former bank building, it's been a mosque since 2002, after the peripatetic congregation spent years renting various spaces. The old Ward still provides a home for new communities.

A block past University sits Toronto Police Services 52 Division, a white glass-block fortress that looks like our homage to the *Miami Vice* style of hostile police-station design. The concrete plaza out front has the potential to be a great people place, but it has instead been intermittently used as a parking lot for both official police vehicles and ones that quite obviously

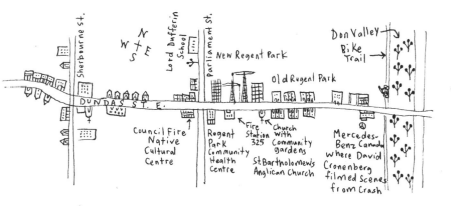

aren't, unless Pontiac Sunfires and Ford pickups are part of the fleet. This has been a problem since 2000, when Julian Fantino was chief of police, but the cars coincidentally disappeared when a corruption scandal broke at 52 Division in 2004. That the cars returned under the rule of chief Bill Blair in the late 2000s seems like a needless PR – and urban – blunder. The vehicles are gone again, but this piece of public space remains tenuous.

The food court that all other food courts should aspire to is inside the Village by the Grange next door. The Village is made up of a series of interconnected condo buildings that stretch almost down to Queen and that boast interesting interior public and semi-public spaces. It's a weirdly wonderful space, with vestiges of the old-timey 'village square' decor left over from when it opened in the late 1970s. Today, the Village is a jumble of everything, like Toronto itself, with a food court to match: Greek, Korean, Japanese, Mexican, Thai, and so on. There's a pho stall and even a Belgian waffle and cupcake bar. Helena's Magic Kitchen offers meat loaf, perogies, latkes, and other Eastern European foods, while Karine's serves an all-day breakfast from what must be the only food stall in the city with a big Victorian chesterfield in it. A few of the places, like Karine's, serve food on proper plates, not Styrofoam, and ask people to return their dishes. OCAD U's annex of classrooms and library are here too, so the place is busy with art and design students.

Around another quick curve, the bulge of Frank Gehry's Art Gallery of Ontario addition dominates Dundas. The Galleria Italia, as the bulge is known, gives visitors a bird's-eye view of the streetscape and a second-storey view of the Victorian houses across the street. Walk along the south side of Dundas and look at those houses on the north side. Then go up to the second floor of the gallery and do the same thing. It's remarkable to walk (nearly) an entire dense city block along the second floor of another building. It's like seeing Toronto for the first time; altering the angle by a half-dozen metres or so can radically change your perception of the city, and makes me realize how often we forget to pay attention to the upper floors of these kinds of common buildings.

The AGO is not just for looking at. The Gehry 'transformation,' as it was called, makes Toronto as much a part of the gallery experience as the art inside. The additions and alterations have opened new views to the north and south of the building. To the north, the timber beams of the Galleria Italia frame those quintessential old Toronto homes along Dundas as if they're works of art themselves. Apart from the occasional views stolen from well-positioned second- or third-floor apartments around the city, we usually don't get to see a Toronto street from this angle.

When you look out the windows on the south side of the AGO, Toronto's skyline appears all around, making it feel as though you're a part of it rather than looking at it from afar. The residents of the concrete slab directly across the park now have a few thousand eyes peeping into their fishbowl lives every day. (As a friend once said when looking out at them, they're close enough to be interesting, but far enough away not to be explicit.) That slab was to be repeated in other buildings along McCaul Street, but then-alderman Colin Vaughan helped turn that proposal into plans for the low-rise Village by the Grange. To the west of the AGO, the Victorian homes along Beverley Street that face Grange Park look like the Toronto doppelgänger of the famous Alamo Square skyline in San Francisco, where Victorian painted ladies (ours are brick) frame the park. In the other direction, architect Will Alsop's OCAD U 'tabletop,' the massive floating school-box in the sky, suddenly looks even more audacious from this close up. It's the kind of building, like the CN Tower and the Ontario Science Centre, that I daydreamed about when I was growing up in Windsor.

The Henry Moore sculpture that graced the corner of Dundas and McCaul until 1973 was moved into Grange Park and replaced by a giant bronze elephant sculpture by Brian Jungen called *Couch Monster*, as it was initially created from discarded sofas. Toronto has a long-standing relationship with Henry Moore, and the AGO houses the biggest public collection of Moore's work in the world. Having *Large Two Forms* sitting here in the park, completely accessible, without a security guard watching, is a bit of a tease. You can't climb on any of his pieces inside, even though some of them seem to be asking for it.

Architect Fred Valentine worked on an earlier renovation of the AGO that was completed in 1973 by Parkin Architects, a descendent firm of Toronto's central modernist architect, John C. Parkin. Large parts of that renovation are still visible in the post-Gehry AGO, including the white concrete 'boxes' on either side of the Galleria Italia, one of which houses the Henry Moore gallery. In 2008, after the Gehry addition was completed, I spoke with Valentine and he told me that he had worked with Moore himself to design the second-floor space. 'Moore had to have uniform natural light,' Valentine said of the gallery. 'He had very specific specifications for it: length, width, height, uniform light – we had proposed an oculus not unlike what Gehry [eventually] did, but Moore was very much against that and felt his pieces should be seen as they were conceived in a dull sky. We wanted to have the path of sun as it went west to east. He was a very interesting man, easy to work with, knew specifically what he wanted.' Valentine went on to say that Moore was upset at how his sculpture *Archer* had been 'theatrically' lit in Nathan Phillips Square. When you visit the gallery today, notice how the light diffuses through the opaque glass squares in the ceiling, creating what can accurately be described as (in view of Moore's stated preferences about the conditions of his creation) 'British light.' Dull and without hard shadows, it's a most British environment in this colonial British city.

The quiet and somewhat austere space along the Dundas side of the AGO – Gehry called it a long 'front porch' – changes at Beverley, where the visual chaos of Chinatown abruptly starts. These two disparate places work well together too, a good example of how Toronto can accommodate radically different spaces so close to each other.

That wonderful chaos continues for a few blocks, but quiets down past Spadina. (Chinatown is a north-south neighbourhood much more than it is an east-west one.) Here, the bottom of Kensington meets the Alexandra Park neighbourhood, yet another large public housing neighbourhood along Dundas undergoing radical change, as new buildings replace the old and affordability is mixed with market units.

Around another bend and past Toronto Western Hospital, Dundas meets Bathurst, where it becomes a mix of small retail and residential homes. Here, Dundas is the kid sibling of adjacent Queen and College Streets, having recently experienced the pressures of gentrification that visited those streets in decades past. Cafés, restaurants, and stores that are endlessly chatted about have opened near old-school places that remain.

Dundas continues like this for a number of kilometres – sometimes the typology is more residential than retail, but it's never exclusively one kind – becoming more Portuguese and Brazilian along the way. West of Ossington, Dundas veers slightly north, now part of the original Dundas that came in from western Ontario, yet many houses and buildings along the stretch up to Lansdowne are still aligned with the grid, meeting the street diagonally as if all turning to look at something at the same time. Be sure to look back east here. Dundas is pointed straight at the cluster of skyscrapers in the core from whose centre rises the white First Canadian Place building. It's an unexpected southeastern perspective on downtown from a street we think of as east-west, and it's especially brilliant at sunset. Past Lansdowne, where Dundas rises to clear the Grand Trunk Railway line, and the smell from the Nestlé chocolate factory often makes the air seem sweet and nutty, the wide-angle view you get when you're looking to the southeast along the tracks presents a different Toronto altogether, making the city seem much more industrial-looking than we know it to be.

Dundas continues to curve elegantly north toward Bloor. At Sterling Road, in the middle of the two-span railway bridge, you can take the West Toronto Railpath as a back route up to Cariboo Avenue in the Junction. Biking or walking the rail path for the first time is like seeing a remixed Toronto: heretofore unseen backyards and factories are in view, and the city seems shaped and put together differently from this new route. Along its northward trajectory, the rail path includes four steel sculptures by John Dickson called *Frontier*, spaced out between stretches of greenery. That mix of neighbourhood buildings and the path itself, designed by landscape architect Scott Torrance with Brown + Storey Architects, is its subtle grace. Wildflowers bloom and other trees and plants have slowly grown in over the last decade. There are even shady stretches now, and the new mass timber building on Sterling dominates; behind it stands the Museum of Contemporary Art in the striking old Tower Automotive Building. When Metrolinx is finished widening its rail corridor, the path will extend further south beyond Dundas to Abell and Sudbury Streets where it will connect to on-street bike paths that lead downtown.

For a different view, follow Dundas past where it meets Roncesvalles (where two long streetcar lines converge) and then crosses Bloor. The street there arcs west into the Junction neighbourhood.

The Junction's change from a working-class neighbourhood into the wealthier one it is now is interesting because of how slowly it happened. Compare and contrast this with the few blocks of Ossington north of Queen that seemed to transform so quickly between 2007 and 2009 that you could almost stand on the sidewalk and watch it happen. The velocity of change was so high that nobody could get a grip on what was happening, and people freaked out, which led the City to place a moratorium on new bars on that strip in 2009. The Junction, however, is a different story. It changed slowly throughout most of the first decade of this century and still maintains a near-perfect balance between old and new, shiny and rough.

Though it has the best name of any neighbourhood in the city, the Junction is hard to pin down. Its borders aren't straight, and they mean different

College St.

DUNDAS ST.

Lansdowne Ave.

Dufferin St.

No Frills

Little Portugal

Cadbury Chocolate Factory

Dovercourt Rd.

Ossington Ave.

Crawford St.

Pope Francis Catholic School

Trinity Bellwoods Park

things to different people. Official versions may look a bit like one of those hard-to-fit *Tetris* game pieces, but for many the infrastructure that gives the railway neighbourhood its name is what truly defines the area. Though the centre of the Junction is at Keele and Dundas, it's good to enter the neighbourhood on foot from an oblique angle along Dundas, heading north from Bloor. The Junction being 'up there' is likely a big reason why the pressures of change have remained lower here than elsewhere for so long.

Until 1968, the Junction seemed a lot closer to downtown and the west side because the Dundas streetcar continued north of Bloor all the way to Runnymede. (You can still see the streetcar loop there, though today the area is served only by buses.) A continuous transit line without a transfer can knit and connect disparate places together. As Dundas curves west from Bloor, you can see retail remnants from days when this was a busier strip, though most storefronts were long ago converted into apartments.

On the side streets close to the tracks, you'll find another reason the Junction's balance has been just right: here, the neighbourhood is filled with small workshops and car-repair garages. (If mechanics were an ethnicity, this would be Little Mechanicville.) Things still get made and fixed and banged out in the Junction, from sausages to rubber to bumpers. For now, anyway. Follow the tracks to Keele and head north under the tracks to the other Junction, which often gets overlooked. Here, there are more little shops and small-scale industry, all coexisting with houses. There are also perfect Victorians that would be right at home in Cabbagetown, though here they're across from the giant concrete Keele Centre warehouse, a rough, industrial place that's also seen its share of arts-and-culture exhibitions and parties. (Take the centre's outdoor stairs to the second-floor roadway for a Mary Poppins view of the neighbourhood.)

The area to the north of this – now home to big-box retailers and fast-food drive-throughs – was once a vast tract of stockyards, and some older Junction folk tell stories of sneaking in as kids and walking on top of a sea of cattle. St. Clair is not far away from Dundas along Keele, but it feels distant

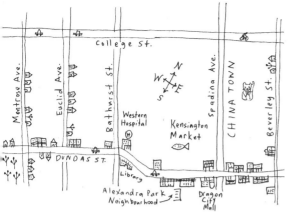

because of the railway-track barrier. Though the big-box land is ridiculously scaled, the older parts of the industrial Junction are very urban; places of stuff-making are tucked in and around places where people live. It's a very old way of living that still works just fine in places like Tokyo, and may just be the future of North American cities.

Back on Dundas, west of Keele, the Junction's main strip is home to some of the most interesting retail in the city. Continuing the theme of making stuff, many of the stores here are cottage-industry outlets and furniture and building salvage shops that are sometimes fancy and sometimes not. Sprinkle in an abundance of cafés (fancy and not), used book and clothing stores, organic and makers markets, electronics repair shops, and restaurants, and it's a near-perfect heterogeneous mix. Another mark of it being a good and healthy neighbourhood is that it offers both daytime and nighttime activities, even though the ban on bars was only lifted here in the late 1990s, as the Junction was famously dry for decades due to its rough-and-tumble railway days.

All this activity is housed in a remarkable stretch of some of the finest buildings in Toronto. The upside of being down for so long is that development was slow here, which has helped to preserve these buildings. Many shop windows still have a film-set quality and seem like they haven't changed since the 1970s.

Further, on the western edge of the Junction, the Maltese flag flies above a small patch of land between Dundas Street West and St. Johns Road. This is Malta Park, in Toronto's Malta Village, which occupies just a few blocks of Dundas. This area was once the vibrant heart of the Maltese diaspora in Canada. Though not many businesses or residents here these days are Maltese, this part of the Dundas strip remains an important part of this small and dispersed community.

The name Dundas Street resonates with all Maltese Canadians; it certainly meant something to me as I was growing up in Windsor, where the only visible Maltese culture was in my relatives' suburban houses. Perhaps that

Saint Paul the Apostle
Maltese-Canadian Parish
Malta Bake Shop
Runnymede Rd
Keele St.
DUNDAS ST. W.
Malta Park
St. John's Rd.
Little Malta
The Junction

explains why Maltese homes are full of wall maps showing the Maltese archipelago, souvenir picture plates, Malta ashtrays, Malta clocks, Malta placemats, and Malta fridge magnets: the smaller the country, the louder the artifact.

The mythic Toronto of my childhood imagination consisted of three things: the CN Tower, Mr. Dressup's house, and Little Malta. We would take yearly trips to see Maltese friends in Milton and make Sunday pilgrimages down to Dundas to eat at the Malta Bake Shop. If you count people like me (half-bred and second-generation), the Maltese population in the GTA is nearly 30,000. Today, most of Toronto's Maltese live out in places like Milton. University of Toronto professor John Portelli, who researches Maltese Canadians, has found there are concentrations of Maltese in Etobicoke, Mississauga, and further out in Brampton – but nothing like the visible concentration that was once on Dundas Street.

Other ethnic neighbourhoods have experienced the same suburban drain. The Italians moved from College Street, roughly following Dufferin out to Woodbridge, while Toronto's Jewish population followed Bathurst from Kensington (once known as the 'Jewish Market') to Thornhill. The first substantial wave of Maltese immigration to Canada occurred soon after the turn of the twentieth century. Many settled in the vicinity of St. Patrick's Shrine Church on McCaul at Dundas, where they held various Maltese events. The Maltese are devout Catholics, and the church exerts a strong pull. St. Paul even found time to shipwreck himself on the island – you can read all about his Maltese adventure in the Bible (in Acts, Chapter 28, if you've got the Good Book handy). New immigrants were helped by Maltese priests and later by the Maltese-Canadian Society of Toronto, which was established in 1922. The society helped purchase and erect St. Paul the Apostle church just east of Runnymede in the early 1930s, establishing the Maltese presence in the Junction and later erecting the current church in the mid-1950s. Its early claim to fame was that it was the only 'national church' (built by parishioners) in North America.

I like to take people to the Malta Bake Shop, a block away from the church, not just to get them to try the pastizzi and to 'Taste of Malta's Delights,' as the sign inside said, but to show them my secret corner of Toronto, one that has a picture of my great-uncle Johnny Catania on the wall. My uncle was a Maltese comedian who entertained the Allied troops in Malta while the Italian Air Force and the Luftwaffe did their best to bomb the island into the sea during the Second World War. In 1964, he gave up his Maltese television show to immigrate to Windsor with my dad's family. Each year, he made numerous trips up the 401 to Dundas Street; he even hosted the Miss Malta of Toronto pageant in the years before he died. That his picture is on the wall of the Malta Bake Shop makes Toronto feel even more like home to me. I often wonder how many other invisible, personal connections people have to places like this. Inside, the Maltese greet each other with an 'All right?' rather than a 'Hello' and speak with a mixture of Maltese and English. It's the aural wallpaper I grew up with.

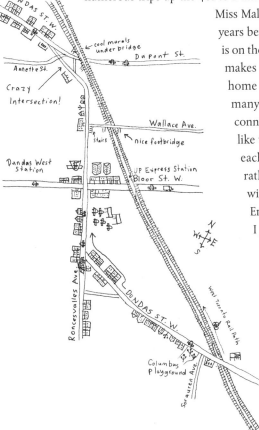

Since the 1920s, when Grazio Borg opened a grocery store here, the bake shop's location has long been a centre of Maltese life in the city. Antoinette Buttigieg, who runs the shop with her husband, Charles, and family, is an active member of the Maltese Canadian Business Network Association. She says they lobbied the city to get vertical street banners installed that mark Malta Village: a little gesture, but important to maintaining a small community's sense of place. Dundas Street is 'like a symbol for the Maltese,' says Portelli, 'even though there is no new blood immigrating from Malta.'

Joseph Cini ran Joe's Barbershop on Dundas since the 1950s, and when we spoke in the late 2000s, he still trimmed the hair of people he shared bomb shelters with back in Malta during the war. He saw a problem when the TTC decided to terminate the streetcar at Dundas West station on Bloor. Instead of a continuous ride from downtown, people had to switch to a bus. 'It's not practical. We had the Dundas streetcar. Nobody knew what the Junction bus was,' he said. Dundas is not a particularly beautiful street, but the sense of place was and is strong. Cini was one of the last holdouts, but after he retired his daughter Joanne opened The Barber's Daughter in the same location. The Maltese Canadian Society of Toronto closed in 2019, however.

Though most of the Maltese residents are also gone, the strip still survives. 'If you come here after church on Sunday, there will be a lot of people,' said George Mallia in the late aughts when we spoke. He was editor and publisher of the local Maltese language newspaper, *L-Ahbar* ('The News'), but it has since folded due to low circulation. 'Some come once a month to hear a Maltese Mass. Certainly, they come on feast days.'

The problem is that people like me aren't moving there, or even regularly hanging out, and I feel guilty about that. Being a member of a diaspora is sometimes a disconnected experience for second-generation immigrants, a kind of shadow citizenship, of being of another place without actually being from there. I like that Little Malta is there, and it's comforting, but my allegiances to other parts of the city are just as strong. When I spoke to him in 2005, Sal D'Angelo of Junction Realty hadn't sold any houses to Maltese folks returning to the neighbourhood, but for him, the culture still played a big role in the area. 'Malta Village should stay in the Junction,' he said. 'Maltese people should stay here.' I hope a few of them stay around too; for me, losing Little Malta would be like losing the CN Tower. I should go to Little Malta more, I often think, but that resolve crumbles as the rest of Toronto distracts me. Maybe more people of non-Maltese descent should visit to help alleviate my guilt. Buy a plane ticket. Go to confession at St. Paul's. Have a picnic in Malta Park. Perhaps pastizzi will become a trendy food like fish tacos or Cronuts, and everybody will flock to the Malta Bake Shop. I hope so. The second-generation guilt can get heavy at times.

Little Malta is all but done by Runnymede, save for the last tiny Maltese sign and banner. Dundas, this most ordinary of streets, continues west, across the Humber, into Etobicoke, and further still into Mississauga, again changing and shifting with the times and places, taking on and discarding characteristics as it goes.

Pearson Airport

 day trip

 dress to impress

 admission

Connecting walks: None, but for fun, try walking into the city someday

Pearson International Airport is Toronto's only true international port. Sprawling into the high plains of Mississauga, it's a place that's half in Toronto, half in some distant land where the grip that familiar places like Yonge, Spadina, and the Scarborough Bluffs have on us slowly loosens as we change our watches to reflect new time zones and anticipate exotic subway systems. It's a liminal kind of place – at once here and elsewhere, and a bit dreamlike too – and a fine place to wander. If you do go there just to wander, though, try to look like a traveller or an eager relative – it's a good way to avoid the attention of those surveilling this most surveilled of places, where anything or anybody that stands out is suspect.

First operational in 2004, Pearson's new Terminal 1 gleams white, and its ceilings soar like the airplanes that taxi away from its gates. The height and arc of the ceiling is stadium-like, and the public art inside is some of the best in the city. Out at the end of Pier F, where the big international jets dock, there are bars with the most expensive cover charges in the city (the cost of an international plane ticket). If you're into art, it's also the most expensive museum admission fee; some seats have a view of a giant Richard Serra sculpture called *Tilted Spheres*, one of only two Serra pieces in the area. (The other, *Shift*, is in a field up in King City.) You can walk through its giant curved metal walls and listen to your voice echo. The spheres are so big they were installed before the walls and roof of the terminal were put up. The bar, with its overpriced drinks ordered from a touch screen, is as jet set as Toronto gets (save, of course, for the lounges that are reserved for first- and business-class passengers).

As impressive as the new terminal is, old Terminal 1, now demolished, has been a hard act to follow. When it opened in 1964, Aeroquay One was this city's bold jump into the jet age. Circular in design, with a parking garage in the middle, it allowed for passengers to be whisked from Pan Am to Plymouth in two minutes. Though it was rendered inefficient by increased passenger volume, an inability to expand, and the spectre of terror that lurks

Richard Serra's Tilted Spheres *may be the last thing you see when leaving Toronto.*

in the corners of our once-utopian air terminals, Aeroquay One was celebrated in aviation and architectural circles alike. Author Arthur Hailey even wrote his blockbuster potboiler *Airport* after getting a tour of the building from his friend, Aeroquay One architect John C. Parkin. The 1970 film of the book evokes the kind of analog-techno thrills the first few decades of the jet age afforded. Journalist George Jonas once wrote a column about the indignities of modern air travel and in it recalled taking a date to Aeroquay One because, he said, it was the kind of slick and mod place you could try to impress someone with. I admit I impress myself drinking that overpriced wine whenever I fly out of the new terminal, and I once took the UP Express train to meet a friend at the airport Sheraton bar in Terminal 3, as she was there on a layover from Amsterdam before heading elsewhere. It was, for a few hours, like we weren't in Toronto, but we weren't anywhere else in particular either.

Once, while dropping off a friend who was embarking on one of those awful Birkenstock-and-backpack tours of Europe, we passed the time by sneaking up automobile ramps to the open roof of the centre garage. We were alone in the dark, high above the runways, feeling like we shouldn't be there, and the terrific sound of the jets moved the hair on our arms as we stood and watched like all those people did when the Beatles arrived at JFK. In modern terminals, you rarely get to feel and hear the jets without the intervention of a thick pane of glass, though some do have outdoor viewing areas. Pearson was the first place I saw a moving sidewalk when I was kid, though today the high-speed ones in T1 are now defunct. Even the future requires proper maintenance. Still, which other airports have given their name to a rock song as this one did for Rush with their 'YYZ' instrumental?

Though airports lend a feeling of being somewhere else, in T1 and T3 pre-boarding, U.S. customs agents admit passengers into a zone where some American laws apply, a kind of embassy territory without the ambassador but complete with small Statues of Liberty. The international arrivals areas, as in all airports, are all theatre. Past customs, passengers are suddenly alone, surrounded by a few hundred faces with expressions that all change from anticipation to *you're not the one I'm waiting for.* When loved ones are finally spotted, people charge up the ramp where they hug, kiss, and cry before moving on in a happy huddle. It makes waiting there a pleasure, and a lovely last moment of strangeness before returning to the normal routine of the city.

I don't recommend it but it's possible to walk out of Pearson on foot. At the back of the T1 parking garage, the brave and ambulatory can stroll out and find Silver Dart Drive, a rather unpleasant airport service road that is at grade and underneath the flying on- and off-ramps that feed the airport with people, though as the airport is always expanding and in flux, routes like this might be blocked at times. An alternate way out on foot is to take the monorail to the Alt Hotel and walk from there. Silver Dart Drive connects to Jetliner Road, which leads out of the airport property and into the kind of wastrel part of town that's adjacent to all airports. As port lands were to cities in the past, the shady landscape around our airports is full of nondescript office buildings and low-rise industrial buildings where the shipping and receiving, importing and exporting of things happens behind unmarked windows. Certainly most of this is legitimate, and there are Hiltons and Petro-Canadas here as well, but the nowhereland around airports is a fine place for doing things under the cover of jet noise.

Walk a little further on and there are the apartment communities along Dixon Road that house many new Canadian families, who live with that jet noise every day, their first steps into Canadian life not far from where they landed.

Exploring more of the airport's perimeter is worthwhile, and though there are parts that won't win any beauty contests, a different view of Toronto's busiest 'port' can change the way we think of the place. Follow Airport Road north to Derry Road in Malton, the place that gave the airport its original name of Malton Airport. In this part of Mississauga, you can never escape the airport. It's the GTA neighbourhood with the coziest relationship to the airport, perched atop its northeast corner. If the wind is blowing from the south, jet fuel can be smelled in the air and the roar of planes darting diagonally into the horizon is a constant presence. This is one part of the GTA where complaints by downtowners about possible jet noise from an expanded island airport or the air show may fall on unsympathetic ears. It's also a good place to purchase a bit of civilization at one of the local South Asian strip malls ahead of an airport adventure: '5 Samosas for $1,' reads a sign at Malton Sweets and Samosa Factory, a block from the airport's northern chain-link fence – quite a bit cheaper than the food in the airport lounges across the runway.

There are references to flight everywhere in Malton, like Our Lady of the Airways Catholic church, with a space-age spire and logo featuring the Latin phrase *Super pennas ventorum* – upon the wings of the wind – and an illustration of Mary standing atop the Earth with two commercial jets flying around her feet. No less spiritual is a vintage 1950s CF-100 Canuck mounted on a concrete pedestal in Wildwood Park, the last fighter jet to be designed and produced in Canada, save for the Avro Arrow, which was to be the next model built here in Malton. When the Arrow was suddenly cancelled in 1959, fifteen thousand people lost their jobs. Some of those workers lived in nearby Victory Village, where wartime houses were built for the aircraft industry. Nowadays, the two-storey peaked homes line the streets much as they did seventy years ago, and the neighbourhood is considered a 'cultural landscape,' meaning all together the homes have historic value.

Malton was first settled by Europeans in the early 1800s near the banks of Mimico Creek; in the 1850s, the Grand Trunk Railway came through and Malton's train station was opened. By the time Malton Airport, later renamed after Lester B. Pearson, opened in 1937, the community centred on the 'Four Corners' where Airport and Derry Roads met. Malton stretches from the airport east to Highway 427 and is often mistaken for being part of Toronto instead of the City of Mississauga, as it's adjacent to Rexdale and doesn't connect directly to any other residential Mississauga neighbourhoods.

There is still some aerospace activity here, though not as much industry as intended; a street called Professional Court is now home to more places of worship than business, including the massive Light Presbyterian Church dominating the landscape. A visitor to the Four Corners can be forgiven for wondering where Malton's historic downtown went: in 1969, a massive natural gas leak explosion destroyed much of the business district, and it never recovered its role as the centre of the community. Malton further disappeared in 1983 when two massive rail underpasses were created for both Derry and Airport Roads, rendering the area a forbidding expanse of concrete. Despite all the physical and economic blows Malton has taken over this past half-century, there's still much life here. Above and around the concrete underpasses at Four Corners are strip malls with busy South Asian businesses like Malton Sweets.

From Four Corners, Derry runs west along the top of Pearson. It's a barren but visceral stretch along the airport fence. Turn south onto Bramalea Road, which dead-ends a couple hundred metres from Runway 23, by the massive FedEx terminal where our various electronic devices likely came through when they, too, immigrated to Canada. At dusk one Sunday, I found a dozen cars parked here watching planes land and take off: kids pressed up against the fence, seniors sitting in back seats, pointing. Many 'plane spotters' also gather at the ends of the runways where the planes fly overhead, at the Tim Hortons on Dixie Road, or in the parking lot behind the Petro-Canada on Airport Road, but on Bramalea there's a wide-angle view of it all. Watching an Air Canada 777 touch down gracefully, as if it weighs nothing, brings the awe of flight back quickly.

Further west on Derry, turn south on Dixie toward that plane-spotting Tim Hortons and find where the entrance to the Etobicoke Creek trail descends from the roadway into a lush prairie of tall grass and sporadic patches of trees across the street. When the trail is low, near the creek, the airport disappears but for the jet noise and a glimpse of the giant golf ball–like structure that houses a weather radar. This part of the airport feels a world away from the one occupied by people standing in long lines just across the tarmac. Signs along the fences keeping trail users out of the active airport lands are bilingual, so you know they're serious. If you're on foot, Courtney Park Drive and Britannia Road, both of which are served by Mississauga MiWay bus 57, bisect the trail should you not wish to do the full YYZ marathon around the airport.

Just before passing under Highway 401, the trail passes by the spot where Air France Flight 358 slid off the runway into the creek's ravine in 2005. All survived, but a similar crash just north of this spot in 1978, Air Canada Flight 189, had two fatalities. South of the 401, the path continues through what seems like deep wilderness, save for occasional views of office buildings or where the trail passes underneath Matheson Boulevard and Eglinton Avenue. Take the steep pathway up to Centennial Park in Etobicoke, or continue south into Mississauga, where creekside trails continue to Burnhamthorpe and the Markland Wood area. One day, the trail may connect to others further south and down to Marie Curtis Park at Lake Ontario. For now, this is one route to the airport that is likely not to be overcrowded.

Markland Wood

 neighbourhood jaunt   Connecting walks: None

 dress to impress

scenic views

There are islands in Toronto that aren't surrounded by water. They're communities that are isolated in some way from the rest of the city. Sometimes it's a cluster of apartment towers surrounded by ravines and a highway, where the only entrances are via bridge or underpass. Other times it's simply a railway line that divides one community from another, which, though relatively narrow, can be as psychologically dividing as a less fraught Berlin Wall.

One such island, on the western edge of the city, is Markland Wood. Toronto neighbourhoods tend to be known either for being superstars – the Annex, Kensington, Parkdale – or for being the spots where crime happens, their names repeated too often in the news. Markland Wood, however, fits neither of these categories. The neighbourhood is surrounded by the Markland Wood Golf Club, which follows the lowlands around Etobicoke Creek that also divides Toronto and Mississauga. There are only four major entrances to the community, one of them via Bloor Street, which bisects Markland and continues into Mississauga. Like a lot of places at the edges of the city, it's serviced only by one TTC line, the 49 bus, which makes a circle around the neighbourhood and returns to Kipling station, a lone bus with no connections once inside the community, almost like a rural collector route.

If you're coming in by bus, get off the 49 just before Highway 427 and walk across the overpass – to get a handle on a neighbourhood it's often good to walk all the way into it from the edge rather than starting at its centre. The 427 is short, fast, and wide here – a quick north-south route between the top and bottom of the city, the view people see when arriving from the airport via automobile – and doesn't have the same mythic identity that the 401 and Gardiner/QEW have. It's the route between places: when you're on it you're either almost at the airport or you're just arriving back in town, and you're wondering which lane you need to be in to get where you're going; there is no time for autopilot or cruise control on the 427. You may feel a profound sense of nowhere standing over the 427 on the Bloor overpass, a big-sky interzone that nobody really owns but that thousands pass through every hour, both underneath and overtop, without much thought of what or who they're travelling past. The West Mall, which runs adjacent to the highway, uses the odd British street-name convention that roughly translates as *wide road, not much going on* (think of Pall Mall in London – fancy, fit for kings and queens, but a bit boring to walk on). To be fair, the West Mall is far better than most highway service roads, flanked at Bloor by a fine example of a Toronto strip mall, filled with a nice mix of mom-and-pop shops. There are also apartment building communities to the north and south between the West Mall and the 427, including the Etobicoke Civic Centre at Burnhamthorpe, one of the former pre-amalgamation city halls. It's a handsome 1958 sprawling building, like the city it represented, clad in Queenston limestone and including a circular council chamber and an almost twenty-five-metre-high memorial clock tower. A decade later, the Board of Education building was built just to the south in a magnificent brutalist style. Etobicoke was *Mad Men*–era cool.

Markland Wood begins a few blocks west on Bloor. The entrance is subtle – the ranch and split-level homes that line the street don't seem much different than the ones a few metres before. Walking through a community like this is a challenge if you're trying to get a handle on the area without having a reason to be there – an appointment or, better yet, plans for visiting somebody – as it's hard to 'read' the neighbourhood. It's private and quiet; people live behind big garage doors and likely travel in their cars more than on foot. Not all of Toronto's outer neighbourhoods are so quiet. Some postwar areas – mixed-income and culturally diverse neighbourhoods especially – see lots of pedestrian activity even though they were designed for car use. In postwar Toronto, the rule is that the more middle-class a suburb is, the less you'll see people out and about. But there are plenty of residents walking through the green spaces adjacent to Markland Wood, especially the Elmcrest Creek trail on the east side, a low-key, not-exactly-a-ravine linear parkland that runs north toward Centennial Park. Here, the 'island' neighbourhood is much more porous, with passageways in and out through the parkland.

Today, the homes in this neighbourhood are over half a century old and show the signs of a mature population: a remarkable number of porches have been glassed in, a particular quirk of retirement-living renovation, and there are other renovations and additions, large trees and landscaping. It feels lived in and comfortable.

This area along the banks of Etobicoke Creek was previously the Silverthorn farm, established in 1807 on land granted to the Loyalist Silverthorn family of New Jersey. It stayed in the family until 1958, when the 400-acre farm was sold for $3 million. This was a few years after the destructive waters of Hurricane Hazel ripped through this lowland, and new residential homes were built only on the area deemed high enough above the flood line, while the rest was given over to the low-risk golf course. The Markland Homeowners Association described the remnants of an old bridge over the creek that can be seen from the twelfth tee of the golf club, though non-golfers miss out on this sight, as they do the sights of many other ravines and watercourses in Toronto that are part of golf courses' private property. There's a slow-brewing movement in Toronto to establish right-of-ways through golf course properties, so perhaps one day they'll be more accessible. Here, trails lead north along Etobicoke Creek to the airport, but could one day connect south to Alderwood and Marie Curtis Park on Lake Ontario and the Waterfront Trail. Golf courses are a prime culprit in breaking up this potential network.

The plaza at the centre of Markland may be the heart of the community, but apart from a McDonald's, it lacks the coffee-shop type of public-private places where neighbours can bump into and overhear each other. A kilometre east, by the 427, the Starbucks is always busy with people, mostly young folks working on their laptops or chatting, proof there's a customer base for this kind of place. The Markland Wood Plaza is a useful one and a classic of the era, with a passageway to a rear parking lot, a barber, hair salon, convenience store, vet, and medical clinic. There's a space out front that could be a fine piazza if some movable tables and chairs were set out. Urbanity, the kind people travel thousands of kilometres to experience, can happily exist here too, but when the car dominates the landscape, it can be hard to make happen.

North of Bloor, in Millwood Park, the 'wood' of Markland Wood is a small thicket of forest, tamed and civilized by street lights that keep the forest bright at night. Follow Mill Road north – the road used to lead to the Silverthorns' grist mill on the creek – and you'll see concrete brutalist towers rise above the 1960s houses, marking where Markland ends and the rest of Etobicoke begins. These towers are 'the Masters,' a zigzagging cluster of condominiums from the mid-1970s with angular balconies, its name inspired by the golf course next door. Back along Bloor, by the park, new mid-rise residential buildings are going in, so more human life is coming to this neighbourhood. If the 49 bus rolls by, hop on and be shuttled off the Markland island back to mainland Toronto.

Alderwood and Lake Shore Boulevard

 pack a lunch   Connecting walk: CNE/Western Waterfront

 bathing suit optional

 few services

Sherway Gardens mall appears like a distant, snow-capped mountain range when approached on one of the expressways that meet in a tangle of ramps next to it. Opened in 1971, it was one of Toronto's first big regional malls and the reason that merchants in Bloor West Village to the northeast invented the concept of a 'Business Improvement Area' to compete with the manicured order inside. Back then, Sherway dominated the landscape, but by the late 1980s the 'intersection' – it's more of an interstellar tangle – of the QEW, Gardiner, and Highway 427 had grown into the beast it is today, obscuring the mall. Like Bloor West Village, Sherway had to do something to get more attention, so they commissioned Eberhard Zeidler and his firm to build an addition that would make it more prominent.

The food court Zeidler created atop the new retail space was a soaring, tent-like structure designed in the postmodern style of the era, with glass blocks, hanging plants, and rich turquoise and brown colours. Incredible light came through the translucent fabric roof and skylights. Though the 'mountains' remain in view from outside, the food court interior was destroyed in a recent renovation, erasing the po-mo style and replacing it with a bland, upscale contemporary aesthetic. A shame, but this is too typically the fate for Zeidler buildings and civic designs that were both ahead of their time and yet not old enough to be worthy of proper preservation – like some of the original details at his Eaton Centre that were renovated away over the last decades.

Sherway's hinterland is typical of malls in the GTA, with numerous tall condo towers sprouting and more condos likely to be built in those parking lots. This mall, once on the edge of town, has turned the area into a kind of urban centre: not exactly a downtown but more somewhere than nowhere. 'We're building Etobicoke's most fashionable address,' read ad copy for one of the condos when it was in the preconstruction state. Definitive marketing copy seems able to will something to be true in the magic-realist world of Toronto real estate. Not far from here is Lake Ontario, but there's quite a bit of civic infrastructure to cross in order to get there. But it's close, and it's always good to see the lake. From Sherway there are two routes to the water: Etobicoke Creek and Browns Line.

Across from the southwest corner of the mall's sprawling parking lots, behind a Tim Hortons, an old road, now free of cars, leads down into the Etobicoke Creek flood plain. It's a pleasant transition from the current somewhat harsh formality surrounding the mall, into a lush, feral-feeling environment. The road leads to the curious Middle Road Bridge. Now a pedestrian crossing, the one-lane bridge was built in 1909 as only the second concrete-truss bridge in North America and is now designated under the Ontario Heritage Act. Most of the Middle Road became the QEW in the 1930s, but this part remains and is in fairly good condition. The other side of the bridge is Mississauga, and a pathway leads up into a quintessential suburban neighbourhood. The multiple landscape transitions in such a short distance from the mall are radical here.

Back on the Toronto side, a path meanders south through the scrubland to the mighty QEW overpass. In between the newer supports that accommodate the widened highway, you can see the original concrete bridge arches of the then-elegant QEW, dating back to 1932. We don't go much for celebrating concrete here, but if this was the United States we might have stylized posters celebrating the overpass the way they do similar Works Progress Administration–era infrastructure projects. South of the bridge, the landscape transitions again to the manicured baseball diamonds of Etobicoke Valley Park, an expanse that eventually narrows beside the creek, where the paved trail continues further south through the thick ravine forest in the aptly named Alderwood neighbourhood.

In 2019, the Toronto Region Conservation Authority (TRCA) completed work on a retaining wall and rock buttresses here to strengthen the creek bank that had suffered from erosion and encroached on the path. The power of water is always working on the land, gnawing at it as it meanders down to and under a rail trestle, then along Lake Shore Boulevard, and ultimately to Marie Curtis Park on the lake. It's a Toronto park, but it's on both sides of the creek, taking up a corner of what seems like it should be part of Mississauga. On that western side, Island Road runs off of Lakeshore (on the Mississauga side, the name is one word rather than two). Island is one of the oddest roads in the city: it undulates like an asphalt roller coaster as it meanders south along the west side of Etobicoke Creek. The road, you see, is sinking in places. Somewhat fun to ride on a mountain bike, less so in a car.

A gently sinking road is one sign that a landscape might be holding secrets. In this case, so does the road's name, as there's no island here today, nor is there a view of an island where the road terminates at a parking lot by the beach. This mystery is 'solved' by looking at the digitized aerial photograph collection online at the Toronto Archives, a stockpile of photos from 1947 to 1992 that often tells this city's stories visually. In 1954, Hurricane Hazel was a rainfall disaster that saw creeks in the GTA rise over their banks, washing away houses and costing eighty-one lives altogether. The most well-known location of Hazel's destruction is the subdivision that was along Raymore Drive near Lawrence Avenue and Scarlett Road, where thirty-five people died when their houses, built in the Humber River flood plain, were swept away. Today, Raymore Park marks the area, as does a plaque on the ruins of a footbridge over the Humber River that was also destroyed.

The geography of the other areas in the GTA tragically affected by Hazel is sometimes less clear, including the area around the mouth of Etobicoke Creek, where seven people were killed when three streets in the Long Branch neighbourhood were flooded by Hazel. Several homes here were also destroyed, some even pushed into Lake Ontario along with trailers from the Pleasant Valley Trailer Park, once located on the Mississauga side of creek, between Lakeshore Boulevard and the railway corridor that today carries GO trains. The aerial photos taken in the years before that event reveal a dramatically different landscape. Today, the numbered north-south streets of Long Branch end at Forty Second Street at the east side of Marie Curtis Park, but before Hazel there were two more streets where the park is now, and in the 1947 photo, the earliest on the Toronto Archives site, Lake Promenade, the street parallel to the lake, extended west, across what is now the park and current mouth of Etobicoke Creek, on a long spit of sand crowded with cottages. Most intriguing is that, south of the railway line, Etobicoke Creek split into two branches, creating an island with yet more houses and cottages on it, eventually flowing into Lake Ontario at the end of the sand spit. The mystery of Island Road was solved (for me, anyway), as was the reason for the roller-coaster road: it's built on unstable landfill that continues to settle over time. It also explains the curious fact that the small chunk of land on the west side of the creek today, all part of Marie Curtis Park, belongs to Toronto, not Mississauga: the city-limit border today roughly follows the old western branch of the creek that was filled in after Hazel. At some point before Hazel, as the 1953 photo reveals, a channel was created in the sand spit, establishing the current mouth of the creek. After Hazel, the streets and homes in the flood plain were razed, and by the mid-1970s, the trailer park gave way to apartment buildings. Today, the beach at Marie Curtis is a pleasant and popular place and even sees the occasional surfer trying to catch a wave on windy days.

This could be considered the semi-natural route to the lake. The other way to get to it from Sherway Gardens is along Browns Line.

I once heard someone describe Browns Line as the ugliest street in Toronto. For a long time, I didn't bother to confirm this fact; I let that idea, like many urban opinions, linger in my imagination and contaminate my impression of the place. Once you hear someplace is bad, it might as well be bad.

Browns Line is rather famous, as obscure arterial roads go, because hundreds of thousands of commuters pass by its QEW and Gardiner off-ramp signs every day – it's one of those landmarks on the way in and out of the city that are noted automatically and peripherally, but rarely given any more thought. Browns Line stands out because it's not a street, avenue, or boulevard – it's a line, a throwback to farm days, the kind of lonely country road where Southern Ontario gothic dramas might unfold.

Evans Avenue begins just south of Sherway Gardens and runs east above the QEW's concrete trench to Browns Line. Looking down on all those QEW cars here – cars filled with drivers who have just seen the Browns Line sign – you really get a sense of how big this city is. Day or night, the cars never stop. Just a few metres beyond the highway, there are homes surrounded by grass and garages, followed by apartment buildings that date to the late fifties and early sixties. The semi-suburban landscape hugs the QEW, but drivers can't see much of it. The cars are harder to ignore, since when you're on foot, the sound of the highway is impossible to escape. These homes and apartments evoke the great postwar age of the automobile – and Metro Toronto's expansion – when Browns Line finally lost the remnants of its rural beginnings.

Browns Line itself begins as a massive off ramp maw, a southern continuation of Highway 427. Maybe this is why that person said it was ugly. But beyond this place, the details tell a different story. Perhaps it's not a story of typical beauty, but it's not an ugly story either. The car is king on Browns Line today, and the strip-mall landscape is never boring. As in Toronto's other strip malls, the variety of stores and restaurants operating here is a completely urban mix. The inner and outer suburbs have an undeserved reputation for being bland and 'all the same,' but, unlike many downtown neighbourhoods, where the chain stores repeat every block or so like the background in a cartoon chase scene, the strip malls here are full of unique, independent, and small-scale businesses, though in recent years some of the shops have become a bit more upscale than they once were.

Just south of the freeway interchange, there are strip malls on either side of Browns Line. There's a Kettleman's Bagel shop with a nice sign made up of bare, almost-Edison bulbs, next to what was once a Miracle Food Mart, then a Chinese supermarket, and is now a Farm Boy. Useful places like a shoe repair shop and a physio office are across from an independent pharmacy, then there's the Morocco House restaurant, and a bit further south a sports café named after Milan's big soccer stadium, San Siro. The overtly commercial gives way to a stretch of tiny postwar bungalows, some with their entire front lawns ceded to paved driveways. Mixed in is the occasional monster home and commercial enterprise. The houses are fortified, calcified even, against the busy street like houses are on traffic sewers like Dufferin, Bathurst, and Dupont in the older city. A few blocks south, the east side of the street turns industrial, but there's also a pub, a schnitzel house, a coffee shop, and even a gentleman's club, fitting of the 'edge of town' feeling Browns Line can still evoke along the way.

Further south, up and over the railway tracks, Browns Line comes to an end at Lake Shore Boulevard. This is Long Branch, where the 501 streetcar route ends. The terminating streetcar loop is just shy of the Mississauga border, a little west of here, where it connects with the Lakeshore GO train line and is a short walk to the Marie Curtis Park beach.

Long Branch could be a film set from the 1950s and 1960s. Relatively few of the low-rise commercial buildings here have been replaced with newer and bigger buildings, as they overwhelmingly have along, say, Yonge Street in North York. Some parts of Lake Shore even have street parking spots at an angle to the curb, which lend a small-town feel to the strip. While walking east, take a diversion south on any street between 39th and 23rd Streets and wander through the pleasant, tree-lined neighbourhood that hugs the Lake Ontario shore. The shoreline is mostly private (save for a few lot-sized parks), hidden behind homes, until Colonel Samuel Smith Park appears with its reclaimed and naturalized waterfront. The park grounds continue on to the Lakeshore campus of Humber College, where buildings from a Victorian psychiatric hospital have been renovated and adapted for use by the college, presenting a new-old landscape that, while familiar in Toronto, is unusual in this pastoral setting. About three kilometres north of the campus is Lakeshore Psychiatric Hospital Cemetery, where over 1,500 patients from the former hospital were buried in near obscurity between the 1890s and 1970s. Neglected for years along the QEW, at Horner and Evans Avenues in Etobicoke, the cemetery has been slowly rehabilitated. A new gate and memorial were installed, and efforts have been made to identify the people – including Indigenous patients – buried here through cemetery records.

The City of Toronto isn't very old, nor does it have much of an empire, but east of the campus and park lies New Toronto, a post-industrial colony that takes up 2.5 square kilometres along the Etobicoke shoreline and is nestled between Lake Ontario and the ten lanes of the QEW. To the east lies the community of Mimico, which, like Long Branch, was an autonomous community before both were swallowed up by bigger municipalities. New Toronto was incorporated in 1913 but technically ceased to exist in 1967, when the entire Lakeshore area (as it is called today, having been rebranded in the 2000s) was amalgamated into Etobicoke.

New Toronto is a streetcar suburb, a form of development common across North America. These communities grew from the late 1800s through the 1920s, just before the automobile became the dominant factor in urban development. The houses have porches instead of garages, the lots are relatively small by suburban standards, and pedestrians can get around comfortably. By the mid-1890s, streetcar service reached as far west as Long Branch (a fine name for the still-operating termination point of Toronto's longest streetcar line). Many New Toronto residents still use that same transit route to get in and out of the city.

Though demographics are changing, New Toronto was a working-class town, one planned for industry from the beginning. The main intersection, Islington and Lake Shore, resembles the four corners of a small Ontario town. Numbered streets spread out in grid formation toward Mimico and Long Branch. The south side of town is largely residential, while vast tracts of land to the north were given over to huge industrial concerns. The factories had mythic-sounding names, some familiar, some just impressive: Anaconda American Brass Limited, Goodyear Tire and Rubber, Continental Can, Gilbey's Distillery, Campbell's Soup, McDonald's Stamping. The town was so focused on industry that Campbell's Soup shared the excess steam it generated with Continental Can, piping it between the plants. At the height of the postwar-production good times, from the 1950s into the 1970s, Goodyear alone employed nearly three thousand people.

When we spoke in 2005, Wendy Gamble, president of the New Toronto Historical Society, described a time when factory whistles sounded around town and workers would walk to work. On 6th Street, the original Gothic revival and bay 'n' gable workers' cottages still exist. The streetscape is unexpectedly similar to that found on Oxford, Nassau, or Wales in Kensington Market. Town lore has it that the Beer Store on Lake Shore used to be the busiest location in Ontario due to all the factory workers heading straight there after work, a story that reminds me of a similar one in Windsor involving a bank and the nearby Ford foundry.

The prosperity of New Toronto made it a desirable place to settle. Large numbers of immigrants came from Eastern Europe, primarily Poland and Ukraine. Today, a large Polish population remains, and the Polish consulate is located in a lakefront mansion just east of New Toronto. Lots of immigrants came from Atlantic Canada as well, including a large number of Newfoundlanders, some of whom frequented the Newfie Pub, a rough-and-tumble draft joint on Lake Shore that closed in the late aughts. New Toronto was a town that worked. Residents were highly unionized, and there were a number of strong credit unions. Service clubs were popular, and there were four active legions.

New Toronto's luck ran out in the 1980s, a time that saw a general industrial decline and the introduction of free trade. When the Goodyear plant here closed in 1987, over 1,500 employees were put out of work. Nearby, Federal Bolt & Nut closed down the same year, laying off 130 other workers, as did the Neptune Meters factory with its 36 jobs. The trend continued up until 2018, when Campbell's Soup Company announced the closure of its eighty-seven-year-old New Toronto plant. In 2005, Bill Worrell, then program manager (now director of Healthy Communities) at the Lakeshore Area Multi-Service Project, described New Toronto as being like a Bruce Springsteen song: 'When all was said and done, ten thousand industrial jobs left, and that shook this place to its foundation,' he said. 'It was a very stable community until this time.' Many of the companies not only closed but tore down their buildings as well. Today, these former industrial sites, known as brownfields, cover much of the northern half of the neighbourhood. Behind hundreds of metres of barbed-wire fence, chunks of concrete and twisted steel are scattered in the prairie-like grass. Many of these brownfields are waiting for redevelopment, but the high cost of the massive environmental cleanup these sites require means they're still empty and languishing. Worrell pointed out that much of the postwar generation picked up and left in the prime of their lives, leaving behind a community that was economically unstable, with a large older population and some very young families.

However, not all of the brownfields remained vacant. The Goodyear site is among those that have been redeveloped, and in the 1990s it became home to Toronto's largest co-operative housing project. The pastel and earth tones of these tall buildings provide a strange backdrop to the traditional storefronts and remaining industrial structures. The residents of the co-ops are largely new Canadians who have changed the face of New Toronto. While the demographics of New Toronto continue to change as more affluent families move in, inflating housing prices and influencing the kind of retail that appears on Lake Shore, the co-ops here are a model of how Toronto and Canada need to address the housing crisis: big, really big, and properly affordable.

Worrell saw New Toronto's future in terms typical of many other inner suburbs: it's either going to go urban or suburban. 'Are we a Port Credit or the Beaches, or are we a diverse urban community with all the mix?' he asked. 'Do we want more Starbucks or do we want to keep the Newfie Pub?' While the Newfie Pub is now gone, Starbucks has appeared on the Lake Shore strip. Neighbourhoods like this, away from the trendiness and development pressures found downtown, gentrify more slowly than those closer to the core because they don't become super-cool super-fast (a blessing more than a curse). Change can take its time, and yet, when it comes, the affordability of the place can be drastically affected.

New Toronto has also had a thriving arts community. The area's relatively low rents and easy access to the city have attracted many artists, and more will settle here as the downtown becomes too expensive. Wendy Lilly, a mixed-media artist, had lived in New Toronto for over thirty years when I spoke to her in 2005, and she liked the variety of environments. 'We're away from the city, but connected to it by streetcar,' she said. 'I don't consider it suburban, but there is a bit of cottage energy here.'

Not being in the middle of everything can offer a unique perspective. Cliff Lumsdon Park, at the foot of 7th Street, has the most stunning view of Toronto's skyline: a perfect cross-section of the city as it rises Oz-like across Humber Bay. In one quick, unobstructed glance, you can take in the city, from Hanlan's Point all the way up to St. Clair Avenue.

East of Cliff Lumsdon, the waterfront is largely private, with intermittent public access to the shoreline at places like Prince of Wales Park and the cute Sand Beach Road Parkette. This stretch was always something of a missing link in the Waterfront Trail, as cyclists were forced to take the highway-like Lake Shore Boulevard for a few kilometres, but in recent years a great protected bike lane was installed. The continuous lake parkland begins again at Norris Crescent, a Montreal-style street with a row of fourplex apartment houses on either side. While the street ends at Norris Crescent Parkette and the lake, the Waterfront Trail for all those not in a car continues on. Until 2012, this wasn't possible, though, and there were few ways to access the water between Norris Crescent and the arched span of the beautiful Mimico Creek pedestrian bridge.

That changed when the new Mimico Waterfront opened, continuing the trail between Norris Crescent and Humber Bay Park, where the bridge is. The linear park was more than ten years in the making and a joint project of Waterfront Toronto and TRCA. What's interesting is that entirely new public space was created for it. This stretch of shoreline was previously fronted by private condo and midcentury apartment buildings, built at a time when we didn't have much desire to preserve public access to a once-dirty lake. To create the park, a strip of property along the lake was either purchased or expropriated. 'We had to acquire the shoreline across the project area in order to extinguish the property owners' exclusive access to the shore, also referred to as riparian rights,' said Nancy Gaffney, head of Watershed Programs at TRCA when we spoke after the opening. 'In some cases it was only one metre wide.'

On first discovering the extended path, there's a sense of revelation: a new part of the city has opened up, one that's quite beautiful, along a lagoon-like expanse of water with the sailboats in the Humber Bay Park marinas as backdrop. Small islands and little peninsulas have been created too, with trees and shrubs all grown in now. Both of Humber Bay Park's peninsulas on the east and west side of Mimico Creek were created by dumping fill into the lake between the 1960s and 1980s. They've naturalized over time and today there are semi-sandy beaches that have formed, with chunks of rock, concrete, and the occasional bit of rebar. Often, there are people sunbathing and even doing a bit of swimming here, sometimes even in winter. As this was once an open lake, the water gets deep quickly. With a little work clearing up the rebar, this could be a functional beach at the doorsteps of the tens of thousands of people who now live just a few minutes away.

Toronto is not, historically, a master-planned city; it just kind of happened. That makes it both interesting and frustrating. Robert Fulford described it as an 'accidental city' in his 1995 book of the same name, meaning it was never supposed to be Canada's biggest city and a cultural and financial capital. The civil infrastructure, like transit, parks, the electrical grid, and even the buildings themselves, are forever catching up with the city that Toronto has become. That's true for transit, the electrical grid, and parks too. Parkland might seem further down the list of critical things Toronto needs to prosper, but these spaces that the great landscape architect Frederick Law Olmsted called 'the lungs of the city' are directly connected to our quality of life. The Mimico Waterfront shows what Toronto can do when it wants to find creative ways to fit new parks into the growing city, here extending the pleasant safety of the Waterfront Trail another 1.1 kilometres. Perhaps one day, all private shorelines in Toronto will get a similar public right-of-way, but those single-family homes along the edge might maintain a fierce grip on their riparian waterfront rights. Still, for the tens of thousands of people living in Mimico, including all the residents in the new apartment towers, this waterfront is a much-needed lung, transplanted into the city with great and worthwhile effort.

The CNE and the Western Waterfront

 day trip

 admission

 bathing suit optional

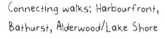 Connecting walks: Harbourfront, Bathurst, Alderwood/Lake Shore

Toronto's western waterfront doesn't have an official beginning, but for me it starts somewhere just west of Bathurst. The Tip Top lofts, housed in the clothier's old textile building with a modern top hat, are the last of the close-to-the-water residential buildings, here among a cluster of affordable co-ops, and they give way to a fairly continuous greenbelt of waterfront parks, disrupted only by Ontario Place and a few other buildings. Coronation Park, the first named park to the west, is built on landfill and has a baseball diamond that's lit up bright on summer evenings, when games compete with the adjacent skyline for attention.

The Queen's Wharf Lighthouse on the strip of Coronation Park between Lake Shore Boulevard and Fleet Street seems to be directing cars rather than boats. Built in 1861, the unlikely lighthouse was originally located at the end of the Queen's Wharf, which ran 215 metres into the lake south of where Bathurst and the Gardiner cross today. In 1912, as infill extended the shoreline south, the lighthouse was moved to its present location, and was then deactivated and almost destroyed before it was eventually renovated to its current working condition in 1988.

The Princes' Gates off Strachan Avenue provide a grand white beaux-arts background to this entire area and serve as the entrance to the vast grounds of Exhibition Place. There are two times to visit here: when the Canadian National Exhibition is on and when it's not. When it's not (or when other events like the IndyCar race or a Toronto Football Club game aren't happening), it has a forlorn, empty, and lonely quality. Like amphetamine users, places of celebration seem to crash when the party's over. These grounds seem extra lonely, and walking easily through the gates seems wrong: there should be somebody here scanning my ticket. During these downtimes, cars routinely use the Exhibition Place grounds as a shortcut in and out of Parkdale, but driving on this kind of civic sacred ground seems like a sacrilege. What to do with the Exhibition Place grounds when the Canadian National Exhibition isn't on is a decades-old unanswered question.

The place changes in late August when the CNE opens. Even far from the grounds, up Dufferin or Bathurst, you can tell the CNE is on by the increase in bus and streetcar service. (It's the best time all year to wait for the TTC, as there's nearly always a vehicle in sight.) The first time I went, in 2005, I was surprised to find out that the CNE is a lot of fun, and I've gone every year I'm in town since. For decades, people have questioned the value of its continued existence as anything more than an antiquated curiosity. The CNE is irrelevant, little more than a stop on the carnival circuit, they say. While it's true that the midway, with its requisite carnies and creaky old swings and Polar Express rides, is the flashy focus for a lot of people, I've yet to attend any event in the city that slams together so many disparate elements into one sweaty, loud, kitschy, fantastic package.

In addition to the Princes' Gates, you can get onto the grounds through the Dufferin Gates. They may be less grand, but I think they're more interesting, as the city and the fair almost touch here, and the gates signal an abrupt shift from normalcy to festival. Here, the Gardiner and railroad tracks are hardly noticeable, sunken below grade in a trench.

Once inside, the scene changes a bit each year. Sometimes there's an immediate farm smell from the Ken Jen Animal Stars and Petting Zoo, strangely inviting in the way gasoline sort of smells good. Every day during the fair, some of the most formidable ducks, donkeys, goats, and pot-bellied pigs you'll ever see endure twelve hours of heavy petting from some very enthusiastic kids.

Over at the farm pavilion there is less fun frottage and more reality. One year, a Pig Mobile charted the life of the average Ontario pig from start to almost-finish. (Even meat eaters don't want to see the last step.) In some of the most honest marketing I've ever seen, the big banner above said, 'Ontario Pork: From Farm to Fork.' There were other signs around that read, 'If you ate today, thank a farmer,' along with nice pictures of the kings and queens from various county fairs. The Ontario hinterland comes to Toronto during the CNE, providing a connection to the rest of the province that goes unheralded. Visitors to this area have also faced aggressive signs that said, 'Farmers Feed Cities.' Well, no guff. Imagine if Toronto did the same and sent out ambassadors to those county fairs with signs that said, 'If you enjoyed the economy today, thank Toronto.' Maybe there's a better way to do this – together.

The strangest place at the CNE is the massive trade show. It's part flea market, part international bazaar, part Dufferin Mall. Many booths are like a live infomercial, with a guy in a golf shirt giving his sales pitch. It's an intimate version of capitalism that's both swashbuckling and desperate. At one of a dozen or so hot-tub displays I visited one year, I stared at a tub that had four built-in speakers and a widescreen TV. 'This is the premier tub in North America,' I was told. I asked if it had a sub-woofer. 'Two hundred watts,' answered the salesman. 'You can really feel the bass in the water.'

In the early part of the century, the CNE constructed its beaux-arts buildings in the tradition of the 1893 Chicago World's Fair, which started the City Beautiful movement. The structures had official-sounding names like the Ontario Government Building (now known as the Liberty Grand event hall) and the Arts, Crafts, and Hobbies Building (now Medieval Times). Toronto architect Alfred H. Chapman built the Princes' Gates in 1927. They're made up of eighteen columns, each set of nine representing the nine provinces of the day. The gates were supposed to be called the Diamond Jubilee of Confederation Gates, in commemoration of Canada's sixtieth birthday, but they were instead named after Edward, Prince of Wales, and his brother, Prince George, who were good enough to pay them a visit when they were in town. Though grander than the Dufferin Gates, the Princes' Gates seem almost forgotten – entering from this side, it's sometimes a bit of a walk before the excitement starts – and now seem more a landmark for motorists driving into and out of the city. Due to environmental damage, the central Winged Victory statue on the top was replaced with a replica fabricated from polymer resin during restorations in the late 1980s.

After the Second World War, a new generation of optimistic buildings was constructed here, this time in the atomic style of the day. We still have wonderful structures like the Better Living Centre, complete with its multi-coloured Piet Mondrian/De Stijl–inspired ornament, as well as the Queen Elizabeth and Food buildings nearby. The displays inside don't always live up to their grandiose names, though. There's a casino inside the Better Living Centre (strangely, the quietest part of the grounds), and the building has housed events during the CNE as varied as an extreme-sports exhibition adjacent to a bunch of vendors selling tube socks. I don't think this is the kind of better living the builders had in mind, though the occasional and legendary rave parties that happened here in the 1990s and early 2000s may be closer to that mark.

The greatest blow to this optimistic age was the 1985 destruction of the Bulova Clock Tower (originally known as the Shell Oil Tower), which was the first example of a welded-steel-and-glass structure in the city when it was built in 1955. The clock tower was destroyed because it stood in the way of the then-named Molson Indy. In fact, Molson paid the $150,000 demolition costs. Many didn't see any architectural value in the structure so today we are without our tower but the Indy still races. In part, it's because of the Indy, and its need for empty space for grandstands, that there is so much empty, treeless, underused space at Exhibition Place most of the year.

Rising above acres of paved and barren CNE parking lot is BMO Field, the soccer stadium where the beloved Toronto Football Club play. Its construction was certainly a good thing – the sounds that come from the open-air stands full of supporters are dramatic – but the new stadium resulted in the demolition of the Canada's Sports Hall of Fame, another handsome, midcentury building that even had heritage status. Too bad we couldn't have preserved a modern gem and put the stadium in one of the many other parking lots. (A similar and convincing argument could be made for the giant spa proposal meant for Ontario Place.)

Near here, the old Exhibition Stadium used to fill up what is now a parking lot. For a time, just to the east of the Better Living Centre, a plaque in the ground showed the footprints of the old grandstands next to some old seats that were salvaged from the stadium, but they were moved when BMO Field went up. In 1988, on our Grade 8 class trip to a Toronto Blue Jays game, the bus dropped my classmates and me off at this spot. We sat in the outfield bleachers, right behind George Bell playing in left field. The Jays lost that day, but I was in awe of it all. Others have memories of seeing Duran Duran, David Bowie, the Jacksons, or U2 at the Ex when they played in the huge bandshell-on-wheels that was moved into place for shows. This whole site is a landscape of our collective memories, the best days of all of our lives memorialized in a parking lot.

At the back of the Enercare Centre, there's occasionally a fairly big historical exhibit from the CNE's vast archives that's curated anew every year. It's the smartest part of the CNE, and serves as its memory. One year, the theme of the exhibit was 'Boomers and the Ex: 1947–1980.' A car from the old Flyer roller coaster was set in front of an old CTV video projection of the ride. Just like being there. What these exhibits do well is show how much the Ex has been a barometer of the times, and a part of Toronto's – and even Canada's – cultural life over the years. The NORAD band even played the fair in 1962. The display isn't always a part of the CNE, but it should be. Toronto has many great achival collections, but they often remain on shelves.

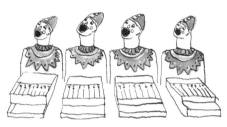

The CNE should stick around because it's fun. What's disappointing is some of the decay and the vast underused space. The buildings were meant for better things. Back in 1893, when the Chicago World's Fair was winding down, a writer from *Cosmopolitan* magazine envisioned what might happen to those grand buildings: 'Better to have it vanish suddenly, in a blaze of glory, than fall into gradual disrepair and dilapidation. There is no more melancholy spectacle than a festival hall, the morning after the banquet, when the guests have departed and the lights are extinguished.'

I felt that melancholy in full one quiet night when a friend and I were wandering around the empty grounds after the CNE was over. Channelling Ninjalicious, a.k.a. Jeff Chapman, the urban explorer and founder of *Infiltration* zine who passed away in 2005, we climbed up the back of the Music Building, one of the few older structures that sports a glass dome. We sat on the roof for a while, looking at the city rise above the empty land, listening to the hum of the Gardiner. I'm not ready for a blaze of glory here, but if we could come up with a way to make the Ex a 'place' all year round, I think Toronto would be better off. In a few years, the Ontario Line subway will terminate by the current Exhibition GO station. With all the new residents living just north of the tracks in Liberty Village or east by Fort York, the pressure for more activity in the area will be intense.

From the Music Building, wander back out the Dufferin Gates – where a sign just north says 'Welcome to Parkdale' – and follow Springhurst Avenue west as it runs along the north side of the railway corridor. The city feels artificially cut off here, so dense and then so empty. Springhurst eventually curves north and meets King Street, which itself soon skirts the top of the railway, above the corporate topiary ads spread out on the embankment that drivers and train passengers see when entering the city. King ends at what feels like the end of Toronto. This corner of Parkdale, where Queen, King, Roncesvalles, and the Queensway terminate in an impossible urban tangle of streetcar tracks and wires, is a most dramatic edge of Toronto. (Somewhere up in Vaughan, Aurora, or Newmarket, the city starts to come together, rolling south, getting thicker and less suburban, acquiring subways, streetcars, more people, and then, suddenly, nothing. A freeway followed by Lake Ontario wilderness.)

This is a good place for the Katyn Monument, a monolithic slab of steel cracked in half that's just east of this intersection, on King. The memorial was built 'in rememberance of 15,000 Polish prisoners of war who vanished in 1940 from camps in USSR ...' Over four thousand were later discovered in mass graves at Katyn, murdered by the Soviet State Security police. This very Polish part of town is home to another memorial a few blocks up Roncesvalles, where a statue of Pope John Paul II looks down on the eastern sidewalk.

Parkdale wasn't always estranged from its lake. However, the construction of the Gardiner resulted in the destruction of 170 homes near the lake, where many of Parkdale's north-south streets crossed the railway corridor and ended as wharves or at the water's edge. Parkdale was once posh and mansion-filled, and many streets are slowly poshing up again as a result of gentrification, after decades of relative affordability.

The Palais Royale sits across the tracks and the freeway, a seemingly lonely lakefront outpost despite being only a two-and-a-half-minute walk from two major streetcar lines and the Roncesvalles pedestrian bridge. Built in 1889, the Palais Royale was originally home to Dean's Sunnyside Pleasure Boats, and the original frames for the boat doors are still visible in the Royale's basement. It was converted into a dance hall in 1922 and drew all the usual big-band names, including Tommy Dorsey, Duke Ellington, and Count Basie.

In a 1988 *Globe and Mail* article on the building, Basil Dolan recalled that 'there were [once] so many people here that you weren't allowed to break into jive. You had to stay close or the bouncers would come over and warn you. "No breaking or you're out."'

After big bands fell out of style, the Palais went downhill, host only to occasional shows like the 'secret' Rolling Stones gig in 2002, for which a temporary air conditioner was installed onstage to keep the millionaires from overheating. In 2006, the Palais underwent a $3-million renovation and reopened with regular live-music bookings and a huge lakeside patio. The renovation also busted one of Toronto's long-held myths: the legendary sprung dance floor wasn't sprung at all, it just had a little give to it. No matter, legends aren't always built on the truth, and it's good to have the Palais Royale back.

West of the Palais, there's another legendary Toronto spot. On hot summer days from the 1890s until August 1950, streetcars would rumble along Toronto streets, stopping for children in bathing suits and carrying towels. They could climb aboard for a free ride to the intersection of Queen, King, and Ronces-valles, where the car would turn south, pass over the railway tracks, and head west down a gentle slope. The destination was not the middle of the Gardiner Expressway, as it would be today, but the Sunnyside Beach area. Toronto provided this free 'bathing car' service to children in order to bring

As immodest as Toronto the Good could get at Sunnyside in the 1920s.

them to Sunnyside – or to three free 'bathing ferries' to the islands – so they could cool down in Lake Ontario. An added bonus: the land adjacent to the beach was home to an amusement park.

To feel truly isolated from the city today, sit on one of the benches in front of the Sunnyside Bathing Pavilion and look directly north. It's like being inside a primitive 1980s video game: two lanes of cyclists, eight lanes of Lake Shore Boulevard, six lanes of the Gardiner Expressway, and, finally, the railway tracks. This is a more formidable barrier than the alligators and floating logs players dodged in *Frogger*. It's not such a far-fetched idea that there could be floating logs here, actually, since the area up to the railway was once all lake. In the early twentieth century, the Toronto Harbour Commission started the Sunnyside Reclamation Project, which extended the shoreline with topsoil that was shaved off a ninety-six-acre Pickering farm through which Highway 401 now runs. By 1922, nearly 197 acres had been reclaimed from the lake between the Humber River and Bathurst Street.

Cut off from the city it still serves, Sunnyside has become a sort of gateway landmark that commuters note peripherally on their way into the city. When you sit on that bench out front, High Park (to the north) and Parkdale (to the east) seem much further away than they actually are. Yet despite being nearly paved over by modernity and progress, Sunnyside is alive and still a part of everyday Toronto, especially in the summer.

When you stumble upon relics like this one in other cities, they often have a melancholy feel of faded glory, as nothing seems more faded than festive architecture. The Sunnyside Bathing Pavilion was designed as a Roman bath by Alfred H. Chapman, the architect who designed the Princes' Gates. It must certainly have stirred up exotic thoughts in staid and provincial Toronto the Good when it opened in 1922. While it was under construction in 1921, an article in the *Globe* suggested the new building would 'look like a compromise between a pseudo-classical villa that should be perched on the steep slopes of some hill looking over olive gardens to the blue waters of the Mediterranean, and a casino at some ultra-sophisticated watering place, through the doors of which should stroll a smartly dressed throng of smart women and blasé men bent on a little turn at the tables.'

Archival photos suggest reality was often a little more down-to-earth and fun: they show huge crowds of people in itchy- and hot-looking bathing suits packing the beach around the pavilion. The photos of the beach here are always jam-packed with people until about the early 1970s, by which point pool culture and the Gardiner (the Sunnyside-area stretch was completed in 1958) had sucked the life out of this most magical of public spaces.

The nearby Sunnyside Amusement Park entertained visitors from 1922 to 1955, when it was demolished to make room for the Gardiner Expressway. At the time of the demolition, Metropolitan Toronto Chairman Frederick 'Big Daddy' Gardiner (for whom the highway was named) said, 'We can't have this honky-tonk at the main entrance to the city on both sides of the main expressway.' But Sunnyside is interesting precisely because it exists somewhere between those high-class Mediterranean looks and a honky-tonk sensibility. And the CNE is great precisely because it's a honky-tonk. During the Depression, Sunnyside was known as the 'poor man's Riviera' – it had been built in a manner that suggested even the common man or woman deserved to feel glamorous. It's fitting that the first Miss Toronto contest was held here in 1926.

After falling into disrepair and having been threatened with demolition in the 1970s, the Sunnyside Bathing Pavilion was designated a historical site in 1975. The city renovated it in 1980, and when you stand in front of it today, it's easy to conjure up the pavilion's old sense of grandeur. Staircases sweep upstairs to the open-air dance floors, where wedding photo shoots and occasional summer electronic-music parties have replaced the big-band swing that you can almost hear echoing up in the rafters, where these imaginary sounds compete with the constant hum of the traffic nearby.

Wandering inside and out on quiet summer days, you get a sense of the people who have passed through this place. What if their ghosts returned to walk the courtyard and dance floor? It's likely they wouldn't notice much change, as the essence of Sunnyside remains, all these decades beyond their heyday. If they went down the front steps, the shock of Lake Shore Boulevard and the Gardiner would probably rattle them – who knew the automobile would go on to change the landscape quite so much? – and the skyscrapers to the east and west along Lake Ontario might seem like a World's Fair dream.

Still, the interior courtyard continues to feel 'exotic,' even if some of the decorative fountains have been filled with cement. Originally, both sides of the pavilion were open-air changing areas for men and women, with 7,700 lockers. Today, only the east side serves this purpose for the massive Gus Ryder outdoor pool next door. Added in 1925, the pool was built to attract more paying customers and people who felt the water in Lake Ontario was slightly too cold for comfort. The concrete breakwalls built offshore were also an effort to keep the water warmer for swimmers. Though good for rowers and dragon-boat enthusiasts, they have the unintended consequence of reducing the circulation in the water, leaving it a bit murky and stale on occasion, and there's more plant material growing in places than at open-water beaches.

Toronto has swimmable and even clean beaches, but Sunnyside isn't exactly one of them. Not many swim here except the swans, who watch, with their patrician aloofness, the beach-volleyball players on the sand. In the café and on the lively patio, Toronto's citizens – now more multicultural than in those old photos – still mix, though some details at Sunnyside aren't quite right. The café uses too-cheap plastic garden chairs, tacky catering equipment is stored in various corners, and the iron railing that runs around the building is flimsy. The gates to this public place aren't always open, as they should be – especially to the grand top deck with its sweeping views of the beach. But the thing about a honky-tonk is it's a wonderful spectacle and great fun that doesn't discriminate. And despite Big Daddy Gardiner's opinion, all the varied activity around Sunnyside is good and should be encouraged. Sunnyside puts on some strong regal airs, but it's not a relic. If our ghostly visitors from the past had some time to spare, they might change into shorts and T-shirts, spike a few volleyballs, and then order a pitcher of beer.

If you walk west from Sunnyside, you'll come upon Sir Casimir Gzowski Park, complete with its modish, railway-inspired memorial. The park is named after the engineer who served as acting lieutenant-governor of Ontario from 1896 to 1897 and who worked on some of the province's most notable pieces of infrastructure, including the Grand Trunk Railway and the Welland Canal. (He is also the great-grandfather of late CBC broadcaster Peter Gzowski.) Near the memorial, there's also a concrete lion that used to sit in the middle of the QEW before the Gardiner was built. When the QEW was opened in 1939 by Queen Elizabeth in 1939 (better known to most of us as the Queen Mum, late mother to the late Queen Elizabeth), it wasn't the utilitarian and jammed freeway it is today but rather a pleasant drive, where the view was as important as getting there. There are still a few grand bits left, like the sculptural elements on the bridge in St. Catharines, posts with art deco-ish 'ER' on them at some of the bridges (the royal cipher meaning 'Elizabeth Regina'), and this relocated lion monument.

This end of the old City of Toronto's western waterfront also doesn't have an official end, though the white bike-and-pedestrian arch bridge that crosses the Humber River into Etobicoke has become a major landmark since it was installed in 1994. It's adjacent to the twin Palace Pier towers that for many mark the entrance and exit points to the city (with apologies to the rest of Etobicoke). When the first of the two towers was built in 1978, it had, true to the spirit of the day, a discotheque in the penthouse. (Today, it's merely called a 'party room.') The decision to put a disco here is not without historical precedent; the towers are named after another lost Toronto landmark, the original, and actual, Palace Pier (named after a pier in Brighton, England, of course), which jutted out three hundred feet into Lake Ontario and included a dance hall that was also popular during the big-band era. The pier was destroyed by a fire in 1963, ending Toronto's version of amusement piers, which were once a feature in many waterfront cities. A monument at the site, just past the bridge, contains one of the original concrete pier footings. Beyond, there's more parkland along the Etobicoke shore, and a new lakefront high-rise community in Mimico that has made the Palace Pier less lonely without diminishing its landmark status.

Bathurst Street

 day trip

 dress to impress

 scenic views

Connecting walks: Harbourfront, Dundas, Dupont, St. Clair, Eglinton, CNE/Western Waterfront, Sheppard

At first glance, Bathurst is not a pretty street. You don't see it on tourist post-cards, and when people think 'Toronto,' it likely isn't the first corridor that comes to mind. But it's a street that means a great deal to the city. It's the line the Jewish community has roughly followed as it migrated from downtown to the suburbs, just as other ethnic groups followed other streets from the traditional inner-city heart to the open spaces and bigger houses outside the city limits. Bathurst is a long road that extends north into rural areas, but its urban delights are often subtle and easy to overlook when you're not on foot.

Today, Bathurst begins at the Billy Bishop Airport dock. A new terminal has been constructed and there's now a tunnel under the western passage, but the original airport building can be seen languishing in the field beyond the runway – it has a design similar to the first Pearson Airport building, back when that international landing strip was still known as Malton Airport.

Down here at the foot of Bathurst, this is all new land, part of Toronto's massive and long-running effort to extend its waterfront southward. At the water's edge, hundreds of metres south of the original shoreline, the passage between the mainland and the island is often rough and choppy. The airport ferry, especially in winter, has a maritime-workhorse air to it, fighting a constant battle against the elements, even if the crossing takes just two minutes. Looking backward, it's nearly impossible to see the original shoreline: Toronto came a long, long way and stopped in a very straight line.

During the Second World War, the exiled Norwegian Air Force had a base here, at what is now Little Norway Park, but only the white flagpole at the southwest corner of Queens Quay and Bathurst Street remains today. A few very wordy plaques commemorate the occasion; in fact, half of one plaque is dedicated to explaining that there is another plaque nearby with more information. Maybe the plaque editors were on strike in 1987 when His Majesty King Olav V was in town for the dedication. After the Norwegians left, and until 1967, this was also the site of Maple Leaf Stadium, home of the Toronto Maple Leafs baseball team that now plays at Christie Pits Park.

These days, Little Norway Park is like a museum to various kinds of playground equipment, some of it unlike anything found in other parks. There's a wire mesh 'ship' that's built into the side of a small hill, complete with what looks like a twisting cement slide. How you're supposed to slide down it is unclear. Bums won't work on the gritty material, the curves are too tight for skateboards, and inline skates weren't yet invented when it was built. If it was just put in for whimsy's sake, Toronto must have been doing all right in the mid-1980s. There's also a slide that's constructed into the head of a giant concrete lion. Nearby, there's a promenade that extends along the western passage and offers scenic views of the airline hangars.

Turn to face north at the Bathurst and Queens Quay corner and you'll see a condo building on the opposite side of Queens Quay. This building is remarkable in that something so big comes right down and meets the sidewalk at a scale that isn't overwhelming, a quality other buildings should emulate. Waterfront condos get a bad rap – and some are indeed terribly designed – but at this end of Queens Quay, many of the buildings are quite urbane. Walk a hundred or so metres north on Bathurst and the half-kilometre-long crossing of Toronto's most intense transportation corridor begins. First up is Lake Shore Boulevard, with its wide, two-stage crossing at which the usual rules of traffic don't seem to apply, as cars come from many directions, obeying traffic signals not visible from sidewalk level. It isn't a fun crossing on foot, and the cozy urban feeling of Queens Quay quickly evaporates.

On the northwest corner of Bathurst at Fleet Street, you'll see two giant toy soldiers, public art created by Canadian author and designer Douglas Coupland. They're cheeky and potentially inflammatory to tourists from Buffalo, as the British soldier is standing, while the American is lying down, defeated. The outcome of the War of 1812 is always a point of debate, but here on a Toronto corner it's been decided in high relief.

A block north of the soldiers, Bathurst passes Fort York. For years, much of the land around the fort was impenetrable to the average Torontonian. Urban explorers and nighttime infiltrators might have entered the old Molson's plant that stood on the north side of Lake Shore Boulevard, or wandered through the St. Mary's Cement yard that helped supply Toronto's late-1990s and early-2000s building boom, but for most everyone else, it was one of those chunks of the city that became a black hole on our mental maps. Add in the Gardiner running along the top of this small, former industrial parcel, and it was an official nowhere. That's changed, radically. Over the last twenty years, those industrial operations between the Gardiner and Lake Shore have been removed. Holes were dug, cranes were erected, and a new neighbourhood was born. One hole even revealed the logs from the Queen's Wharf that stuck out into the lake, as well as an old schooner, buried by fill more than a century earlier.

What's most remarkable is that what was impenetrable is now permeable, with streets and other passages crossing the area. The 509 Harbourfront streetcar line stops two blocks south of the fort, and from there the fortifications and tops of the blockhouses are visible. These new, albeit narrow, vistas are as close as we can get to seeing the fort as somebody might have during the War of 1812, aboard a ship a few hundred metres out in the lake, perhaps on the attack. The Gardiner marks where the original shoreline was and is conveniently high enough to see under. It has also allowed for new development to be created underneath the roadway on the east side of Bathurst, where the former Weston warehouse has been given the adaptive reuse treatment as a grocery store and other shops and services.

Back on the west side of Bathurst, Grand Magazine Street has a view corridor through new condo buildings that frame the Tip Top Tailors lofts, a perfect terminating view. Grand Magazine, like other streets such as Bastion and Gzowski, reference Toronto history. Sloping Sky Mews is named after an Indigenous ally of the British during the Battle of York, a Mississauga warrior also known as Nawahjegezhegwabe. Bruyeres Mews is named after Colonel Ralph Bruyeres, a military engineer who oversaw the fort's rebuilding in 1814. Angelique Street is for Angelique Givens, remembered as 'being fearless in confronting the American troops in 1813 as they plundered her house of its contents including the clothing of her seven children.' The mix here is made up of townhomes along some of the mews and taller, mid- and high-rise condo buildings along Lake Shore. People walk their dogs to the Garrison

Common, the space to the west of the fort gates. New buildings have made the Gardiner largely disappear into the mix rather than dominate the landscape. Even the awkward triangular parcel of land at the corner of Fort York Boulevard and Bathurst has a mid-rise building on it, just about the closest building to the Gardiner now, as some of its units look out at the roadway only a few metres away. One can imagine a David Cronenbergesque film about a young insomniac financier on amphetamines staring out at headlights all night long ... though the view really isn't much different for the thousands of people in other buildings on busy arteries across the city, the busy streets where Toronto has forced most multi-unit residential towers. The Gardiner, after all, is often slow-moving. Underneath it, the Bentway linear park straddles the fort and continues to grow east and west, not just helping erase whatever barrier the Gardiner presented before, but creating a new kind of public and cultural space for Toronto.

In the middle of the new neighbourhood is another linear plot of land running from Lake Shore to Fort York Boulevard, home to June Callwood Park. This is our memorial to the life and work of the great Toronto writer and social justice activist who died in 2007. Before her death, Callwood stated that she wished for the park to be designed for toddlers and their caregivers, and to reflect one of her mottos: 'I believe in kindness.' The voiceprint of that phrase is mapped into the landscape and can be seen from above. This raises the ongoing issue in Toronto's new condo neighbourhoods of unit size: Will toddlers even live in these buildings if some units aren't built family-sized? Developers have said the market will not bear these larger, more expensive units, proving once again that, in order to have inclusive housing in our city, we once again need robust public housing initiatives like the massive, nationwide effort that occurred in the decades after the Second World War.

The original, much shorter version of Bathurst Street began near here and was named after Henry Bathurst, 3rd Earl Bathurst and secretary of war for the colonies. Though he never had the courtesy to visit Canada, he's the guy who granted the University of Toronto (then King's College) its charter while waging distant wars from the Home Office. North of Queen Street, Bathurst was known as Crookshank's Lane until 1870, when it, too, became Bathurst as the city grew up and around it. The first bit of old Bathurst we can still see is the bridge that runs alongside Fort York.

Though the city's identity doesn't embrace them, Toronto is a city of bridges. Some cities, like San Francisco and Vancouver, are known for their iconic bridges, but our only famous bridge is the Prince Edward Viaduct – the one Michael Ondaatje wrote into our collective consciousness in his novel *In the Skin of a Lion* – which leaps across the Don Valley, affording magnificent views few cities can match, whether you're on it or looking up at it. We think of our other workaday bridges only when they're being repaired and aren't available when we need them, or when some cataclysmic bridge collapse occurs in another city and we cast a wary eye toward the cracks in the concrete holding up the Gardiner. All around Toronto, there are unsung bridges that cross the city's ravines and, while perhaps quotidian on top, they're often works of engineering beauty when seen from below.

The Sir Isaac Brock Bridge, one of the city's oldest, is one we never worry about letting us down. Its 680 tonnes of solid steel and concrete are not hidden behind euphemistic or sexy architectural forms more pleasing to those with delicate sensibilities. So much visible structural metal seems too industrial and almost obscene, but this is what old Toronto the Good looked like. To David Spittal, a retired City of Toronto archaeologist, the bridge is a sort of living museum: 'There used to be dozens of these old truss bridges around town, down along Spadina and other places,' he says. 'But fewer and fewer remain. It's part of our cultural landscape, like overhead wires and wooden poles. People want to bury them, but that alters the historic look. It's a conundrum – we want to improve the city, but we want to preserve things, too.'

The Bathurst Street Bridge is about as solid as anything in Toronto gets. Take a walk along it and hold on to the handrail as a streetcar crosses the bridge. This is what Toronto feels like when streetcars roll over its civic body: your hands vibrate from a direct connection to those heavy steel wheels. When large trucks go by, the bridge gently bounces and sways, making it seem awake, responsive, alive. Built in 1903 by the Canadian Bridge Company in Walkerville, now part of Windsor, the bridge originally crossed the Humber River, where Lake Shore Boulevard is now. In 1916, the trusses were taken down and reassembled in an expanded fashion at the Bathurst location to replace an earlier truss bridge that dated to the 1860s.

In 1931, the bridge was realigned twenty-two degrees to allow Bathurst a straight slope down to the lake. In 1985, it was designated a historic structure, worthy of preservation. Though it is structurally sound, the bridge has suffered from a lack of maintenance but recently had a refurbishment. The iron handrail is ornate and as solid as the rest of the bridge, but children would be wise not to run their hands along it lest they embed chunks of old Toronto in their soft palms (as it's rusty and its paint is flaking off). Stand under the bridge and you'll realize that what's underneath is as important as what's on top: this bridge, which was designed to get us over the railway land, is the best place to see that Toronto is still very much a rail town. The main span of the truss floats over ten sets of tracks that make up a disconcertingly empty view as you look east toward downtown.

From here, you really get a sense of how much land the railroad takes up; suddenly the Gardiner seems like a patsy, not the barrier to the waterfront it's made out to be. The Bathurst Street Bridge continues south beyond the truss section as a standard-issue, steel-plate-and-concrete structure that dates to 1930.

At Fort York Boulevard, a ramp takes you to the base of the fort walls. The walk down to the fort lands gives a sense of the enormous earthworks that American soldiers so desperately wanted to scale during the War of 1812. Here there's access to the underbelly of the bridge, the part you're not supposed to see. The southern section of the bridge is cathedral-like below, with a series of concrete pillars holding up the roadway. Though the ground is littered with what one expects to find under an urban bridge – assorted garbage, the odd condom, and dirty Y-front underpants – it's often a bucolic and nearly rural experience. David Spittal pointed out that 'people have been living under there for generations, it's not a new phenomenon.' He recalled that during his university days, he saw folksinger Murray McLauchlan sing a song called 'Under the Bathurst Street Bridge.'

This area has much to reveal, and the occasional encampments here are just one layer of many that extend back through railroad, colonial, and First Nations history. Spittal considers it one of the most dangerous sites he has ever seen a dig take place, as it's also the site of the original mouth of Garrison Creek, which still runs underground. 'As soon as you dig a hole,' he said, 'it fills with water.'

From the mouth of the original creek, by the concrete pillars that hold up Bathurst Street, walk west along the south side of Fort York's ramparts and the Gardiner Expressway, along the Bentway and by the new Fort York Visitor Centre whose weathered corten steel wall is meant to evoke the mild escarpment of the former shoreline. From here, eyes wide shut, it's easy to imagine Lake Ontario only a few metres away. The hum of the Gardiner even sounds like the surf. But open your eyes and the freeway looms on its concrete columns, and you must look between condominiums to catch a glimpse of the distant water.

On the north side of the fort, you see hints of why we have Toronto terra firma where the shoreline once existed: nearly a dozen rail lines cross Toronto here; one branch heads along the lake toward Hamilton, the other curves northwest toward Weston and Georgetown. The latter follows part of the route of the historic Grand Trunk Railway, Toronto's first railway and a piece of infrastructure responsible for much of the city's early development. In the middle of that wedge is Ordnance Triangle Park, with a new vista of downtown, backed by a cluster of new high-rises and their podiums that have created a rather grand and busy entrance to Liberty Village, all connected by a double pedestrian and cycling bridge called Garrison Crossing.

The name Grand Trunk still sounds expansive; it is a reminder that after the War of 1812 it was railways, not armies, that started to decide Toronto's future. The Grand Trunk grew, as planned, into a main trunk line – becoming, for a time, the world's largest railway system – and finally morphed into CN. But when it was first built, the Grand Trunk didn't even cross what is now downtown Toronto. It swung down toward the lake from the northwest and stopped at a terminal on the south side of Fort York. Evidence of the rail line that led to this important terminal is mostly gone, save for traces of it underneath the southern part of Strachan bridge, where a passage leads from the Bentway west to where the main GTR tracks once curved north, through what is now Liberty Village.

The Grand Trunk was originally chartered under the name Toronto & Guelph Railroad Company, and became part of plans for a railway between Toronto and Montreal and southwestern Ontario. Between 1853 and 1856, lines were built in two sections: Toronto to Montreal and Toronto to Sarnia. Engineer Casimir Gzowski was the contractor who worked on the western section, and the lakeside park west of Sunnyside bears his name. The large terminal yard for the Sarnia line was constructed in front of Fort York on twenty acres, about half of which was landfill, thus beginning the shoreline's slow move south to its current point across from the Billy Bishop airport.

More than anything else, the railways were responsible for the extension of Toronto's waterfront, because the rail companies had the political and financial muscle to get what they wanted. (The term *to railroad* means what it does for a reason.) There was a gap between the Sarnia and Montreal sections of the GTR for only a short time before the railway bullied Toronto city council into letting it lay tracks across the front of the city along the newly created Esplanade, a development that marked the beginning of the city's estranged relationship with its waterfront. In the late 1850s, the view from the fort's bastions was still of the lake, but also of a busy Victorian industrial scene.

The Fort York yard was formed when workers dumped fill behind a line of sixty-two massive timber 'cribs,' which were then filled with dirt also from Garrison Common, a vast tract of land that included what is now Exhibition Place and the residential neighbourhoods to the north of the fort, and from the GTR itself. Archaeological issues were not considered then, so Grand Trunk was able to carve the railway's trench through the heart of the 1813 battlefield. That's the equivalent of paving the Plains of Abraham in Quebec City or Gettysburg in Pennsylvania, and it's probable that the fill still contains cannonballs, artifacts, and even human remains. The site is so historically important that the City of Toronto began a campaign in 2009 to have Fort York recognized as a UNESCO World Heritage Site, a process that's likely to take years. As for the railway itself, we tend to either take it for granted or else complain that the tracks cut the rest of the city off from the lake. According to David Monaghan, curator of the House of Commons and former curator of the land transportation collections at the National Museum of Science and Technology, 'one of the great tragedies of Canadian industrial and transportation history is that so little remains of the original infrastructure that played a critical role in the development of the first railway networks in Canada.'

With this sentiment in mind, that lonely trench under the Gardiner and Strachan suddenly echoes loud with meaning, as it was one of the reasons Toronto grew as a city. The Grand Trunk connected Toronto to Sarnia, where a ferry (enhanced in 1891 by a rail tunnel) crossed the St. Clair River to Port Huron, Michigan, allowing cargo to connect by rail to Chicago, a big market for Toronto's industrial might.

North over the bridge and a block east of Bathurst sits Victoria Memorial Square, which was designated a national historic site in 2003. Though it looks like a pleasant grassy square, as unassuming as the ground under the bridge, it's Toronto's first military cemetery, holding nearly four hundred graves of people connected to Fort York who died between 1793 and 1863. While installing a wading pool in the square during the 1930s, city workers horrified onlookers when they accidentally unearthed human remains. History may often be buried, but not very deeply.

Bathurst continues north as a mixed residential street, albeit a busy one. More stores and restaurants have appeared along the way, as well as landmarks like the massive Toronto Western Hospital, but it is mainly lined with a jumble of houses, from high Victorian homes to workers' cottages. North of Dundas Street, Bathurst meets Nassau Street at Kensington Market's unglamorous back door.

In the 1920s and 1930s, Kensington was known as the Jewish Market, and some sixty thousand Jews lived in and around the area, worshipping at over thirty nearby synagogues. After the Second World War, people wanted their own versions of the Canadian Dream: more space and a better life. In turn, Bathurst became an extremely long ethnic strip, as the Jewish community moved up along it toward Thornhill.

Bathurst remains remarkably uneventful up to Dupont. Apart from a few exceptions, Bathurst is a private kind of street whose address doesn't come up much as a destination, even though it's a road often travelled. It can be hard to live on a busy route like this. The little front yards tend to be treeless and paved, and this stretch has a batten-down-the-hatches look, as if it's taking the hit of pollution, traffic noise, and graffiti taggers so the leafy streets to the east and west can keep real estate agents salivating.

Under the tracks north of Dupont, Bathurst softens into a more genteel, quieter, and leafier kind of urbanism. The white building at the northwest corner of Davenport Road and Bathurst is the Tollkeeper's Cottage. Once part of a nearby residence, it was returned to near its original location by the Community History Project, a volunteer group that restored the circa-1835 building. Now a museum, the cottage is a reminder that Davenport is one of Ontario's oldest roads, originally an Indigenous trail called Gete-Onigaming, Anishinaabemowin for 'the old portage,' as it was a route between the Don and Humber Rivers, that ran along the shore of ancient Lake Iroquois and was used long before European settlers arrived and gave it its current name.

Past the top of the Davenport hill, Vaughan Road splits off from Bathurst, heading diagonally to the northwest. The wonderful – and rare – V-shaped intersection could be home to a stunning flatiron-type building, but instead has a remix of the standard Toronto midcentury high-rise with triangular balconies rising out of a giant cement base. High-rise haters have nightmares about this exact building multiplying and destroying the Annex like an army of architectural Godzillas, but they house a lot of people comfortably and we need many more. With a little work, this boring pedestal could be fixed up and become a people place. For a visual pick-me-up, look across Bathurst and you'll see the lovely, recently refurbished, and expanded Wychwood branch of the Toronto Public Library – possibly the city's cutest branch – which was built with a Carnegie grant in 1916. Even more colourful is the public artwork in the orphaned plot of land at the bottom bit of the V: *Three Points by Two Lines* by artists Christian Giroux and Daniel Young, which generated some aesthetic controversy when installed in 2018.

Bathurst enters its golden stretch north of St. Clair, where it's lined with a few blocks of walk-up apartments and beautiful modernist high-rises. Just before Bathurst flies over Cedarvale Ravine, it's home to 1599, the building where Ernest Hemingway lived for a few years in the early 1920s while writing for the *Toronto Daily Star*. In the *National Post* in 2003, Robert Fulford explained that Hemingway originally 'came to Toronto as the male version of a governess, hired to babysit a young fellow whose rich parents believed he needed a masculine role model.' The Connable family lived a few blocks southwest of St. Clair and Bathurst. Their son Ralph walked with a limp, and they hired Hemingway, says Fulford, to give their son 'the right slant on life, especially as to his sports pleasures.' Fulford goes on to explain that Hemingway's mentor, Ezra Pound, held a certain disdain for Toronto and addressed his letters to Hemingway 'Tomato, Can,' while Wyndham Lewis suggested he was toiling away in a 'sanctimonious icebox' of a city. Hemingway shared his own view of Toronto in verse he penned for the *Star*: 'I like Canadians: They let women stand up in the street cars / Even if they are good-looking. They are all in a hurry to get home to supper / And their radio sets.'

Just past Papa Hemingway's place, the Holy Blossom and Beth Tzedec temples, two massive synagogues built in 1938 and 1955 respectively, are the first major indications of Jewish life on this street.

At Shallmar Boulevard, a few blocks north of Eglinton, there's a collection of brilliantly white buildings fronted by huge Caesars Palace–style fountains. They all hold many stories. In one of these buildings lived Sidney Raykoff, whose family owned Raykoff Hardware in Kensington Market until the 1950s. Raykoff remembered neighbourhood boys Joseph Berman (his family owned a chicken store down the street at Augusta) and Eph Diamond joining the navy during the war and 'every night getting the hell kicked out of them as they were the only Jews on their ship.' He also remembers them each borrowing $2,000 from their grandmothers after the Second World War to build their first house, founding the Cadillac Fairview development empire, and eventually erecting the building Raykoff lived in when I met him in the 2000s. (Raykoff, too, was part of that Jewish migration up Bathurst.)

The area between Eglinton and St. Clair Avenues was the site of a very public 1970s battle between the car lobby, who wanted to widen Bathurst, and those who supported more urban-friendly visions like the Stop the Spadina Expressway movement.

North of Glencairn, the signs of Jewish migration, and the references to Kensington Market, increase. In Lawrence Plaza, which Queen Elizabeth II visited in the 1950s, lives United Bakers Dairy Restaurant. A Toronto institution since 1912, it first opened at Bay and Dundas, then moved to 338 Spadina in 1920, where it stayed until it relocated to this plaza in the 1980s. Behind it is the Barbara Frum branch of the Toronto Public Library, named after the legendary Canadian broadcaster who lived nearby before she moved to to the York Mills and Bayview area with her husband, dentist-turned-developer Murray Frum.

The Baycrest Centre for Geriatric Care, a bit further north on Bathurst, is a sort of bookend to Kensington in the south. Though it's true that there are thousands of Jews living in this area and well into Thornhill – the Holocaust memorial in Earl Bales Park at Sheppard West is a powerful spot – the sprawling collection of buildings that make up the Baycrest Centre is a storehouse of memories of Jewish life in Toronto like no other. Inside the heads of the residents here lives a library of memories that detail a lost Toronto. There's even a recreation of an old-time Kensington peddler scene, complete with chickens, produce, and a sign that says, 'All the bones you want for free.'

Established in the early twentieth century, Baycrest was originally located are at 29–31 Cecil Street, where it was then known as the Jewish Old Folks' Home. In the 1950s, the home purchased almost twenty-five acres of

farmland north of Toronto, and Baycrest has been expanding there ever since. With halls full of contemporary and abstract art – even some Andy Warhol prints – it feels more like a big public gallery than old-age home. Hang out by the papier mâché peddler long enough and a resident is bound to tell you his or her Bathurst story too.

North of Baycrest, the wonderfully named Neptune Drive winds through a treeless 1950s and 1960s apartment development along the south bank of the gas, steel, and rubber river that is Highway 401.

From here, you can walk north up Bathurst under the twelve lanes of the 401. It's a tight squeeze – the sidewalk is wedged between the 401's supporting wall and a little steel fence. Pedestrians almost have to rub up against people coming the other way. The underbelly of the 401 is like a cut tree with its growth rings exposed: you can see the original overpass, a reminder of when the 401 was the King's Highway and carried my mother and countless other Maritimers to Windsor during the 1960s, and the lanes that were added later, turning it into the bloated express-and-collector-lane beast it is today. This mythic Canadian highway can make a pedestrian feel very small.

The 401 is so big and formidable, it feels like it has always been there, as if it's a land formation left over from the glacial retreat. Humans built it, of course, and kept expanding it to the incredible, never-ending behemoth it is today. Highway 401 connects southern Ontario, end to end. So wide, so fast, it's a deadly and dangerous beast. Do a quick Google News search of it and words like *killed*, *injured*, *crash*, and *wrong-way* come up over and over. Travelling it my entire life, I've had some frightening moments, and I bet everyone else has too. It scares me, more as I get older, but it's also a perversely fascinating piece of postwar megaproject engineering.

To pass the time on countless trips along the 401, mostly to Windsor, I've idly wondered how highway engineers weaved it through existing farmland, noted how many small concession roads were disconnected by it, and considered where it altered the topography in major and minor ways. Ontario has an amazing landscape – subtle by Canadian standards, but varied and beautiful – though not much of it is really seen from the 401, a road designed to pass through it fast, annihilating the nuances of landscape for straight lines. In his memoir *Son of Elsewhere*, author Elamin Abdelmahmoud wrote that the 401 has been a constant presence for him, a kind of connective tissue of his life, and a looming presence for all of us. 'A town of 150,000 people can pass by you in four exits, then it's in your rear-view, and you're returned back to the trees,' he writes. 'It's hard not to be romantic about this – a perspective of human life that lets you swing out wide and see a whole city, and how fleeting it is.' The 401 has also never stopped growing since work on it began in the 1940s. It's alive.

Where it crosses Bathurst Street is a particularly interesting place to see how this beast of a freeway and the city have grown up with each other. Bathurst here is relatively dense, not much different than, say, the Danforth, with mixed retail and apartments on the main street, and detached residential homes on side streets. When you are approaching from the south, the highway seems almost tucked into the neighbourhood, as the buildings hug it closer than most parts of the 401. There's just one eastbound on-ramp too, without the usual long approach lane. It wasn't always like this.

In 1956, when the 401's Toronto portion opened – then called the Toronto Bypass, as it was an alternative to Highway 2, which ran through the centre of the city – farmland around here was just beginning to be urbanized. Originally only two lanes in each direction, the 401 passed just south of the Bathurst Street and Wilson Avenue intersection. The Toronto Archives' online aerial photograph collection reveals the story of how quickly Toronto expanded. In 1947, Bathurst and Wilson was rural, with just a scattering of residential houses and faint traces in the landscape of the subdivisions that were being prepared. Three years later, as 401 planning was well underway, the area was a patchwork of brand-new housing tracts and streets waiting for houses, some where the 401 would be built just a few years later.

Pull out your phone and type 'Carhartt Street' into a map app. This tiny, dead-end street was once an on- and off-ramp for the eastbound 401, in addition to the on-ramp on Bathurst that still exists today. Highway 401 traffic was funnelled along adjacent Marquette Avenue, a residential street. Similarly, on the north side, wee Brightwood Street was the on- and off-ramp for the westbound 401, funnelling people up to Wilson. People actually lived on both 401 approaches – unbelievable today, but it's telling how tranquil the highway was originally imagined.

However tame it was when first opened, it congested quickly and, by 1964, construction was underway for the collector lanes. The aerial photos show wide swaths cleared out, as if a giant eraser was dragged alongside the highway, destroying roads and houses. The ramps at Carhartt were closed on the south side, and a massive off-ramp that leads directly to Wilson today was created where Brightwood was, clearing away some houses in the process.

Brightwood still exists as a small loop of a street next to the ramp. Two blocks east of here, Richelieu Road is another loop running south of Wilson that was altered by the 401 expansion, and just two houses remain of the original five that were on its east side. All along the 401 and its sound barriers are streets that were truncated as the highway expanded. This is easier to follow with a map app open, but the speed of city growth is apparent in how quickly relatively new houses and streets were completely torn down and removed to make way for the expansion of a highway that now seems as if it's been there forever. If there is one constant here, it's that the city has always changed, but time has a funny way of covering up the traces of change.

A westbound on-ramp on the north side of the 401 at Bathurst and Wilson was also removed, and the triangle of leftover land that was created eventually became what is now the Bathurst-Wilson Parkette. In 2016, it got an update with a Mabuhay (Welcome) Garden to recognize the presence of the Filipino community that has made this area – sometimes called Little Manila – home, and includes more seating, a pergola, and new landscaping. A massive mural designed by artist Ian Leventhal was installed on the 401's retaining wall here in 2005, a project under former mayor David Miller's 'Clean and Beautiful City' program. It has tranquil scenes that, at times, resemble Seurat's famous 1884 painting of Parisian swimmers, *Bathers at Asnières*. From farmers' fields to Little Manila in seventy years, the change here is remarkable, even if the 401's vehicular river isn't exactly Paris's Seine.

Continue up Bathurst, past mini-malls and the 1960s apartment buildings on the west side of the street that overlook Earl Bales Park, site of some of the most dramatic topography in Toronto. This street would have done well with a subway, but instead the trains run a few kilometres west in the middle of a low-density freeway corridor. Toronto's ravines are celebrated for giving the city deep fissures of mystery, but at Earl Bales Park, one ravine – part of the west Don Valley – is also home to the Earl Bales Ski and Snowboard Centre, complete with chairlift and rope tow. Though folks in the Rockies might scoff, it's an impressive slope in a city that's often thought of as flat. Earl Bales Park was previously the site of York Downs Golf and Country Club, and the ghost shapes of tees and greens can still be seen around the park. The snow machines here keep pumping as long as the cool weather will allow, and strips of dirty, glacial-like snow often last weeks into the warm almost-spring weather. You can walk north along the Don River, under Sheppard, and along the odd little Don River Boulevard, a kind of mini–Hoggs

Hollow made up of just one street of modest homes. When the street ends, a path through the 'Hinder Property' leads through Bathurst Park and ultimately to Bathurst Street.

In the basement of the midcentury plaza at Sheppard and Bathurst is the Ambassador Club, a Russian sauna. There are a number of Russian saunas – or banyas – in the Toronto area. Though some Russian Jews emigrated to the area in the 1980s, it wasn't until the fall of communism that Russians came to the city in large numbers, so their presence is much more recent and mostly found outside of the central core. The Ambassador's grandeur is not architectural. The lobby is wood-panelled, with three clocks telling Toronto, Tel Aviv, and Moscow time. After you pass through the change rooms, there's a cold, backyard-sized plunge pool. Here, naked men bob around in surroundings that look much like an old school gymnasium, as the club dates to the 1960s. Through another passage are the doors to two small saunas. It's friendly, and often we're the only non-Russian speakers there. Men ask if we've been here before or if we're 'Canadian,' then tell us about sauna culture. One fellow told us that because everyone is naked, 'we are all equal.' He paused and laughed, grabbing his privates, saying, 'Except for this.' We all laughed too, I think.

North of Sheppard Avenue, Bathurst thins out even more, crossing the west Don Valley before it passes by Bathurst Park. At the bottom of the valley, you'll find the Bathurst Jewish Community Centre, a sprawling complex that's partially on stilts over the flood plain. It meets Bathurst at grade with a rather impressive pedestrian entrance into the Toronto Holocaust Museum, though few people other than transit riders likely ever use this entrance, as the main entrances are down in the valley near the parking lots.

Nearing Steeles, Bathurst exits Toronto's limits as it started, with a collection of residential apartment towers, including some remarkably modern white towers on Antibes Drive that rise high above the nearby bungalows and houses that belong to the large Russian community here. In Thornhill, residential subdivisions were allowed to 'turn their back' onto Bathurst, so the streetscape is a topology of backyard fences. It's no way to honour a street as important as Bathurst, but this treatment doesn't last long, and Bathurst is soon semi-rural, eventually meeting up with Yonge Street near the village of Holland Landing. Henry Bathurst, 3rd Earl Bathurst, ought to be pleased at how long the street he never knew in the city he never visited grew.

Dupont Street

Dupont is the back-street/alternate route of western downtown Toronto. For drivers, it's a shortcut across the city that avoids busier routes like Bloor and St. Clair. Cyclists and pedestrians trying to cross mid-block will tell you it's fast, maybe too fast. As with the servants' side of a British manor house, things get taken care of on Dupont: it's a working street that keeps the prettier parts of the city running. Though this has been its role for years, Dupont is changing, and its current look is a heterogeneous mix of styles and uses sometimes referred to as 'messy urbanism.'

My favourite approach to Dupont is to walk north on St. George and meet it at a rare-for-Toronto T intersection. There, the old sign for People's Foods diner has been repurposed for a more expensive restaurant now, keeping just the word *Food*. Next door, the giant Victorian pile that is the Pour House pub – almost-old-timers will remember it as the former home of the Red Raven – is a perfect example of a storefront extending out from an old house and meeting the street, residential transformed into commercial. Finding hints of the former 'houseness' inside buildings like this one provides some amateur archaeological amusement. There are a lot of these conversions on Toronto streets like Dupont.

Nearby, there's a big LCBO liquor store (people from small, compact European countries will find it amazing and endless, or perhaps obscene, but it's still a small version of the Summerhill mothership), an interior-decorating store, various dry cleaners, and a suburban-style gas station whose design is so cookie-cutter and inappropriate that its south-facing doors and windows are blocked by a fence along the sidewalk. This is about as mixed up as a Toronto street can be.

Dupont begins just east of here, at Avenue Road, in another T-intersection that faces the Hare Krishna Temple. The little sign for the temple always seems to stand out on the old stone building, but it's a high-traffic example of how old British Toronto adapts and accommodates the new. The temple has been a local landmark since the 1970s, in a very un-seventies building.

Built in 1899 by Toronto firm Gordon & Helliwell (builders of many a local church, such as the Anglican one across the street, as well as the West End YMCA), the building held a Presbyterian congregation until 1941, when it became the Avenue Road Church of the Nazarene, founded by famed Canadian evangelist/politician/broadcaster/cartoonist Charles Templeton. (Templeton later declared he was agnostic.) The Nazarene's congregation is now part of the evangelical Bayview Glen Church in Thornhill. On summer days, you can hear the Krishna chants floating out of the open windows here. Just to the north of the temple is a park named after poet Jay Macpherson, with passages from her writing inlaid on the sidewalk.

This first bit of Dupont west of Avenue is a rather nice residential street that has evolved into a busy thoroughfare. A dip in the landscape marks where the now-buried Nordheimer reach of Castle Frank Brook once ran. A bit further west, downtown-bound cars heading east on Dupont whip around the corner where it meets Davenport; the streets don't meet at a right angle, and a few degrees can mean a lot to a car, and they can turn around that corner fast, so watch out. It's one of those places where you can stand still and feel why big streets are called 'arteries.' This intersection collects traffic – both automobile- and human-powered – and feeds it into the city like an asphalt aorta. Trains moving along the CPR tracks just to the north seem almost airborne, and make the urban layers here feel almost like a movie set.

It's worth it to detour from Dupont and head up Davenport, past the tracks, and, after a quick right, north on Poplar Plains. It's all uphill here as you climb the shores of ancient Lake Iroquois. At this point, Toronto's street grid gets wonderfully disorganized – analogous, in a way, to the twisting streets of the Hollywood Hills above L.A.'s street grid. Take another short detour up Glen Edyth Drive, where there are fine city views when the trees are bare of leaves. Glen Edyth climbs high rapidly, with only a steel crash barrier on one side keeping the Teslas and Audis from tumbling into the ravine below. Up at the top, you can see a cross-section of midtown Toronto – the Four Seasons Hotel, the Manulife Centre – from a weird, unexpected angle and height. Directly below, trees and houses spread toward Avenue Road. During the day, when the area is deserted, save for the few tradespeople working on lonely homes, you can feel like the only person in the city, which is laid out in front of you almost too perfectly, like a Currier & Ives lithograph. Nobody seems to live in these big houses – I never see the owners, that is – but they're always being fixed up.

Walk back down to Spadina and Dupont, where you'll see the unique plexiglass entrances to Dupont subway station. The two Dupont subway station bubbles, located kitty-corner from each other, invite us into a subterranean 1970s fantasyland where there are no sharp edges and everything is rounded and soft. The station interior is the architectural manifestation of the tail end of that laid-back decade. Opened in 1978, the station's orange interior includes a somewhat hippie-inspired lush and flowery tile mosaic by James Sutherland called *Spadina Summer Under All Seasons* that starts at track level and grows up into the mezzanine. Remarkably, the thousands of bits of glass that went into the mosaic are still intact. Dupont station is one of the last stations built into the urban fabric rather than on it: two buildings were removed for the bubbles and everything else was kept underground. Today, subway stations seem to require vast spaces and pavilion-like surface buildings.

Beyond the station, Dupont turns into a heterogeneous, sometimes ugly, sometimes pretty street that runs parallel to the railway tracks all the way to the Junction. Much of the industry that once lined Dupont is gone, most of it from an era when a 'mixed-use neighbourhood' meant a factory could be next door to a home. This is the Dupont that Alfred Holden so wonderfully evoked in his 1998 *Taddle Creek* magazine essay 'Dupont at Zenith,' in which he wrote, 'Enterprises, as great as Eastern Airlines or as lowly as a corner store, will often die pathetically, with no ceremony or celebration of their achievements. Dupont Street in Toronto at the close of the twentieth century is an open graveyard of such industries, most of which collapsed without so much as a pauper's funeral. Their skeletons lie exposed. They are the parking lots, warehouse loft condos, and retail joints of the post-industrial age.' As though itemizing a hero's feats in an elegy, Holden goes on to list the industries that left Dupont in the 1990s, after the Free Trade Agreement of 1988 sent manufacturing jobs out of the city en masse. When I lived on Dupont a few years after Holden wrote his essay, the street was already changing, as fancier bits of the Annex to the south and Forest Hill to the north (the area in between is sometimes called South Hill, a name straight out of a realtor's fever dream) started appearing. The trains in the rail corridor would shunt at all hours, shaking our apartment in Richter-measurable magnitudes. Dupont didn't become a graveyard after its de-industrialization: the autobody shops and warehouses all remained useful, and many are still there, though in diminished numbers as they've been replaced over time. It's probably still ugly to those who don't find the Toronto jumble of architectural styles beautiful in its heterogeneity. The trains still shunt here, and Dupont is always interesting to walk along.

Over the twenty-five years since Holden wrote 'Dupont at Zenith,' Dupont has started to sprout again. It hasn't experienced the wholesale makeover that Queen Street West has; rather, it's as if the high-ended York-villeness of Avenue and Davenport has seeped west and collected sporadically along Dupont. Little shops selling small, cute, middle-class things dot the street now, sometimes sprouting up between lumberyards and luxury car dealerships.

The fancy and fey places become less frequent the further west you go – though this, too, is a changing experience – and the 1970s Quaalude bubble entrances of the Dupont subway station seem a distant memory. Brick homes give way to ones with cheaper siding as the Annex and Seaton Village neighbourhoods become places without such widely known names, like Wallace Emerson. Just east of Ossington, peek into auto-shop windows to see a Ferrari on the hoist and a showroom full of Lotuses (you can even buy an Aston Martin if you want), while further west there are little European shops where old vw beaters go for life support.

In Dionne Brand's 2014 novel, *Love Enough*, she writes of a beautiful sunset glimpsed in a rear-view mirror on Dupont Street. 'Because it's such an ugly street, in some regards the sunset is even more magnificent,' explained Brand in an interview when the book was published. This working street, where the gas stations and parking lots that wouldn't fit on Bloor were established, is looking quite different now. On larger sites along Dupont, mid-rise residential buildings have sprouted up, often to the chagrin of residents of the single-family homes in adjacent neighbourhoods, comfortable with their front yards and backyards but grumpy about new neighbours. These buildings have turned Dupont into a different kind of street, a post-post-industrial place.

In the summer of 2023, I passed by 888 Dupont as the setting sun lit the building's faded green siding and graffitied windows with a melancholic beauty. Melancholic because it was the twilight of this building's life, one that's been incredibly important to Toronto. Built in 1921, 888 has had many lives. It's played big roles – including as a yarn-spinning factory and the Canadian National Institute for the Blind's broom-making works – but it has also had numerous small firms operating out of the building, and, over the last decades, it evolved into a dense concentration of arts and culture workers. Ask anybody in Toronto's creative community about 888 Dupont and they'll likely have a connection: they lived there, they worked there, they knew somebody who lived there, or they partied there. It was a machine of culture. There were studios, workshops, and small arts outfits, but it was also home to individual artists living loft-style. Real, hard loft-style. The kind depicted in 1980s films, not the renovated, all-mod-cons units marketed as lofts today. Along the Ossington side of the building, some of those loft windows opened onto the sidewalk and passersby could see Toronto's art scene at work. There was even a fellow who raised tarantulas in his basement unit. One was named Lucy. I thought about them every time I passed by the building.

And then it was gone – just a shell of itself the last time I passed by, completely gone not long afterwards. In its place a fourteen-storey building with 155 units is going up, each designed as live-work space, with 10 per cent, or twenty units, being affordable and run by WoodGreen Community Services. Those twenty affordable units are good, of course, but they're only the tiniest fraction of the amount of truly affordable spaces needed in Toronto for living, working, or both. A drop in the paint can, if you will.

The loss of 888 Dupont was met with both nostalgia and grief, very familiar feelings in this community. Nostalgia for a time when there were a lot more 888 Duponts around, and when life here was generally more affordable. It was a bit easier, once. Boomers and early Gen-Xers speak especially fondly of the late 1980s and early 1990s in Toronto, when buildings like 888 were far more plentiful, and having a creative career was more easily sustainable. There was a serious recession during part of that period, so it wasn't great for everyone, and Toronto was always more expensive than other Ontario cities, but there were plenty of spaces like this to live and work in. Old and messy buildings that nobody but the artists thought or cared about fostered an exciting and deep arts and culture scene, though their availability also meant there was a previous economic trauma for a different kind of worker. Today, though, places like 888 have been devoured, in part because of Toronto's restrictive zoning that forces most new major housing onto main streets like Dupont and post-industrial sites, while leaving 'house neighbourhoods' nearly untouchable. The art scene and beloved retail strips suffer. The grief being experienced is what the tenants of 888 felt when they were evicted, and what other people felt, not just for those who lost their homes, but for how hard it is to make a living in Toronto working in the arts.

We celebrate innovation-incubating institutions like MaRS (College and University) and the Centre for Social Innovation (Spadina and Queen), but this part of Dupont was another kind of incubator for small businesses, artistic or otherwise, and a natural one that passed under the radar. Behind many of these old industrial facades – inside the old subdivided warehouses on Lansdowne Avenue, or in noble old buildings like 888 – there were, until recently, start-ups that couldn't afford rents elsewhere in Toronto. Some of that still exists, but it's harder to find.

As the gentrifying flow from Ave and Dav moves west, this low-rent incubation will move on, as transient as it is necessary to the city. Even in the Junction, where Dupont ends in a complicated five-point intersection by the West Toronto Railpath, much of this kind of space is now priced out of reach.

Stand above Dupont on the West Toronto Railpath overpass, itself a relic of a mighty industrial age, and notice the view back east is of an entirely new skyline, with clusters of high-rises sprouting at Lansdowne and at the old Galleria Mall site at Dufferin. Dupont has slight zigs and zags in it, so these clusters now become terminating views along the corridor.

In 2009, the rail path, a 2.1-kilometre marvel, opened alongside the Georgetown GO Train rail corridor. Like an expressway just for bikes and pedestrians, it's integrated into the city, near where people live and work. Ultimately, it will connect to a larger network of paths and trails, if plans, and some dreams, are realized. Currently, it extends down to Dundas Street, but will eventually connect further downtown, while north of Dupont Street at Cariboo Avenue it ends in a landscaped parcel of land along a short stretch of autobody repair shops. Just west of here, two major railway corridors crossed, creating a diamond shape where the tracks touched each other. Though an underpass has separated them now, the last 'diamond' section was relocated a few dozen metres and embedded in the path's pavement here.

South of Dupont the rail path passes by old warehouse buildings and new loft-like office spaces, reaching the great Wallace Avenue footbridge, built in 1907 with fantastic west-side views up top. Here, the rail path runs alongside the train station for the Bloor GO and UP Express, and commuters can walk right from the platform onto the path, a nice bit of integration. Here, too, is *Gradation*, one of the most impressive artworks along the rail path, covering an entire building's cinder-block facade facing the train plat-forms. The work, as described on the artist Lynnette Postuma's website, is composed of 14,508 blocks painted in variations of blue and green to 'better integrate the building into its adjacent landscape,' giving it a sense of movement. Existing trees, shrubs, and vines were outlined, meant to be a 'growth marker' to monitor changes in vegetation since the mural was installed, though most were cut down in 2022 to facilitate expansion of the rail corridor and station. It will be interesting to see how new plantings work with the art over time.

Back up at Dupont, this was once one of the 'busiest industrial crossroads in Toronto,' according to Heritage Toronto, though passenger trains dominate now, and the remaining industry is small. The long-awaited expansion of the rail path will make this even more of a commuter supercorridor, especially if it can connect north to St. Clair and beyond, more new city fabric knitted out of the remains of the old city.

Dupont remains a series of snapshots representing disparate views of Toronto, a sort of museum of its various forms of cityness. Walks along Dupont don't feel like an isolated back route, but rather dense and almost humid, like being in the thick of where things happen.

Northish

Spadina

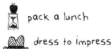
pack a lunch

dress to impress

scenic views

Connecting walks: CN Tower, Harbourfront,
Dundas, Dupont, St. Clair

Spadina is a strange word. Say it. *Spa-die'-nah*. Now repeat it a few times. You'll soon wonder how we use it in conversation without pausing in curiosity. Yet we say 'Spadina' easily, and it feels 'Toronto' just as much as the Anishinaabemowin word it's derived from, *Ishpadinaa*, which means 'a place on a hill.' In 2015, the Ogimaa Mikana Project began pasting Anishinaabemowin words and names around the city, including on both Spadina and Davenport street signs below Casa Loma. As occasionally happens, a guerrilla public-space project became permanent and today the official City of Toronto signs here have *Ishpadinaa* and *Gete-Onigaming* (meaning 'at the old portage') written on them, along with their colonial names, Spadina and Davenport. To get a perfect view of Spadina, climb the Baldwin Steps at Davenport, stand next to Casa Loma, and look south over Toronto and the southern, downhill length of Spadina (a 'road' at the north end and then, south of Bloor, an 'avenue') to its glittery, skyscraper end. It looks as if somebody cleared a wide swath of land through Toronto to make the street – in a 1996 *Toronto Life* article called '1966: The Tunnel of Endless Pleasure' the late writer Matt Cohen wrote, 'Spadina is Toronto central, the cosmic spine' – and, in a way, that's true.

Spadina's girth is due to William Baldwin who, in 1818, cleared a royal-scaled driveway from the lake, through what was then a forest, to his 'Spadina House.' (The word is pronounced *Spa-dee'-nah* in reference to this house on the hill, which is now a city-owned museum.) Baldwin's family got a clear view down to the lake, but the effort also gave the city a rare street that matches the proportions of today's Toronto.

Toronto was never supposed to be a metropolis, and its infrastructure is forever catching up. It's why we've got wooden hydro poles (which some of us think of as nice artifacts of our industrial and humble past) and, less romantically, small sidewalks. Even Yonge Street – Toronto's main drag – can't match Spadina's wide sidewalks. Strolling on Spadina's broad concrete walks is like being in another city, because sidewalks, and their comparative size, affect how a city behaves.

Spadina meets Lake Ontario with a wave.

In an entry in his *Moscow Diary* dated December 17, 1926, philosopher and urban observer Walter Benjamin wrote, 'It has been observed that pedestrians [in Moscow] walk in "zigzags." This is simply on account of the overcrowding of the narrow sidewalks; nowhere else, except here and there in Naples, do you find sidewalks this narrow. This gives Moscow a provincial air, or rather the character of an improvised metropolis that has fallen into place overnight.' He could have been writing about most places in Toronto.

On Spadina, however, Torontonians can walk proudly, like world-class pedestrians. Yet, as Spadina starts by the lake, near one of the most intense development zones in the country, it also seems to, as Benjamin wrote, fall into place overnight. We hardly notice skyscrapers going up anymore until somebody moves in and flicks a switch, at which point a light glows in the sky where it didn't before. The city was shocked (shocked!) in 2008 when Waterfront Toronto opened the Spadina WaveDeck at the foot of the street, on the shores of Lake Ontario. Not only did it bend the rules of what a sidewalk can look like, but it confused people who were adamant in their belief that waterfront development would never move forward, a sentiment that still exists despite the addition of more evidence to the contrary since. Waterfront Toronto says the WaveDecks – also located at the bottom of Simcoe and Rees – created a 'total of 1,780 square metres of new high quality, diverse fish habitat,' and that 'riverstone shoals, tree logs, and embankments were installed to provide shelter and increased feeding and forcing opportunities for lake fish.' The wooden waves at the water's edge cause people to stop, look, and linger, where before they may have carried on without noticing that this is the beginning of Toronto's spine.

The first leg of Spadina has become a crystal entrance to the city for those coming off the Gardiner or heading up from the lake, in an area that twenty years ago was either parking lot, golf driving range, or urban scrubland. West of here lies a vast cathedral-like space, hidden underneath the Gardiner that has been transformed by the Bentway and other projects into places people linger in rather than pass through or avoid.

The Concord CityPlace condo development – which is made up of nearly two dozen buildings – is clustered on both sides of Spadina. Skyscraper- and condo-haters have derided City-Place since the first towers started going up in the late 1990s. Part of this sentiment is certainly due to Toronto's fear of heights, which, when applied to places completely appropriate for towers, becomes ideology rather than good city planning or thoughtful opinion. The other reason for the hate seems to be a kind of underlying misanthropy. Phrases like 'Ugh, more condos' are often heard but rarely interrogated. Are we talking about condos in general, or just the badly designed ones? Replace *condo* with *people* and suddenly we have one group – presumably made up of those living in tidy two- or three-storey houses – sneering at another group of people who want to live downtown and don't seem to mind spending their money on glass perches in the sky. *Condo dweller* is the new sloppy epithet for *bourgeoisie* or, worse, for *uncool*. The word *luxury* is routinely used by those in opposition to new housing, including politicians trying to ride NIMBY populism, but how a tiny box in the sky is considered luxury when the only real and wide-spread luxuries are the on-the-ground houses, in all their various forms, is an urban puzzle. A few buildings in this area even have government affordable housing in them, though not enough, but it complicates the high-rise-hater narratives, which have also been applied to rental and even truly affordable buildings, revealing the misanthropy behind the sentiment.

It's true that at ground level, the east side of Spadina, the condos closest to the SkyDome (or the Rogers Centre, as some insist on calling it) are imperfect and feel too much like a Supercentre entrance. But take a walk through the newer development on the west side and you'll see fountains, townhouses, pathways, and a grocery store. Here, CityPlace has learned from its mistakes and has created a more urbane neighbourhood where it's easy to forget there are dozens of floors overhead.

The extension of Fort York Boulevard that connects Spadina to Fort York – only a few hundred metres west at this point – passes Canoe Landing Park, designed by Douglas Coupland and landscape architects Phillips Farevaag Smallenberg of Vancouver in collaboration with Landscape Architects and the Planning Partnership of Toronto. The park continues Coupland's Canadiana theme with giant fishing lures, a pathway named after Terry Fox, and a memorable Toronto landmark: a big red canoe on a hill that points directly at the Gardiner traffic – certainly an unexpected site for motorists passing by. Coupland has been busy in Toronto: nearby at Lake Shore and Bathurst, his War of 1812 soldiers are in front of a condo, while up at the Shops at Don Mills, his *Starburst Clock Tower*, made up of an explosion of model houses, is a scrambled take on postwar suburban Canada.

The vast scale of the CityPlace development can be seen across the rail corridor along Front Street. There, a massive concrete wall containing a honeycomb of hidden parking garages rises out of the ground. As in many parts of Toronto, the ground we walk on may be real or human-created. A pathway here extends underneath Spadina and is part of the growing east-west bike-trail network.

At Front Street, the Well, a massive retail, office, and residential project, is something Toronto has never seen before. Or have we? The scale of the project, just one development but with many parts, is remarkable. In dense downtown terms, it's on the scale of the Eaton Centre, taking up an entire block. Its various architectural styles make it seem like a cluster of separate buildings. The Well reminds me (in a good way) of the New York New York Hotel and Casino in Las Vegas, where a pastiche of the Manhattan skyline is created by amassing its most famous landmarks. It's whimsical, with homages to famous architects and their important buildings, like Richard Rogers's Lloyd's Building in London, with its exposed external staircase, or the cantilevered floors of Norman Foster's HSBC building in Hong Kong. The steel-and-glass canopy over public areas is reminiscent of structures by Santiago Calatrava, including his atrium at Toronto's Brookfield Place.

The materials, from brick surfaces to the perfectly smooth poured-concrete columns, are better than the usual Toronto standard. Montreal's late urban designer Claude Cormier, who passed away in 2023 before he could share more of his brilliant visions with the world, worked on parts of the project with his firm CCxA. The Well includes the tiny, lot-sized Draper Street Park on the west side. Draper Street is a unique, block-long enclave of wee, Second Empire–style homes that are a dramatic contrast to the Well, but one that shows how small and big can work well together. Along the south side of the Well is the wide rail corridor (site of the failed 'Rail Deck Park' plan of the late 2010s that may yet live in a different form), another dramatic contrast – here of emptiness – giving the closely packed site a vista south. Cormier's whimsical park on Draper is also of a quality that doesn't seem quite like Toronto and includes a single cat sculpture welcoming visitors, a nod to the Cormier-designed Berczy Park, with its beloved dog fountain, on the east side of downtown.

The part of the Well most people will see are the three floors of retail space partly covered by that steel-and-glass canopy, an indoor-outdoor kind of space relatively new to Toronto. The wide entrance facing the Spadina and Front intersection turns what was a busy if nondescript crossroads into a memorable coming-and-going place. But what is the Well? Is it a mall, like the Eaton Centre, or something else? In Toronto and North America, urban retail tends to work only if it's 'at grade' (sidewalk level). A floor below or above promises diminishing returns for shopkeepers here, but in other places, such as many Asian cities, going up multiple floors to find a store, café, or restaurant is as common as going next door is in North America, where only big malls tend to work on multiple levels. In this sense, the Well must be thought of as a mall in order to work: that makes sense to North Americans.

Perhaps we can evolve, though. Essentially, the retail, public part of the Well is a giant podium, a kind of megastructure. Dozens and dozens of residential buildings put up during the twenty-five-year Toronto boom have podiums: a blockish building, sometimes housing commercial units or residential amenities, from which more slender towers rise. It's very Toronto. It's also very Hong Kong. These kinds of structures can be filled with all kinds of activity – retail or otherwise – and blend into the urban fabric. In Toronto they've tended to be a bit boring and sterile, but more of the Hong Kong variety is beginning to appear as these structures evolve with a variety of interesting services inside, often independent, that feel like an indoor city rather than simply a generic mall filled with corporate chain stores. In a few places, like Yonge Street in North York, this is already starting to happen. One day, we might not even have to call them malls for them to work.

The Well includes the former McGregor Socks factory on its Wellington corner, the first bit of old Spadina that begins to appear with familiar turn-of-the-last-century warehouses and new buildings mixed in. The Toyota dealership and surface parking lot here are remnants of a time when cars ruled the area and there was near-contiguous pavement from the CNE to University Avenue. Today, much of the space in and around those old warehouses has been filled in with new buildings. Some, like the Morgan, which sits on the northwest corner at Richmond and boasts a massive penthouse that looks like the lair of an art deco villain from an Ayn Rand novel, match the older form. Others, like the District Lofts just east on Richmond, with its soaring catwalks that link mid-rise towers, are completely contemporary.

The Queen and Spadina intersection is, for many, the heart of Toronto. It was an early Toronto landmark for me as a visiting kid – I worried that the thick web of streetcar wires hanging overhead would electrocute lost skydivers. The east side is Toronto at its most old-school beautiful. The former bank building's facade on the northeast corner is part of the new Queen-Spadina station of the Ontario Line subway, while on the northwest corner is the world's ugliest McDonald, housed in a turd fortress. Knowing this was once the Mary Pickford Theatre, built in 1908 but demolished in the uncaring 1950s, doesn't help attempts at appreciation. The subway station also sprouts up on the southwest corner, behind which begins Graffiti Alley, now officially named as such after years of the city resisting what has become an ever-changing tourist attraction.

The Cameron House bar a block west of Spadina on Queen has also served as one of Toronto's largest canvases for four decades or more. The lower facade regularly receives paint treatments by different Toronto artists, and ten giant ants crawl over the upper floors. The ants are by Napoleon Brousseau, a co-founder of Toronto art collective FASTWÜRMS, and were in part a response to the City of Toronto inspectors who routinely visited the Cameron House to check on the ten 'illegal dwellings' that housed a variety of artists. The ants were installed in advance of the Pope's 1984 visit to Toronto, and also symbolized the tenants – or ten ants – of the aforementioned dwellings, who were eventually allowed to legally stay in the building.

North of Queen, Spadina becomes a relatively quiet zone. While still busy, it's an in-between space, tucked just south of Chinatown and just north of the Queen-King cluster of old and new residences and offices. Both sides of the street have some fine old warehouse buildings, some of which have been renovated and modernized into loft offices, while others still wait for the same treatment. Of note is the Robertson Building at 215 Spadina. It's the one with the Dark Horse café on the main floor and the green wall in the lobby. In the winter, your eyeglasses will fog up immediately when you walk in, due to the humidity created by the wall.

The Chinatown Centre across the street is one of Toronto's more interesting malls. Inside you'll find shops, cellphone accessory boutiques, and other hard-to-categorize businesses, another bit of Hong Kong in Toronto. Unfortunately, the white facade is perpetually dirty and the large open courtyard – a space that could be Chinatown's public square – is an unhappy, treeless, and often garbage-strewn area. To get an idea of its squandered potential, go inside and find the original Chinatown Centre architectural model on display, complete with trees, crowds of miniature people, and open second-floor patios. Maintenance is the Achilles heel of every utopia.

The Dundas and Spadina intersection has a mild Yonge-Dundas Square look, mostly due to the other Chinese mall located on the southwest corner, which routinely has advertisements flashing on it. (The mall replaced a Hungarian church as the area gave way to the influx of Hong Kong money that poured into Chinatown during the 1980s.) On the northeast corner there's a standard-looking drugstore, but look behind it and notice the graffiti-covered fly tower, which betrays the theatre within. This was originally the Standard Theatre, which operated from the 1920s onward and hosted Yiddish and vaudeville productions. In the 1940s, it became the Victory Theatre, and by 1961, it had morphed into the Victory Burlesque, where strippers often mixed with the likes of Rush, the New York Dolls, Peter Frampton, the Soft Machine, and Iggy and the Stooges. Its last incarnation was as the Golden Harvest Cinema, which showed Hong Kong films until the cinema finally closed in the 1990s. It's spooky to stand nearby and imagine that vast, empty theatre space behind the bank, a portal to a lost and dead world, though there is a lingering proposal to bring it back to life.

Chinatown peaks north of Dundas, where it's filled with the overlapping signage and bustle commonly found in Chinatowns everywhere. There is much worry over preserving Chinatown as new places move in among more traditional businesses, traditional being relative, as Chinatown only established itself here from the late 1950s onward after being forced out of Toronto's original Chinatown at Dundas and Elizabeth Streets. Other Chinatowns around the GTA also compete for business, drawing visitors away from Spadina, and new, larger developments have started to take away some of the older, smaller retail spaces. Yet, there are deep roots here in the form of Chinese family associations that are largely invisible to casual visitors but represent a permanence that might be Chinatown's staying power. Many of Toronto's family associations can trace their history to the nineteenth century, when the first major waves of Chinese immigration came to Canada, primarily to work on the railway. For families arriving in a land that needed their work but resented their presence, the associations were a place to escape the racism of their new home, a role that is now often fulfilled by settlement agencies.

'The family association became a one-stop shop,' Greg Wong told me in 2014. Wong was then director of the Wong Kung Har Wun Sun Association, or, as it's more commonly known, the Wong Association, located just north of the Standard Theatre building, marked by a Heritage Toronto sidewalk plaque. 'When they came, they didn't speak English, know how to ride the streetcar, open a bank account, or see a doctor.' The family associations would arrange for a bed, food, or medicine if the new immigrants were sick. There were even informal credit unions and job search assistance. Greg Wong's own grandfather first immigrated to Canada in the 1890s and was assisted by a Vancouver association. There are now six independent Wong Associations across Canada that meet every three years in a large reunion. The Wongs and other family associations that assisted immigrants before the 1970s are sometimes known as 'Lo Wah Kiu,' which translates to 'old overseas Chinese' or 'old Chinese bridge,' connecting the two countries. In Toronto, larger associations can be found on the upper floors of buildings on Spadina or Dundas, with smaller ones in houses on the adjacent streets. Keep an eye out for the signs that indicate which family, or clan, a location is associated with. All but the Lem Si Ho Tong Society eventually moved from their original location by City Hall to the Spadina area (look for their small green mailbox at 121 Dundas Street West, tucked in next to and above a Denny's restaurant).

Today the associations have become social and cultural hubs. The busiest days for the Wongs are Sundays, when you'll find elders playing cards or mah-jong, the clink of the latter's tiles a ubiquitous sound throughout their Spadina Avenue building. As with a lot of ethnic organizations, the focus now is on attracting youth, as membership skews older. When people reach university age, life often gets busy, affording little time for cultural events, especially in a city like Toronto where the list of other pursuits is long. 'Young people get married and there's not much time to come here. That's the hard question,' said Helen Wong, the first woman to be president of the Wong Association. For organizations that also once functioned as a bachelor society, helping single immigrant men find a wife and start a family, Helen Wong's election as president was a source of pride for the association.

So are people like Christina Wong, author of the novel *Denison Avenue*, set in Kensington Market and Chinatown, who first came to the association when she was ten years old but remains active after finishing a PhD in music. She took lessons in how to play the Chinese fiddle here. 'I've met a lot of people here, they've become my family,' she says. Rollerblading, book clubs, and learning about older traditions are all part of the mix at an association. The Wongs' strategy is to catch people again when they're a little older, in their forties and fifties, when they have more time to explore their cultural roots. As the city changes, as it always has, and populations shift, the Lo Wah Kiu might be the anchors that keep Chinatown's identity intact, as many of the associations, like the Wongs, own their own buildings, even renting out the lower floors as a source of income and stability in Toronto's inflated real estate and rental market. With so much ephemeral in this city – here one day, gone the next – the Lo Wah Kiu are a layer that runs deep.

Buildings, if they can avoid being torn down, can have many lives. Sometimes they can change so much they're unrecognizable; if they were landmarks, that can be a shock. Such was the case in 2018, when the green construction mesh was removed from the former Bright Pearl restaurant at 346 Spadina, revealing a renovation that dramatically altered the look of the building. 'I'm really disappointed they just ripped out the Chinese architectural features,' Arlene Chan told me, shortly after the reveal. 'There were animal symbols on the eavestroughs. When it was first opened, the whole design was by Taiwanese restaurateur Yen Pin Chen, who brought in artisans and created a real landmark in Chinatown.' Chan is the author of seven books on the history and culture of the Chinese in Canada and often leads tours through Toronto's Chinatown. Chen's Yen Pin Place restaurant didn't fare well when it opened in the 1970s, and a series of different restaurants followed.

From 1924 to 1971, the building was Toronto's Labour Lyceum, the centre of Toronto's labour movement. Famed anarchist Emma Goldman once gave a speech called 'The Youth in Revolt' here during the time when she was exiled from the United States and living in Toronto. (After her death in 1940, her body lay in state at the Lyceum.) Slip down tiny Glen Baillie Place off Spadina and follow the alley behind the Lyceum for a secret entrance into Kensington Market. 'The building hasn't had any good luck,' said Chan of this supposedly haunted structure. 'There have been exorcisms, and feng shui masters [were] brought in to bring more luck.'

Chan points out that after they were evicted from Toronto's first China-town, when New City Hall was built, the Chinese didn't build from scratch, instead moving into existing buildings at Spadina and Dundas. 'When I lead my tours, people ask me why Toronto's Chinatown doesn't look like San Francisco's, with all of its architecture features,' she said. 'I remind them that San Francisco's was rebuilt after the 1906 quake and done in a style that imagined what a Chinatown should look like, with exaggerated and unusual details. [346 Spadina] was one of the few buildings we had like that here.' It's a place with many layers, but the renovation has erased most of them, turning it into something that looks like a generic condominium podium. Real estate brokerage firm Metropolitan Commercial was behind the renovations that caused considerable community outcry, as have other developments nearby on Spadina. But 346 is currently one of the Scott Mission's locations, so the slick look belies a community function.

'We're in the early transition,' said Chan of the process of Chinatown gentrification. 'It's bound to happen, but so far it isn't happening as fast as in other communities.' She did note that some of the many Chinese family associations in the area are feeling the pinch of rising costs. She's largely hopeful, though, pointing out that there have been many older Chinese businesses in the area replaced by new ones owned by younger Chinese entrepreneurs. 'I don't see them being changed over to non-Chinese,' she said. 'I find that very promising. With all the new condos going in at the end of Spadina, it's bringing a whole new group of potential customers into the city.'

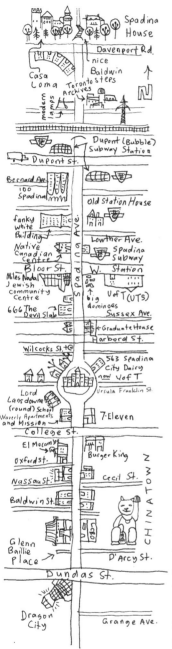

Chinatown continues north to College Street and fades out by the venerable old El Mocambo nightclub, a legendary Toronto dive and yet another historic local venue where the Rolling Stones have played. A recently separated Maggie Trudeau attended one 1977 performance, and a recording of that show was released as the album *Love You Live*. Their opening act that night, April Wine, also recorded their performance and released it as *Live at the El Mocambo*. There was a great fanfare in the mid-2000s when the El Mo's palm-tree sign was relit, and the building has since received a complete renovation.

Beyond College, 1 Spadina Crescent is the bulge that makes Spadina (the road) interesting. Without this building – built in 1875 and formerly known as Knox College – sitting in the middle of the street, the Spadina streetcars wouldn't need to make their wild and graceful arcs around it. One Spadina gives our eyes somewhere to rest when scanning the urban horizon – another rare terminating vista, and for a long while it was home to the Ontario Eye Bank. Today it's been renovated and expanded to house the Daniels Faculty of Architecture, Landscape, and Design. Look for the *Pole Colonnade* public-art piece by Stephen Cruise on top of the streetcar poles just to the north at Willcocks Street; the one entitled *Bottle/Mold* refers, in part, to the period when the Connaught Laboratories produced penicillin at Knox College. The history of this building is rife with tragic and strange stories: a U of T professor was murdered here in the early 2000s – the case is still unsolved – and, in 2009, a woman trying some amateur (is there any other kind?) urban exploring was killed when she fell from the roof.

Lord Lansdowne Junior Public School, located on the west side of the circle, is sometimes known as the 'crown' school due to its round modernist design. (It so evokes the postwar era that parts of the 2007 remake of the movie *Hairspray* were shot here.) The huge Precambrian boulder in its front yard was unearthed during excavation of the lot and takes Toronto's new-old theme to the extreme.

Around the top of the circle, Spadina becomes a mix of residential and institutional, with the U of T lining the east side of the street. The old part of New College (north of Willcocks Street – a new New College is to the south) was built in 1964 and presents Spadina with a nearly blank brick wall. That barrier seems like a mistake now, but in 1964, this part of Spadina was slated to become an expressway, so building a wall between cars and students seemed like a good idea. A rather beautiful interior courtyard is hidden inside, protected from whatever the city might do outside the walls.

The U of T's Grad House hangs out and over Harbord Street at Spadina, the architectural equivalent of a loud and bold grad student elbowing their way into a conversation. When it opened in 2000, the building, by Los Angeles–based and Pritzker Prize–winning architect Thom Mayne, was controversial because of that un-Torontonian overhang. Yet, as the following decades passed, one rarely heard a word about it; buildings of this average size tend to fade into the background, even if they're bold. A block away, the much higher and chubbier Robarts Library still has the lovers and haters nattering away more than a half-century after it was built. I've always thought that all the concrete poured into Robarts keeps the books safe. When I'm in a library, I like to feel that I'm in a cocoon where I can't hear the outside world, kept safe and sound in a place where the books can take over.

Just north, on the southeast corner of Bloor and Spadina, a small parkette was formed when the underground Spadina streetcar line was installed in 1997. The giant granite dominoes by Susan Schelle and Mark Gomes are an homage to the checkers and dominoes players who would gather here before the inter-section was re-engineered to accommodate the streetcar line. Behind the domi-noes there's a grassy knoll surrounding a TTC vent that bears metal leaf imprints – a reminder of the Carolinian forest that once grew here. Just south, there's a small parkette named after writer Matt Cohen, who lived and worked along Spadina and who wrote a short story called 'Spadina Time' in 1972.

A block east of here, on the other side of the University of Toronto School, sits a concrete high-rise that's one of Toronto's most unsung landmarks. From 1968 to 1975, what today is the Senator David A. Croll apartment building was known as Rochdale College, Toronto's 'vertical Haight-Ashbury,' as it's sometimes called. An experiment in alternative education and communal living, its baby-boomer idealism degenerated into a culture of bad drugs and squatting bikers, culminating in a massive police-led eviction in 1975. The only physical vestigial remnant of the Rochdale days (there are other cultural and individual echoes throughout Toronto today) is the *Unknown Student* sculpture out front. The statue originally faced toward the building, but it was reoriented to face the street when the building reopened.

North of Bloor, Spadina becomes a mix of homes, low-rise apartment buildings, and a couple of very tall landmark towers by late Toronto modernist architect Uno Prii, whose curving buildings can be found around the city. Along Spadina Road, the 'tower in a park' quality of these buildings has been augmented with townhouses and low-rise tower infill, and what was once a somewhat open stretch of street is now home to many more people. Along here it's clear Toronto doesn't treat its streets well, even the nice ones. This stretch between Bloor and Davenport Road could be one of the city's grandest boulevards, complete with a castle at the end, but instead it's a drab arterial, overbuilt with four lanes for traffic and those narrow Toronto sidewalks again. This part of Spadina has been in a kind of urban purgatory since 1971, when plans were scrapped for the Spadina Expressway, which would have run in a massive ditch where the road is now, requiring the demolition of many homes, some still owned by the city due to the expropriation process that was stopped just in time. Despite this, there's lots of potential here.

Consider the cultural institutions on the street, like Alliance Française and the Spadina Theatre at Lowther Road. And just north of Bloor is the Spadina Branch of the Toronto Public Library. Notice the Cree syllabics and 'Mahsinahhekahnikahmik' written on the facade, which translates to 'the lodge or place of the book.' Next door to the library is the Wigmawen Terrace apartment complex and next to it the Native Canadian Centre of Toronto in the former Ontario Bible College building. An enhanced Spadina could create a more prominent Indigenous presence here. Spadina is home to some impressive houses and buildings, lined as it is with nearly mansion-sized Victorian and Edwardian homes that have been carved up into multiple apartments. The upside is they provide much-needed rental units, but some are in poor condition, with squadrons of rubbish bins scattered out front. The Spadina Gardens apartment building at 41–45 Spadina Road is one of the most elegant in the city, a rare specimen from 1906, an era when Toronto didn't build many residential buildings like this because of a deep anti-apartment bias.

Toronto's most homey subway station entrance, formerly a grand Annex home, can be found at 85 Spadina Road. Once you pass the automatic turnstiles, you'll find Joyce Weiland's huge and sprawling quilt, called *Barren Ground Caribou*. It's puffy-soft public art from 1978 that furnishes the soul with the warm feeling that Pierre Elliott Trudeau is still in power and offers the fantastic illusion that the University-Spadina Line extends all the way north into the Canadian Shield and the caribou land beyond.

A few blocks north of here, take Bernard Avenue to Jean Sibelius Square Park, which is tucked away by Kendal Avenue in the deepest Annex, a neighbourhood named as such because the part east of Brunswick Avenue was annexed to the City of Toronto in 1883 along with Yorkville. Three years later, developer Simeon Janes named his new subdivision Toronto Annex. Jane Jacobs lived a few blocks west at 69 Albany, and it's worth the walk to see the inner parts of her neighbourhood. The park is named after the Finnish composer, and his bust can be found near its north end.

At Dupont, Spadina dips under the railway, and here you'll find *Spadina Line*, a public artwork installed in 1991 by Brad Golden and Norman Richards. It consists of various references to the railway, including a clock that tells time both digitally and by the sun, and a stainless-steel archive. Here Spadina intersects with the east-west hydro corridor along the railway that may one day be home to the proposed Green Line, a linear park that could really be something if plans aren't watered down. North of the underpass, a series of light standards illuminate bronze words inlaid into the sidewalk that mark the development of both the adjacent City of Toronto Archives and Spadina Road, and that refer to Casa Loma builder Henry Pellatt with the word 'Power.' (Pellatt made his money electrifying Toronto.)

Toronto has its share of great museums and great libraries, and straddling the line between the two is the Toronto Archives. Housed in a postmodern fortress on Spadina Road, underneath the Davenport escarpment, the archives contain Toronto's official memory, which is deep and extensive. You can research your house there, look at sewer photos from the 1920s, read past council debates, and browse reports on just about anything city-related. The best part of the building is the large atrium, which hosts rotating year-long exhibits curated by in-house archivists that ensure that even when you're not looking for something in particular, you'll find something interesting. The building is set back from Spadina, a remnant of zoning that created a right-of-way for the Spadina Expressway, which would have burst out of the escarpment here as it headed south through the heart of the Annex. This part of Spadina ends at Davenport, and though the road jogs west and continues on further north as a narrower road, pedestrians can use the Baldwin Steps that start here to climb up the steep hill. Once at the top, winded or not, don't forget to turn around and look down the wide swath of Spadina, just as Baldwin once did. (That's his house on the east side of the street, while Casa Loma is on the west side.) The view is now more electric and packed-in than he'd ever have imagined. Spadina, like Yonge, belongs to all of us now; it just has more elbow room on some of those sidewalks.

St. Clair Avenue

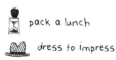 pack a lunch

 dress to impress

offspring friendly

Connecting walks: Yonge, Dundas, Bathurst, Spadina

St. Clair Avenue is a street in two acts, with the Don Valley as entr'acte between the St. Clair that starts in East York and heads east into Scarborough, and the part of the street that starts in upper Rosedale by Mount Pleasant at the Moore Park Ravine and heads west. The folks along the Scarborough stretch likely carry the burden of always saying, 'No, we live along the other St. Clair,' when they're asked where they live.

The St. Clair most people think about is initially the high-rise edge of Rosedale and Forest Hill, boasting a long row of upscale pre- and postwar residential buildings. There's no cute nickname for Yonge and St. Clair. Blessedly so, perhaps, as neighbourhood nicknames are often created in an effort to make them trendy. Sometimes it's best to lie low in this hyperinflated city. Still, considering how impressive the cluster of buildings and people are here, it's an overlooked part of Toronto. In any mid-size city, Yonge and St. Clair would be 'downtown,' but in Toronto it's just another node, another cluster along the knuckled backbone that is Yonge Street from the lake to Richmond Hill.

There's a restaurant on the main floor of the Weston Centre – the building that housed the Loblaws headquarters before it consolidated operations in Brampton – with one of the best views in the city. The centre's octagonal high-rise is a unique bit of mid-1970s late modernism, with a lobby ceiling of chunky stalactites that make it feel like Superman's Fortress of Solitude. The restaurant is in one of the also-octagonal pavilion buildings off the lobby and, with its giant windows, the room is a perfect vantage point from which to watch streetcars feed into and out of St. Clair station. I can imagine set-in-Toronto films using this room for a big meeting or intimate conversation scene, so Torontonian is the background. When you take in the view from the restaurant, Toronto looks like an idealized city with transit that runs frequently and fast. Before it was a restaurant, the space was a series of coffee shops, the kind of useful but forgettable businesses that often populate the bottom of office towers. Restaurants could bring interior drama to other corporate towers, though they won't all have a public transit show for patrons to watch. The rest of the Weston Centre underwent a recent renovation too, giving the Loblaws store a lunch counter with Yonge Street frontage, another good place to sit, though it's mostly indistinguishable from other subway-connected mini-malls now.

The St. Clair subway station across the way is one of the originals. From either St. Clair or Pleasant Boulevard, on the south side, its low-slung 1954 lines are visible, a time capsule surrounded by the higher and bigger buildings its opening unleashed. With subways, streetcars, and buses all feeding this station, it's a total TTC experience. All of this thick urbanity is just a few hundred metres from the Vale of Avoca Ravine, one of the most profound transitions from big city to urban wilderness around. Down in the ravine, the occasional deer and coyote can be spotted.

The ravines feel eternal, but Yonge and St. Clair's place in Toronto has shifted. Though it feels like a downtown, it's decidedly the city's midtown now. However, it was once considered the suburbs. A 1972 newspaper article titled 'Granite Club Has Again Gone Suburban' marked the club's move from St. Clair, just west of Yonge, to its present location on Bayview Avenue north of Lawrence. In 1926, after the club had moved to St. Clair from its previous location on Church Street, the present-day 519 community centre, this was considered the suburbs of Toronto. The city is never static, except when the forces of change are resisted.

When Imperial Oil was moving into their new building at 111 St. Clair West in 1957, the company's *Imperial Oil Review* newsletter declared that the

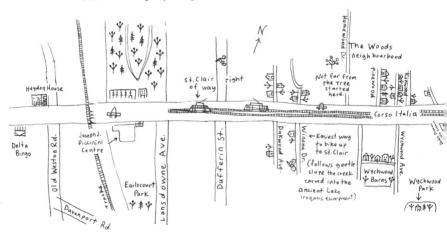

'uptown hustle and bustle' they were creating 'was fascinating for the passers-by.' Originally a contender in the New City Hall design competition in the early 1950s, this building was designed to double as a hospital in the event of a nuclear attack (its hallways were built wide enough for beds). It's been renamed the Imperial Plaza, the oil folk having decamped to Calgary in 2004, and the now-residential building has the second-most ornate LCBO in the city after Summerhill. Located in the building's lobby, the booze sits underneath the massive *Story of Oil* abstract mural by artist R. York Wilson. Luckily it didn't go to Calgary. Next door, a former Presbyterian church has become part of a residential building; this is something of a conversion district.

Outside, a 7.5-metre-tall sculpture of a man holding up a thin skyscraper that was installed in 2019 generated some controversy. *Toronto Man* (also called 'Condo Man' by many), a work by German artist Stephan Balkenhol, might be too on the nose in this city that is constantly adding new buildings and causing anxiety. Since the city focuses so much development on clusters like Yonge and St. Clair, rather than spreading it around to neighbourhoods that are mostly off limits to change, the sculpture could be viewed as the burden a place like Yonge and St. Clair carries for the rest of the city. St. Clair, along here, has now become a big-city canyon of buildings.

The Park Lane apartments at 110 St. Clair, between Yonge and Avenue Road, are notable because of their streamlined deco look, but also because pianist Glenn Gould lived in the penthouse here, when he wasn't at his perch at the nearby twenty-four-hour Fran's Diner (now split into a pub and café). Toronto could be called Glenn Gould City. In addition to the statue of Gould

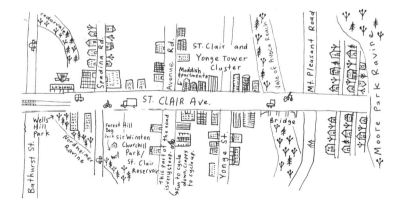

by the CBC building down on Front Street and the studio inside that same building named after him, there is also Glenn Gould Park, at the corner of Avenue and St. Clair, which is often known as 'Peter Pan Park' due to its statue of the pan pipe–playing boy. Just across the street is Amsterdam Park, named when that city's burgomaster met then–Toronto mayor David Crombie here when the two cities were twinned in 1974.

At Avenue Road stands the unoriginally named the Avenue – not a road, but a condo that was billed as 'Distinctly Forest Hill' and 'The ultimate address' when it was being constructed. Clad in stone and brick, it's tall but nondescript enough that it fades into the Toronto wallpaper, as most good buildings should. Here, especially, where there are lovely pre- and postwar buildings as far as the eye can see, being subtle is okay. The stretch of Avenue north of here will lead you to exclusive Upper Canada College, a private boys' school. Follow the road toward its fine terminating view of the school's preppy, private, and privileged clock tower, but don't forget to look around you as you go: this part of the road has some of Toronto's best stock of midcentury apartment buildings (and a few from later on too).

Further along St. Clair, at Spadina, two unique 1960s apartment towers rise out of green Nordheimer Ravine like super-modern white monoliths. Though large and indeed monolithic, one of the Tower Hill buildings seems ready to float into the air due to its original white iron wraparound balcony rails (and the glass walls behind them), which makes the building seem honey-combed and light. In the summer, the towers here rise out of the green fabric, just like those utopian science-fiction cities in *Star Wars* or *Star Trek* do, especially when viewed from the ravine below.

At Sir Winston Churchill Park, on the southeast corner of the St. Clair and Spadina intersection, you'll find one of Toronto's hidden lakes. Though it looks like a standard park, with tennis courts and fancy Forest Hill dogs romping around, it sits atop one of Toronto's ten water storage reservoirs. The reservoir was completed in 1931, at a time when we built public works with great style. The pumphouse buildings toward the southwest corner of the park are miniature versions of the famously grand R. C. Harris Water Treatment Plant out in the Beach. Stand on top of the south 'cliff' to see the magnitude of the structure, and then look down into Nordheimer Ravine, under which is buried Castle Frank Brook.

To the right of and below this lookout, you'll find the Spadina Road Bridge. Near the base of the bridge, notice the Russell Hill subway escape hatch. It was through this passage that the victims of the 1995 Toronto subway crash escaped the superheated tunnels (three were killed and many more were injured). It's quiet now. Every few minutes the sound of the subway rushing by somewhere deep inside will echo up this unnatural cave, and if you stand close enough, you can feel the warm air blow through the grate. There's a hidden plaque memorializing the tragedy here, located behind the exit door, but it really should be public and visible. According to the inquest into the disaster, an overall cause was the underfunding that allowed the TTC's 'state of good repair' to decline. Toronto subsequently got its repair state in order back then, but the plaque should be publicly visible, not just because it remembers the victims and responders, but because decades later it's again a warning we should be heeding as Toronto's underfunding and deterioration have become widespread. Though it seems as though you're immersed in nature here, deep below the city's surface, Toronto's artificial arteries are pumping people through the city like blood through veins. There is a bit of wetland regeneration here too, and the long-buried creek surfaces in some areas. The path leads northwest to the Loblaws supermarket on St. Clair, past a locked subway station exit through which people could go directly from train to forest if it was open, or southeast to Poplar Plains and Davenport Roads. This is a zenith of Toronto's urban ravine system, with green passages in many directions.

Back up at St. Clair, take a short walk north on Spadina to Forest Hill Village. Once the hub of the autonomous town of Forest Hill, it's now an exceptionally cute enclave that feels a bit like a summer cottage town, its small and intimate scale overwhelmed by people jockeying too many cars into position in front of the Starbucks or the wee grocery store. When I was on a stroll there once, the elderly widow of a flamboyant Toronto millionaire was pointed out to me by a long-time Forest Hill resident as she walked along with her rhinestone-encrusted dog, anonymous to most – Forest Hill Village feels like a soft place to land when the bold-face society columnists no longer want to write about you. Contrary to Forest Hill's manse-filled image, there's a remarkable number of old walk-up apartments here too, complete with vintage light poles that bear the old Forest Hill insignia.

Further west along St. Clair, the street dips low by the Loblaws and the St. Clair West subway station, a sort of land bridge of fill between Nordheimer Ravine to the south and Cedarvale to the north. The giant underground bus and streetcar bay – a dreamy 1978 discotheque-era palette of gold, brown, and orange – would be above ground had the ravine not been filled in. Getting the Bathurst bus from here is one of the most awkward transfers on the TTC system: riders must walk a few hundred metres on St. Clair to get from the station to the bus. There tends to always be a northbound crowd waiting for the number 7 bus, as if perpetually in protest that the Spadina subway goes up the middle of an expressway instead of up Bathurst, where the people who use it are.

West of Bathurst, St. Clair's retail strip comes alive, at first without a discernable character – a typical Toronto jumble – to eventually become Corso Italia. The neighbourhood to the north of this stretch has been called 'the Woods,' as its streets include Humewood, Pinewood, Wychwood, and Kenwood. Laura Reinsborough, founder of the urban fruit-gleaning organization Not Far From the Tree (NFFTT) and a former resident of this neighbourhood, saw these woods through her 'fruit goggles' – her group harvests thousands of pounds of fruit from private urban properties each season. Reinsborough got into the fruit-picking business by accident when she volunteered at the nearby Wychwood Barns farmers' market and was asked to pick apples from the heritage orchard at nearby Spadina House, near Casa Loma. Back at the market, they were sold with a sign that read 'This was biked here from 1.3 kilometres away – trying to put to shame the 100-kilometre diet.'

NFFTT's fruit-picking activities have spread to other neighbourhoods – Reinsborough estimated there are 1.5 million pounds of 'edibles' growing around Toronto that could be harvested. She had a theory that there is such good fruit growing around St. Clair because it's up on the escarpment, just like the Niagara peninsula and its vineyards.

Thankfully, Toronto doesn't welcome gated communities (as long as condo buildings don't count), but Wychwood Park, just south of St. Clair, is the exception we can live with. This bucolic historical anomaly is hidden between Christie and Bathurst Streets, climbing up the shore of ancient Lake Iroquois, the escarpment that runs across the city just above Davenport Road.

Unless you look for the 'Wychwood Private Road and Park' sign, you're likely to mistake the two entrances to the neighbourhood for somebody's driveway. The circular road climbs up the old Lake Iroquois escarpment from Davenport through a forest of old trees and multi-million-dollar homes. When it's icy, I've slid down the steepest part of the road, by the only ultra-modern bungalow in the park, with its low, horizontal windows that afford a perfect view of the owner reading in bed. Designed by Toronto architect

Ian MacDonald, 4a Wychwood Park won the Governor General's Medal for Architecture in 2008. It sits upon the footprint of the site's original house and carries on this city's tradition of successfully mixing old and new.

Wychwood Park was established in the 1880s as an artists' colony by Marmaduke Matthews and Alexander Jardine. It's the only place where Toronto's long-buried Taddle Creek is still visible. A pond, thick with algae and quicksand, was created by damming the creek. Descendants of goldfish deposited by Matthews's grandson on the eve

Marshall McLuhan's house in Wychwood Park.

of his departure to fight in the First World War are said to still swim it. Toronto's finest have lived here, including Marshall McLuhan, at number 3. Just outside the north gate, at 41 Alcina Avenue, lived R. York Wilson, the artist behind the *Seven Lively Arts* mural that is in the lobby of Meridian Hall and the mural in the Imperial Oil building mentioned earlier in this chapter. The conversion of the Wychwood streetcar barns into an arts-and-culture centre keeps that tradition alive.

Unfortunately, some of Wychwood's residents seem to have forgotten the neighbourhood's artistic heritage. When the abandoned TTC streetcar barns to the north were in the initial stages of being repurposed into the indoor-outdoor arts-and-culture space there now, a group called Neighbours for a 100% Green Park mounted a ruthless campaign against the plan. Their true colours became visible when a Wychwood resident told the *National Post* in 2002, 'What if my friend Fran wants to have a dinner party? Where are her guests going to park?'

Back along St. Clair, the street does have the feeling of being high up above the rest of the city. There are fewer buildings on the skyline (though more continue to be added) and no hills in view. Further west, closer to the heart of Corso Italia and just before Oakwood Avenue, there's another dip in the road, this time where the headwaters of the Garrison Creek once flowed. Though the ravine is now filled in, its legacy is seen in the gentle slope of Winona Drive, which is the easiest way to bike up to St. Clair from the south.

St. Clair moves at a slower pace than other parts of the city, which may be the most Italian thing about it. Cafés, restaurants, and bars are quieter; you know you're coming up on one when there is a cluster of folks standing around, smoking or talking, a human trickle that spreads down the sidewalk. Kids, too, will sometimes be with their dads at bars, running around while the adults talk. I grew up partially in Canada's Maltese diaspora, a culture with a similar Mediterranean sensibility, and for me these were the most magical times to be a kid, extended ultimate freedom while parents nursed their highball glasses. Updated places like the Tre Mari Bakery keep this vibe alive with a new generation in charge, as does a venerable restaurant like La Bruschetta, a decades-old family operation with signed photos of famous people on the walls that has sometimes been rented out entirely, and quietly, when stars are here for the Toronto International Film Festival.

St. Clair continues beyond the railway underpass, and though this stretch certainly won't win any urban design awards, it might yet be the most exciting part of the street. Until recently, it was an under-the-radar landscape of evangelical storefront churches, automotive stores, and bingo halls, not unlike Ossington Avenue was until the late 2000s, when it became the epicentre of hipster gentrification, but change is coming on St. Clair too, with new midrise residential buildings, particularly a cluster at Old Weston Road. There, Heydon House is a secretly beautiful Gladstone-like hotel that was once on the frontier of Toronto. Rundown, beat up, and carved into numerous unglamorous uses (such as a convenience store), it's easy to imagine it getting the kind of loving renovation treatment that the Gladstone or Broadview Hotels on Queen Street West received.

Further west, St. Clair gets big. Like the part of North America we call the West, this is big-sky country and big-box land. Some of the giant retail operations here are built on former railway lands and stockyards. At the south edge of the Rona Stockyards parking lot, just west of Keele, two remnants of the CPR West Toronto depot can be found. Once a sprawling place with industrial shops and a roundhouse, all that is left is a turntable and transfer table, a bit forlorn and partially obscured by shipping containers. 'There were very few transfer tables in Canada, as they were only at main shops,' said Raymond Kennedy, a CPR historian. 'West Toronto was one of the very few shops that had two transfer tables. Thus, the greater significance for its historical preservation.' In the late 1990s, when CPR was selling off some of their land, Kennedy was brought in to inspect the site and make recommendations for what should be preserved. Small items were sent to the former CPR roundhouse near the CN Tower and these two pieces were incorporated into the new commercial developments.

Today they're publicly accessible as a sort of walk-through museum with a sidewalk crossing over both, though the fence is deteriorating and the operator's booth is caving in on itself. Toronto redevelops so quickly that derelict scenes like this are rare, but even the remnants are deteriorating at a worrying rate. There is no plaque here, though Kennedy said he wrote text for one that was planned at the time of preservation, with CPR agreeing to pay $5,000 for it, but it didn't happen. 'Nobody knows what these things are, nor the historical significance of this important industrial site and the role it played in the Second World War,' he said. The raised sidewalk between the two pieces provides a good view of what remains of the much smaller, still-working railyard to the south. Engines snort and idle, but nothing indicates what was here before, only the 'Stockyards' name itself, and the name of West Toronto Street running west from Keele, remain – references to both the old railway depot and the fact that the Junction was once a separate municipality called West Toronto until it was annexed by the City of Toronto in 1909.

There are still some meat-packing plants near Gunns Road, but housing tracts have replaced many of these operations. The mix of large-scale retail, light industrial, some scattered residential homes, and even co-op complexes from the last great era of affordable-housing building more than three decades ago continues until St. Clair ends at Scarlett Road, not far from the Humber River and the start of Etobicoke.

Eglinton Avenue and the Borough of York

 pack a lunch   Connecting walks: Yonge, Bathurst

 dress to impress

 scenic views

Where Eglinton crosses Black Creek Drive, down by the waterway valley that lends it the name, Toronto feels like a very different place than it was just a few years ago. When you walk next to the giant, grassy berm that seems to eject the elevated concrete railbed of the new Crosstown LRT line eastward like a launch pad, the sprawling new train yard at the old Kodak lands feels airport-sized. At the opposite end of the yard, the new Black Creek Crosstown station connects with the Kitchener GO line, knitting the region together a little more. Suddenly, there is a major transit node where there was once just a big intersection, underpass, and a shuttered industrial site. There's even more down here in the valley now too.

'It's a place out of no place,' said architect and project manager Phil Fenech of the York Recreation Centre that he and his firm Perkins&Will designed at the behemoth intersection of Black Creek Drive and Eglinton Avenue when it opened in 2017. Planning for it went back more than twenty years, to pre-amalgamation, when the site was part of the City of York, a scrap of provincially owned land that ran alongside Black Creek and was used for years as a ragtag baseball diamond. Though a former 'no place,' the site really is in the middle of things: on top of all the new transit, at least three neighbourhoods surround it, more depending on how you define neighbourhood boundaries.

Occupying the other two corners of this busy intersection are Keelesdale Park to the northeast and a large No Frills big-box grocery store with a sprawling parking lot to the southwest, a space that will see dense, transit-oriented redevelopment once the Crosstown is running. 'There were a lot of constraints on the site,' said Duff Balmer, design architect of the recreation centre, also with Perkins+Will's Toronto office. 'The TRCA (Toronto and Region Conservation Authority) regulated a line and we worked with them to moderate that line.' That invisible line exists next to creeks and rivers across the GTA and prohibits building in floodplains to prevent, at worst, a Hurricane Hazel scenario where buildings and people are swept away by torrential floods.

After hydrology and heritage studies were conducted, a bit more room was found for the building. Still, during the major storms and flooding a few summers ago, Fenech says he came down to see the water, and though it was halfway up the property, the building site remained high and dry. Such effort to build close to the creek is a reminder the ravine and valley watercourses in Toronto are a force to contend with, but the recreation centre will also help connect people to Black Creek itself. Perhaps Toronto's most alienated creek, it's encased in concrete in some places or poorly treated otherwise. Some people are even surprised there's an actual Black Creek and that it isn't just a fanciful name for one of our baby expressways.

'We wanted it to have the sensation of being set in nature,' said Balmer of the relationship of the centre to the creek. The side of the building that faces it has a pergola-covered patio along the entire length that multi-purpose rooms, including a kitchen, open up onto, and that allow for indoor activity to spill outside. Pathways lead to the edge of the creek where TRCA has strengthened the banks, and swatches of green glass and panelling on the building are abstract echoes of the ravine. The building design also reflects what the surrounding community asked for. 'This was one of the busiest public engagement processes we've had,' said Balmer. 'We went to schools, and they were very vocal about what they didn't want: a high school gym.' Instead, the gym has plenty of glass, inside and out. From the central sign-in desk, it's possible to see people playing in it, as well as views of the exercise room, front lounge, and twenty-five-metre pool. There's an ant-farm-like feel to all the activity going on at once.

Fenech described the centre as a Swiss army knife: one building that does many things. During consultation the community said they also wanted a track, a pool gallery so parents could watch their kids swim, a dance studio, and a music room. Change rooms are universal, meaning they are gender-neutral and have individual cubicles. There is light throughout, and the cars alternately speeding or idling on Black Creek are visible to people using the facilities – but the folks in those cars can also see all the action inside, as the gym, pool, and exercise room are lined with windows. 'You want to attract participants,' said Fenech of their open and 'playful' design. 'Centres like this used to be just a blank box. You can't market and maximize participation if people can't see in.' Compare the new building to the Chris Tonks Arena just across Black Creek: opened in 1956, it looks like a bleak collection of Quonset huts attached to a cinder-block base. The least appealing part of the new centre is the large parking lot on the south side, but it remains a necessity in parts of present-day Toronto.

If the omnipresent name *York* is curious around these parts, head east, up the big Eglinton hill, passing by an entrance to the Crosstown tunnel, to the York Civic Centre perched at the top on Municipal Drive. Out front is a marker for a time capsule buried in 1997 as a 'farewell to the City of York.' Alas, poor York, we hardly knew it.

Toronto is built on York. The word, that is. It's everywhere: there's Fort York, York University, even the landmark Royal York Hotel. Names and nicknames like Yorkville and Muddy York are splashed all over our mental maps of Toronto. But the one place that probably isn't on that map for most Torontonians is the former City of York, as it was known in its later years. It is, and was, Toronto's forgotten lost city, an underdog of a municipality that lived in the shadow of its bigger, richer neighbours Etobicoke and – there it is again! – North York until all were amalgamated into the Toronto megacity in 1998.

York wasn't easy to find: it was completely landlocked and asymmetrically shaped, and displayed very few overt physical signs, stretching roughly between St. Clair and Eglinton Avenues, and extending west from Bathurst Street to the Humber River and Weston area, with a few municipal tentacles reaching in various other directions.

The name York originally referred to the township established in 1850 that stretched from the Humber River east to Scarborough Township and from Lake Ontario up to what is now Steeles Avenue. As Toronto grew, it annexed communities in the township like Parkdale, Deer Park, and Yorkville, continually encroaching on York until the Municipality of Metropolitan Toronto was created in 1954 and established the City of York out of what was left over. In the final edition of the York Municipal Code – a sad book, now without a city – the preface boasts, 'York is a pleasant surprise in Metropolitan Toronto, with a future that holds promise!' The future still holds promise, as the long-awaited Eglinton Crosstown opens. Eglinton is a long street, crossing much of Toronto, right through the middle. The Crosstown elevates Eglinton from a major street to a street that, despite Toronto's numbered naming scheme, will also be known as a major transit line. These streets live in our imagination more because they become trunk routes to get places, on top of the local destinations.

York's poor financial lot was due in part to the fact that its southern border with Toronto was established just north of the lucrative tax base of the St. Clair retail strip. There's a similar shift in wealth starting from Eglinton West station, again just outside the borough's boundary.

If you approach the station from the east, Eglinton Avenue does a gentle Forest Hill fade-out as it rolls out from Yonge Street, where it is dotted with upscale boutiques and shops. The affluent neighbourhood of Forest Hill's main street and spiritual heart is nearby Spadina Road, but this part of Eglinton fills out the rest of the area's proximal needs. The low-rise retail is on a relatively wide sidewalk (a welcome change from Toronto's tendency for narrowness in this regard), which makes the area feel like a neighbourhood despite the width and busyness of Eglinton. Just before Bathurst, Eglinton crosses over the Beltline Trail, the former rail cut that is now a diagonal park and trail through Forest Hill. (The trail provides a quick route southeast to Yonge and Davisville or, to the northwest, deeper into York.) Around the Beltline there are modish and deco-inspired apartments, much like those on St. Clair to the south. Though known as a neighbourhood of mansions, Forest Hill has some of Toronto's best pre- and postwar residential apartment buildings. Between Bathurst and the Allen Road Expressway (and Eglinton West station), the Forest Hill–ness of Eglinton is still evident, and there are obvious signs of its Jewish character, but the north lanes of the street begin to seem like the freeway on-ramp they become as they get closer to the Allen.

The TTC's best advertisement to entice motorists out of their cars and into public transit may be Eglinton West station, which is more spaceport than subway station, with a floating concrete roof and glassed-in platforms. It's one of a handful of buildings in Toronto that were designed by Canadian architect Arthur Erickson – a starchitect long before that term existed – and a vestige of the heady days in the late 1970s when subways were built not just to transport people from here to there but to inspire futuristic utopian visions. Erickson's work, here and at Yorkdale subway station, Roy Thomson Hall on Front Street, and the King's Landing condos on Queens Quay, still feels like a future we've yet to reach. Below this odd island in the middle of the planned Spadina Expressway, which was cancelled before it was to be extended south in 1971, lies another future Toronto didn't get: the first tunnels for the planned Eglinton subway line, which were dug out in the early 1990s, only to be filled in when the Conservative provincial government of then Premier Mike Harris cancelled the project in 1995. The station is now joined by more LRT glass pavilions, one to the west and another on the south side of the road, finally allowing subway access from that side without having to dodge traffic.

Arthur Erickson's Eglinton station spaceport.

Directly south of the station, across Eglinton, is the Ben Nobleman Park Community Orchard. An urban farming project, the orchard is also where Toronto should erect a statue of Jane Jacobs if it ever decides to do so. This patch of land is where the Spadina Expressway, which the legendary Jane Jacobs and hundreds of other activists campaigned against, was stopped in its bulldozer tracks after the province, under the leadership of Bill Davis, bought up a small strip of land, effectively blocking the proposed road. 'If we are building a transportation system to serve the automobile, the Spadina Expressway would be a good place to start,' said Davis. 'But if we are building a transportation system to serve people, the Spadina Expressway is a good place to stop.' Here, on a nondescript part of Eglinton, the province has both given and taken away subway and freeway megaprojects. Now you can quietly pick fruit here. Walking the residential streets to the south is like being on death row after the governor calls to pardon everybody. These roads were spared when the expressway was called off, and somewhere deep below, the subway rumbles along, roughly following the diagonal path of the Cedarvale Ravine, which begins a block south of Eglinton. Formed after the last ice age by the Castle Frank and Cedarvale streams, the ravine eventually leads back to Forest Hill Village.

More than forty-five years after the expressway was cancelled, ghosts of it exist in the form of properties that were expropriated for it. There's a ghost at 543 Arlington Avenue. It's a narrow, empty lot with a chain-link fence and a wooden gate on a street that's a mishmash of architectural styles, typical of the Toronto neighbourhoods where homes were built by individuals rather than by a large developer all at once. The lot, its grass trim and litter-free, is an undeveloped vestige of the expressway that had been planned to cut through Cedarvale Park and Ravine, running behind Arlington.

In 2017, the City of Toronto issued a report titled 'Disposition of Spadina Expressway Properties – Memorandum of Understanding with Infrastructure Ontario.' The report reads like a map to lost graves of old political battles and was issued 'for the efficient and effective management and disposition' of the remaining fifty-eight Spadina Expressway properties. In previous years, more than $27 million worth of Spadina properties were sold off. That there were still fifty-eight left is a testament to how deeply a freeway can affect a city, even if only a stub of it was actually built.

The Glen Cedar Pedestrian Bridge south of Ben Nobleman Park is designated under the Ontario Heritage Act and was the first bridge over the ravine. It was built as part of Casa Loma–builder Henry Pellatt's development scheme for the area. (Called 'Cedar Vale,' his plan imagined the construction of a 300-acre exclusive subdivision.) For years, the bridge was closed and condemned, but it was renovated in 1989 as a pedestrian-only crossing with commanding views of the ravine below.

Back on Eglinton, west of the station and orchard, you cross the old border between the City of Toronto and the City of York. Though Eglinton contains a typical Toronto mix of influences, Little Jamaica begins here and includes Reggae Lane, taking on a visual identity that extends to Keele Street. Construction for the Crosstown LRT profoundly impacted businesses and the community here. Though the street itself is largely back to normal, the disruption caused community members to call for help in preserving the neighbourhood's identity and livability. In 2023, the City completed the Little Jamaica Cultural District Plan, meant to help protect this unique community. At Oakwood, a new mid-rise residential building is the first sign of what more will come as trains start operating, so there may be growth pressure of a different kind now.

At the corner of Eglinton and Dufferin streets, tiny St. Hilda Square is now a plaza for the Fairbank Crosstown station. Here, Vaughan Road stops just short of what was once a five-point intersection. Previously known as the Vaughan Plank Road, it used to connect Davenport, one of Toronto's earliest roads, with Vaughan Township to the north of the city, following an early Indigenous trail. Vaughan crosses York on a diagonal, like Rogers Road does just to the west, breaking with the standard Toronto grid just enough to throw off those with an untrained sense of direction.

The intersection of Eglinton and Dufferin marks what was once the centre of Fairbank, one of the many hamlets that were eventually consumed by Toronto's growth. The name survives here and there, most prominently as the name of the Crosstown station, an act that will surely bring the name back more than in past decades. The part of Dufferin that runs north from here is one of Toronto's least beautiful stretches of streets, one you don't want to show visitors. Many of Toronto's high-end interior design shops are hidden here in York's old light-industrial landscape, well-known to all those Forest Hill homeowners.

All along Eglinton, a handful of surviving Italian businesses hint that this was once a third Little Italy, behind the celebrated College Street Little Italy and St. Clair's Corso Italia.

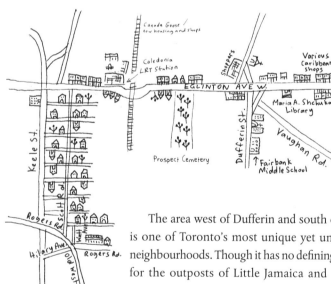

The area west of Dufferin and south of Eglinton is one of Toronto's most unique yet uncelebrated neighbourhoods. Though it has no defining style, save for the outposts of Little Jamaica and the Italian community, the topography makes this area very charming. Built on a series of hills and valleys, surrounding streets make sharp turns and dead-end abruptly, sometimes at a grade that looks too steep for cars. Toronto has been called 'San Francisco upside down' because of its many deep ravines, but this part of Toronto could easily be 'Little San Francisco.' There are surprise vistas across rooftops, and parks with secret escapes up or down outdoor, *Exorcist*-like staircases.

Back on Eglinton, before it slopes down into Black Creek Valley toward the Etobicoke skyline, there's a break in the continuous streetscape: a large plaza that includes a Canadian Tire is by located beside the Caledonia Crosstown station. It's another node in the transit network, as GO Trains on the Barrie line will connect here too, making this the kind of place where Toronto likes to build very dense and tall neighbourhoods. Just north of here, on Bowie Avenue, a large mixed-use development is planned for the Canada Goose factory site. Build transit, and they will come. A busy café in the plaza looks across the street at a rise in the land that exposes a strip of residential backyards in an almost obscene manner, as if the houses have been caught with their pants down by an accident of topography. Also by Caledonia, Eglinton skirts the top of Prospect Cemetery, a green corridor that runs south to St. Clair and Earlscourt Park. A few blocks north of here is the first section of the Beltline Trail, making this area an active (human-powered) transit node too, with proximity to off-grid routes.

At Keele, just before the Black Creek lowlands, 'main-street' York reaches south to Rogers Road, where there's a strange architectural oddity: a multi-coloured apartment building on top of a huge concrete parking garage. It's a little bit of Holland in Toronto, or someone's Dutch nightmare, depending on your tolerance for kitschy landmarks. There's an edge feeling here, where the Grand Trunk Railway cut and Black Creek Drive create an informal border. A left on Rogers Road leads east, back into old York and the complex five-point intersection where Rogers meets Old Weston Road and Watt Avenue. A chaotic, European-style mess of roads with North American traffic remains a great place to walk around, with a café, pizza joint, Portuguese and Caribbean restaurants, and more. Had York developed sufficiently before the age of the automobile, this could be one of Toronto's greatest intersections, maybe even marking the centre of York, but the cars are still bullies here and you should be wary when you cross the street.

Eglinton is the Yonge Street of the east-west, stretching from near the Scarborough Bluffs all the way to the western edge of Mississauga. The west-side Toronto stretch of Eglinton is a bit of an analogue to Eglinton east of Yonge, which takes on a much more domestic character again, with residential buildings and occasional retail, mixed with an increasing number of smaller homes. At Bayview Avenue, there's another dip in the road for a buried creek that runs under the Leaside High School yard. At Laird Drive, the south side of Eglinton becomes big-box land, a curious contrast to the genteel North Toronto residential neighbourhood that continues on the north side. After Brentcliffe Road, Eglinton becomes more highway-like and heads downhill into the Don Valley. There, the LRT makes a dramatic appearance in the slope, much like it did at Black Creek, carrying on above ground toward Scarborough. These two high-tech maws in Toronto valley slopes are like billion-dollar bookends after decades of cancellations, delays, and waiting, vaulting Eglinton into the big-name-street league.

Yorkdale Mall and Lawrence Heights

 neighbourhood jaunt   Connecting walks: None

dress to impress

offspring friendly

Can a mall have history?

Malls are all about fashion – and fashion changes fast. New clothes, new decor, and new facades are erected out of once-familiar stores like an ever-changing Hollywood backlot. There's no looking back, unless a retro style is in for a season. Yet Yorkdale Shopping Centre is over half a century old, and though it doesn't look its age, there's some history to be found there. Some of it can be felt on the bridge from Yorkdale subway station, opened in 1978, where the original circular terrazzo floors are worn smooth like rocks on a beach and the steps have deep indentations where millions of feet have landed. Walking here feels as if you're sharing a moment with everyone who came before. It's the kind of wear more commonly seen in the ancient stone floors of European cathedrals, a testament to how busy this place is.

Yorkdale subway station is one of a handful of Toronto structures by famed Vancouver architect Arthur Erickson. The design originally included 158 colourful neon glass tube arches installed along the length of its 570-foot-long transparent ceiling. When trains arrived and departed, a computer connected to the TTC's signalling system caused the lights to pulse, reflecting the speed and direction of the train, like a launch pad from a science-fiction film. Designed by artist Michael Hayden and called *Arc en ciel* (*rainbow* in French), it was dismantled in the early 1990s and remains in storage, neglected and unelectrified because the TTC's public art budget doesn't cover maintenance costs and, like many of Toronto's 1970s-era future-forward elements, the future has become the past, though there has been talk of reinstalling the work.

Some of us might not want to admit it, but the best place to see Toronto might be at the mall. Where else does a nearly complete cross-section of the city exist in one spot? On those rainy, overcast Sundays when melancholy blankets the city, I like to ride the Spadina subway line to Yorkdale Mall and walk in circles with some of the 18 million people who visit each year.

When Yorkdale opened in February of 1964, it was on the rural outskirts of Toronto and, for a short time, the biggest enclosed mall in the world.

Lester B. Pearson addresses the crowd in the Simpson's Court in 1965.

Within a decade, the city had built to those outskirts and quickly raced further north. Yorkdale was designed by John Graham and Company, the Seattle architecture firm that did the Space Needle and, two generations earlier, the Ford factory and showroom at Dupont and Ossington. Not much of the original Yorkdale is left, but the third-floor food court, built into the rafters of the old Eaton's building, has an outdoor patio overlooking the patchwork quilt of building roofs that makes up the mall. It might seem an odd place for a patio, with views of Highway 401 traffic on the near horizon, but there's an openness to it not normally associated with malls and, better yet, an up-close glimpse of the midcentury modern geometric brickwork of the old Eaton's exterior. Today's new malls are often little more than metal sheds, so this kind of detail – that few got to see up close – hearkens back to a time when such things mattered.

Adam Sobolak, an activist in Toronto's modern preservation scene, speaks in glowing terms of what some see as just a mall: 'Yorkdale always seemed more ample and luxurious than the usual Graham fare … What intrigues me is, from photographic evidence, how astonishingly Kennedy-era suave, stylish, and timelessly fresh their graphics and accoutrements were.' Sobolak also points out that the interchange of Highway 401 and the Allen Expressway that fed into Yorkdale's 7,000-car lot was called, in the space-age parlance of the day, a 'turbochange.'

From the outside, that suave style is now hidden by various additions and inconsistent tacked-on facades; it's become a classic Vegas-style 'decorated shed,' with the vernacular stylings of the Cheesecake Factory or the metastasized Restoration Hardware that inhabits the former Sears store. Yet, inside, the utopian modernism is still evident: the ceilings are wider and higher than in most malls, and light floods nearly all corridors through nearly continuous windows above all the stores. Even the latest addition, carved out of the hulk of the old Eaton's store, has a massive glass atrium that hangs from an exterior skeleton and 'floating' benches made of smooth Jatoba wood.

Unlike the rest of Yorkdale, the Simpsons Building (now Hudson's Bay) was designed by CN Tower architect John Andrews while he was at Toronto's legendary modernist architecture firm John B. Parkin Associates. In an essay on Yorkdale she wrote for the 2007 book *Concrete Toronto: A Guide to Concrete Architecture from the Fifties to the Seventies*, architect Veronica Madonna writes that the building 'demands to be seen while driving at rapid speeds. Its repetitive vertical piers stand like a fortress holding thousands of eager shoppers inside [where] the concrete vaulted ceilings made Yorkdale a shopping cathedral.'

Parishioners at this cathedral of commerce can still pay indulgences in the ruins of the old Simpsons Court. In what was once one of the best rooms in the city, the lamps that hung from each 'stalactite' are long gone, and the fountains there were reorganized and partially covered as the Bay colonized more space. The old Simpsons restaurant once overlooked the Kresge's across the court, which sold giant helium balloons to children whose slippery hands let many escape up to the ceiling. 'My parents always refused to buy me the balloons,' recalled Miriam Verberg, who went to the mall as a child in the late 1970s and early 1980s. 'So when we ate at Simpsons, I would stare at the balloons above me and wonder how many people the size of my dad would have to stand on each other's shoulders to reach one for me.'

Outside, you can walk among some of the 75 per cent of Yorkdale patrons who drive to the mall rather than taking transit. Few places seem more sinister than the lawless Wild West of a mall parking lot, where even the Ontario Highway Traffic Act doesn't apply and cars battle for choice spots. There always seem to be lone men sitting in idling cars, the streams of runoff from their air conditioners pooling together in the middle of the pavement. The sun and asphalt conspire to create a blast-furnace microclimate, the opposite of the controlled environment inside.

Yorkdale's paved wilderness is mitigated by a twenty-foot-high sculpture with amusingly obscene genitalia called *Universal Man* by the west entrance. Created by Gerald Gladstone, the sculpture was originally located by the CN Tower to 'give balance of human scale' to Andrews's more famous free-standing masterpiece.

As Yorkdale has aged, it has progressed from middle- to upper-middle class, and now into the retail stratosphere. The Dominion gave way to Holt Renfrew and the everyman's Eaton's and Kresge's became stores a rung or two up the ladder, even as the mall's visitors still range across class lines. Today, big brands, including electric car manufacturers, use Yorkdale as the place to try out experimental retail environments. It's worth the walk across the parking lot and south down Dufferin a block to Orfus Road, where Yorkdale's working-class slack has been taken up by outlet stores with giant block-letter signs that advertise liquidation blowouts and 'urban wear' 50 to 75 per cent off. If Yorkdale and the turbochange are the utopian future of the 1960s, Orfus is the hinterland that feeds off the commerce the mall lets get away, as remora suckerfish do with shark leftovers.

Yorkdale's history can be found in another unexpected place: the mall's archive. Decades of unorganized material was stored in a basement room of the mall, and for the fiftieth anniversary in 2014, Yorkdale's management hired archivist Ellen Scheinberg to sort through and catalogue it, with the intention of donating it all to a public archive. 'I thought I'd find ten or twenty boxes, but there were over fifty,' said Scheinberg of the trove of documents, photos, advertisements, video tape, films, posters, and other ephemera she found, much of it in salvageable shape. So much of it reflects Toronto as it grew rapidly into the mixed metropolis it is today. 'There were more events than I ever imagined, and they were very eclectic. Lots of international days. There was Japan Week, Israel Week, Danish Week, and so on. Also, art displays from the ROM and AGO.' Though not a true public space – there were no protests or political rallies at Yorkdale – the mall became a community hub. Art Starts, an organization that uses the arts to bring about social change, is even housed in the basement.

The Yorkdale archive also contains a number of large scrapbooks, with pictures of various fashion and news articles. One scrapbook Scheinberg found was simply emblazoned 'SPADINA' and contained clippings, beginning in the early 1960s, of the debate around the Spadina Expressway that would have linked Yorkdale with downtown, followed by the subsequent Spadina

Subway debate. The news clippings are depressing to read through – they remind us we've been having the same debate over transit for more than fifty years. Even so, the scrapbook demonstrates developers have always been keenly tuned in to the endless politics of it all.

Another Yorkdale transit connection can be found at the GO bus terminal below the mall, though it is decidedly less glamorous than the subway station. Signs direct people to buses bound for Barrie, Gravenhurst, and Sudbury. Malls like Yorkdale were often built in what was the middle of nowhere, and the city eventually surrounded them. With its bus station, Yorkdale (like other Toronto-area malls) has become a regional hub.

It's also part of a neighbourhood. At the southeast corner of the Yorkdale property, outside of the bus terminal, a crosswalk leads to Yorkdale Park, a small strip of land between the residential neighbourhood and the Allen Road on-ramp. The park runs down to Ranee Avenue and the top of Lawrence Heights, a neighbourhood undergoing massive change as the fully affordable, rent-geared-to-income housing is being transformed into a mixed-income and mixed-use neighbourhood, one that will ultimately have four times the amount of housing than previously here. The same model as Regent Park's redevelopment is being employed: tearing down the aging social housing and building a blend of social, affordable, and market (ownership or rental) housing in its place. Lawrence Heights is also a neighbourhood where the Spadina Expressway was never really cancelled, despite the Toronto mythology it continues to have, as Allen Road is still an expressway in all but name.

'I'm sorry, if they can put trees on top of buildings, they can put trees across the Allen,' Denise Bishop-Earle told me. She was standing on Varna Drive in the northeast corner of Lawrence Heights one overcast afternoon in the winter of 2020 just before the pandemic, looking at the first phase of the neighbourhood's redevelopment. The empty space where buildings had once been provided panoramic views of the two new large residential buildings flanking Allen Road near Yorkdale, like a northern gateway to the neighbourhood. The towers had the effect of minimizing the highway, so it no longer dominated the landscape as it once did. It was still there, though, its dull roar sounding like the white noise of ocean surf, if you used your imagination.

'You can hear the cars speeding on it sometimes,' said Bishop-Earle, a resident of the community for over thirty-five years. 'Oh, somebody's racing someone else down the highway. You can hear all the noises.' Bishop-Earle was musing about what to do about the road that cuts her community in two. What if it disappeared under a park? 'It would buffer the noise. They have sound barriers now but they don't really do anything. Then there's the dust and the dirt that ends up on all these windows.' Talking about what to do about Allen Road has been a Toronto tradition for generations. The section of the Spadina Expressway south of Casa Loma would have passed through the Annex, a Toronto neighbourhood of considerable political and cultural clout, filled with just the kind of university professors, lawyers, and media-savvy sorts who could mount a campaign to stop a freeway, even if it was already under construction and advancing toward the city centre.

The drama and rhetoric around the fight was intense. The famed urban thinker, writer, and activist Jane Jacobs, who had recently moved to Toronto from New York, joined the fight, fresh off her victorious battle against Robert Moses and his Lower Manhattan Expressway. *The Bad Trip: The Untold Story of the Spadina Expressway*, published in 1970 by David and Nadine Nowlan (two of those savvy Annex sorts), includes an opening blurb by Toronto resident Marshall McLuhan. 'Citizens of Toronto, reach for your Cass-masks,' he wrote, referencing transportation engineer Sam Cass, Toronto's version of Robert Moses. 'Get ready for the world's most supercolossal car-sophagus – right here on old Bloor Street. Toronto will commit suicide if it plunges the Spadina Expressway into its heart.'

In 1971, as construction was set to advance south of Eglinton, Premier Bill Davis halted the expressway there at the eleventh hour. The Stop Spadina movement is a story told and retold in Toronto. It's a feat people in few other cities in North America were able to pull off, perhaps one of the greatest symbols of citizen resistance to top-down, midcentury planning. The mythology around the victory is so strong it makes it seem like once Davis's decision was made, all was well in the land. And indeed it was for a large part of the central city. Since then, however, the Lawrence Heights neighbourhood has lived with a freeway running through its heart, an ongoing story not often told that continues to have a profound effect on the community.

In a series of aerial photographs at the Toronto Archives, you can trace the evolution of Lawrence Heights and the freeway that divides it. In 1956, the area where the neighbourhood would eventually be located still bore traces of the farmland that existed just a few years prior. Where the Allen would eventually be located, a dirt or loosely paved road stretched from Lawrence to Ranee Avenue, the latter already sporadically lined with houses.

Jump forward four years and Lawrence Heights is under construction, its circuitous road pattern laid out, the words 'Spadina Extension' written on the photo's centre road to indicate where it would go. In 1962 the neighbourhood was complete, with space in the middle for the eventual highway, and by 1966 the highway was completed from Lawrence Avenue north to where it meets the 401 next to the brand-new Yorkdale Mall.

South of Lawrence, a tight grid of residential houses that had already been developed was expropriated and razed. Three hundred homes were destroyed in this more affluent neighbourhood. But of the eight streets that once crossed the highway's right-of-way, seven overpasses were built to replicate the connections. In the public housing project of Lawrence Heights, just two crossings were built – the expressway effectively slicing the community in half. 'A lot of my friends were on my side of the highway,' remembered André Darmanin. 'I hardly ever crossed to the other side of the highway unless I was going to school. For utilitarian purposes I would go over there, but it was a barrier for a lot of social activities.' Darmanin grew up on Leila Lane, in a now-demolished apartment adjacent to the highway on the east side, and lived in the community from 1972 until 2000. Trained as a planner himself, he's gone back to the neighbourhood on occasion to observe the place he grew up in and recall some of its patterns. 'People travelled in north and south directions in the neighbourhood,' he said. 'You're going north to Yorkdale Mall or its subway station or you're going south to Lawrence West station or Lawrence Square. You never really go east or west.'

The divide created by the highway produced its own mythology over time, with the west side known as 'America' while the east side was termed 'Canada.' 'It's the American side because there are no resources, basically,' said Bishop-Earle. 'There's only townhouses and a few apartment buildings. Whereas, if you go on the east side, you have a school, the maintenance building, the office, the rec centre, the high school, and the public school. There's the health centre too, which used to have a store and a cleaners.' The two highway crossings came to be known as 'Overbridge,' where Flemington Road crosses over the highway, and 'Underbridge,' where Ranee Avenue crosses underneath it. 'You have to walk all around to get anywhere,' said Bishop-Earle. 'You just can't go through the middle of the community.' As we walked the ring roads, Flemington and Varna Drive, the distances became apparent. Although the other side of the community is seemingly a stone's throw away, it takes considerable time to get from one side to another as there are no direct routes, a small thing at first glance but enough of a trek that mobility and social patterns change.

Darmanin recounted a childhood episode walking back home via the underpass when a stranger in a car followed him, giving it a sinister air from the 'stranger danger' era, though today the walls of the underpass are brightly coloured with murals that read 'HOME' and 'LIMITLESS.' Like Bishop-Earle, Darmanin believed the ideal solution for the Allen problem was to cover it up. 'Making it one community, connected through a green overpass, that would be the biggest and best solution for that neighbourhood,' he said, pointing out that the two new 'gateway' residential buildings at the north side of the community are by the same developers and have a visual cohesion that brings the two sides together.

'One of the things that we were kind of surprised about, but it was an important thing to learn, was that the community felt very strongly that they wanted the revitalization to be done all together,' said Carmen Smith, former manager of community renewal and revitalization at Toronto Community Housing (TCH). 'Part of this was because the Allen divided the community.' Smith started working there in 2008, early on in the Lawrence Heights revitalization process. TCH had seventeen community animators who facilitated the consultation process, undertaking community surveys to find out what residents hoped and feared as change was coming, and what positive things they thought could be brought in. 'Like with any progressive and positive plan, you need the funds and financial resources to bring the vision to bear, along with the political will,' said Smith of the Allen question. They looked at a variety of options, including a park that straddled it or simply making the highway more of an attractive urban road, with cycling paths, a park, and green spaces alongside it that both sides of the community could share. They even talked about filling it in. Still, much can be done. 'Certainly from the community there was a lot of interest in what revitalization could do with the Allen. Residents were showing up, deputing and speaking out, saying, "We want our community to be united."'

Attempts to cover up a transportation corridor that passes through where lots of people live are not unprecedented. Toronto made an unsuccessful effort to cover the downtown rail corridor west of Spadina in 2021, though 'Rail Deck Park' may yet live again in a different form. Since the Allen was paved in a Detroit-style freeway trench (below grade to allow surface streets to pass over without long overpass approaches), it's easy to imagine it being completely covered. In downtown Chicago, Millennium and Maggie Daley Parks were built over a massive railway yard, creating a much-celebrated public space with the Pritzker concert pavilion and *Cloud Gate*, the bean-shaped reflective sculpture by Anish Kapoor. Similarly, in Melbourne, Federation Square and the Australian Centre for the Moving Image were created by covering that city's main rail corridor. At the tip of Manhattan, Battery Park is built over both the Battery Tunnel and FDR Drive. In Seattle, the appropriately named Freeway Park was created over Interstate 5, and other American cities, including Pittsburgh, Dallas, St. Paul, and Atlanta, are considering 'deck parks' to cover freeway gashes in their urban fabric. Why not in Lawrence Heights?

While some of these locations, like the failed Rail Deck Park in Toronto, are in shiny downtown neighbourhoods, some of the proposed land bridges seek to correct historic planning wrongs that saw highways built through lower-income neighbourhoods where people of colour lived. Lawrence Heights is an interesting case because, though the neighbourhood came first, it was built with the expectation that the highway would pass through the middle of it and was designed to accommodate it, at least spatially.

Back in 1991, Eb Zeidler, the architect behind Ontario Place and the Eaton Centre, began looking at ways to make the underperforming University subway line more financially viable. He suggested housing could be added to land adjacent to the Allen to increase ridership and profitability, but the city didn't bite. Fast-forward to 2007, when Zeidler and his firm produced a more detailed proposal and gave it to the City for free. The plan centred on Glencairn station, a subway stop surrounded by single-family homes. On either side, between Eglinton and Lawrence Avenues, they proposed putting mid-rise buildings of twelve to fifteen storeys in the 'wasted' land alongside the expressway.

Zeidler figured around eleven thousand units could be added along here, housing twenty to thirty thousand new people in the area, residents who would also contribute to subway ridership. Zeidler also proposed decking the expressway and subway line with a slab covered in sustainable landscaping. 'This new "roof" covering the expressway and transit line would reduce the sound and visual disturbance that is now created by these corridors and keep them clear of snow during the winter,' wrote Zeidler in his 2013 autobiography, *Buildings Cities Life*. 'The newly created living units above the line would overlook a landscaped area instead of the noisy expressway and subway.'

'Eb tried so hard to make this happen,' said his daughter, Margie Zeidler, who is also an architect. 'He did the cost analysis, structural analysis, and talked to developers who were very interested and said it would work for them financially, even back then, with far lower land and housing values. He flogged it at City Hall and the TTC for months to no avail. Then he got terribly ill and was never able to pick it up again.' One of the aspects of this plan that makes it not just appealing, but in the realm of the possible, is that the City already owns the Allen and can pretty much do what it pleases without worry of purchasing air rights. Around the same time Eb Zeidler was pushing this project, former area councillor Howard Moscoe was advocating the Allen be covered as part of the Lawrence Heights revitalization, then in the planning stages.

Though Lawrence Heights is fully planned out, there's no reason the Allen couldn't still be decked with a park north of Lawrence Avenue, while Zeidler's green space and housing plan could be added atop the highway to the south, making sure to include lots of affordable units – the two competing rail deck visions, together. Would there be opposition from those detached, low-density homes nearby? You bet, but with a heavy-duty subway line running nearby for nearly forty-five years, higher-density residential should be expected. Margie Zeidler, trained as an architect herself, suggested the city could carry out her father's vision by creating a master plan with short deadlines and have developers bid on different pieces, the way the St. Lawrence neighbourhood was built. A variety of developers and architects would also make it more interesting.

So here it is, plans and ideas, nearly fully formed, waiting for a champion that would cover the Allen Expressway from Eglinton all the way to Yorkdale Mall. It's not downtown, but that shouldn't be a problem, right? It provides a new park for a lower-income area and creates new housing during a profound housing crisis. More residential will surely be built in the Yorkdale Mall parking lot with the closure of Downsview Airport to the north, unlocking height restrictions in the area and increasing the need for public open space for all the new residents who won't have front yards or backyards of their own. For residents like Denise Bishop-Earle, what's certain is that current plans aren't enough to connect the community. 'They're building a big park on both sides of the Allen and the only thing that's going to connect them is a footbridge,' said Bishop-Earle. 'It all comes down to who's going to fund it, where the money's coming from, and the will of the government.' As the subsequent phases of the revitalization are carried out and even completed, there's an opportunity to do something better for the community and city. If there's will downtown, why can't there be will up here too?

The Sheppard Line

 neighbourhood jaunt   Connecting walks: Yonge

dress to impress

offspring friendly

The city constantly creates, devours, and recreates itself, and the velocity of this cycle can be as quick in Toronto's inner suburbs as it is downtown. If you stand at Yonge and Sheppard in North York, you can see the change happening in one 360-degree glance: lots of big, shiny new buildings that quickly give way to tiny midcentury bungalows and front lawns. If urban planning were like a game of chess, these older homes would be the pawns that only a few generations ago were the first line of Toronto's expansion into Ontario farmland.

As they do in many areas of the city, long-time residents quibble with the boundaries and proper definitions of the neighbourhood. This isn't actually Willowdale, they might say, but Lansing. They've got signage on their side – the city has marked area streets with this historic designation – but neighbourhood boundaries (and even the idea of a neighbourhood) change as populations shift. It's easy to forget that neighbourhoods we think of as historic are human creations that have evolved over time.

Historic Lansing was centred at Yonge and Sheppard, and its last immediately visible vestige, Dempsey's Hardware Store, stood on the northwest corner until the late 1990s, when the store was moved a few blocks north. A local landmark, the store was a symbol of old North York, a place whose civic ontology was made up of a number of small hamlets and villages like Lansing and Willowdale.

To head east on Sheppard is to walk above Toronto's great 'subway to nowhere,' the five-station line that runs from Yonge Street to Don Mills Road. That term was (and still is, occasionally) used by detractors because, at the time of its construction, Sheppard Avenue passed through a part of Toronto where density was relatively low. However, it's important to remember that when the Yonge line opened between Union Station and Eglinton in 1954, density along parts of that line was not much greater than it was along Sheppard when the subway opened in 2002. And those who still refer to this area as 'nowhere' either haven't been here in a long time or hold a grudge against the newer parts of Toronto.

Only a few blocks east of Yonge, at Bonnington Place, the office-and-condo landscape shifts into the familiar bungalow landscape that many North Yorkers grew up with. Yet urban growth is more like Monopoly than chess, ruled by a market that decides what has value and what can be discarded. Some of those bungalows along Sheppard are showing signs of these market effects, now sitting uncomfortably close to streets that have grown fat and eaten up their front lawns. The nuclear families they were intended for have long since departed, and now some are offices for dentists and lawyers, while others offer shiatsu and psychic readings. People, it seems, don't like to live in a tiny house on a big road.

Directly south of here, between Yonge and Highway 401 – an area that's three to five blocks wide – the transition from postwar to postmodern development is stark. Small, single-family homes sit across the street from thick new townhouse developments and condominium towers. The houses on the front lines tend to look a little battered and worse for wear, as if their owners saw the approaching development and decided not to bother fixing the roof.

The land immediately adjacent to the 401 and Yonge was once slated for the Toronto Maple Leafs' new arena, but when a more appropriate downtown location was chosen, the land was developed as residential. From the highway, the condo towers seem to hug and almost lean over the road, leaving those who have never been there on foot to wonder if the situation is too close for comfort. While the view from many units includes the 401's express and collector lanes, it's likely the unencumbered city view to the south that makes it desirable to live there, save for the exhaust. If and when all vehicles go electric, the experience of living by a highway like this will be much different.

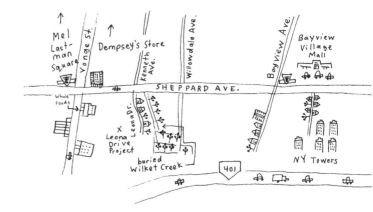

Still, when viewed from above, this stretch of the 401 is impressive, a twenty-four-hour river of steel that I could stare at for hours. It has a beauty in both its contrasting rhythms and gentle curves. Those constantly worried about Toronto's world-class status can take solace; our main expressway is bigger than most.

On the ground, wandering between the towers around Harrison Garden Boulevard, the experience is typical of many new developments: everything seems new. Jane Jacobs said neighbourhoods take a generation or two to grow into themselves, a sentiment first expressed a century ago by landscape architect Frederick Law Olmsted. Trees grow, people make subtle alterations to their properties, and the place acquires a patina that only comes with age, the one that makes buildings seem like they belong. Though new-seeming, there's the foundation for a good community here, with a mix of buildings and townhouses that, perhaps most importantly, are not dominated by the car. Unlike in the traditional landscape of North York, parking is hidden underground in this area, and much of the public space around the buildings is car-free and dense, the spaces between the townhomes often sidewalks rather than roads. Borrowing ideas from the New Urbanism movement, these smaller developments may actually work because they are located within walking distance of the shopping and entertainment locations on Yonge. This area is a nice change from many New Urbanism communities like it, where services are all a drive away and urbanity is only an illusion.

For two weeks in October 2009, the transition from not-so-old to new was explored on Leona Drive, two blocks east of Yonge. The street hosted the kind of public art project that Toronto needs more of, one that is ephemeral

rather than permanent, and that explores and raises ideas and then disappears – an arts event staged as much for the local community as it is for people who come from elsewhere to experience it. The *Leona Drive Project* was a temporary, large-scale art installation that took over six 1940s bungalows that were slated for demolition to make way for newer, slightly more dense housing. The vacant houses, interpreted and transformed by over a dozen artists, explored the territory of this suburban landscape, the one we're led to believe (at least by popular mythology) has no worthwhile stories and isn't interesting. What was most striking on the block was a bungalow painted entirely green, like a real-life Monopoly piece waiting to be bought, sold, and replaced by something bigger.

The remarkable project was organized by the collectives Public Access and L.O.T.: Experiments in Urban Research. The green Monopoly house was by artist An Te Liu, and though it was made of solid brick, wood, and plaster, a simple paint job rendered the house plastic-seeming, as if it really were as disposable as it was being treated. Next door, Daniel Borins and Jennifer Marman impregnated a living room window with a white Honda Civic, evoking a too-common news story where an errant car drives up over a lawn and crashes into a house, a David Lynch *Blue Velvet* view of the tranquil suburbs, where the very instrument that gave rise to this kind of development later destroys it.

Janine Marchessault, one of the project curators and a professor at York University, cobbled together various small arts grants (to a total of around $50,000) and many in-kind donations to make the project happen. Marchessault and her colleagues' greatest work of art may have been getting a developer to agree to the project. As Marchessault explained, 'The risk for him was if this project caused people to take too much of an interest in these houses.'

Leona Drive was part of the first wave of residential development that took place after farmland here was subdivided and most indications of rural life were bulldozed and covered up. The headwaters of Wilket Creek used to flow alongside Leona Drive, but the watercourse has been long buried and entombed in concrete tunnels. You can follow its path south along a slight depression in the land; it meanders through parks and between bungalows to the giant 401 sound barrier. There, a metal grate blocks access to a culvert under the highway, beyond which this nearly lost vale continues to meander through middle-class neighbourhoods to York Mills and Bayview, where the stream finally sees the light again. Along the way, there are oversized drains that, coupled with the vast size of the 401 culvert, give a spooky sense that this infrastructure is waiting for the flood, a kind of semiotics of potential disaster.

Here and elsewhere, following Toronto's lost and buried streams and creeks is like navigating the city with an old, outdated map written in another language, where only vague symbols and signs guide the way. Many of the bungalows along the Wilket's path have been replaced with monster homes, another way the stability of a neighbourhood can be thrown off. Many downtown residential neighbourhoods have historic designations, meaning a walk down the street today feels like it did in the past and, if the bylaws hold up, what it will feel like decades in the future. Younger neighbourhoods don't have this kind of protection, so something that has been the same for over fifty years can quickly change, though it is most often with another house, not, say, a modest apartment building.

Back on Sheppard, by the Leona Drive TTC escape hatch – a small brick building that leads deep below the buried creek to the subway – Sheppard dips slightly, marking where Wilket Creek passed. Cross Sheppard and follow the vale north all the way up to the Empress Walk mall on Yonge, site of North York's first municipal buildings. The streets around here – a royal quartet that include Empress, Duchess, Princess, and Kingsdale – are part of an early North York suburban development. Kingsdale was billed as a place of fresh air and open spaces only thirty-five minutes from King and Yonge by electric streetcar. Today, the streets are a mix of new monsters and old craftsman homes that date back to the 1910s and 1920s – a sense of history not often associated with North York. Further east, on newer streets, there's a utility hole cover emblazoned with '1947' on it (such covers often contain dates and are a small, if unreliable, clue to when the area was created).

The mishmash of converted bungalows and small apartment buildings continues east along Sheppard, a distinctly modernist typology that, like the stories inside the surrounding neighbourhoods, hasn't been celebrated much yet. As change comes to Sheppard, buildings are disposed of without challenge. Perhaps many don't have value, and it's smarter urban planning to replace them with more density, but the net waste of energy that comes with demolition is a hidden but large factor in what's happening up here. How to preserve these bungalows while acknowledging what the market wants is a tricky riddle to solve.

At Willowdale Avenue, a planned subway stop was nixed by neighbourhood opposition that predicted that too many new residents would want to move in. NIMBYism has many direct effects, not just a housing crisis. At Bayview, where there is a subway stop, it's evident their prediction was correct. Like the area around Yonge, Sheppard, and the 401, North York's constant, skyward transition is evident here. Bayview Village, once a small neighbourhood mall, has evolved into an upscale shopping centre, a kind of indoor Yorkville but without whatever grit Yorkville has left in the corners. There's an interesting vibe inside; it's the kind of place you might expect to see Dustin Hoffman's parents shopping in an updated version of *The Graduate*. Out in the parking lot, by the subway station, an oval blue-and-white condo tower sits like a cross between a cruise ship and Philip Johnson's famous Lipstick Building in Manhattan. All this on land that, during the Second World War, was used to grow potatoes, and where horses were raised.

Starting in the 1950s – a decade or so later than the homes on Leona Drive were built – the farmland here was turned into a meandering housing development that gave the mall its name. Designed by Eugene Faludi – the planner responsible for much of the postwar low-density development in cities across Canada – it's quintessential suburbia, a sort of utopic museum for a Canadian dream. South of the mall, Faludi's landscape collides with more of the change brought by the so-called 'subway to nowhere.' A 1950s-style ranch house (not the sight you generally expect when exiting a subway station) had white development signs out on its lawn in the spring of 2009, complete with the familiar bureaucratic poetry describing the proposed tower that would be built there soon (and, as of 2024, the sign and house are remarkably still there, one of the few projects in this town taking its time coming to fruition). There's still a handful of these houses on streets running south of Sheppard, before you bump into the development known as NY Towers.

It's a startling transition, as if the sets from two different movies are sitting next to each other. The NY Towers hug the 401 and look vaguely like the Chrysler Tower in NYC. In fact, one is called the Chrysler, while others are the Waldorf and the Chelsea, correcting any thought that the NY part of the name might stand for North York. The name and style may be embarrassingly un-Torontonian, but even in New York there are buildings that are supposed to look like somewhere else. (Think of all those European-looking courthouses and museums.) Walking through this area isn't unpleasant; townhouses and their barbecues, hedges, and patio doors wrap around the bases of all the towers. It's still a version of the Canadian Dream, just packed in a little more tightly. Nearby, the North York YMCA has some cool 1980s design elements in the 'high tech' style, along with Kenaston Gardens Parkette out front and slim Kenaston Park along Sheppard, a parkette in all but name.

Back on Sheppard, the buildings soon give way to a landscape of mod walk-up apartments and attached homes, the kind of places so many baby boomers started out in in the second half of the 1900s, when this was Mel Lastman's North York. Sheppard starts to slope downward here, and there are dramatic views a few kilometres west to Don Mills Road. This is a valley as vast as the Don River Valley to the south, but the development here hides the topography well. For many Torontonians, the intersection of Sheppard and Leslie means only one thing: IKEA-land! The hinterland disappears at this goal-oriented intersection: get in there, buy exotically named furniture, get out. Once a bit lonely, it now feels a little out of place, a big box in what has become a residential neighbourhood.

Named after a short road nearby, Bessarion subway station was once a desolate outpost on the way downhill, one of the least busy of the TTC's seventy stations when it opened, but not anymore. The sprawling Canadian Tire distribution warehouses here were replaced by a glass-tower community very much in the style of the CityPlace development that's adjacent to the Rogers Centre. It's the kind of place that the IKEA next door seems destined to furnish.

Here, too, is Ethennonnhawahstihnen' (Etta-nonna wasti-nuh) Park, which all this new development surrounds. Originally called Woodsy Park, it was renamed and means 'where they had a good, beautiful life' in Wendat. It might be Toronto's biggest outdoor gallery too, and includes work by the Dutch art collective Demakersvan, who created intricate maple leaf trellises and fences. Anishinaabe artist Michael Belmore also created carved granite boulders that evoke water moving over surfaces, and artist Ken Lum created stained-glass-like panels called Cracked Ice that surround the park, as well as a massive sculpture of Lake Ontario in front of one of the nearby condo buildings.

IKEA seems to be the only big-box store that can evade the heat of the urbanist anti-big-box attack, safe because everybody secretly likes it. Though it's on the subway, the North York location's connection to Leslie station is still awkward: shoppers who come by transit have to walk about ten minutes from the station. The walk isn't much in urban terms, but the scale of the roads and the underpass suggests you shouldn't be here on foot.

If you are, though, you'll see the entrance to the East Don Parklands at the intersection of Sheppard and Leslie. Head south along the trail and you'll come upon a cathedral-like passage underneath the 401. Walk north and a path leads down under the humid tree canopy to the Don River, whose rushing can't drown out the sounds of traffic coming from Sheppard and Leslie. Further north, a network of trails expands octopus-like into northern North York. Most of this Sheppard walk is scored by a long motor symphony. Yet walking north of Sheppard on the trail is a bucolic experience punctuated by the smell of trees, the chirping of birds, and little footbridges that cross the stream, all of this below the soaring railway bridges crossing everything else up above. As wilderness-like as this all is, it too was once farmland and dotted with mills. But during redevelopment, trees were allowed to sprout up rather than homes. The landscape here has long been altered and is untrustworthy (is this real or human-made?), but the bigger picture is true: this is a river valley. Twists in the river or sugarloafs in the ravine wall may be natural, or they may not.

Not far from Sheppard, a staircase leads up to a cluster of new residential buildings. This was once the Villaways, a public housing complex that looked a bit like *A Clockwork Orange* meets *Sesame Street*, but was razed and redeveloped in the mixed-income model of Regent Park. *Unarmed Verses*, a 2016 NFB documentary by the late Toronto filmmaker Charles Officer, documents the time just before the demolition of the complex and the displacement of its residents.

Back at IKEA, I sometimes come up here with only one thing in mind: to eat at the IKEA restaurant. It's an odd experience, unlike most dining experiences today, and it plays on our nostalgia (much like some of the furniture sold here). Cafeteria-eating was once more common – most famously in New York's Automat locations, but also at old department stores – and it's sometimes comforting to slide a tray along stainless-steel rails and eat food from the Swedish machine. IKEA also offers interesting people-watching opportunities: tragic and heartbreaking domestic squabbles are routinely fought in public here, a good counterbalance to the romantic North York nuclear-family ideal that may blossom on this walk.

From the restaurant's windows, you can glimpse a fine view of the valley around IKEA-land, an area that's home to the Canadian College of Naturopathic Medicine building – a perfect specimen of 1970s concrete architecture surrounded by the requisite institutional pine trees that were the style then – and North York General Hospital, which was one of Toronto's ground zeros during the 2003 SARS crisis.

The walk up out of the valley east along Sheppard is decidedly boring, as the adjacent neighbourhoods were allowed to turn their backs on the street, so it is lined on both sides with backyards. Only near the crest of the hill before Don Mills Road do things improve, where a corner of the Henry Farm neighbourhood provides Sheppard with more than just a fence to look at. Though the whole neighbourhood here is known as Henry Farm – it was named after Henry Mulholland, who settled it in 1806 and whose great-grandson, George Stewart Henry, was Ontario's tenth premier – the area spreading out from the southwest corner of Don Mills and Sheppard is most interesting. Unlike the typical detached homes of the surrounding area, this corner is a multi-layered maze of townhouses. It is a wholly pedestrianized community, where the residences have been built into the hills and parking is hidden in a lot underneath. It compares favourably with the apartment tower and townhouse community on the east side of Don Mills, where care-taking is not at the same level.

On the northeast corner of Don Mills and Sheppard sits Fairview Mall, the terminus of the subway line. Though many Torontonians' subway dreams would see this line extend to the Scarborough Town Centre, where it could connect to the Scarborough subway, for now the station is a kind of exotic transportation hub, with buses to the most distant corners of North York and Scarborough. To ride one of these bus lines is to realize just how big Toronto is.

If you opt not to board a bus, getting into Fairview Mall is a little odd. The subway doesn't offer a particularly glamorous route, letting passengers out into the parking garage, where they must walk briefly outside (interrupting what could be a completely indoor experience from the downtown core to this mall).

Though North York sidewalks are far from desolate, they don't have near the amount of pedestrian traffic you find downtown, and thus far fewer conversations to overhear. As a result, you may come away from this walk without a sense of who lives here. At Fairview, the aisles are just like Bloor or Queen on a Saturday afternoon: busy. To distort the lyrics of a Neil Young song, everybody knows this is somewhere, and the subway to nowhere led there.

The Finch Hydro Corridor

 pack a lunch

Connecting walk: Yonge

 rough terrain

 few services

If you look at a map of Toronto, you'll see that two bands run across the top of the city. One is the fat and wide Highway 401 that all Torontonians and most Canadians are familiar with. The other is the Finch Hydro Corridor, which runs across the city just north of Finch Avenue and looks like a continuous green line on maps, bisected at predictable points by longitudinal streets. In Google Earth, the corridor seems like a linear park, though you can make out the steel hydro towers and follow the line of them right out of the city. I once started a walk of the corridor at Finch station at about 2:00 p.m. on a nowhere, no-time Sunday afternoon, and I finished about three hours later. (Days like this are often the best time to walk, a much better way to spend the day than sitting around a cramped brunch hot spot.) I was going to exit the station at the round, spaceship-like kiss 'n' ride passenger pickup area because I'd never done that, but that seemed presumptuous. (Who exactly can you kiss and ride? Also, they don't call them kiss 'n' rides anymore but rather the more chaste passenger pickup area.) Instead, I exited on the east side of Yonge.

The hydro corridor extends to the horizon in both directions, but I decided to walk east. Just outside the northern exit of Finch station lies the expanse of the TTC commuter parking lot, so vast that it rivals the one found at the Canadian National Exhibition. If it weren't for the power lines, an Airbus A380 could land there, or at least crash without much collateral damage. The scale is more airport than urban. Except for the spots closest to the subway, this lot is nearly empty on a Sunday afternoon.

There's much to notice in an empty parking lot, like the tight black rings of rubber tire tracks (what else is there do with a small, front-wheel-drive car with an overpowered four-cylinder engine in an empty lot but make doughnuts?), the massive footprint of power towers (about the size of a downtown duplex), and the puddles of broken safety glass (smash-and-grab surprises at the end of the day).

After the parking lots ended, I continued east along Bishop Street, which runs parallel to the grassy hydro corridor. It's impossible to get lost on this walk: just follow the lines. The grass here is taller and wilder than a lawn, though it's still not quite a prairie. Many houses nearby have garages with opaque glass transoms over the door. So many Toronto subdivisions have a subtle, admirable trait like this one that shows that some unsung architect cared. Like a lot of places in Toronto, this place has a small-town-Ontario, almost exurban feel. A braided metal wire fence attached to rough wooden posts marks the perimeter of the hydro area. If these old fences could talk, they might express surprise that they are, in fact, part of a giant metropolis now. This far from the city's core, Toronto has grown so quickly that traces like this, things that suggest this wasn't supposed to be a big city, are common. When I first walked this route, it was hard to tell whether I was allowed to walk here or not, but the fence was passive and Canadian-looking enough to not scare anybody off. We're taught to think power lines and corridors are dangerous or private – like railways – but they are so inviting. Today, a multi-use trail leads out of the parking lot through the hydro corridor, like a miniature highway complete with a dotted or broken line down the middle, so the invitation to explore is official.

After passing some community gardens around Maxome Avenue, the trail meanders through rolling hills. This is about as close as I've ever come to feeling like one of the early Romantic peripatetics like William Wordsworth, who wandered through the rural Lake District in England. That this place so close to the action of the city feels so shockingly rural makes it seem more rural than true rural places, where ruralness is expected. However, Wordsworth never had the buzz of the power lines above to keep him company as he ambled along. A funny thing happens when walking alone here and passing by other solitary hikers – mostly dog walkers – out along this natural passage through the cul-de-sacs. We greeted each other with hellos like people do on trails in Algonquin or the Bruce Peninsula (and not like on most Toronto sidewalks), so perhaps it's more like a bucolic Wordsworth ideal than not. Perhaps it's being in the 'hike' mindset rather than the mindset of the city walk.

There's quite a bit of hilly terrain in North York that former mayor Mel Lastman's boosterism didn't celebrate much, if at all, but should have. When I first explored this area, I found myself climbing down a muddy path, then blocked by a somewhat-raging brook, forcing me to backtrack and take to the streets for a spell. Today the trail passes over a bridge, crossing this tributary of the Don River.

Once across Bayview Avenue (about the only place commercial activity was in view during most of this walk), the trail passes by a Swiss Chalet, familiar Toronto 1960s apartment clusters, and chains of backyards. The rhythm of the path is broken only where it intersects with the other north-south Don Valley trail. It's a great car-free interchange deep in a valley that affords amazing views on either side of this northern part of the Don, vistas across the landscape with, when looking back west, the Yonge Street skyline rising like some kind of emerald city. The trail still comes to a full stop at the Old Cummer GO station, where I broke the law and crossed the train tracks once so I didn't have to break my stride, but there are signs directing hikers and cyclists who wish to continue west up to Cummer Avenue, a rather out-of-the-way detour that should really be fixed with a proper, signalled crossing so no one else is tempted to sneak across. Old Cummer has a vast parking lot of its own, a paved paradise that no longer has a proper trail either. Beyond Leslie Street is a giant power substation, where that electric hum buzzes as loud as the planes in the Pearson flight path above. The official trail has ended (for now), so continuing east under the wire requires walking through the tall, somewhat unkept grasses below until Don Mills Road.

My own walk ended after I'd ambled through more vast parking lots that begin here – an eastern bookend of sorts – and found myself at the Seneca College campus and the sound barrier of Highway 404. A few pine trees, some lawn, and a giant wall kept me safe from the no-person's-land of the speeding expressway. (It should be noted that in the latter 1970s, the Seneca College Field House booked rock shows, including the Grateful Dead, Thin Lizzy, Blondie, Iggy Pop, and David Bowie.) Though the wall is ugly, its presence conjures up thoughts of other walls around the world of a similar look that have much different meanings, so perhaps there's little to really complain about here. The power lines carry on east, over the 404, but I backtracked through the Seneca campus to Don Mills and Finch, where I sat with a Tim Hortons coffee and waited for the bus down to Pape Station. I was 8.4 kilometres from Finch station, where I'd started, having walked through some of the best countryside Toronto offers.

Eastest

Rouge Park

 day trip

 rough terrain

 scenic views

Connecting walks: None

The opening lines of Robert Frost's poem 'Stopping by Woods on a Snowy Evening' read, 'Whose woods these are I think I know / His house is in the village, though; / He will not see me stopping here / To watch his woods fill up with snow.' Though he's writing about a semi-rural area, there's something about the proximity of those quiet woods to the nearby village that makes Frost's poem seem cozy and urban – a quick escape into the wild, but never far from civilization. How wonderful it would be to walk through a forest on the way to a friend's house, or to a tavern or movie in another part of the city.

In Toronto, the best of nature and the city often intersect, and if you're willing to head into one of the city's ravines – some of which are strategically poised between various points A and B – you can easily take the road less travelled (it's the one that's more wooded). The wildest and deepest wilderness, the one closest to that Robert Frost moment, is found in Rouge Park, one of the world's largest natural-environment parks in an urban area and the first national park (that is, run by the federal government through Parks Canada) in the country. Rouge National Urban Park – its full name – runs from the Oak Ridges Moraine in the north down to Lake Ontario along the far east side of Toronto, where Scarborough meets Pickering. The park ends at a nice beach where the sand spit changes every year, and with a good view of Pickering Nuclear Generating Station to the east, a fine backdrop for any picnic or urgent romantic moment. Up the Rouge River, in the northeast corner of the city, there's a series of hiking trails that start just off Meadowvale Road, across from the Toronto Zoo, and are easily accessible by the 85A or B Sheppard East bus. The landscape here is closer to that of cottage country (and of Algonquin Park) than to Yonge and Bloor or even Trinity Bellwoods, even though it's partly within the city limits. Since taking over the park in the mid-2010s, the federal government has considerably expanded the park's footprint too.

The route to the zoo up from Sheppard is wide open, with lots of traffic lanes (overbuilt in the 1970s by a metro government that expected more cars

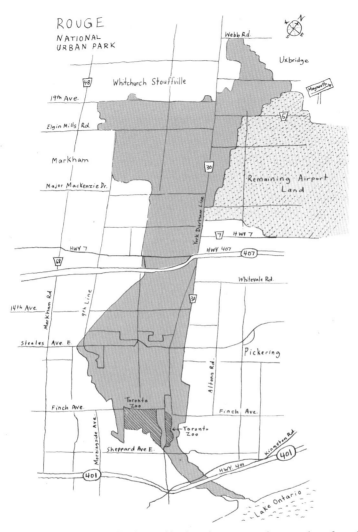

ROUGE NATIONAL URBAN PARK

Webb Rd.

Uxbridge

Maynooth

Whitchurch Stouffville

48

19th Ave.

Elgin Mills Rd.

Markham

Major Mackenzie Dr.

30

Remaining Airport Land

York Durham Line

7   HWY 7

HWY 7

HWY 407   407

68

Whitevale Rd.

14th Ave.

Markham Rd.

9th Line

30

Steeles Ave. E.

Pickering

Altona Rd.

Finch Ave.

Toronto Zoo

←Toronto Zoo

Finch Ave.

Morningside Ave.

Kingston Rd.

Sheppard Ave. E.

401

HWY 401

401

Lake Ontario

to travel here than actually do) and high-voltage wires that pass by a few old homes on Sheppard that were there when the road was only two lanes, back when this was a seldom-travelled part of Scarborough. There's even a bike lane out here. The housing development on the north side of Sheppard was built in the New Urbanism style and tries to mimic older, pre-car neighbourhood typologies. But like many of these developments, it's located far from the services that would make this place actually walkable. Still, the density here on the edge of Toronto is welcome. This corner of the city is the only one that touches rural Ontario; the rest of the 416 and 905 area-code borders have been entirely consumed by sprawl. The Pickering Airport Lands north-east of here have seen their development restricted since the early 1970s, when the federal government expropriated vast tracts of land for the proposed airport, which has yet to be built.

Though dormant since the 1970s, the Pickering Airport simmers on a back burner, threatening to come alive again. In June of 2013, then–federal finance minister Jim Flaherty held a news conference and announced Pickering was going to get an airport. It was a surprise announcement about something that wasn't a surprise. 'Local people phoned me and asked for help because I wrote the book,' says Sandra Campbell. That 1973 book was *The Movable Airport*, about the then- and still-controversial process by the (first) Trudeau government of expropriating 18,600 acres of farmland, including two villages, for a new airport to supplement Pearson. New airports were in vogue then, but not so much now. Mirabel airport, the result of a similar expropriation process outside of Montreal, was opened in 1975, but commercial passenger traffic stopped in 2004 due to lack of demand. Though Flaherty's announcement came and went without any real movement on the new airport, this massive tract of land adjacent to the northeast corner of the expanded Rouge Park is still in limbo.

There's a strangeness to a visit to the airport lands; it's quieter than most Southern Ontario farmland, and a keen eye will see traces of the houses and communities that were removed. More visible are the boarded-up homes with Transport Canada 'No Trespassing' signs out front and the security men who patrol the dirt concessions in trucks, all paid for by us, appearing and disappearing like sinister agents in a 1970s paranoid thriller film. As you move around this high country, there are vistas southwest that look past the tower cluster of Scarborough City Centre to the downtown skyline. Other times, the rolling landscape looks like a Turner painting, had he tramped about the edges of Toronto with his easel.

Tenant farmers still grow on the land, and some still live here. Nearly 10,000 acres of the original parcel have been given to Parks Canada, but 8,700 remain designated for a future airport. Advocacy groups point out that putting a hold on this land for so long has inadvertently preserved some of the best farmland in the country, and they envision this becoming a food hub for the millions of people in the region. Building a new airport is the kind of megaproject politicians can hitch election hopes to, with the promise of jobs and economic prosperity, but the Greater Golden Horseshoe already has underused international airports in Hamilton and even Kitchener-Water-loo. Pretend we're in Europe or Japan and imagine if the GO train network connected to them – the case for a Pickering airport diminishes quickly. As for jobs, in the GTA the 'food and beverage cluster' does $17 billion in annual sales so we should take care not give away the farmland that helps sustain it. At the time Campbell wrote *The Movable Airport* she was living in Claremont, just to the east of the lands. Campbell recalls taking the 8:05 a.m. CPR passenger train to Union Station while attending U of T. Though there's no longer passenger traffic, the line still carries freight, so there's potential for that line to connect farm and city. In 2016 Jim Miller, who was still farming on airport land, said something prescient to me: 'Southern Ontario's only permanent source of wealth is its farm soil.' The problem is, selling that soil to developers can make quick wealth too, as we've seen with the Greenbelt.

Back in Rouge Park, the Vista trailhead is a short distance up Meadowvale from Sheppard, across from the zoo. Though the zoo is the best-known place for wild animals, there are some truly wild landscapes nearby. You can visit a number of these landscapes starting from Pearse House, a historical and natural interpretation centre housed in the 1869 Ontario farmhouse that was the homestead of James Pearse Jr., a stonemason who, along with his brothers, operated a sawmill nearby. The sign at the beginning of the Vista Trail lists a number of organized tours that start from the Pearse House, occasionally including an 'animal tracks- and scat-reading' winter walk that must be geared toward an audience of hardcore nature enthusiasts.

A few minutes down the Vista Trail, there's a bench that boasts one of the best views in the city, but not of the city. The bench doesn't face the CN Tower or any part of the Toronto skyline; rather, it faces across the hundred-metre-deep gorge created by Little Rouge Creek. Sheer and dangerous cliffs drop down to the creek below, whose constant whitewater rush rumbles back up to the trail. The bench is dedicated to Rouge Park employee Patricia Joy Brooks with a little plaque that reads: 'Tragically taken August 2001, she fought and won so many battles, both personal and for the Rouge. She will remain forever young.' Finding her bench makes a solitary country walk less lonely.

Beyond the bench, the trail continues, following the gorge, and soon enters a forest of evergreens that's different than most of Toronto's deciduous forests and that can be a bit of a shock in the winter months – so much green and thickness at a time when we're used to ravines stripped of foliage, revealing the usually hidden topography beneath. The trail gradually slopes downhill through the forest, and as I walked it, I passed other hikers, usually in couple or family form.

The Vista Trail ends down at Twyn Rivers Drive, a curvy and extremely steep street that cuts through the park and connects the two parts of Sheppard Avenue. A short walk across a narrow pedestrian-unfriendly bridge to the Pickering side of the river brings you to the Orchard Trail, which heads back upstream. This trail is flat and low, and follows Little Rouge Creek quite closely, allowing for numerous side trips to the water's edge and good views up to the cliffs where Brooks's bench sits. The trail eventually leads to a long, straight road that's flanked by the former Beare Road Landfill hill, now part of the park with meandering trails up to the top and a view not to be missed. Turn left here and you'll arrive back at the Vista trailhead, the zoo, and the TTC, which will carry you back to places much less wild. After a walk through the Rouge, gigantic Toronto seems, impossibly, even bigger. After all, it can contain all this too.

Kingston-Galloway, Guildwood Village, and the Bluffs

 neighbourhood jaunt   Connecting walks: None

 rough terrain

scenic views

'No access to bluffs.'

Signs advising this can be seen all along streets leading south of Kingston Road throughout Scarborough and are an off-putting welcome to the most striking geological landmark in Toronto. Torontonians love to complain that the buildings downtown block the lake, but there's a near-continuous public lakeside realm from the Beaches to Mimico. It's the further western and eastern ends of the city that are largely privatized by houses. The proliferation of the 'No access' signs are evidence of a desire to see the bluffs, despite some of the difficulty. A favourite spot is a stretch of the Waterfront Trail running between Brimley Road and Chine Drive, just south of St. Augustine's Seminary with its own skyline-dominating dome. The trail partially runs alongside the top of the ravine that Brimley follows down to Bluffer's Park and has a few fantastic vantage points overlooking it all.

I walked that path with some friends during a stunning midsummer moonrise over the lake, the clinking of masts from the marina and sounds of happy summertime voices wafted up from below. It felt almost Mediterranean. The area around here is a bit wild too, not manicured parkland but a mix of forest and meadow, with other paths that allow hikers to scramble up and down the hills. In a lot of Scarborough, the word *waterfront* along the marked waterfront trail should be in quotes as it really isn't all on the waterfront, instead weaving along adjacent residential streets. A similar situation exists in Etobicoke. This meandering part of the trail, more a route designation on regular roads, creates important connections that allow cyclists and pedestrians to avoid fast and dangerous roads like Kingston. But this stretch between Brimley and Chine is one of only two unpaved sections of the trail I can recall between Pickering and Mississauga, the other being in the Harrison Properties park, a few kilometres west of here, closer to the beginning of the bluffs.

Back in 2011 there was a city plan to pave the trail here (known as the Chine Meadow), just as trails through sensitive ravines and natural areas

404

Markham Rd.

Yonge St.

Don Valley Pkwy

Danforth Ave.

Kingston Rd.

Gardiner Expwy

Lake Shore Blvd.

Fool's Paradise

Kingston-Galloway

N W E S

across the city are, making them accessible and passable to all, not harming beast or plant (as unpaved trails tend to do more damage, spreading wide as people avoid puddles). But area residents objected and today this key connection remains in rough shape. If Chine Drive and paving sounds familiar, residents of that street fought to prevent the installation of a sidewalk leading to a school on the street around the same time as the meadow path came up. It's as if residents here don't think they live in a city. That sidewalk was eventually installed and today is perfectly fine – the sky did not fall – yet these kinds of battles are fought all over.

Apart from Bluffer's Park, there are just a handful of places to get to the bottom of the bluffs relatively easily. West of Chine Drive, following the Waterfront Trail, there is an unmarked roadway running south off Glen Everest Road, between Fishleigh Drive and Wynnview Court. Another steep slope, it leads to the base of the bluffs, where rocks have been installed to prevent erosion. On a kayak trip along here, I saw a number of groups out for an adventurous evening hike – another place to feel far from the city while still in the middle of it.

One place that seems very far away from the city is Fool's Paradise, the former home of artist Doris McCarthy, to the east of Bluffer's Park and reached by that meandering almost-waterfront trail. In the summer of 2019, I spent a week living on the bluffs among deer, foxes, geese, chipmunks, birds, and a waddling groundhog. I was lucky to get a short residency at Fool's Paradise, set high atop a sheer section of the bluffs and along Gates Gully, a deep ravine at the foot of Bellamy Road. McCarthy purchased the property when it was near-treeless farmland in 1939 for $1,250, a large sum for a single art teacher at the time. Her mom thought it was a folly and referred to it as a 'fool's paradise,' a name McCarthy kept. It felt like being in a far-flung cottage, yet just a short walk from the bluffs took me to busy strip malls and urban life. Toronto is ahead of most places in the way the ravines weave natural landscapes throughout the city, but Scarborough has the most wonderful and extreme blend of 'town and country' to be found here.

McCarthy designed and built a small cabin on the site, which she later winterized and expanded over the decades into her home and studio. In one of her biographies, she boasted of getting her plans approved by then-Scarborough Township's council. It's a special place that couldn't be replicated today, and in 1998 she willed the house, a portion of its contents, and five acres of property to the Ontario Heritage Trust. She continued to live there until 2010, when she passed away at age one hundred, and afterward it was turned into a residency for artists, musicians, and writers as per her wishes. Her own $500,000 endowment maintains the property in perpetuity. In 1986, she had previously donated seven acres of the property to the Toronto and Region Conservation Authority.

The quirky house is preserved just about as McCarthy left it and is open to the public only on Doors Open weekend in May, worth visiting if you can make it. I thought a lot about what it must have been like to be her, alone but resilient on the bluffs. I, a city person, got spooked at night by various animal sounds and the lack of other people around. A silly thing, but it takes a bit of time to get used to being alone. Over the years, she took advantage of the conservation authority's program to plant trees to prevent erosion, and today the site is ringed by them, save for the expansive lake view. Adjacent farmland was also subdivided into lots, and a residential neighbourhood now surrounds Fool's Paradise.

I spent a lot of time looking at Lake Ontario while there. It has a real personality. On hot and humid days, when the air is heavy and still, the lake was so calm and tranquil, with large swirls in the turquoise water like the ones I've seen in the Mediterranean Sea on similar summer days (see, it's a theme in Scarborough). On an overcast day, grey waves crashed over erosion barriers, and it felt like Nova Scotia and the Bay of Fundy. I frequented nearby spots like Cudia Park, with its panoramic view of Bluffer's Park and its deep, forested ravine, and the Doris McCarthy Trail that follows Gates Gully to the lake, named after the Gates Tavern that existed on Kingston Road in the early 1800s. There are rumours of loot and stolen goods hidden here. These places, along with nearby Sylvan Park, are publicly accessible and may give a sense of what the bluffs were like for McCarthy before the city built up around her.

I also liked the opportunity to explore the city from Fool's Paradise. Though I've been to Scarborough countless times, day-tripping is different from staying put in a place for a spell, doing errands and getting to and from places. What struck me most when walking or biking up from Fool's

Paradise is how fast the transition from 'country' to 'city' is. Kingston Road is wide and fast, and when speeding along in a car it's easy to miss the subtleties, like the cozy bars tucked into strip malls, and busy multicultural bakeries and restaurants.There are also places like Stop 17 Variety near the St. Clair Avenue East intersection, and the Stop 20 Plaza a little further east, both ghosts of the old Kingston Road electric tram and its numbered stops, though it's been many decades since it ran. Venturing further north in the evenings to plazas on Eglinton and Lawrence Avenues revealed the urban oases I know mostly by day but that were often as busy as downtown streets in the evening, with people coming and going. Clusters of towers on the busy streets, as is the Toronto way, rain down the sounds of domestic life on warm evenings when balcony doors and windows are open, allowing the tinkling of utensils and the blare of TVs to escape. Then there are abrupt shifts to quiet, meandering streets of detached houses, or vast light-industrial neighbourhoods where autobody shops bang late into the night, and the occasional creek-side paths that connect neighbourhoods safely. It goes on and on, and it was a treat to wander.

At the bottom of Gates Gully, far underneath Fool's Paradise, is *Passage*, a large corten steel sculpture by artist Marlene Hilton Moore that resembles the ribs of a fish or boat. Installed in 2001, it's an homage to McCarthy as well as the bluffs and geological time. If the lake is low, a glimpse of the *Alexandria* wreckage, a sunken steamer just off the shoreline, can sometimes be had. East of here, a gravel path runs a few kilometres along the bottom of the bluffs to Guild Park and Gardens and is a wonderful place to feel completely alone. On walks or rides here, I've often not passed a soul, despite being surrounded by the 7 million people who live in the greater metropolis, and it is like a secret alternative route across a portion of Scarborough. Further on, at East Point Park, there is another access point to the informal beaches below the bluffs. Though people do swim here, the water quality is not regularly tested, something that should change to facilitate more swimming areas, but the steep roadway up to Guild Park and Gardens reveals yet more Scarborough artfulness and the Kingston-Galloway neighbourhood beyond where some old Toronto myths are slowly being busted.

Neighbourhoods are like people – bad reputations are easily acquired but hard to shake. But with neighbourhoods, there's the added injustice that a reputation can be spread by relatively few individuals. The crossroads of

The ruins of old Toronto reconstructed at Guild Park and Gardens.

Kingston and Galloway Roads would likely not have risen to notoriety had it not been for the Galloway Boys, the local gang that knew how to pick a memorable name and gave the neighbourhood a bad reputation in the 2000s. The Galloway Boys' activities brought the area into Toronto's wider consciousness.

The curious thing about Kingston-Galloway, and a lot of neighbourhoods like it, is that when you're there, in middle of it, you'd never know it had such a reputation. There are apartment towers, bungalows, townhouses, strip malls, used car lots, Starbucks, Tim Hortons, and high schools – all things that resemble what a lot of Canada looks like. The landscapes of Canadian distress don't match the cinematic picture that's been painted of 'bad neighbourhoods,' so there's a sense of cognitive dissonance when you're there. The 1970s Bronx-on-fire is nowhere to be seen.

In the western side of Scarborough, Kingston Road is something of a divide: higher income to the south, by the lake, lower to the north. Here, the train tracks south of Kingston-Galloway play that role. Walk south on Galloway a few blocks, across the GO and VIA tracks, and you encounter the big lawns and bigger trees of Guildwood Village, one of the wealthiest postal codes in the city. 'The other side of the tracks' is, as many clichés go, a reality.

At the south end of Galloway, where the road to the bottom of the bluffs connects to Guildwood Parkway, sits Guild Park and Gardens high atop the Scarborough Bluffs, among eighty-eight acres of manicured grounds and woodland strewn with chunks of old Toronto buildings – the sculpture garden of lost Toronto. (Try visiting late at night during a full moon for the full ghostly experience.) The sculpture garden was started by Rosa and Spencer Clark, who collected bits of old Toronto buildings that were being torn down in the name of progress and set them up here. The main Guild Inn building, the Bickford residence, is an Arts and Crafts building that was constructed in 1914 and used by the Clarks as a Depression-era arts colony. In recent years, it's been refurbished and expanded, now serving as an event venue.

On Galloway Road north of the tracks, sits BGC East Scarborough, formerly the Boys and Girls Club of East Scarborough. On a June day in 2009, I met Trichelle Primo there and she took me on a walk. Primo had lived in Kingston-Galloway – sometimes known by its older name, West Hill – all of her nineteen years, and she ran an after-school program out of the club. 'It's not as bad as people make it seem,' she said. 'Everybody knows everybody.'

As we zigzagged around the neighbourhood, down a quiet postwar suburban street with the disproportionally mythical name of Overture Street, through the Gabriel Dumont Co-op along Kingston Road (home to one of the highest concentrations of First Nations residents in Toronto), and near public housing buildings, she greeted people and pointed out the obvious: the area is clean, it's quiet, and it's more like the rest of Toronto than we think.

The reasons this is a distressed neighbourhood are somewhat hidden at first glance, but as now-retired BGC executive director Ron Rock explained to me in 2009, it's due to a lack of services. 'Downtown, you can walk a kilometre and you'll hit all kinds of services,' he said. 'In East Scarborough, they are few and far between.'

In 2017, I sat in on a discussion group in the neighbourhood, convened by the Toronto Community Foundation and focused on how a lack of services of various kinds, as well as, simply, places to hang out, can lead to isolation. 'Social inclusion,' as it's termed more formally, can be difficult to come by. On top of her full-time job at a large retail store, Mary (not her real name, as participants were offered anonymity in order to record their thoughts) ran an after-school soccer program to bring neighbourhood teens together, but she struggled to find suitable spaces for them to play. 'In summer it's okay, but winter is a challenge,' she said. 'School gym use is a problem. The hours are bad and the fees are outrageous for our non-profit.' She had help from social service organizations and even a sympathetic school principal in the area who wanted to help but whose hands were tied because of school board rules that make opening up underused school facilities during off-hours difficult.

'We're not a rich neighbourhood, but we help each other,' said Mary, referring to West Hill by its other, newer nickname, KGO, a reference to the Kingston and Galloway Roads intersection. 'After seven years of doing this, it's nice to see the kids you've helped. Maybe I don't recognize them, but they say hi to me. These were angry kids before. We just need a space to play. They're alienated from the spaces they can see, and they ask, "Why can't we use it?" If we can't find space here, then what are we doing?' Cities like Toronto are rich with public resources already built into the urban fabric, but they are often managed in ways that prevent easy use by the wider community.

When I was riding in Ron Rock's car, we went up Galloway Road north of Kingston Road to where it ends at Lawrence. He showed me around this part of the neighbourhood, pointing out Toronto Community Housing buildings and the East Scarborough Storefront nearby on Lawrence. Located in a former police station, the Storefront is a collection of a few dozen social agencies – 'a one-stop shop' – that share resources and offer services. Sahar Vermezyari was the coordinator of programs and services at the Storefront when I spoke to her (she's now the director). She said they received seventeen thousand requests for services in 2008, everything from 'how to find a lawyer to belly-dancing classes. We want people to feel comfortable enough to ask for help.'

Like Primo, Rock also seemed to know everybody, engaging people along the way, asking a fellow at the Storefront how his job search was going. As the community catches up to the rest of Toronto service-wise, it's obvious there's already a strong network of people here who provide the solid human infrastructure that is as strong as the kind that small towns are romanticized for having. *King of Kensington* was set in downtown Toronto, Al Waxman's strut down the sidewalk in the opening credits evoking that traditional neighbourhood feel. If the CBC decided to reboot that sitcom today, it could be set out here, because everything would be the same except for the topology: it's just wider and taller and there are lots more cars.

Wander the neighbourhood and you'll see physical traces of a small town. West Hill is a name that lives on here and there, on street signs and school buildings. It was a busy stop on the road to Kingston, but it was eventually subsumed by Scarborough and, later, Toronto. On Lawrence, between community housing towers and townhouses, sits St. Margaret's church and park. Its adjacent cemetery is not fenced in, so the park blends into it. These are the kind of fuzzy boundaries we don't see as much in cities.

A Festival Market was held in the park each Thursday during the summer for a few years. Local vendors selling either produce or crafts and small items could rent a table for two to five dollars. In 2019, I met with Sandra Hutley, one of the organizers, while wandering along. Hutley had lived in the area for thirty-five years and still called it West Hill, a name, she said, that started to disappear when they lost their post office in the 1990s. Like many long-time residents of Scarborough, she noted changes in the buildings that sprouted up between the houses over the years. When you look at the area on Google Maps, you can see that Highland Creek wraps around West Hill, and it's easy to imagine that, when this was one of Scarborough's rural post-office crossroads, it was isolated and very much its own place.

This market was important to the area, as there are few public places available for community gathering. In 2007, nearby Morningside Mall was torn down, replaced by an outdoor strip mall with little room for formal and informal community gatherings. We may have looked down our noses at mall culture, but for many places that developed rapidly when the car was king, they became town squares. Because they are privately owned, however, they can disappear in an instant, no matter how much they matter.

The lack of all-season public spaces in this neighbourhood makes a place like the BGC East Scarborough critically important. Primo had been going there since she was seven and said she felt like she grew up there. The club serves over three thousand families annually and, before he retired in 2017, Rock led a campaign to double the club's size and open up the nearly window-less 1970s building, add new program rooms, arts, media, and dance studios, and expand the gym. The area's former councillor and onetime mayoral candidate, David Soknacki, revealed his old-fashioned Red Tory self by donating his $30,000 councillor's severance to kick-start the campaign.

The club's motto, when I first visited, was 'A Good Place to Be,' and today it's 'Great Futures Start Here.' Both embody the feeling I got when hanging around people from Kingston-Galloway, and either could be the whole neighbourhood's motto. It's town-and-country Toronto, and deserves a walk or two.

Scarborough City Centre, Bendale, and the Meadoway

 neighbourhood jaunt   Connecting walks: None

 dress to impress

🐕 👶 offspring friendly

You could forgive a visitor driving eastward into Toronto on the 401 for thinking they've found downtown as they approach Scarborough City Centre. The cluster of skyscrapers surrounding the Scarborough Town Centre mall would be the envy of many mid-size midwestern American cities. They shimmer on the horizon from kilometres away, and some are even lit up with phosphorescent colours at night. Should that visitor arrive and be told that this is Scarborough City Centre, you might also forgive them for being confused. Like North York City Centre, Mississauga City Centre, and a few other malls that are transforming into clusters of density, Scarborough City Centre has followed the 'If we call it a city centre, the city centre will follow' model of city building.

The Scarborough Town Centre mall and the adjacent Scarborough Civic Centre both opened in 1973 and are separated by Albert Campbell Square, the Nathan Phillips Square of the then-city of Scarborough. Both squares are named after a former mayor and come complete with a skating rink. In 1985, the Scarborough Rapid Transit line continued the path of the Bloor-Danforth subway line to this area with a new not-really-a-subway, Ontario-built technology that was supposed to be the future of public transit. (Few cities bought it, Detroit being a notable exception.) When the SRT train pulled into the station on its monorail-like track, it made a strange electric hum that, paired with its late-1970s space shuttle styling, evoked low-budget science-fiction effects from that era and suggested that this was Spaceport Scarborough rather than a rail stop. The future ended in 2023, when the SRT was shut down prematurely after a derailment, and this city centre will be without proper transit until the Scarborough subway opens.

The civic centre was used as Scarborough's city hall until amalgamation and was designed by Raymond Moriyama of Moriyama Teshima, the Toronto architecture firm that designed both the Toronto Reference and the North York Central libraries. Though the civic centre came first, all three of these buildings have central atriums with zigzagging staircases. In keeping with the science-fiction theme, a sculpture by James Sutherland called *21 Points in Equilibrium* is made up of reflective triangle shapes that begin outside and make their way up to the atrium ceiling. When Terry Fox ran through Toronto on his Marathon of Hope, he gave a speech by the pond full of goldfish (there are still big ones swimming in there today) as onlookers crowded every level up to the ceiling. Seven years earlier, in 1973, Queen Elizabeth II stood in the same square to officially open the building. Inside, in a locked glass cabinet (as if waiting for eBay), there's a shrine to this event that includes the pen the Queen and her consort used to sign the opening documents. The faded pictures and dusty Union Jack are now memorials to Scarborough's former WASPy demographic makeup, which has radically changed since this place was built.

When the civic centre opened, it was the symbol of Scarborough's bright future. Inside, there's still the architectural model of the 'site development concept,' which has a complicated keypad that used to light up various sections when you pressed the right numbers – more space-aged 1970s technology. It doesn't work anymore, as its electric power is unplugged, just as the building's political power was in 1998. Though the building is still busy and used for municipal offices (there's even a wedding chapel), it once aspired to loftier civic ideals. A 1970 proposal letter from architect Moriyama summed up this spirit: 'We are very conscious of the contribution the new civic centre will make to Scarborough and our interest in the centre goes beyond the normal provision of Administrative Offices ... As a municipality, Scarborough has come of age. In just two decades it has been transformed from a rural agricultural area into one of the fastest growing municipalities on the continent ... It will be Scarborough's contribution toward making Metropolitan Toronto a World city.'

Somewhat sad to think we've been plagued by thoughts of our world-class status for more than half a century. Scarborough was the bright future and it was big, so big that if we could fold it over the rest of Toronto, it would cover almost the entire city to the Mississauga border. Made up of a few dozen smaller communities – farm country post offices or tiny crossroads, in some cases – Scarborough was merely a township until it was incorporated as a borough in 1967. Though that farm heritage is just about gone (there are still a couple fields left in the far northeastern corner of the city, past the zoo), it isn't so far in the distant past that it doesn't live in Scarborough's collective memory.

In the summer of 2004, I was in an upper-floor room of a retirement residence on Sheppard Avenue in Agincourt, just north and west of the civic centre. I was there to see Bill Walton, a farmer born in 1919 and on whose land the mall and civic centre were eventually built. There was a little metal Ford toy tractor by the window that looked out and over the sprawl to where his farmhouse once was, an area that's easy to find because of the condo skyscrapers. 'We raised grain and hay and we had pigs and quite a big orchard. The orchard was quite a thing at one time. It kind of petered out,' he told me. Farms in Scarborough often petered out like this, but this is no Depression-era story. Most farmers, including Walton, sold their properties. The Walton farm eventually became what the retail industry calls a 'super regional shopping centre.'

Back on Walton's former land, it's like a casino inside the mall: except for skylights that let in hints of the outdoors, this is an enclosed and self-contained universe. If you want to see Scarborough – not just the buildings or the highways, but the people – walk laps here, because it's Scarborough's downtown core. This mall was home to the very first Second Cup kiosk in 1975, and today it's where the Scarborough Walk of Fame is laid out in the floor.

Make your way east across the parking lot past McCowan Road and the open country, where the loudest sound is the hum of the highway. Though you're still surrounded by buildings, taking a walk here is not unlike walking through rural country: it's all big skies and wide vistas and the lingering feeling that walking isn't what you're supposed to be doing in a place like this.

Consilium Place is made up of the first cluster of high-rises that were constructed in the area, and they shoot out of the parking lot plains like the Rockies do when you're driving west through the Prairies. They were built in the mid-1980s and wear that era's style boldly: J. R. Ewing from the soap opera *Dallas* could have had an office here. It's a landscape made for the car, yet the steps leading to the front entrance are massive and wide and make you wonder what percentage of people going to this office walk up these grand steps instead of driving into the parking garage. Can you really know a building if you don't walk through its front doors?

Further east, you'll see the newer condo buildings along Lee Centre Drive. These buildings hug the edge of the 401 and, while they're impressive from a distance – two of these towers appear to arc toward each other, as if about to hug and kiss – they meet the sidewalk awkwardly. What could be urban isn't, and the busiest parts of the sidewalk aren't full of pedestrians but are where the constant car traffic enters each building (gated communities in a city that isn't supposed to have any). At 94 Corporate Drive, perhaps not the most bucolic-sounding address, is Hillsborough Park. It's wedged in between one of the large condos and East Highland Creek and has a commanding view of the 401 traffic if you walk to its northern edge. Peer through the lobby windows and you'll see that these modern buildings are decorated in a decidedly ticky-tacky style. Two of the indoor pools are done up in Roman temple style, complete with pillars and paintings of what looks like the Tuscan countryside. If you walk past the condos and south on Bellamy Road, you'll see real temples of a radically different style: many of the light industrial and commercial buildings here have been converted into evangelical churches that suggest this is, in fact, God's country. Just as ethnic neighbourhoods like the Danforth and Little Italy are branded with their own special street signs, Bellamy and Ellesmere could be called the Big-Box Jesus District.

It's lonely heading back east along Ellesmere on foot. The cars fly by, but there are few people to bump into. Knowing how many there are in the mall nearby is like being in a stadium parking lot on game day: crowded inside, quiet outside. Behind the civic centre, there's a stand of trees that were saved when the farmland was developed. The area to the south is Bendale. If you want to see how Toronto works, how its past and its present coexist, take a walk through Bendale, where the layers of our city are as visible as they are in Kensington Market or Corktown, but in a different form.

The name Bendale doesn't resonate with everyone who lives there – the word is scattered throughout the area, attached to schools or retirement homes, though the post office that bore its name is long gone. It's anachronistic and, like the neighbourhood itself, mostly overlooked by many of the people who live here.

Bendale's most striking feature is its sense of space. There's the city-centre skyline to the north and the downtown bank headquarters far to the west, the latter visible only on days with minimal smog. Instead of the CN Tower as a geographic landmark, Bendale has high-voltage power lines. They cut a diagonal swath through the neighbourhood, and through the rest of Scarborough, and never linger or come down to a human level; instead they're cold and reserved, headed straight for those towers downtown, feeding the empire all the electricity it can eat up. Standing in the middle of the hydro fields is like being in Montana, big-sky country again. You can even see the horizon, something that generally isn't in view anywhere within the built-up areas of the old City of Toronto.

It was here in Bendale, where the hydro corridor passes through Thomson Memorial Park, that the Meadoway was born, a transformation of what was once a utilitarian strip through Scarborough, treated as leftover space, into a natural corridor. 'I think my favourite part is the original Scarborough Centre Butterfly Trail,' said Katie Turnbull when we spoke in 2021, referring to the initial pilot project that launched the Meadoway. 'That portion has been established since 2013. There's wildflowers and grasses, a couple of allotment gardens, as well as shrub nodes, and the grass buffers are all nicely mowed. To me, that's the spot that I just love to walk with family and friends. But I also love taking them through the sections that we haven't restored yet and showing the difference between the mown grass and what could be there.'

Turnbull had been working on the Meadoway since the beginning, as a Toronto and Region Conservation Authority (TRCA) senior project manager. She's witnessed it grow from that butterfly trail into a plan to turn sixteen kilometres of the Gatineau Hydro Corridor into a linear park of continuous green space and meadowlands, along with a walking and cycling trail, that cuts across Scarborough, connecting downtown Toronto to the Rouge National Urban Park on the eastern edge of the city. Hydro corridors are ubiquitous in cities, and the Meadoway is a new way of thinking about them as sites of recreation, connectivity, wildlife habitat, animal migration, and a unique melding of human and natural landscape. 'It's an industrial reuse project,' said Corey Wells, also a senior project manager at TRCA. 'We've taken what has been typically viewed as not a place where someone would want to ride their bike or hang out, and flipped it on its side.' Wells points out there are more than five hundred kilometres of hydro corridors in Toronto, and the Scarborough project is something that can serve as a blueprint for how they can create new space for parks and wildlife. Toronto is known for its ravines, wild fissures that weave their way from north of the city down to the lake, generally running from north to south but not connecting laterally. The hydro corridors that cross Toronto are like human-made ravines, portage routes over the tablelands between one ravine system and another. As Wells said, 'It's the backbone of Scarborough.'

The Gatineau corridor climbs out of the Don Valley at what will be the Bermondsey Road 'Western Gateway' to the Meadoway, connecting to the East Don Trail that will lead right to downtown Toronto. From here the corridor runs east, linking seven rivers, fifteen parks, thirteen neighbour-hoods, and what will be more than two hundred hectares of cultivated meadows on its way to Rouge National Urban Park. Though not yet completed, much of the Meadoway can already be followed on foot or by bike to experience the various stages of this seven-year project, taking the traveller along a series of long and gentle grades rising from and lowering to the watersheds. Cycling the trail is a meditative experience as it meanders through the hydro towers, passing dozens of 'no mow' signs along the way that protect what Turnbull called this 'central habitat.' There's much more to the Meadoway than simply letting the grass grow, though.

Before the Meadoway, the Gatineau corridor would typically be mowed six times a year. 'It's pretty in-depth, what needs to be done,' said Turnbull. 'We look at it as a three- to five-year process. In year one, we start off doing farming practices and actually use farm equipment to remove the turf.' After the existing turf is taken care of by mowing and tilling, a cover crop of oats is planted. Its role is to reveal what other seeds are in the soil and might grow in place of the turf. The oats allow invasive species like dog-strangling vine and Canada thistle to grow, but also keep them in check, making them easier to remove. That crop will be mowed, and the process repeated four times throughout the summer, until they are satisfied they have suppressed all the non-desired and invasive species.

Then it is seeded in the fall to allow natural stratification – a process by which a period of cold and moist weather breaks seed dormancy through freezing and thawing, cracking the seed shell to allow it to absorb moisture – and then subsequent germination in the spring. 'We use a variety of seed mixes depending on the moisture regime in the soils and where we are within the sixteen kilometres,' said Turnbull. 'All seeds used are from local nurseries that provide native species sourced within Southern Ontario. We try to pick species that will help to increase species diversity, improve ecosystem health, provide a variety of bloom times throughout spring to fall, provide plant host species for pollinators and birds, have long root depths to help stabilize soils, be resilient to drought, and provide food sources in the winter for birds.'

There are dozens of different species planted, and the choice depends on the particular landscape, such as butterfly meadow, wet meadow, dry grass mix, upland slopes, and so on. The most seeded species are big bluestem, New England aster, oxeye, wild bergamot, evening primrose, switchgrass, black-eyed Susan, cup plant, blue vervain, common milkweed – and there are many more. At this point, TRCA moves to an adaptive management and monitoring phase, watching for more invasive species, monitoring how the meadow is coming up and doing infill seeding where necessary. While this is happening, the City of Toronto mows a 3.25-metre grass buffer along the trail, as well as a 5-metre buffer edge along homes that back onto the Meadoway. Ongoing maintenance is needed because, as Turnbull explained, every meadow will want to turn into a shrub thicket and then a forest.

'A big thing I always find in talking to residents along the path is that they are hearing pollinators,' said Turnbull. 'A lot of residents hadn't seen a lot of these insects or heard birds calling before, and all of a sudden the meadow brings a whole new habitat.' This effect is part of what Turnbull called enhanced ecological services: increasing the biodiversity and ecosystem resilience along the corridor. With taller meadow plants, birds, along with butterflies and other pollinators, now find a home there. For those staying through the winter, the meadow can now help them through the cold season; for migratory birds and butterflies, it provides a feeding and resting ground as they pass through. Deer and other larger wildlife can travel between ravine systems.

'For me, its power lies in its connectivity,' said Nina-Marie Lister, a professor at Toronto Metropolitan University's School of Urban and Regional Planning and director of the Ecological Design Lab, which ran a design workshop for the Meadoway. 'It's a space of connection across communities, but it's also a space across landscapes and topography.' Because a meadow has so much open sky, Lister said there's opportunity to see birds in ways we can't in the forest, and the open quality allows for sunlight that is good for growing things both for human consumption, through urban agriculture, and for enjoyment. 'I would describe it as a very different landscape experience,' she said. 'On the one hand it's physical, about connectivity, but visually it's about openness. The Meadoway is a kind of counterpoint to the ravines, which are folds in the landscape, whereas this provides a view across the tablelands.'

'A lot of the classic industrial reuse projects globally are ones where there was a historical industrial usage that has now stopped and it's been converted into a public space, like the High Line in New York,' said Wells. 'The Meadoway is unique in that it's still functioning for its primary purpose.' Wells points to Hydro One's 'Provincial Secondary Land Use Program,' which provides opportunities for other uses in the corridors as long as the primary one – transmitting electricity – can still function. These could include, for example, an adjacent developer building a parking lot, or the city maintaining playing fields under the wires. 'I think Hydro One is learning a lot, just as much as we are, about becoming a little bit more comfortable about what has typically been seen as a place where no people really spend any time,' said Wells. Apart from not planting trees that could interfere with the wires, Wells says the locations of plantings and trails are designed to be in harmony with maintenance needs, and that a meadow is a perfect in-between landscape that is compatible with all these uses.

The Meadoway is also an example of a public-private partnership – a concept more common in U.S. parks than in Canada. This public-private partnership was first created through the Weston Family Parks Challenge, a city parks initiative that funded the Scarborough Centre Butterfly Trail pilot. The success of that first revitalization led to a pledge of up to $25 million from the foundation to revitalize the entire two hundred hectares. The project is even more complex when considering how much ongoing public consultation goes into it. 'We developed something called the community liaison committee, reaching out to a number of local organizations, residents, NGOs, groups like WalkTO and BikeTO, and Scarborough bike repair groups,' said Wells. 'Like-minded individuals with different perspectives on how they might be able to utilize the space. We used them sort of as an initial sounding board.' All of this outreach produced buy-in and a sense of ownership from residents.

After the Meadoway's designers digested the input they had received, details were sorted out: benches, bike lock-ups, litter bins, and the design of trail intersections, where the Meadoway crosses north-south trails, to include ample seating, play areas, and more manicured garden sections. A wayfinding system is still in the planning stages. It will include educational signage telling people where they are and where they can go, but also informing them of the natural and Indigenous heritage of the area, as well as the geomorphology of the waterways the Meadoway traverses. There are some big obstacles in the way of creating a seamless natural corridor through a crowded city. Lister notes there are more than thirty road crossings along the Meadoway that pose challenges, not just for humans but for wildlife. 'If we prioritize pedestrians, and we prioritize the creatures who are most vulnerable to traffic, it's done by slowing the traffic,' said Lister. 'If the Meadoway is a priority, we need to think really big about what it means to have a healthy, accessible green space for the safe movement of people and wildlife, and that it's worthy of capital investment – as important as sewers and railways.'

While tunnels under roads are not a preferred solution, bridges are expensive. A smaller but useful example of the traffic slowing Lister mentioned can be seen where the Meadoway crosses Crockford Boulevard in the Golden Mile neighbourhood, a few kilometres west of Bendale. Rather than a signalized crossing, the road is 'pinched,' or narrowed, and the usual asphalt replaced with bricks, all of which push drivers to slow down. Highway 401, with its expanse of express and collector lanes, is perhaps the biggest barrier to a continuous Meadoway. It crosses the hydro corridor just north of the University of Toronto's Scarborough campus, as the corridor nears its terminus at Rouge National Urban Park. TRCA may route active transportation users through the campus, in harmony with the school's master plan, including the new switchback path that leads from the ravine floor up to the campus and onto Conlins Road, where protected bike lanes were recently installed to provide a route over the highway.

The TRCA is also hoping the Meadoway takes on a life of its own and becomes a catalyst for other changes along its path. 'In ten or fifteen years, I'd like to see a fully connected and seamless trail system from east to west,' said Wells. 'When new developments are being planned and parks are being enhanced, I hope they're all thinking of ways to connect to the Meadoway. I'm really hoping it becomes the veins of a leaf right across Scarborough.' Lister called it the 'ultimate teaching garden,' one that will influence not just other cities, but individuals and their private property. 'If the City and TRCA can do this, we can all do it.' She saw it as a literal, and metaphorical, seedbed for natural gardens. As for Turnbull, she hoped it will inspire people. 'I'm hopeful it will be a place where the community and the public can come and enjoy nature and biodiversity,' she said. 'I hope it will help them visualize that a different type of habitat in cities is possible. Bendale is neither the beginning nor end of the Meadoway, but rather Thomson Park is the middle and a good place to start an exploration of it, not just the Toronto town-and-country mix, but also an active industrial one.

Long before the power lines were put in, Bendale was one of the cradles of Scarborough civilization. Most of the activity took place along St. Andrews Road, a bucolic lane that curves around the small patches of forested ravine that run between McCowan and Brimley Roads. When you're strolling down St. Andrews, the city might as well be a thousand kilometres away. On misty mornings, the road feels and smells like rural Nova Scotia (another Scarborough theme, along with the Mediterranean vibes). In the middle of this sits

St. Andrew's Church, built in 1849. It still welcomes a Presbyterian congregation, some of whom are descendants of the Thomson family, the first European settlers in the area.

The Thomson clan's homes are still on St. Andrews Road and date back to the mid-1800s. Some bear historic plaques put up by the Scarborough Historical Society. The owners had great nicknames like 'Stonehouse Willie' and 'Springfield Jimmie,' names that referenced the geography and building materials of their houses.

Despite many thousands of years of pre-settler activity, and a sizable Indigenous population residing in Scarborough today, Indigenous peoples' presence and history isn't immediately visible, eclipsed by both colonial development and mythology. The cemetery stones in the St. Andrew's yard describe the taming of an untamed land, though one stone acknowledging who was here before has been added. Perhaps the most conspicuous site of the long Indigenous history in all of Toronto is near the intersection of Lawrence Avenue and Bellamy Road in Scarborough, where Tabor Hill rises above bungalows in the Bendale neighbourhood. As Scarborough's development marched on in the mid-1950s, a bulldozer disturbed the hill, revealing it was an ossuary with the remains of over five hundred humans buried here. Today a plaque at the top of the mound tells the story. There are other sites in Scarborough, some along the creek and river valleys, with ossuaries, though they are unmarked, both out of neglect and to preserve them from grave robbers who would disturb the remains for a variety of nefarious reasons.

The second wave of Bendale pioneers who filled up the new modern postwar homes were looking for the Canadian dream, the one we borrowed from America that involved backyards and driveways on winding cul-de-sacs. Some came from downtown or from the streetcar suburbs around the Danforth or St. Clair and started families here. Their backgrounds were mostly English and Scottish, but some Greek and Italian folks were attracted to the area too.

One of the developments east of McCowan Road is known as the Ben Jungle because every street begins with the prefix Ben; there's Benlight, Benlark, Benfrisco, Ben Nevis, Ben Stanton, Benroyal, and even Benhur and Benorama.

As the European families grew up and out, in came the Filipinos, Chinese, Sri Lankans, Indians, Afghanis, Persians, West Indians, and Somalis, and in the last couple decades, Bendale has gotten more and more interesting. The built environment suggests a *Leave It to Beaver* modernism designed with the car in mind. The plazas were built as rest stops on the way to bigger centres like Cedarbrae Mall or the Scarborough Town Centre. Yet so many of these new residents don't own cars and can't make it to these malls without a long journey. There are often long queues at windswept bus stops. Some of the plazas that are often criticized as bad urban planning have actually become centres for many people who lead what amounts to urban, or possibly èven village-style, lives in a suburban landscape.

Today, these fifties- and sixties-era plazas better emulate the idea of Main Street than do downtown neighbourhoods like the Annex or Little Italy. If you look past the parking lots, these places are often ungentrified, old-fashioned urban streets, places that people without cars, or without a lot of extra money, can get to.

These small businesses can survive and prosper in the shadow of the chains and malls because the rents out here are considerably cheaper than those downtown. The affordable nature of these malls opens up room for innovation, low-budget eccentricity and services that cater to individuals rather than broadly defined demographics.

If you stand still, even for a short period, you notice that everybody seems to know each other here. People say hi or nod to each other the way you do when you run into someone you don't know that well but see every day. The stores are busy. The big mosque nearby on Lawrence (it was first housed in a former car dealership but now has an impressive new building) holds barbecues in the summer. It, too, feels like a small town at times, but the another era of massive change may be here.

The Lawrence Avenue and McCowan Road intersection has had two incarnations over the last century. It's about to enter a third; how it will look and work is still a bit of a mystery, but some change is definitely coming. During its first colonial incarnation, the intersection was a rural crossroads. Then Toronto's postwar boom began to change Scarborough. Farm after farm became a sprawl of suburban-style houses, but, in the particular Metropolitan Toronto way, there were new hubs that were and are quite dense – city versions of the villages that were here before. At Lawrence and McCowan, apartment buildings of various sizes are served by the strip malls as another branch of Highland Creek passes by the intersection. Today, it still resembles this familiar Scarborough with one addition: a massive construction site for the Scarborough subway extension that will usher in its new era.

Toronto has been talking about the Scarborough subway for so long it seems like a lifetime – so long it doesn't seem real. A Toronto unicorn, talked about but never actually seen. Standing at the intersection in 2024 blows all that mythological inertia away, as piledrivers pound the earth and diggers excavate massive holes for Lawrence Station. The project is so enormous it took over the east side of the Scarborough General Hospital site and required the demolition of commercial buildings and a gas station on the southern corners. Lawrence Station makes sense geographically and for bus connections, but the area around it brings up another particular Metropolitan Toronto thing: we've built extremely expensive subway stations that are literally a stone's throw from houses with front and backyards, conditions that haven't changed much in a half-century along many parts of the current subway. Big infrastructure for a low population. Today, the tallest thing by forthcoming Lawrence station is the hospital's cool, round midcentury tower. Otherwise, it's all quite low. Low but interesting.

With the Highland Creek and Meadoway cycling and walking trails, as well as vast Thomson Park, Lawrence will become one of the best subway stations from which to begin an exploration of Toronto's urban natural and semi-natural areas. The question will be whether or not that very low density will give way to more places for people to live, for more Scarborough. The immediate area around the subway station was designed as a 'transit-oriented community' and should welcome dense housing developments. A good, small start, but Lawrence Station will be an expensive test to see if Toronto has learned anything over seventy years of subway- and city-building since this was farmland, so it's an area to watch to see if change will really come again.

Dorset Park

 neighbourhood jaunt   Connecting walks: None

 dress to impress

offspring friendly

When eastbound Highway 401 enters Scarborough at Victoria Park Avenue, its twelve to sixteen lanes move at high velocity in close quarters. Here, the Highway of Heroes is a city on wheels where the smallest mistake can be catastrophic. Out of the corners of their eyes – a glance any longer than a peripheral one is too long – drivers glimpse bits of Scarborough: the rooftops of houses, factories, townhouses, apartment towers, strip malls, big-box stores, and more roads.

As eastbound cars pass Birchmount Road, passengers and particularly skilful drivers may take a longer look at the leafy area to the south. Large trees – including giant willows – catch the breeze on rolling grassy hills. Behind them there's a wide, balconied apartment tower, and more like it scattered further south. There isn't any time on the freeway to wonder about this pocket of the city – it's gone before an impression of it can sink in – but this is the top of Dorset Park, a Scarborough neighbourhood of just over 25,000 people.

Though the City of Toronto designates it as such, the term *neighbourhood* is not the most accurate descriptor for this large area that runs from the 401 south to just below Lawrence Avenue East. It is made up of a relatively narrow strip of residential land that's sandwiched between an industrial area to the west and the former Scarborough RT line to the east. The southern part is largely made up of single-family bungalows, while the northern section above Ellesmere, the one that's in view of the 401, features a mixture of apartment towers and townhouses.

When you stand in Glamorgan Park, by those aforementioned towers and willows, the traffic on the 401 is white noise in the background, not terribly unpleasant, almost like the ocean surf (with the occasional down-shifting sputter from one of the big rigs – the asphalt-sea version of foghorns). You can see the highway and its blur of traffic in the gaps between the trees. From the park, the highway looks as fleeting as the park looked from the highway. The two places are close to one another, but they might as well be a real ocean apart; they move at different speeds and there's no communication between them. Here in the park, with that white noise in the background, it's not immediately evident why Dorset Park is one of Toronto's 'emerging neighbourhoods' (a designation evolution that was previously called a 'priority neighbourhood'), designated for focus because it doesn't boast the social services other parts of the city do.

You can reach Glamorgan Park from Kennedy Road via Antrim Crescent, which ends in a cul-de-sac by Glamorgan Junior Public School. The school, its parking lot, and the park blend together, creating a large public space. Apart from the trees, there are baseball diamonds, swings and other equipment, a splash pad, and washrooms in a rather cool mod building: everything you'd expect from a typical Canadian park. The Canadianness of this park – the bucolic semi-rural vibe that's often our shared image of this country, even if it's not nearly universal – seems almost cartoonish: witness the groundhogs that peek out of the dens they've dug around the park. When I was first in the park in the summer of 2009, one of them had even created an elaborate den and tunnel near a landscaping boulder at the entrance of the school parking lot. Though it had built its home in the path between the school and the park – hundreds of kids must have passed by it every day – this groundhog seemed at home and comfortable. Across Antrim, the grounds of the apartment tower also help put the 'park' in Dorset Park.

Back then, I met up with three neighbourhood women and some of their children near the groundhog boulder. They were part of a local group that had led a recent Jane's Walk, the community-led walking tours that happen in the city every May. Abeer Ali, originally from Egypt, Feriba Mirza from Afghanistan, and Abeer Abukhaled from Saudi Arabia all call Dorset Park home, and, within minutes, their love for their neighbourhood and the care they devote to it was clear.

'This is our hub,' said Ali, gesturing to the school and park. 'If you come late in the afternoon, there will be five or ten families here.' Mirza continued, 'Here in the park, each picnic table will have a different family from a different place – Afghanistan, Saudi Arabia. Everybody shares sweets, and our kids play with each other.'

Yodit Tsegaye was a community engagement worker with Action for Neighbourhood Change, a United Way–funded organization that operated in nine of the city's then-priority neighbourhoods. She had also been along for the tour. 'The school has ESL classes and space for community meetings,' she said. 'No services are provided in the area, so we use the schools as well as Toronto Community Housing buildings that provide us a little space.'

This is why one experiences some cognitive dissonance when standing by the park, wondering why this is a priority neighbourhood. The unseen things, those that are missing, are the problem. Downtown neighbourhoods, and those that are older and more compact, have services – community centres, libraries, public health facilities – that are usually just a short walk away from the homes of those who use them. Neighbourhoods like Dorset Park are so spread out that the same services are much further away. Enter the fundamental design flaw in suburban planning that makes life difficult for the people who live here: areas such as this were built on the assumption that all residents have cars and will use them to get to the distant services, shopping malls, and other activities. With the influx of new Canadians and less affluent residents, a pedestrian culture has been grafted onto an automobile landscape, and sometimes it's a hard fit.

We strolled along the side of the school to a place where the walking residents of Dorset Park collide with its poor design. A narrow sidewalk, fenced in with chain-link on both sides, runs a few hundred metres between a condominium property and industrial land, then turns left for a similar distance. It's an important passageway between the school and park and the residential area to the south. For those on foot, it cuts travelling time down considerably, but with only two entrances/exits and poor lighting, it can be an unpleasant and almost claustrophobic place.

'This is the most important problem,' explained Ali. 'During the winter and summer months, there is no maintenance. Along here, this factory hasn't cut the grass for five years, so we don't know what might be hiding in there. When we walk through, it's one child at a time in a line because the fence is broken and it isn't safe for them.' The women pointed out that the bottom of the chain-link fence was installed quickly and cheaply likely decades ago, and the sharp ends of the wire were now ready to catch the pant leg or skirt of pedestrians. Mirza said her six-year-old son got caught on the fence and fell face-first into the concrete, winding up with a bloody nose. 'In winter, we all hold on to each other to get through,' she continued. 'They do plow it, but at ten o'clock at night. What about at 8:00 a.m., when everybody uses it?' Further down the pathway, the fence bends in where the condo parking-lot plow pushed the snow, further encroaching on the public space. Walking the same route fifteen years later, we see that the fences are still in poor shape and still block what might be natural routes between buildings – and to the rundown but absolutely vintage 1970s playground equipment between the towers. A utility cover with '1974' marked on it in steel gives an indication of when this all came to be. A bench of the same vintage suggests no one has thought to take care of or update this area for residents.

In 2009, we continued through the neighbourhood to a spot where the towers give way to townhouses. Today a new, long-awaited modular housing project at 39 Dundalk Drive provides homeless people with a first stable home until something more permanent can be found. The project is long-awaited but not enough. To the south, at Kennedy and Ellesmere, a plaza has imperfect connections with the neighbourhood: more fences and dirt paths despite the importance of this place for the community (though, post-pandemic the retail wasn't as filled out as it was in 2009).

Like much of Scarborough, Dorset Park was nearly all rich agricultural land just over fifty years ago. Scarborough Township, as it was known, was dotted with small villages like Wexford, Bendale, and West Hill. When I visited her in 2009, Doreen Brown had been a resident of the area since 1955, when Dorset Park was preparing to welcome the first wave of post-development residents. Brown had pictures of herself sitting on the foundation of her house as it was being constructed in 1955, only months after it was farmland. Of the days before and during the transition from rural to suburban, Brown said: 'Since the late 1800s, the areas of the present community of Dorset Park

and the Kennedy Commons Plaza were all farmland. Eventually, around the turn of the century, several commercial merchants began to locate along Kennedy Road – especially between Sheppard and Lawrence Avenues. Lansing Buildall, a lumber and building supply business operated by William Kitchen, was one of these merchants. His lumberyard was situated on the east side of Kennedy Road, just north of Ellesmere.'

When I visited Brown's house on Exford Drive, full of Scarborough artifacts, the one-woman Dorset Park archive showed me cardboard displays of the area's history that detail where the old can be found among the new, as well as the places that go back further than the Second World War. There's the original Rutherford Farm farmhouse at 34 Kecala Road (now the manse of St. Giles Anglican Church), which is today surrounded by standard suburbia. It requires a leap of imagination to see it alone in the fields as it once was. Brown then took me on a walk to Rutherford Farm and around her neighbourhood. You can't catch all the details on a quick pass through a place like this, details that, in fact, make it a place. Bits of history are scattered here and there – old homes, churches, graveyards – and even these 1950s bungalows are beginning to feel the weight of history. Entire families have moved in, grown up, and moved out, and the cycle has begun and even finished again in some cases. New becomes old (though not yet 'historic,' as that would imply a kind of universal admiration).

One of a rare breed of Dorset Park resident even in 2009, Brown was an 'original' who lived in the house that was built for her family. (They added a second storey at one point and now tenants live upstairs – an example of the kind of densification that happens downtown too.) One of her cardboard displays detailed the wooden milk chutes that each of these houses have, though they are no longer used for their intended purpose. The postwar and modern features on most of these homes make these tiny doors for milk-bottle delivery seem anachronistic. Brown had documented what some of her neighbours had done to them: some used them to collect mail, others stored yard tools in them, and one told stories of her son squeezing through the chute when he was locked out of the house as a boy.

Brown was active in organizing the local community but lamented the difficulty of getting people out to meetings. She was conscious of the new vs. old, high-rise vs. house divide among residents, and noticed that many 'old-timers' weren't present at meetings. She tried to bridge those gaps when she could with events like 'get-to-know-your-neighbour night.' 'We don't want to think of this as North and South Dorset Park,' she said. Of all the new families moving in, including the women I had met earlier (Brown had also participated in the Jane's Walk with them), she said, 'To me, it's like going back to when we moved in here. Everybody raising wee kids. It's just we were Anglo-Saxon and they are Middle Eastern.'

When Highway 401 was completed across the top of Toronto in the 1950s – it was then known as the Toronto Bypass, and later officially named the Macdonald-Cartier Freeway, though no one ever calls it that – it looked much like the standard four-lane highways that cross the Ontario countryside outside of major population areas. The 401, as well as the expansion of small country roads into arterials in the township, fed Scarborough's dramatic and quick growth. Though those groundhogs in Glamorgan Park seem out of place in an urban wilderness, fifty years is a blip in nature, so perhaps they're just waiting for us to move on again.

In what is now the Kennedy Commons shopping plaza, there's no longer a lumberyard at the site of Lansing Buildall. It's now a Chinese supermarket called Foody World, though William Kitchen lives on in the name of the street that bisects the parking lot.

Outside of Kennedy Commons' controlled retail environment is a more unpredictable retail environment. The Kennedy Road Business Improvement Area (BIA) organization, one of a handful of such organizations found in Scarborough – most BIAS are located within the old City of Toronto boundaries – describes the area as having 'a wide variety of businesses to meet your needs' and as 'recognized as one of the most diverse shopping districts in the entire GTA. We have over three hundred businesses and services to choose from.'

It's a strange but enticing description to read – a Wild West of unfettered retail – and just as strange a walk. The blocks are extremely long here, with few breaks for intersections. There's even a painted moose, a Mayor Mel Lastman project from the turn of the century, greeting drivers as they exit the 401. A walk down Kennedy is not unlike a walk in the country, where your path is rarely disturbed by traffic lights or obstacles. Such meditative, if loud, strolls seem at odds with the suburban environment, but these streets are good for ambulatory thinking. There's lots to look at too: there's GO SMASH, which bills itself as Scarborough's first 'rage room,' where you can shatter glass and crush old electronics, as well as an abundance of neon yellow and green lawn signs lining Kennedy that advertise various stores and products, and are perhaps a result of the numerous sign-making shops that do business along this road.

The BIA has made improvements along Kennedy that include stylized light poles and fixtures, streetscaping, and boulevard planters filled with lush and colourful flowers. Though they're meant more for car passengers than pedestrians, such flourishes do have the effect of taming a huge street like Kennedy and making it less of a pavement desert. The BIA represents only the businesses along Kennedy and has no responsibility to Dorset Park itself, and it's telling that the priorities of urban beautification still revolve around automobile routes, while residents struggle for years for simple solutions to their pathway problems.

South of Ellesmere, you'll find the bungalows where long-time Dorset Park residents live next to the successive waves of residents who have made this place home. Black-clad European widows sit on their porches, across the street from houses flying Tamil flags. As we walk around the quiet streets, it's clear that suburban neighbourhoods like these are to present-day Toronto what College Street, Dundas, and Cabbagetown were to the city fifty or a hundred years ago: places that can absorb a varied population, where working-class Canadians and new Canadians – overlapping groups, for sure – can perhaps afford to buy homes and live out their version of the Canadian dream. It's a less expensive place in Toronto terms, though not by much, but it's the 'blank-slate' nature of these areas (which unsympathetic folks might call 'sterile' or 'boring') that lets new forms of neighbourhood and urban culture flourish without the heavy, prescriptive history that some downtown neighbourhoods have. Out here, history is very much happening now, and there is no official guide to what comes next.

At first, Dorset Park seems not very different from the suburban Windsor neighbourhood I grew up in. It feels the same and, though I've never lived here, being in Dorset Park is like visiting a familiar haunt I haven't been to for a while. The landscape makes sense to me.

My old neighbourhood, though, was somewhat more exurban, with fields and forests nearby. Dorset Park is more urban, with curbs and strip malls. And while the suburb I grew up in has grown over the years, it's remained a quiet, suburban kind of place. Dorset Park and other neighbourhoods like it – some 'priority,' some not – have stayed largely the same in their landscape and infrastructure, but are really urban at heart, with all the mix and needs of any big city. Kids in exurbia can play in fields and forests, while the kids in Dorset Park – and there are a lot of them, many more than in downtown neighbourhoods – have less space for this activity, so places like recreation centres become critical.

The future for a place like this is bright because of its residents. In 2008, Abeer Ali won a community-building award for her work in the neighbourhood. 'I didn't sleep until I called my mom in Egypt,' she told me not long after she received her award. 'I scanned it in and emailed it to her.' The award was a small gesture, but, according to Ali, 'what it also did was get a lot of other women to join in and help.' Here we see the beginnings of community activism that may one day evolve into a formidable organization like the high-rise-developer-hating Annex Residents' Association downtown. If that happens, small things like that walkway won't take years to fix. The residents I met have just that kind of commitment to Dorset Park. 'Before, this neighbourhood was a place people came and left,' says Ali. 'But now people try to stay.'

Thorncliffe, Flemingdon Park, and Don Mills

 pack a lunch   Connecting walk: Danforth/Crescent Town

 dress to impress

 scenic views

According to Graeme Stewart of ERA Architects, driving on the Don Valley Parkway between the 401 and Bloor is the most modern moment you can have in the city, perhaps even the country. As the road curves through the ravine, hundreds of high-rise apartments poke out above the forest, channelling one of those futuristic and utopian *Star Trek* cities. A number of these high-rises are located in the neighbourhood of Thorncliffe Park, just north of the Leaside Bridge, a span that's nearly as impressive as (but much less celebrated than) the Prince Edward Viaduct a few kilometres south.

Standing on the bridge affords a beautiful view not just of the valley but of the DVP itself. The highway is a stunning piece of engineering as highways go, a two-way steel river that runs next to the slower Don River. Torontonians who don't want to drive to the country to engage in 'leaf peeping' can still see all the fall colours from this bridge, where the white mod high-rises of Thorncliffe Park contrast with the blazing colours below.

Thorncliffe is like a huge apartment island and is surrounded by deep ravines on three sides. Light-industrial land separates it from Leaside, its upscale neighbour to the west. It's hard to imagine walking to Thorncliffe from anywhere, as it seems so cut off from the rest of the city, but when you walk up from the Danforth, it turns out that the valley is a bigger psychological barrier than it is a physical one. If you're at the northern end of the Leaside Bridge, stay left and you'll get to Leaside proper. But turn right at Overlea Boulevard and you'll find yourself where Thorncliffe begins. In the early 1800s, George Taylor named the house he built here 'Thorn Cliff.' Later, his daughter and her husband turned it into Thorncliffe Farms and then sold it to a Baltimore concern who built a racetrack that remained until 1952, when it was torn down so the area could be developed into apartment complexes. All that's left of the racetrack era are two short streets – referred to as 'places' – named Milepost and Grandstand.

Thorncliffe became, and still is, one of Toronto's largest rental districts (though there are some condo buildings), comprised of over thirty low- and high-rise buildings totalling nearly six thousand units that are home to 21,000 residents, though it was designed for far fewer. In her book *Leaside*, former Toronto councillor and mayoral candidate Jane Pitfield wrote that 'a unique piece of history … all but disappeared' when East York Council renamed Thorncliffe 'East York Centre' in 1993. Unlike most of Toronto's family-friendly neighbourhoods, which are generally made up of detached or semi-detached dwellings, in Thorncliffe, housing is almost exclusively in large apartment buildings. Though Thorn-cliffe is located relatively close to the central part of Toronto and remains an imminently walkable neighbourhood, it's somewhat geographically isolated, surrounded on the south and east sides by the lush and sinuous Don Valley, and to the north and west by a light-industrial landscape.

The Don Valley pathway passes through E. T. Seaton Park below. A connecting route runs up a long and steep driveway that starts from the lower parking lot and leads up to Thorncliffe Park Drive. In the summer, you can watch people play cricket in the shadows of the tri-footed towers down in the valley and observe the mountain-bikers who regularly pop out of the forest after riding the single-track trails along the Don.

All the buildings in Thorncliffe surround the East York Town Centre, a mall that serves as the area's high street. Though many of Toronto's suburban tower communities were built for the car, Thorncliffe is remarkably walkable, as each building is no more than a few hundred metres from the mall.

Inside, the whirl of the blender at Real Fruit Bubble Tea intermittently drowns out the din of conversation in the mall's airy food court. It's a busy place. People nurse coffee they brought over from the Tim Hortons that always seems to have a lineup by the mall entrance. Others eat food out of plastic containers from Chester Fried Chicken or Kandahar Kabab. The joyous

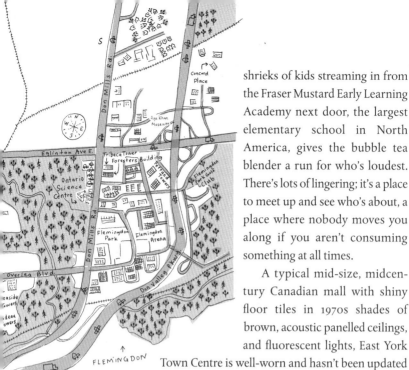

shrieks of kids streaming in from the Fraser Mustard Early Learning Academy next door, the largest elementary school in North America, gives the bubble tea blender a run for who's loudest. There's lots of lingering; it's a place to meet up and see who's about, a place where nobody moves you along if you aren't consuming something at all times.

A typical mid-size, midcentury Canadian mall with shiny floor tiles in 1970s shades of brown, acoustic panelled ceilings, and fluorescent lights, East York Town Centre is well-worn and hasn't been updated much. Nevertheless, the mall has become Thorncliffe Park's de facto town square. 'I think East York Centre is the one of the essential parts of the neighbourhood,' said Sabina Ali, chair and one of the founders of the Thorncliffe Park Women's Committee. 'It is like a recreation space, especially for the seniors.' There are indoor walking groups for seniors and women. During cold winters, parents pick their kids up from school and bring them to the mall, feeding them meals brought from home. 'It's a really important place to meet with friends and neighbours and spend quality time talking while having a coffee or some food,' she said.

The mall's draw as a social space isn't a new phenomenon: for decades the Thorncliffe Bowlerama was a near-perfectly preserved subterranean recreation lair with both five- and ten-pin bowling lanes and a bar in the middle. Throughout the mall's history, discount department stores have acted as anchor tenants – the kind of big retailers malls covet, not only because they're a draw unto themselves, but also because two or more anchors draw people between them, increasing circulation, browsing, and spending. Sayvette, a now-defunct Canadian discount department store, handed the discount baton to Woolco in the mid-seventies. That space later became a Zellers. And in 2013, the mall got an injection of retail star power when Target moved in, part of the American chain's much-heralded expansion into Canada.

Malls like East York, with their varying mix of independent retailers and chains, are found all around Toronto – Eglinton Square in Scarborough; Sheridan and Centrepoint Malls in North York; Albion Mall in Etobicoke; Lawrence Allen Centre, and the demolished Galleria Mall, in the old City of Toronto – and all play similar roles in their communities. When Target announced the closure of all their Canadian stores in 2015, however, many malls were left with enormous holes to fill in their floor plans. At East York, the upper two floors of a key anchor space were left empty. Then, in 2016, the Bowlerama closed its doors too. Coupled with a new Costco big-box retail location that has opened across the street, drawing more people away, the future of this mall might seem like it's part of the 'dying mall' phenomenon occurring across the United States, where once-prosperous malls have lost their anchor tenants, starving smaller stores of a critical mass of shoppers.

At East York, the cheaper rents have allowed independent mom-and-pop shops to flourish, businesses that couldn't afford the overhead of Toronto's high-rent main streets and more prosperous malls. But while the small spaces are ideal for individual ventures, vast anchor spaces are harder to fill. A Dollarama eventually moved into some of the main floor space, keeping the discount retail tradition alive, as did an A&W franchise, but there was still more space to fill. Enter the Flemingdon Health Centre (FHC) and the Neighbourhood Organization (TNO), two health and social service agencies that saw an opportunity to serve local residents in the languishing retail space.

'Maybe five or six years ago there was a recognition in the Thorncliffe community that there was a lack of comprehensive primary care,' said John Elliott, then the executive director of the FHC, in 2018. Health care in the community was scattershot: there were physicians treating people at walk-in clinics, and others operating at independent offices, but nothing that looked after the long-term health of the community as a whole, no central place that would promote social and physical health and illness prevention in the community as much as treating colds and pulled muscles. Since everyone was already at the mall, it was a natural place for a hub where all of this could be centralized and coordinated: a one-stop shop for getting better and staying healthy.

Within living memory of some Torontonians, Thorncliffe Park has gone from a rural landscape to the dense urban form that exists today. As the region grew rapidly in the postwar years, the town of Leaside, a former municipality now part of Toronto, redeveloped the land into a then-innovative modern apartment neighbourhood that could house entire families, a living arrangement common in Europe. Initially marketed to young and upwardly mobile couples keen to start families, the yuppies of their day, the neighbourhood has since seen massive demographic changes that were not part of the original plan.

Over the years, Thorncliffe has attracted newcomers, including a substantial number of recent Syrian refugees, drawn by the large apartments and slightly lower rents than those found in the city core. Today, Thorncliffe Park is one of the densest clusters of people in Canada and a 'landing pad' neighbourhood for immigrants. Toronto's multiculturalism mix is profound here: based on the 2016 census, 73 per cent of the population has a mother tongue that isn't French or English, with Urdu speakers leading the way, followed by Persian, Pashto, Tagalog, Gujarati, Arabic, Punjabi, Bengali, Spanish, and Greek. It's a young, family-oriented community, with 26.8 per cent of the population under fourteen years old.

While bus service is good, many people don't leave the area much due to the costs of travel, said Elliott. On a sailing excursion for neighbourhood youth, some of the kids had never ridden the subway before or seen Lake Ontario. 'A lot of the kids, when they saw the lake, said, "Oh, we didn't know it was a sea next to the city,"' said Ahmed Hussein, executive director of the TNO, a multiservice provider that offers programs and assistance to newcomers, refugees, and youth. 'Even though they live in the city, they also don't.'

While the eventual opening of the Ontario Line subway will include a Thorncliffe station and make the neighbourhood less isolated, the mall's health hub offers a unique opportunity to treat a community where they live. For forty years, the local health centre has operated out of Flemingdon Park, the community adjacent to Thorncliffe, providing a wide range of primary health care and health-related activities. In looking to address the needs in Thorncliffe Park, the health centre worked with the TNO to build something different. The model they created, called Health Access Thorncliffe Park, is a hub that will bring together a variety of health and social services in the former Target store. 'That was the unique piece of the HATP model,' said Elliot. A visit to a walk-in clinic won't happen in isolation. Instead, it will be integrated with the hub, so follow-up visits can be arranged and the patient's long-term health prospects can be monitored and improved. Other partners have come onboard, including the Toronto Healthcare Clinic located in the mall, a group of midwives, the local schools, Sunnybrook and Michael Garron hospitals, the United Way, the Toronto Central Local Health Integration Unit, and Toronto Public Health.

The ultimate plan is to provide primary health coverage, chronic disease management, newcomer services, mental health care, maternal reproductive care, and newborn, child, and youth services, all in the former department store. 'No one who lives in Thorncliffe has to walk more than two hundred metres to get to the mall,' said Hussein. 'People are coming to the mall anyway, to socialize and to shop, so why not bring all those services under one roof? Having our hub in the mall will help the stability of the mall, which has nothing to do with our intended outcomes, but it will be good for the community.' In a sense, it's a reinvention of the traditional mall by tapping into what malls do best: bring people into the same space. Spending time in a mall may seem like an insignificant pastime, but malls are places where community is built, especially in postwar, car-oriented cities where the traditional public realm – places you could bump into neighbours and where you might even promenade – either doesn't exist or is substandard. That, and in winter Toronto gets rather cold. It may seem obvious, but judging by architectural and landscape renderings of new developments, you'd be forgiven for thinking we live in a perpetual June, as so little thought is given to cold-weather public spaces. Just south of the mall is R. V. Burgess Park, famously revitalized by Sabina Ali and her women's committee, even getting a tandoor community oven installed, though the park sometimes suffers from the same lack of civic maintenance much of Toronto's public realm endures.

True town squares are located in public space and owned by everyone, while these malls are private, so the rules and management's tolerance for the community life flourishing under their roofs could change arbitrarily. It's a provisional kind of community space, and one that isn't sexy either. Malls like East York don't get the kind of attention newly landscaped parks and squares created by internationally renowned designers do, but they mean just as much to the fabric of the city. Health care isn't particularly sexy either, nor should it need to be. What's exciting here is the creation of a more permanent, public-focused space inside of a mall that, by chance, became the vital, if precarious, community space it is today.

Back outside, the twin slabs of the Leaside Towers located to the east of the mall stand out like giant monoliths from *2001: A Space Odyssey*, though instead of solid black they're glass and concrete. When they opened in 1970, they were Canada's tallest apartment buildings, and the penthouses could be rented for $750/month. For many newcomers who call this neighbourhood home, the idea called to mind by the word *Canada* is not rural, pastoral, or small-town, but an intensely modern place like this one.

This landscape continues across the Overlea Bridge to Don Mills Road and Flemingdon Park, so it connects two of Toronto's densest apartment neighbourhoods. The bridge is a busy four lanes, with narrow sidewalks and no provision for cyclists. It feels precarious to cross. 'This bridge is our community sidewalk,' said Zanib Zaakia, a seventeen-year-old student who was, along with other students, presenting their ideas to make the bridge better, as it's slated for refurbishment. The students pointed out that three thousand pedestrians cross the bridge daily and that the sidewalks are so narrow there was no way to physically distance during the pandemic. Plus, there's bad drainage, so vehicles routinely splash pedestrians with water and slush. Students also said their family and friend connections are located on both sides of the bridge.

Walking up Don Mills toward the Ontario Science Centre gives a sense of what a lot of Toronto outside the core is like: six to eight lanes of fast arterial traffic. For an alternate route, go back down that valley driveway to E. T. Seaton Park and walk up the ravine path toward Sunnybrook, past the civic archery range, but take the Science Centre exit (there are way-finding signs all along) and come up past all the cascading concrete that was poured down the side of the ravine to form the Science Centre, a 1970s brutalist building designed by Toronto architect Raymond Moriyama. The Science Centre is a great example of how brutalism actually brings the inside outside and closer to nature better than other architectural styles. As you descend between the building segments inside, it's as if you're moving through the forest itself, but then you're deposited into another exhibit room en route to the bottom of the ravine. It's always curious to me why natural rocky environments are appreciated and held in wonder, but human-made ones are often the target of contempt.

The intersection of Eglinton and Don Mills is a ten-lane-wide no-man's-land that is being tempered somewhat by the arrival of the Eglinton Crosstown tracks and attendant cycling and pedestrian improvements. The former IBM and Celestica campus on the northwest corner is being turned into a massive residential and commercial complex, retaining some of the midcentury IBM heritage facades.

Behind and southeast of the intersection is Flemingdon Park, Toronto's first planned apartment community, built between 1958 and the early 1970s on the farm of 1890s mayor Robert John Fleming. It's a maze of townhouses and apartment buildings, with underground parking and courtyard playgrounds where, in 1965, *Ontario Homes and Living* said, 'Mothers can watch their children play from their windows.' Today many chain-link fences that block movement – there's a strip mall here, but all the fences make it hard to figure out how to get to it – suggest that utopia has not yet been reached, or, perhaps, has been blocked. Flemingdon Park is worth a walk-through to find the niches that are rather cozy: small courtyards with trees, say, or the vast open space under the wires in the hydro corridor.

Nearby, a $200 million donation from the Aga Khan facilitated the creation of a centre for Toronto's expatriate Ismaili community, along with a stunning museum and landscaped grounds. This is something of a cultural precedent in Toronto, with the Aga Khan Museum and the Japanese Canadian Cultural Centre tucked in behind (its original Moriyama-designed building, a brutal beauty, is just across the DVP), though it's set to be integrated into a new development.

All the land to the north of here is Don Mills, Toronto's (and perhaps Canada's) most influential suburb because it both invented and came to define what suburban living was in this country. While it's the geographic centre of Toronto, to walk Don Mills is to go back to the future, back to a modern vision of the future that's now over sixty years old.

The parkette on the northeast corner of Don Mills and Lawrence, in the centre of the community, is named after urban planner Macklin Hancock, a local hero. When he was just twenty-seven years old, Hancock took a leave from his graduate studies at Harvard to work for Toronto tycoon E. P. Taylor, the financier behind Canada's first planned suburb. Built between 1952 and 1965, Don Mills was, and is, a modern wonderland that garnered postwar headlines in local papers like 'The Suburb That Is to Become Canada's Most Perfect City' and 'Toronto's Bright Satellite between the Forks of the Don.'

E. P. Taylor lived a few kilometres east on Bayview at his Windfields estate – now home to the Canadian Film Centre – and began purchasing working farms in 1947. Taylor's plan was to build a new brewery – his holding company, Argus Corporation (later owned by Conrad Black), owned the O'Keefe Brewery Company – but in the end, a massive new community was planned instead. Hancock's plan, though brand new for Canada, was a modern take on the English Garden City model developed a half-century earlier, where residential, commercial, industrial, and agricultural uses were balanced with greenbelts throughout.

Though it's relatively close to downtown, Don Mills is also physically isolated, surrounded by ravines and railways. Turn onto any of the residential streets and you soon lose your sense of direction due to the twists and curves of the streets. Low-rise apartment buildings mix in with townhouses and single-family homes. Some of those homes have fantastic space-age designs, with massive panes of glass and roofs that slope to the ground.

This place is mother to most Canadian suburbs that followed. In 1977, John Sewell (who would become mayor two years later) said in a *Globe and Mail* article that already 'it is difficult to overestimate the influence of Don Mills on urban development in Canada. By the 1970s, the planning of every Canadian city was dominated by the suburban form espoused by Hancock.' Walking around the neighbourhood, you begin to notice subtle but important differences from many of the suburbs that came after. Over two hundred different home designs were built in Don Mills, far more than are offered in contemporary suburban developments. You can still see the gentle roll of the Ontario countryside here. Homes and apartment parking garages are built into hillsides. For Sewell, developments that followed similar principles were 'the ghosts of Don Mills – but in a sad way.'

If you travel up to the fringe of GTA sprawl, north of Major Mackenzie Drive, you'll find landscapes that look like images from clear-cut Brazilian rainforests, where the land is shaved down to an empty, muddy, uniform plain, waiting for streets and houses. In Don Mills, efforts were made to preserve and work around mature trees, and in some spots the narrow tentacles of ravines reach up between homes to the street.

The problem with suburbs is that they are neither city nor country; they try to do the impossible by being both. Don Mills might come as close as possible to attaining a balance. In the southeast quadrant, take a walk down to Moccasin Trail Park – it's tucked underneath Don Mills, by the DVP. An artificial pond was constructed here in the early 2000s to contain stormwater, but it's already natural-looking and home to at least one rather extroverted beaver. If you follow the path nearby, you'll come across a long cement tunnel that smells of pot and teenagers and that passes under the DVP into a clearing that leads to the Rainbow Tunnel (which northbound highway commuters can see from their cars). Through this looking-glass passageway you can see a quiet and hidden near-wilderness crossed by the paths along the Don that lead under what is likely Toronto's most impressive railway bridge. Look across the shallow river and you'll see the rusting ruins of the old Don Valley Ski Club.

Hancock's design incorporated nature and people from the very beginning. Karl Frank, a landscape architect who worked with Hancock and has lived in Don Mills since 1970, noted that many of the residential streets were narrower in Hancock's original design and that the natural watercourses were preserved. 'They wanted to avoid costly infrastructure,' recalled Frank in 2007. 'They tried to use as much of the topography as possible for drainage.' However, in the 1980s the soft shoulders and ditches were replaced with curbs and gutters for aesthetic reasons, and the natural absorption of runoff was curtailed. 'People just didn't like the ditches.'

Though it was built when the car was king, many residents of Don Mills, such as Jeanetta Vickers, who had lived here for forty-eight years when we chatted in the late 2000s, get along just fine without cars. 'It's very handy here. I don't drive, but I can walk everywhere,' she told me. 'There are a lot of seniors here who don't need a car.' Vickers said she raised her children in Don Mills, and now they and her grandchildren live there – 'once a Don Miller, always a Don Miller.'

Joan and Ernie Simpson lived at 57 Jocelyn Crescent in Don Mills for sixty years. They purchased the house in 1959 for $19,000, the second owners, and not long after Don Mills became the most talked- and written-about new suburb in Canada. They lived in it until they passed away in 2020, and, with some mixed emotions, it was sold a few months later by their son, Jeff Simpson. 'I was brought home from hospital to that house,' said Simpson. 'They were in an apartment on Brentcliffe Road in Leaside and picked Don Mills, as it was new and affordable for a young family. Their best friends told me my parents hosted all the parties back in the day, as they were one of the few couples to own a home.' Jocelyn Cresent was one of the first streets developed there, so theirs was a very early Don Mills–style house. It's something of a celebrity too. The Simpson home was featured on a 1998 Canada Post stamp, part of a series that paid tribute to the evolution of housing history in Canada and a recognition of 'more than fifty years of service by Canada Mortgage and Housing Corporation (established in 1946).' The house also served as a filming location, including for the Our Lady Peace video of their 1999 song 'Is Anybody Home?'

Ernie was an architect and keen on modern Don Mills, while Joan was an artist. 'My dad did have the studio built for my mom,' said Simpson of the small, house-like structure in the backyard. 'He was working with Viceroy homes at the time, so if the studio looks like a "Lakeland" [model house], that's why.' As in many neighbourhoods not locked down by blanket heritage conservation district protections, many perfectly mod homes have slowly been replaced by highly renovated ones or McMansions. That's why 57 Jocelyn was so remarkable: the owners largely kept the exterior as it was when brand new. It makes for a heterogeneous architectural landscape now, but perhaps that's more like than unlike most of Toronto. Living neighbourhoods all change to some degree: people plant trees, add windows, change the siding.

Fifty-seven sold for just over $2 million, around $500,000 over the listed price. That $19,000 the Simpsons paid in 1959, when Ernie was thirty-two years old and Joan twenty-seven, plugged into the Bank of Canada's inflation calculator in 2021, was worth the equivalent of $171,620. Housing, of course, follows its own wild inflationary patterns, but that's something to remember next time the question of why it's harder for young people, or anyone without a lot of cash, to afford the city today: the playing field is radically different. Remember, too, that stamp celebrating the CMHC: there was a time when Canada put maximum effort and money into helping Canadians house themselves, something that's missing now. Any time you hear older generations say it was just as hard to buy a house or rent in their day, they should be asked to show their math. The Simpson story is also one of 'aging in place,' a future many of us hope for. 'Their wish was to die in their home and not move to long-term care,' said Jeff. 'It took a lot of support to keep them there, as dementia for both was making it tough. But with some great personal support workers and support from family, they were able to stay in the house.' Later in 2021, the new owners applied for a permit to build a new house at 57.

The utopian view of Don Mills is not shared by everyone, however. Author Lawrence Hill devoted a chapter in his book *Black Berry, Sweet Juice: On Being Black and White in Canada* to the neighbourhood. His parents moved from Washington, D.C., and settled in Don Mills in the early 1960s. 'It was a challenging terrain to navigate,' he told me. 'Nine out of ten days, it was a normal [suburban] life, hanging out at the rink, playing on teams. Then on the tenth day, somebody would spit in my face and call me a n——. It happened enough to keep me off balance.'

For many ethnic groups who were here during the WASP-dominated Toronto-the-Good era, this is a city-wide phenomenon. 'I may have faced similar things in other places,' said Hill. 'It's strange that my parents were fleeing one of the most highly charged racial places in the U.S., and they took us to Don Mills. They were looking for an escape hatch. Well, they found it. Then we had to find a way out.'

In the late 2000s, Don Mills Centre, a lower-tier enclosed mall in the middle of the community, was transformed from a place that welcomed the mall-walkers and seniors sipping coffee in the food court to a high-end outdoor mall. Locals mounted a campaign to save the dowdy mall from what ultimately became the Shops at Don Mills, a busy place, but one that caters to a different demographic than it previously served. Similarly, the residential and commercial development that replaced the Galleria Mall at Dufferin and Dupont raised questions about what will happen to the community – in the Galleria's case, a swath of Toronto's west-side working-class population – that uses malls like these as their town square on both a daily basis and special occasions (like watching World Cup games on a widescreen TV set up in the central court).

The Shops at Don Mills is an interesting and new exercise in planning for Toronto, the retail equivalent of New Urbanist ideas, recreating a series of traditional 'main streets,' though instead of being home to a variety of mom-and-pop stores, it's dominated by chains and large retailers. While there are still places for people to gather, they are generally all outdoors, and this is (occasionally) wintry Canada, after all. Still, people were able to gather long before malls were invented. Maybe the sense of community Don Mills residents felt can endure just fine. For now, the Shops have a film-set quality to them: they seem like real streets, but slightly off. Things are too new, the street signs and bike stands look like Toronto's but just a little different. In the middle of it all, there's *Starburst Clock Tower* with its 'exploding' model houses flying in all directions, designed by Douglas Coupland. Like the sculpture, walking around the Shops is a little like a dream, where reality is skewed just a bit, and that's probably a lot like how Don Mills itself felt when it was first built.

Eastish

The Danforth and Crescent Town

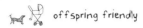 neighbourhood jaunt

dress to impress

offspring friendly

Connecting walks: Thorncliffe/
Flemingdon Park/Don Mills, Castle Frank/
Brick Works

Somewhere on the Prince Edward Viaduct, Bloor Street becomes the Danforth. There's no marker, but Torontonians shift from a western to an eastern state of mind while on this bridge. Michael Ondaatje used it as an inanimate character in his novel *In the Skin of a Lion*. 'The bridge goes up in a dream,' he wrote of its construction. 'It will link the east end with the centre of the city. It will carry traffic, water, and electricity across the Don Valley. It will carry trains that have not even been invented yet.' One moment the pavement is soaring eastward above the valley, the occasional train rumbling underneath, and the next it's part of a dense urban street. The change in topography is unmatched in Toronto. What's most remarkable is how flat and straight and perfect the road is throughout these changes, as if the road came first, and then the Prince Edward Viaduct and the earth rose up to meet it.

At 1 Danforth Avenue, you'll find the City Adult Learning Centre, a mountaintop of modern institutional architecture completely surrounded by the on-ramp to the Don Valley Parkway. Various modish wings of the building lead back to community gardens and a secret pedestrian bridge over to Riverdale Park. Though it's somewhat neglected, this is one of Toronto's most unsung modern buildings, perhaps because of its island-like location. Opened in 1963, it was designed by Peter Pennington, then the lead designer for the Toronto Board of Education. Pennington was involved in a number of designs during this burgeoning era, when the school board had in-house architects and there was a real, determined effort to build well and beautifully for the future. Some of his other schools include the sharp and cool École élémentaire Pierre-Elliott-Trudeau on Grace Street and Lord Lansdowne School on Robert Street, with its whimsical crown shape. Sadly, Pennington's fine Davisville Junior Public School was allowed, like many schools, to deteriorate and wasn't renovated to contemporary standards. It was razed a few years ago, replaced by a school of inferior design quality. They don't generally build schools like they used to, but they should. Between the school and the ultra-bright Pizza Pizza, there's a curious building that houses a Greek organization called the

Thessalonikeans Society of Toronto. The building's original purpose was somewhat more corporeal in nature: if you've ever wondered how Toronto built public washrooms in 1921, they did it like this, with this kind of style and elegance (today we build them – if we build them at all – with the hope that they work when and if they're open). In front of it, a bike lane with traffic signals has made what was once one of the most fraught cycling passages in Toronto, crossing a freeway on-ramp, much safer.

At Broadview, two buildings, the CIBC building on the north side and the Playter Society building (where Guy Lombardo's orchestra played the third-floor hall regularly in the 1930s) on the south side, welcome visitors to the part of the Danforth they make tourist brochures about. It's one of the streets people use to define Toronto, bearing an iconic name with that definite article in front of it – *the* Danforth – as if it has an importance of place beyond that of being a major street. It's like a colonial territory or a realm of great consequence, perhaps awkwardly echoing the way the British referred to *the* Sudan or *the* Levant back in the days of empire. It also appears in a line from a Barenaked Ladies song, where the fellas from Scarborough sing of going down to the Danforth. The use of *the* could be a local Anglo-Saxon hangover – in the *Toronto Star*, writer Robert Thomas Allen described the character of the area up until the 1950s as overwhelmingly working-class, 'a flat suburb of English, Irish, and Scotch cops, TTC motormen, and T. Eaton Company tie clerks.'

The Danforth had been the hardest stretch of 'destination' road in Toronto for me to cozy up to. It perpetually seemed one lane too wide for walking and one too narrow for driving, but that bike lane and the CaféTO outdoor dining program has made it a much more humane and lush strip.

Just west of Broadview, at number 121, there's a tiny passageway that leads north/south to A & V Aluminum, an infill development *avant la lettre*, and a bit of very old-fashioned mixed-use heritage. Across the street and a bit east of here, at Playter Boulevard – the Playters were an original Loyalist family – the 'All Canadian' Mister Transmission was replaced in the late 2000s by a Shoppers Drug Mart building that, while it does meet the sidewalk, is a glorified big-box structure along with the adjacent LCBO, only one storey tall in a place where there should be three or four or more floors above the retail. Though Mister Transmission is gone, it and A & V represent what Toronto once was: a provincial working-class city. Businesses like this were, and sometimes still are, located on our main drags, not tucked away in a hidden district.

It's details like these, some of which you don't see at first, that make the Danforth worth getting to know.

In the 1950s, waves of Italian immigrants settled in those working-class houses surrounding the Danforth, replacing the tie clerks. The Greeks who followed eventually turned the area into what the local BIA calls the largest Greek neighbourhood in North America. At its height in the 1970s, there were around forty thousand Greeks living in the area. But like so many other inner-city ethnic enclaves, the first- and second-generation Greeks started to move out – to suburbs like Scarborough and North York in the late seventies – selling their homes to 'white painters' who moved in and fixed them up, shifting the prices and demographic in a decidedly upwardly mobile direction. The ethnic strip remains, as they have in other neighbourhoods, anchored here by the restaurants and Alexander the Great Parkette at Logan.

The Carrot Common is a good example of this transition. Opened in 1984, it won a City of Toronto urban design award soon after. Inside the Big Carrot – a worker-owned co-op, and the guilt-free version of the corporate Whole Foods – terms like 'wellness' and 'well-being' are printed on nearly everything, and customers shop with their bike helmets on. An employee once told me, on condition of strict anonymity, that when she started working there, 'it felt like Sesame Street, everybody cheerfully saying hello to me by name.'

A bit further east, at Pape, the Ontario Line station will bring big changes, as it already has, and around Jones Avenue, the Danforth returns, somewhat, to its working-class roots. Gone are the high-end coffee chains and mid-scale restaurants; instead, a nearly continuous line of independent stores, bars, and low-rise architecture styles stretches to Victoria Park. This is where the east side's great unsung view starts: to the south, Lake Ontario has a looming presence, a rare thing in most of Toronto's urban areas, where the lake might

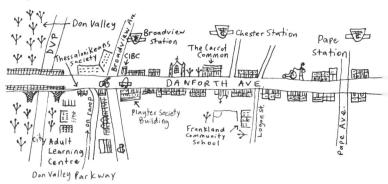

as well not exist. Here, too, the minaret of Madinah Masjid pierces the skyline, and the sidewalk out front is often busy.

A few new residential buildings have created more activity, including filling in a Beer Store parking lot that sucked life from the street on the southwest corner of Greenwood. The former Allenby Theatre (later known as the Roxy) has been turned into a Circle K and Tim Hortons combo, complete with gas pumps. For a while the still-intact marquee advertised a 'Double Double,' an oddly graceful nod to the lost cinematic roots here.

Things change in a city, sometimes fast, sometimes imperceptibly. In the late 2000s, I spoke to Madeleine Callaghan, who lived near the Greenwood intersection with her husband and two kids. She remarked that when they moved here in 1997, they 'were the second young family on the street. Slowly, it became all young families. Everybody said the intersection was just about to turn for the better, but it didn't.' Then, suddenly, it did change.

The Danforth continues past Greenwood. This post-Greektown stretch of relatively low rents, called 'the Danny' by the area's BIA, is important and looks a lot like a museum of small-time capitalism in some places.

At Main Street, on top of the Hakim Optical building, a pair of huge red eyeglasses watches over the street omnisciently, like the billboard eyes of Doctor T. J. Eckleburg do in *The Great Gatsby*. Main Square, opposite the eyeglasses, is a dense community of high-rise towers whose utopian plaza has been neglected and is now host to underutilized retail spaces and unkept concrete planters. Even the pool area has been filled in.

Main Square was a public-private project of the Canadian Mortgage and Housing Corporation (CMHC) during the heyday of the Crown corporation's public investment in large housing projects. The building had subsidized, affordable units for people with less income, part of a profit-sharing program.

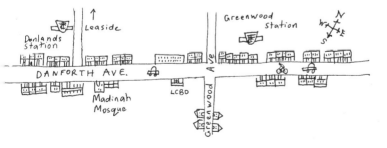

Opened in 1972, Main Square was planned with the most utopian and egalitarian aspirations of the day. A 1971 brochure boasted the community was being built around the 'Communicept' program, 'a totally new idea in community living' that included the apartment towers, a shopping level with thirty stores, a swimming pool, a gymnasium, space for hobbies and community meetings, and a daycare centre, with thirty different apartment layouts to choose from.

In 1998, CMHC sold its share of the project to a private company. Located between Main subway station and the Main GO train station, and at the terminus of the 506 streetcar, this residential cluster is a logical place for density, and the open space in front – the square – is a prime candidate for infill development. It would be a shame to lose what could be a great public space, but Main Square is one of the handful of dense anomalies along the Bloor-Danforth subway corridor, now here for a half-century, but mostly lined by two- and three-storey low-rise buildings, and street after street of houses to the north and south that have been prevented from adding real density. Hubs like Main Square do the heavy lifting for a city that prospers from people wanting to live here but that doesn't want to share that 'burden' equally. Main Square has provided a home for many thousands of Torontonians over the decades. With five new towers proposed for this site alone, and adjacent single-family-home neighbourhoods remaining largely the same as they've always been, it's important to ask why these residents are asked to do the heavy lifting while others aren't.

Just past Main hulks a large Canadian Tire store, one of the biggest crimes against Toronto's urbanity. Though it seems like a Crown corporation, the way Tim Hortons does, and so should have our best interests at heart, this company enjoys plunking down big-box stores where a more detailed touch is needed (though the LCBO, an actual Crown corporation, is certainly no

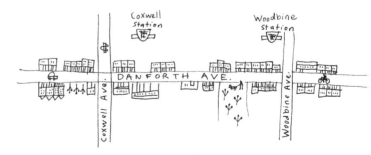

model of urban design sensibilities either). Like the Shoppers back at Playter Boulevard, the Canadian Tire meets the sidewalk but gives the pedestrian a lot of nothing, just a blank wall and one entrance. But there is a development proposal here too – for two towers that would incorporate a Canadian Tire in the shared podium and, hopefully, make more of an effort at the sidewalk level.

Past Warden Avenue, the Danforth becomes just Danforth Road. Looking back into the city, you can see the slope down toward the Don and enjoy a perfectly straight view all the way into the heart of midtown. Though it's a mall with a big parking lot, the Shoppers World Danforth at Victoria Park is an interesting hybrid of a strip mall and what must be the city's shortest mall – there are just a handful of stores in its truncated arcade. This was once a Ford factory, but when Shoppers World was built in 1962, it was replaced by what was the second Eaton's store outside of a downtown area. It would also become home to Murray Koffler's drugstore empire, which adopted the plaza's name to become Shoppers Drug Mart.

The old City of Toronto, East York, and Scarborough all meet by the corner of Danforth and Victoria Park Avenues – not exactly a 'four corners' kind of place, but three will do. Walk north on Victoria Park a few blocks and you'll find Crescent Town, a self-contained mod spaceship of a community that rises high above the ravine of Taylor Creek Park, a landmark last bit of East York concrete before the former borough gives way to Scarborough. Crescent Town is attached to Victoria Park subway station by a long covered walkway, and it's the first thing you see out the north side of the train when it exits the tunnel.

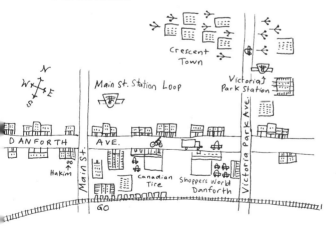

Much of Crescent Town's public space is raised up on pillars, hovering above mud and parking lots, allowing for grassy parkland and passageways. Yvonne Bambrick, now a registered downtowner, spent her first eighteen years happily positioned with her parents in a condo on the twenty-ninth floor of a building in Crescent Town. 'It was as hip as lofts are today, but with a lot of young families,' said Bambrick. 'There were lots of three-bedroom units.' Places like Crescent Town demonstrate that when units are built big enough for families, kids can live happy vertical lives too.

Bambrick would walk her dog in the Taylor-Massey Creek ravine and take swimming lessons in the pool at the attached Crescent Town Club. A few years before she arrived, a young Kiefer Sutherland was one of the development's first residents, and a student at Crescent Town elementary school.

This area was once named Dentonia Farm. The farm was owned by the famed Massey clan in 1897 and named after Denton, Susan Massey's maiden name. It was here that the Masseys raised the cows that provided the milk for their City Dairy Company, which was located on the northeast side of Spadina Crescent, in a building that's now owned by the University of Toronto. In 1933, Susan donated her mansion and forty acres of Dentonia Farm to the Crescent School (for Fancy and Exclusive Boys). In 1969, the private school moved to its current location on Bayview near the Bridle Path, and this land was redeveloped as Crescent Town. The name Dentonia lives on in the moniker of the adjacent city-owned golf course.

Sadly, the Crescent Town restaurant, snug in the centre of the neighbourhood, with laminated placemats that listed cocktail suggestions from the swinging era when this place was built, is gone.

The public spaces around Crescent Town have received some updates and renovations of late, and it remains busy, especially the passages that come and go from Victoria Park station. Here, the pedestrian-oriented mix of modern concrete utopian space next to forested ravine – a very Torontonian kind of place – is largely intact.

Downtown East Side Zigzag

 pack a lunch

 dress to impress

 offspring friendly

Connecting walks: Yonge, Harbourfront, Nathan Phillips Square/PATH, Dundas, Castle Frank/Brick Works, Gerrard

Standing down where the Esplanade meets Yonge Street, you feel like the bulk of the city is towering above you, more so than anywhere else in Toronto. The east side of the city core has a special view of downtown – from the west the buildings gradually build up to the core, whereas on the east it's an abrupt rise, like an electric mountain range next to low-lying plains. The effect is dramatic, and ever so big-city, a valuable feeling in a city like Toronto, which is eternally preoccupied with how it measures up. Parking lots here have been converted into new condos and what was once a back-alley kind of place is now dense and filled with people.

A few steps east of Yonge, between the Esplanade and the railway corridor, there's a large condo building that's remarkable because it's Toronto's larger, yet unsung, flatiron building. Our famous flatiron, the Gooderham building, is only a block away, on the corner just east of Yonge where Front and Welling-ton Streets meet. It gets all the tourists snapping photographs, while this one looms unheralded, almost invisible despite its size, looking like the prow of an unreal ship slowly passing in front of the skyline.

Across from the unsung flatiron on the Esplanade, you'll find yourself at the back door of what was once the O'Keefe Centre, later the Humming-bird Centre, then the Sony Centre, and, more recently, Meridian Hall (anybody who still calls it the O'Keefe Centre can be forgiven for sticking to one name). This building hosted legendary Russian dancer Mikhail Baryshnikov after he defected from the Soviet Union in June of 1974 and was spirited away, first to journalist John Fraser's apartment and then to the Caledon Hills just outside of the city before he finally found his way into the arms of Leonard Bernstein, Jackie O, and the rest of New York's arts society. This door is the tiny passage to that notable life. That Cold War drama was able to play out down here because Victorian-era Toronto-nians decided to extend the city south of Front Street, where the original shoreline of Lake Ontario was located.

A little further east from here, you'll find the beginnings of Church Street. There are two Church Streets in Toronto – the one below Gerrard Street and the one above. People talk about the northern section of the street more, since it's where out-of-towners go during Pride Week, the part locals are perpetually worried is becoming less gay, or straighter. People have been worried about the state of the Village for at least a decade now, and every time a bar or gay-owned shop closes, the fretting begins anew. Neighbourhoods like Church Street are delicate, as community interests and the free market have to be synchronously directed in order to produce a beloved neighbourhood.

Far from these queer concerns, Church Street has a rather unglamorous beginning in a parking garage. Though it's unsung (perhaps we should brand this area of Toronto the 'Unsung District'), the view from down here in the St. Lawrence Market neighbourhood shows Toronto's urbanity at its zenith, as a bowl of buildings – some old, some new – rises in each direction. It feels safe and solid: we are protected by buildings here. The steep slope up to Front

DOWNTOWN EAST SIDE

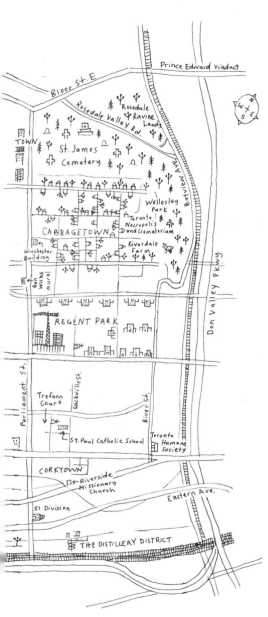

Street is the result of fill that softened a eight-metre cliff to the original beach below, where the Town of York's first substantial wharf was built. Tucked into a nook on the west side of the street here is a public artwork by Paul Raff called *Shoreline Commemorative*.

Though the lake view from Front is gone, the Gooderham building is still photographed hundreds of times a day. This part of Toronto is the city's most Parisian quarter in terms of scale, but it also feels like a 1980s period piece. Maybe it's the font of the St. Lawrence Centre for the Arts logo, or Derek Michael Besant's 'peeling facade' mural on the back of the Gooderham flatiron building, but Front Street evokes the last days of Toronto's 1970s 'City That Works' era (though the Claude Cormier–designed renovation of Berczy Park, with its beloved dog fountain, has brought the area right into the present).

North of here, Church Street quiets down, and it remains in this calmer state for quite a number of blocks. Just below King Street at

Colborne Street, look west down tiny Leader Lane – once the brokerage centre of Toronto – to the side of the King Edward Hotel, up to the penthouse ballroom. It's another bored-out urban canyon view and a glimpse of a sheer part of that electrical mountain range.

At King Street, Cathedral Church of St. James – the first of three churches that give Church Street its name – was, for a time, the centre of social life in old York, and the source of all things Toronto the Good (it remains so for a few). A few blocks north, the Metropolitan United Church at Queen remains a hub of community meetings – it was home to the anti-amalgamation rallies of former mayor John Sewell's Citizens for Local Democracy group in the 1990s.

A block north, St. Michael's Cathedral is the Catholic counterpoint to St. James's Anglican redoubt. These three churches form a kind of religious triumvirate that, like Toronto itself, seems to effortlessly contain a variety of divergent viewpoints. In the middle of this, the Spire condo building rises above all their steeples, the triumph of civic secularism in a city that still seems to dig the churches, but whose steeple shadows no longer dominate the streets and the culture.

On the west side here, at 167 Church Street, was the Athenaeum Club. Originally an athletic club built in 1891, this building was known as the Labour Temple from 1904 to 1968 after the club was purchased by the Toronto Trades and Labour Council by selling shares to members of associated unions. 'A library was set up, many unions had their offices located here, and for the sixty-four years it operated as the centrepiece of the Toronto labour movement, many meetings were held here to discuss the key issues of the day,' said labour historian David Kidd. Those issues included public ownership of the TTC and Toronto Hydro, and whether to support conscription during the two world wars. Today the facade of the Athenaeum Club is preserved as part of the Jazz apartments.

On the southeast corner of Church and Dundas, a condo completed in 2023 represents why people often don't like new developments: it makes the street boring. The view from the street is often a uniform glass wall, even some utility areas, and big retail units that attract repetitious chains like banks – none of the chaotic variety that makes cities vibrant. In 2016, before this corner was razed, it was a quintessential collection of Toronto shacks. Cheaply built, like so much of Toronto, the jumble was ugly to unsympathetic eyes. Ugly but useful and adaptable: just this one quotidian corner housed more Toronto life than seems possible in one place. A visit to the deep wells of civic memory stored in the old city directories on the second floor of the Toronto Reference Library, randomly selecting volumes about a decade apart, from 1915 until 1993, revealed that life. Here's just a sliver of it.

Part of the redevelopment parcel included an unpaved parking lot along Church, and buildings on both the north and south sides bore ghost traces of the structures that once abutted them, addresses numbered 215 to 221. In 1915, Ebenezer Chesney's cigar shop, the Porter Plumbing Supply Company, and various apartment-dwellers were here. In 1925, Porter was still a going concern, but the cigar shop was vacant, Hawley Auto Supply had moved in next door, and Samuel Barrett had a wholesale confectionary. By 1936, Seto Kwan had set up his tailoring business in Ebenezer's old place, and Tire Chains and Accessories had opened next door, along with the Collins Printing Company next to it. Porter was still in the plumbing business.

In 1947, Kwan had become a 'Designing Tailor,' and Church Cleaners and the Lewis Fur Company had moved into the block, while Porter Plumbing had evolved into Good Specialties Plumbing and Heating. By 1958, Master Brothers Business Machines was in operation here, alongside M & R Enterprises Clothing and Novelties. In 1968, the Club Coffee Company was operating where Kwan once sewed, and next to it Athens Photo Studio had opened, and Art Electric Construction had slipped in here too. In 1980, the Toronto Resale Centre, Metropolitan Coin Exchange, and the Wheel Silverware and Antiques shop were operating alongside Master Brothers. By 1993, 215 was not listed and 217 was vacant, no doubt the slow birth of the parking lot that replaced it.

Up until they were torn down in the late 2010s, the buildings continued to overflow with life and enterprises both spiritual and commercial. At 223, you could rent a room in 2016 for $79 at the Toronto Central Hotel, but back in 1915 the Baptist Book Room and Baptist Missions Office shared the building with the Standard Publishing Company. Floyd Robinson was the live-in caretaker in 1925, and Arthur James had taken over the job by 1936. The Baptists and their many arms (religious education, publications, foreign missions, etc.) were here until at least 1947. In 1958, 223 had become the Canadian Insurance Building, housing said insurers, but also, over the years, the Downtown Businessmen's Association of Toronto, Talco Importers, Masterpieces of Music, Custom Elevator Services, the Top 10 theatrical agency, the Architectural Millworkers of Ontario, Felix Photo Products, Ip Ken commercial artist, Brown Security Services, and Amalgamated Eye Services. By 1993, 223 Church had become the Toronto International Hostel.

At 225 Church, where the Thai restaurant Sabai Sabai most recently was, Thos B Trumphour sold cigars and Godfrey Hattie was a dressmaker in 1915. For 1925, the listing was simply 'Chinese Restaurant,' and it was vacant during the Depression; but, by 1947, it was back in action as the Arena Pool Room until sometime before 1968, when Parthenon Jewellery and Gifts was in operation. Harts Restaurant operated here in 1980. Next door, Ethiopiques Restaurant operated at 227 in 2016, but over the decades the location saw Peter Harakas's confectionary in 1925, the Liberty Lunch in 1936 (though Peter Harakas still lived at this address, so perhaps he rebranded), and later the U N I Grill. In 1993, the Amalfi Restaurant opened and their giant A was still visible at the peak of the roof above Ethiopiques before the demolition. Everything leaves a trace, if it's allowed to.

Directly on the Church and Dundas corner, the space was divided into addresses on both streets. Number 229 Church saw a succession of grocery, cigar, and variety shops over the decades. In 1915, Dundas was called Wilton Avenue along here and this block started at number 81, where Robert Ringland operated a shoemaker business next to a Chinese laundry. By 1925, Wilton had become Dundas and been renumbered, so Evan Tanaseff shined shoes at 99½, next to what was TACOS 101 before the demolition. Chinese laundries, subsequent shoeshiners, and barbers such as Percy McGovern in 1936 and Sam Ho in 1947 filled these small spaces. In 1958, the People's Open Kitchen operated at least into the 1980s. From the 1960s into the 1990s, the Toronto Invisible Weavers operated above where Jesmin Hair and Nails Spa was. At 117 Dundas, where Curry Kitchen most recently was, numerous restaurants such as Ash, Star of Bengal, Rhodes, and Sun Avon have operated over the years. And before that, Sim Ho (the directories don't say if he was a relation to Sam – the stories here are always between the lines) ran his laundry in this location until at least 1947. So much activity happened at this one corner it's hard to follow.

This is just a sliver of what was here. Old Toronto was able to adapt to all kinds of uses, especially small, independent businesses that could afford rents and make a go of it, even if the turnover of some businesses shows how volatile retail life has always been. The trick for Toronto will be to find a way to make sure the new buildings, with much more needed housing on top, can play the same ultra-flexible role along the sidewalk as they once did.

North of Dundas, the Toronto Metropolitan University campus dominates both sides of Church, and the George Vari Engineering and Computing Centre is a block-long addition on the east side of the street – it filled in a parking lot between Church and the magnificent Merchandise Building, which was once a Simpsons, and then a Sears warehouse, and is now a residential loft conversion. The building is a four-storey glass fishbowl of student life that was designed by Moriyama Teshima Architects, of Toronto Reference Library and Scarborough Civic Centre fame.

North of Gerrard, Church becomes busy and diverse again. This stretch used to be residential all the way up to Bloor, but over time the big houses were either torn down or converted into stores and bars.

As Toronto's gay scene moved from Yonge to Church in the 1980s, that old sensibility of queer bars behind darkened windows evolved into a much more conspicuous street presence. It's been suggested that this was always a gay area, from the early 1800s, in the legendary days of possibly gay magistrate Alexander Wood (whose statue once stood at Alexander and Church but was recently removed when debate arose around his involvement in the organization of residential schools), to the fifties and sixties, when the City Park Co-Op and Village Green apartment complexes were built (the latter includes a round building endearingly nicknamed 'Vaseline Tower'), residential structures where a single person could live alone and in relative privacy.

Church-Wellesley's kind of urbanism is ideal. Church along here has one of the liveliest streetscapes in Toronto (it filled in for Pittsburgh in all five seasons of Queer as Folk), with enough bars to keep people around until late at night, but enough of everything else to keep it populated and functional by day. With a few grocery stores, restaurants, and other services, it's a completely self-contained neighbourhood – it's not a surprise that lots of not-so-gay folks want to move into this kind of Sesame Street urban landscape.

If you look at the changes in the neighbourhood through the 'Diversity Is Our Strength' motto lens, it's all good, but for those worried about the demise of Church, it's useful to think of how Toronto's other ethnic strips have evolved. The Greeks don't live en masse on the Danforth anymore, nor do the Italians along St. Clair, but the ethnic strips remain, and people visit because the areas still feel Italian or Greek. Bars may come and go, but the Church-Wellesley area is anchored by visible institutions and places like the 519 community centre, the AIDS Memorial in Barbara Hall Park, the AIDS Committee of Toronto, and the ArQuives (Canada's LGBTQ2+ Archives). Even the CBC's *Battle of the Blades* figure-skating show that put life back into Maple Leaf Gardens in 2009 was good for the community because it was the gayest event the place had witnessed since Liberace performed there in the 1950s. Though the need to stick together in one area for security is much less powerful now, the Village is still critical, if only for this moment: imagine a gay kid from a less tolerant place arriving at Church and Wellesley and, for the first time, seeing this vibrant, celebratory strip. This is why cities are salvation: you can see, immediately, that you belong here, just as you are (though this area has often been criticized for being too white and too male, so belonging is always subjective and a continued evolution).

As Church moves north, its overtly gay vibe fades into the institutional feel of Bloor Street East. Here you'll find the typical Toronto mix of old Victorian houses that have been converted into bars, restaurants, or businesses next door to taller, modern buildings, proof the two styles can coexist close to each other without offence. On the northeast corner of Church and Bloor, a large stainless-steel sculpture by Kosso Eloul called *Meeting Place* is the kind of public art kids like because they can run up and touch it and, in this case, look at themselves in it. Further east, on the north side of Bloor, the Manufacturers Life Insurance Company building has the finest putting-green-style lawn in Toronto, which is kept safe behind a tall wrought-iron fence.

A little further on, there's a relatively rare-for-Toronto T-intersection where Jarvis, one of Toronto's most contentious streets (for a brief period of time), meets Bloor.

Jarvis, once the most beautiful street in Toronto, has been reverse-gentrified and turned into a wide arterial traffic pipe between North Toronto and downtown. The City's 2009 Jarvis Street streetscape improvement plan aimed to return the street to some of its pedestrian-friendly glory, but like many utopic plans, it languishes. Even the bike lanes that were here briefly were removed during Rob Ford's reign, and the car reasserted its dominance and urban-design influence.

As early as 2000, then-councillor Kyle Rae told Christopher Hume of the *Toronto Star*, 'What [the plan was] trying to do is bring back something the city lost many years ago … a dignified and safe street with a park and a boulevard.'

What the four-wheeled folk of Toronto, who want to keep this a fast and dangerous traffic sewer, hadn't noticed was that a 'residential urbanization' had taken place along the strip in the preceding decades, a change that was easy to miss while speeding by in a car. Walk Jarvis and you quickly notice the incredible residential density, and how much of its past grandeur still remains.

Today, Jarvis still begins in grandeur of a kind, along Bloor's Insurance Company Row. The Manulife building is now the most impressive building here representing the industry. (The Rogers headquarters on the corner used to give it a run for its money when it was Confederation Life, a company that went under in 1994.) Here, Mount Pleasant Road, opened in the early 1950s and once referred to as the city's first expressway, funnels all that Rosedale and North Toronto traffic onto Jarvis, traffic that was the reason behind the widening of the street in the 1960s.

Artist Michael Snow's best-known pieces of public art in Toronto are *The Audience* (the grotesque figures shouting and hanging off the building formerly known as the SkyDome) and *Flight Stop* (the famed flying geese in the Eaton Centre). But hidden behind the Rogers corporate campus at Mount Pleasant and Bloor is *Red, Orange and Green*, the giant stainless-steel tree sculpture Snow built for Confederation Life in 1992 that includes cut-outs of his equally famous 'walking woman' figure from the 1960s. The sculpture was originally placed in a very public spot, where Mount Pleasant splits off from Jarvis, but you can now find it on the Huntley Street side of the Rogers campus, near where the Christian talk show *100 Huntley Street*'s studios once were. Snow once told me that the building owners, 'without discussion or permission, moved the sculpture to the backyard. This was a big deal: the street needed to be closed for big cranes. The title of the sculpture refers both to traffic lights and the seasonal colour changes of tree leaves. It was explicitly designed for that corner – in the work there are references to nearby shapes. It was made to be seen driving by, as well as more contemplatively from the sidewalks.' On another occasion he joked that when Rogers bought the SkyDome, he was afraid that they would move *The Audience* as well.

South on Jarvis and opposite Rogers, there's a block of wonderful midcentury modern apartment buildings made from angular yellow brick and glass that looks as sharp as Glenn Gould's *Goldberg Variations* of the same era. One of the buildings is appropriately named Massey House, as the Massey family lived just down the street in the Keg Mansion, what is now one of the most unique chain-restaurant locations in the city.

I spent eight years living at 105 Isabella Street, south of Massey House. Built in 1959, 105 was a handsome eleven-storey yellow-brick building with symmetrical windows and balconies located at the corner of Jarvis Street. In my imagination, it looked like a perforated computer punch card from the era, though now it has been reclad in awful white stucco and black balcony treatments, destroying the original look. Mine was a standard-issue Toronto apartment and had the parquet floors to prove it – ubiquitous here, especially in apartments built between the 1950s and 1970s. The living and dining area had a panoramic view north and there was a huge balcony by current standards. There was always light in my apartment. It had a big-enough galley kitchen and one bedroom that was just separate enough from the living area to seem like a distinct place. Most importantly, everything was at a right angle and it was easy to fit furniture inside. The proportions were just about perfect, and, living there for so long, I began to admire how much thought went into what seems like a deceptively simple design. I've become obsessed with windowsills and size them up now: Can you put plants on them, as I could in my apartment? Are they at the right height so a couch can naturally be put in front of it?

There are many thousands of apartments like this in Toronto and beyond, with either near-identical layouts or remixed versions, as if each room was a piece of Lego that could be rearranged. They are instantly recognizable as kin to anybody who's lived in one. If you go to a party in one of these units, they seem to fit more people than you'd think possible, like a Holly Golightly party in *Breakfast at Tiffany's*. At one a friend threw a few years ago, I mentioned how similar his place was to mine, commenting on the minor variations. 'A machine for living,' he said, using a phrase coined by the architect Le Corbusier, who, along with others, pioneered the design of modern apartment buildings like ours. Le Corbusier is sometimes maligned for his 'Plan Voisin,' a 1925 scheme that called for large areas of central Paris to be demolished and replaced with many cross-shaped towers surrounded by green space. That didn't happen, but those towers later inspired residential buildings in the Parisian suburbs and around the world. Here, these kinds of buildings, sometimes called 'towers in the park,' have housed an awful lot of Torontonians, and relatively affordably too.

These buildings fell out of fashion, though, as Canadians continue to like, love, and obsess over single-family houses. As for apartments, condos have been in fashion for the last twenty years, as have single-family homes that have been carved up into quirky individual units, sometimes lovably called 'dirty mansions.' (The signs of a dirty mansion are subtle: multiple hydro meters or a cluster of mailboxes by the front door are the telltale clues that what was once a single-family home has been divided up into apartments inside.) Troubadour Corin Raymond referred to 'dirty mansions' when writing about musicians leaving Toronto for cheaper Ontario cities, as he did when he moved from Toronto to Hamilton. It's such a brilliant term – not one meant to be taken literally or morally – as the house pride every house is anointed with, whether big or small, is wonderfully undermined. Toronto has long had an anti-apartment bias, where houses are valued above all, so the term *dirty mansion* has such a subversive edge to it, a bit of shade thrown toward a culture obsessed with aspirational home ownership. Sadly, they are being re-amalgamated and turned back into single-family homes at an alarming rate.

Though buildings like 105 Isabella may not be in fashion and generally don't have granite countertops or ensuite laundry (though sometimes landlords are installing these sorts of things as an excuse to raise the rent), these midcentury buildings still have style. Near the front door of 105 is a subtle nameplate noting it was built by Bregman + Hamann Architects, a then-young Toronto firm that has gone on to become the large international firm B + H Architects. The building is connected to its sibling at 100 Gloucester Street to the south, and the two share an underground parking garage and a grassy 'backyard' overtop of it. (A third building of identical vintage and style is found on the north side of Isabella at 550 Jarvis, and still retains its original name, Massey House.) Numbers 100 and 105 were once called the 'Cawthra' and 'Mulock' Apartments, references to early-1900s millionaire Cawthra Mulock, whose mansion was torn down to build these two buildings, though those names have been lost over the decades and they just go by their street numbers today. Pictures of the mansion reveal a grand old building, razed during the postwar apartment boom; though, before that, it was used as a shelter for newcomers and refugees. A grand mansion is a lamentable loss, perhaps, but after it provided me and my hundreds of neighbours a home for so long, my feeling of regret is low. These three buildings are the true Jarvis mansions today.

My building was a microcosm of Toronto: there were young office workers, flight attendants, blue-collar workers who came home wearing steel-toed shoes, nurses, a fellow who collected recyclable material in his truck, and some older and elderly folks who had lived in the building for decades. Immigrant families with strollers made it their first Canadian home too, and a variety of languages could be heard in the elevator. There were a few drag queens living here, often seen leaving in full regalia, heading for the

Church Street bars and pulling their suitcases full of gowns behind them. The building was even name-checked by Scott Thompson's Buddy Cole character in a *Kids in the Hall* TV skit, as it was long part of the Gaybourhood.

The Church-Wellesley neighbourhood is full of these kinds of buildings, and there are great clusters of them around Toronto in places such as Davisville, High Park, along Marlee and Cosburn Avenues, and at Crescent Town. Some have many amenities while others are more humble. Not all are kept up to the same standards as mine was, and constant maintenance is key. I loved that when something broke in my apartment, I just filled out a form and it was fixed.

Some similar towers are Toronto Community Housing properties and are in desperate need of rehabilitation by the underfunded agency. Often the green space and other common areas are neglected too. These buildings unite parts of the city together. Now that I've moved to a dirty mansion where no lines are straight and the floors are slanted, I sometimes miss 105 Isabella and the shared experience of living in one of Toronto's many fine 'machines for living.'

To understand the Jarvis story, stand across from the Keg at the corner of Cawthra Square (which leads back to the AIDS memorial in Barbara Hall Park). From there, you'll see two massive Richardsonian Romanesque mansions (they look like smaller versions of Old City Hall), high-rise and low-rise apartment buildings, and then, south of Wellesley, Jarvis Collegiate Institute, the public high school where so many Torontonians of note went and where so many Canadians of future note currently study. These buildings are slightly diminished by one of Toronto's ugliest parking lots, which sits in front of the Keg Mansion like a blunt piece of public art representing the crimes against Jarvis. Yet, in one glance, there's an incredible diversity of building types.

Nearby, the details that make Jarvis great are abundant. At Wellesley, on the northeast corner, Plaza 100 – a narrow, wide, and high concrete building, complete with rooftop swimming pool – is surrounded by mod parkettes defined by Expo 67–era avant-garde sculptural shapes. Sit on one of the benches and the potential that Jarvis has to return to its former, welcoming state is obvious.

Until I walked Jarvis to write about it – that is, until I paid close attention to the street – I hadn't noticed the SickKids Garry Hurvitz Centre for

Community Mental Health just south of Wellesley at number 440, a children's mental-health facility that's housed in a brutalist masterpiece tucked away behind some trees. A few steps down, at 432–438, the Jarvis Court apartments have gorgeous prewar De Stijl tile and window designs. (So many details only reveal themselves when you're on foot.) Across the street, round apartment towers rise behind a Second Empire mansion that could have been the inspiration for the house in Hitchcock's *Psycho*. At this point, Jarvis begins to seem like it should be a cherished architectural museum rather than Toronto's shortcut.

The celebrated jewel in Jarvis's heretofore secret crown of gems is Canada's National Ballet School, a perfect collision of new and old, with glass and steel surrounding old mansions and the former CBC headquarters, itself once the Havergal College school for girls. The condo towers that rise behind – appropriately named RadioCITY – are yet more additions to this dense residential neighbourhood.

South of Carlton, Jarvis begins to look more fortified. The Inglewood Arms rents rooms daily and weekly, and the Allan Gardens park has an underwhelming street presence. Meanwhile, the fenced-in Moss Park Armoury is a bad urban neighbour, taking up space and giving nothing back. A friend of mine refers to the Ontario Court of Justice building at 311 Jarvis as 'the saddest place in Toronto.' What I've thought of as a really lovely example of 1955 modernism by architect Peter Dickinson is home to family court, a place where last-ditch emotional pleas are heard and life-altering custody decisions are made. Since hearing that, I can't walk by without thinking about it, and knowing what happens inside darkens the day when I'm near.

In 2006, Toronto gave Lombard Street – a short street between Victoria and Jarvis south of Richmond – the honorary title of Gilda Radner Way. Radner, the comedy legend of *Saturday Night Live* fame who died of ovarian cancer in 1989, performed at 110 Lombard, an 1886 fire hall that was home to the Toronto location of the Second City comedy troupe from 1974 to 1997. This location was also the launch pad for Canadian comedians Mike Myers, John Candy, and Eugene Levy.

Back on Jarvis, the fine and urbane St. James Park flanks the west side of the street as it moves back into the St. Lawrence neighbourhood, where there's no questioning the street's vibrancy. Here, Jarvis no longer has its magic centre lane that changes directions during rush hours, and traffic is forced to squeeze into two lanes – and further south into one – during non-rush-hour times when street parking is allowed. All that fuss over a street that wasn't really a highway, after all? The tamed almost-highway passes agreeably by St. Lawrence Hall, built in 1850, and down to Front Street.

Across the street from the beloved south building of St. Lawrence Market, which houses a fine selection of fresh fish, vegetables, and meat, sits its northern counterpart, the long-awaited replacement of the dowdy and stern 1968 building that itself replaced an earlier market building. Toronto-lovers have long held on to the dream of a museum dedicated to the city. Until there is political and public will for such a place, Torontonians can remain content with the City of Toronto's Market Gallery, a gem of an exhibition space on the second floor of the old St. Lawrence Market that has been putting on city-centric shows since 1979.

Jarvis slopes along the side of the market, another hint of the long-buried beach that was once adjacent to the building. The Esplanade, which runs behind the building, may be one of Toronto's most beautifully and grandly named streets, but when you're here, its narrow width and relatively short length do not live up to that fine name. The street is a fraction of the wide waterfront promenade it once was. By the mid-1800s, the railway had pushed its way across the front of the city, laying tracks along the Esplanade. Landfill eventually extended the waterfront away from the Esplanade, leaving the city with what we have today: a cute urban street with a very big name. East of here, the Esplanade runs alongside David Crombie Park, named after the 'tiny perfect mayor' of 1970s Toronto who presided over the construction of what has become a not-so-tiny perfect neighbourhood. One of Toronto's largest-ever urban projects – a peek at archival photos shows much of the St. Lawrence neighbourhood was just parking lots by the 1970s – the area combines rental housing with condominiums, co-ops, and even a school and community centre built into some of the mid-rise buildings. It's a kind of urbanity we don't see much of in Toronto.

The park and the Esplanade are a natural corridor leading east to the Distillery District. As the West Don Lands build up, the isolated, island feel of the Distillery is diminished and the city grows up around it. Soon it will get its own Ontario Line subway stop too. Walk through Parliament Square Park at the end of the Esplanade, past the subtle plaque that explains that this was the site of Ontario's (then Upper Canada's) first Parliament building, which was burned to the ground by American attackers during the War of 1812. Then travel across Parliament Street to the corner of Mill Street, where you'll find the Toronto condo that is most likely to poke you in the eye. The Pure Spirit condo and loft tower includes a glass flatiron-style podium that comes to a perfect and dramatic point at Parliament and Mill Streets. Historical-architecture purists may not like where it's located, but modern structures adjacent to the preserved Victorian industrial buildings of the Distillery occupy a space in the growing tradition of a unique Toronto look, a look that should be celebrated (when it's done right) for preserving historic buildings and making them part of the evolving and living city. The building replaced an ugly parking lot, and it opens up a grand entrance into the Distillery District that properly connects the site with the St. Lawrence neighbourhood.

Apart from a few places like the Distillery complex, the 51 Division police station in the renovated former Consumers Gas Station A building from 1898, and other old warehouse buildings, Parliament Street's lower half is not particularly pretty. Some of the older parts of the street are rundown, while newer bits are often clunky and ugly. There have been tragedies here too. On the northwest corner of Queen and Parliament, keep your eyes to the sidewalk and find the granite plaque that bears the names of the ten residents of the Rupert rooming house who died in a December 1989 fire. After the tragedy, concerned tenants, landlords, community workers, and housing advocates formed a group called the Rupert Coalition, which fights for increased safety inspections of rooming houses and the development of more safe and afford-able housing units.

Parliament's quieter feeling ends north of here, with the Regent Park revitalization project's new glass-and-brick buildings. As people and stores moved (all former residents were given the option to move back in, though not without considerable disruption to their lives), and the rest of the project is continued by further razing the older parts and replacing them with mixed-income housing (and a return of the old street grid), the Parliament streetscape will change dramatically, and the rebuilding will also shift the psychological boundaries of this neighbourhood and that of Cabbagetown, its neighbour to the north.

North of Gerrard, Parliament sometimes seems to achieve a tenuous and ever-changing balance between gentrification and the urban hodgepodge that makes cities exciting. Old-timers argue that the real Cabbagetown was south of Gerrard and was destroyed when Regent Park was created. But the idea of a neighbourhood is what's important; the borders that define a place often shift.

Old Cabbagetown was an Orange bastion of mostly working-class Irish Protestants, a Little Belfast devoted to crown and empire. Cabbagetown was political currency, as the Toronto writer Morley Callaghan explained in a newspaper article in 1987: 'If you were from Cabbagetown, it meant you really belonged to Toronto … [I]t was the working man's area, where there was a neighbourhood feeling, where people were sort of proud to be living, and they produced politician after politician … To be a member of the Orange Lodge and born in Cabbagetown had all kinds of splendid possibilities. A man like Tommy Church could become mayor six times, always proudly announcing that he was a Cabbagetown boy.' I don't recall 1990s-era Toronto mayor Barbara Hall ever mentioning she lived in Cabbagetown for decades in the same way.

The most visible workers in Cabbagetown now are tasked with the eternal upkeep of those old homes (the sound of hammering will never cease), many of which still have genuine McCausland stained-glass windows (a very special thing, Cabbagetowners will tell you). At Halloween, a candied version of noblesse oblige plays out as the neighbourhood welcomes a flood of children from neighbouring (and far less affluent) St. James Town. None of this will solve class divides, but the mix that plays out between the very different Parliament neighbourhoods is Toronto at its best.

From many vantage points in Cabbagetown, you can see the towers of St. James Town peeking out from between Victorian gables. Wellesley is the divide, with high-rises to the north and low-rises to the south. From a distance – especially from the east, across the Don Valley – St. James Town looks like a cluster of skyscrapers quickly giving way to a low-rise suburban or rural landscape. It looks as if it's a solid mass, but up close, from any direction, St. James Town is porous: there is no right or wrong way to get in, no main or backdoor entrance.

On a number of occasions, people who should know better – smart newspaper columnists or even friendly city-minded folks – have suggested that walking through St. James Town is something that just should not be done, as if they'd be embarking on some kind of wild urban adventure through the set of a 1970s Charles Bronson film. That isn't the case. There are around seventeen thousand people living in this cluster of towers. It's the area with the highest residential density in Canada, and there are always people around, whether it's noon or midnight.

To grasp how it's put together, St. James Town is best explored without a plan. Subway stops make for good official entrances to neighbourhoods, and the Glen Road exit of the Sherbourne subway station at the top of the neighbourhood should be St. James Town's grand entrance. Instead of being welcomed to the neighbourhood, people exiting the subways were for years met by Victorian houses – once long abandoned and now mostly renovated – that line Glen Road, and some rather handsome walk-up apartment buildings.

Though many, if not most, of St. James Town's residents are pedestrians and transit users, it took many years before a safe crossing of Howard Street was installed. Across from where this crosswalk should be, there is a row of Second Empire buildings, some of the few remnants of the original neighbourhood that was cleared out in the 1960s to make way for the swinging-sixties vision of bachelor apartments that were the first incarnation of St. James Town. Today, only a handful of buildings – like the New World Laundry on Parliament at Wellesley – remain from this era. The buildings along Howard appear as though they were prepared to be demolished when the march of towers suddenly exhausted itself.

Ghosts of those razed streets can also be found all around the neighbourhood. Though cars can't make it through, Ontario Street still cuts a straight line down the middle of St. James Town and, with a little work, could become a fantastic linear neighbourhood plaza if the city invested here as it docs in other neighbourhoods. Walk down off Rose Avenue or Bleecker Street, which still connects Wellesley and Howard.

Inside St. James Town, there are apartment buildings called the Winnipeg, the Halifax, the Quebec, the Calgary, the Edmonton, and the Vancouver. Never let them say Toronto doesn't think about the rest of Canada – we do, and we proclaim our connection to other cities via the most appropriate form: the skyscraper. The northernmost tower, the Toronto, has a mature pine forest (as do many institutional and residential buildings from this era) in its rather large front yard along Howard Street, along with half-round planters and interesting angular pathways through the trees, with benches for resting. However, what might be a well-used space is often empty because of the fences that surround it, which leave nowhere to go once inside. To the north, there's a new almost-flatiron tower wedged in between Howard and Bloor, a rather impressive entrance to the dense centre of the city if arriving on Bloor from the east.

The white tower cluster of St. James Town.

While St. James Town is porous at its edges, wandering around inside can be a challenge because there are even more fences separating the various tower properties, making natural and desired routes on foot often impossible. More than once, I've walked a logical route through the buildings, only to be blocked in by chain-link or a cheap knock-off of a wrought-iron fence. Some of those fences have been turned into inadvertent and somewhat beautiful sculptures by people who have locked their bikes – many dozens of them, all in varying states of disrepair – there.

In the middle of St. James Town, along that ghost of Ontario Street, there are often impromptu markets selling fruit, vegetables, and other items, while closer to Wellesley, by the Food Basics grocery store, a flea market runs when the weather is good. All this hints at the tremendous capacity that is locked up in the surrounding towers. The people in them know how to make and do things and, given the chance, could likely create a flourishing local economy.

It wouldn't take much to make this area nice: remove the fences, make sure landlords keep their properties in shape (and plowed in the winter, which is often a problem) while not raising the rents, get some lighting that doesn't burn the retina, and keep it clean. The city life is already here, it just needs some respect. Nicer spaces will bring more people out. Add in some infrastructure that would support the markets that already exist, and we have the potential for a new Toronto attraction.

At the southeast corner of St. James Town, a neglected parkette with a modish concrete sculpture marks the transition back into the deep Victorian jungle of Cabbagetown. Follow Wellesley east to Sackville Street, which bisects the neighbourhood as well as the entire east side of town. Sackville begins at a brick-walled dead end and it's downhill from there, as all of Cabbagetown's northern edge is pressed up against St. James' Cemetery, one of the city's finest burial places. The first block of Sackville is a little stub of road that extends north of Wellesley for a hundred metres or so. To the south, the street is a consistent line of Victorian pleasantness made so by pioneering gentrifiers – so-called 'white painters,' people who moved into the rundown houses and painted everything white – in the early 1970s.

Sackville does run noticeably downhill. On a bike you can coast all the way to Gerrard if you're liberal in your interpretation of what a stop sign means. On foot, the grade results in effortless walking. It feels strange to say this, but one of the nicest things about Sackville, and Cabbagetown in general, is the fences. These aren't the two-metre-high suburban fences I grew up with, but proper low wrought-iron fences with squeaky gates that close with a bang and rattle. They mark the divide between public and private in the gentlest way, inviting and allowing the exchange of pleasantries between residents and those passing by. From spring until late summer, the southern entrance to Cabbagetown, at Sackville and Gerrard, is a fertile gauntlet created by rival corner stores that display an explosion of portable foliage for Cabbage-folk to pick up in their red wagons.

Though the area was completely redeveloped in 1948, and the southern part of Cabbagetown – what Hugh Garner called 'the largest Anglo-Saxon slum in North America' in his novel *Cabbagetown* – was razed, you can still follow Sackville Street continuously through the changing neighbourhood. Midway through Regent Park is Oak Street, once lined with old homes (made famous by the 1953 NFB film *Farewell Oak Street*), the four quadrants of Regent Park spread out in each direction. At Dundas Street you'll find St. Cyril and Methody, a Macedonian-Bulgarian church where you can see and listen to wedding receptions taking place under fluorescent tube lighting if you're passing through on a Saturday night, an older remnant amid all the new.

Just south of Dundas, Sackville passes through an early, and completed, phase of Regent Park with mid-rise residential buildings, townhouses, a new park, and a community centre. Toward Shuter Street, Sackville passes though Trefann Court, an area whose planned redevelopment in the 1960s was halted by a historic community effort to keep the small neighbourhood intact (led in part by John Sewell, who would become mayor in the late 1970s). In what is now the yard of St. Paul Catholic School on Queen at Sackville lies the burial ground of hundreds of Irish refugees who came to Toronto in 1847 after fleeing the Great Hunger. Today, they're beneath a paved playground with an asphalt baseball diamond nobody would ever want to slide into home on. Here, Sackville faces the twin elevated roadways of Richmond and Adelaide. Directly in front is the impenetrable green berm the roadway is built on. However, head east and find a secret passageway that feels illicit but allows pedestrians to pass through to King Street via a parking lot under the highway.

The lot skirts the side of the Riverside Evangelical Missionary Church, best known for its 'Prepare to meet thy God' sign, which drivers up on Richmond pass on their way into the city. Just east on King is the Sackville Playground. This park was created in the 1960s when Richmond and Adelaide became super-arterial roads; existing streets and buildings were removed, leaving this new space. With the continuation of Sackville through redeveloped Regent Park, following its historic route, this is now the only break along the street.

There is a crosswalk on King here that leads to that last existing bit of Sackville, which extends one block down to Eastern Avenue, where it finally comes to an end. Remarkably, and with the exception of the traffic lights at Gerrard, Dundas, and Shuter, the pedestrian has the right-of-way, through either stop signs or push-button crosswalks, the entire length of Sackville, from the cemetery to Eastern Avenue.

The area south of Queen is called Corktown, and below it is the Distillery District, which we encountered from the other side on Parliament earlier. I once spent an afternoon following Dennis Keliher around Corktown circa 1890. Keliher was the sole character in *A People's History Distilled*, a wonderful historical mobile play in which he led an audience on a walking tour of the Distillery District, where he worked, and out into Corktown, where he lived.

When the play ventured outside the preserved Distillery confines, his Toronto mythologizing got exciting. At Mill and Cherry Streets, we encountered the unrelenting wooden wall that surrounds the West Don Lands development. The wall went up seemingly overnight in the mid-2000s, and everything inside it began to be removed to make way for a new community. Keliher mentioned living here, a nod to the fact that this area was residential over one hundred years ago. Once, in the early 2000s, I tagged along to a late-night warehouse party in this area. I can't remember if it was any good or who threw it, but the building it was in is now gone, and with it most of my memories of that night. Today, this is the dense Canary District – home to thousands of people and Corktown Common park – and I have to remind myself how recently it was a very different landscape.

The West Don Lands regeneration has been forty years in the making but not begun in earnest until the mid-2000s. In the late eighties, the 'St. Lawrence Square' scheme – later renamed Ataratiri – was a City of Toronto proposal for a massive mixed-use and affordable housing development that saw more than $300 million spent on a project that didn't happen. Planning fetishists can visit the library and look through report after report on Ataratiri: 'Social Structure Analysis'; 'Noise and Vibration Study'; 'Soil Management Report'; 'Flood Protection Options.' Reading them is like listening to George and Martha talk about their non-existent son in *Who's Afraid of Virginia Woolf?* When the economy and local housing market collapsed in the early 1990s, the project was unable to get private investors on board, and in 1992, Bob Rae's provincial government cancelled Ataratiri. Toronto's never-ending housing boom and the catalyst that was the 2015 Pan Am Games, an event that used some of the buildings as athlete housing, finally got things built here.

Before the fence went up here, Bayview Avenue and Front Street met in a derelict, post-urban kind of place where one could imagine bad guys in noir films dumping bodies, unnoticed in the darkness. These days, the frogs in the lush ponds of Corktown Common can be heard croaking on summer nights. This is one of many spots around the city where the relatively recent changes are almost too vast and swift to comprehend. The frogs sound like they've been here forever.

One time, I revisited the area alone and wandered the streets, going up alleys, finding original Corktown cottages, and sneaking under the flying Eastern Avenue roadway where film crews store New York City cabs. Getting lost and a little dizzy, I repeatedly forgot I was in Toronto until I'd turn a corner, and Toronto's skyline, so sheer when viewed from the east, came into view. There's lots of Corktown left, but you have to find it among all the concrete of elevated expressways.

At River and Queen Streets, on the edge of Corktown, you'll find the Toronto Humane Society building, which bears a dedication to pianist and benefactor Glenn Gould. It reads, in part, 'The Toronto Humane Society gratefully acknowledges the generous legacy left to thousands of abused, lonely, and abandoned animals ... a musical and humane legacy to the world.' Surrounding it are heartbreaking 'Pawprints on our heart,' memorials to Toronto pets that include 'Gigi Mak – Beloved member of our family,' 'In memory of Benny Bergman – A gentle soul,' and 'Porky Alfino – Our funny little man. We'll miss you.'

This urban edge of Toronto, along the Don Valley, shifted over time, just as the Don River itself was altered and industrialized, and though the history of exactly how the city evolved is not written out on a chronological ledger, oblique glimpses come in unexpected moments and ways. For instance, during the deepest, darkest days of the pandemic, I would watch live, virtual tours of the Cranbrook Center, an education and museum campus in suburban Detroit, Michigan, that was designed by Finnish architect Eliel Saarinen and includes buildings by Frank Lloyd Wright and Albert Kahn.

As an aside one day, curator and tour guide Kevin Adkisson mentioned that Cranbrook's founder, the newspaper magnate, arts advocate, and philanthropist George Gough Booth was from Toronto, a tidbit that I didn't know until then. After I inquired further about this, Cranbrook archivist Laura MacNewman dug up what she could about Booth's early life in Toronto. He was born to a 'modest household' in 1864 to what became a large family, and to trace his existence in Toronto via archives in Michigan is to see a very early version of Toronto that is largely gone today.

The archives indicated he was born at what would now be 8 McGill Street, just off Yonge Street, in a house that no longer stands. When aged two and a half, he lived with his family above their store at 84 Seaton Street, in a humble house that appears to have been replaced. His final residence in Toronto was at the corner of River and Bell Streets in 1871, a few blocks north of where the Humane Society is today, 'though the location was principally on Gerrard Street.' Bell Street no longer exists, and maps of the time show it was by the southeast corner of Gerrard and River, on the edge of the Don Valley before the Don River was straightened. It was a wild edge of town then, almost entirely rural.

When he was thirteen, Booth moved to St. Thomas, and at seventeen he finally moved to Detroit, where he made his fortune, which included owning a half interest in an ornamental ironworks in Windsor for a time. There, he designed and fabricated the ornate iron fence that stands outside the Hockey

Hall of Fame at Front and Yonge Streets today, a former Bank of Montreal, along with its interior metalwork. History and geography mix and connect in endlessly fascinating ways.

Speaking of ornate metalwork, when commuters cross the Don at Queen Street, the bridge they travel on is part of a 1990 artwork called *Time and a Clock* by Eldon Garnet. It includes the stainless-steel words 'This river I step in is not the river I stand in' and a clock. Across the river, in South Riverdale, at Queen and Broadview, more phrases alluding to time are embedded into the sidewalk, the words 'Time is money, money is time' perhaps contributing to some east-side anxiety. At a third site, by Jimmie Simpson Park near Logan Avenue, Garnet installed four steel pennants, each emblazoned with the one of the following words: *coursing, disappearing, trembling, returning*. The pennants announce that the Don River is near. This work, which begins at the river that serves as the city's physical divide, and which creates an even more significant psychological one in many Torontonians, helps drag the two sides of the river, and the city, together. Looking back, the skyscraper cluster doesn't seem so far away, but there is much to find in between.

Castle Frank and the Brick Works

 neighbourhood jaunt

 dress to impress

scenic views

Connecting walks: Danforth/Crescent
Town, Downtown East Side

If you don't have a sense of the local history, Castle Frank subway station might seem like a misnomer. There is no castle in sight when you exit, though some of the Rosedale manses to the north might think they're castles. It's a swell station, though, with a little dome and a lot of horizontal glass: a classically modern mid-1960s TTC structure from the transit commission's Kennedyesque era of station-building and design (for some reason, 'Diefenbakeresque' doesn't have the same ring of modernity). South across Bloor, Castle Frank Crescent sits on the edge of the Don Valley and is home to the Rosedale Heights School for the Arts, a Toronto version of the art school from the movie *Fame*, and formerly Castle Frank High School, a trade school. This whole area is the end of a ridge that's surrounded by buried creeks and ravines, though modern development obscures some of it. The obvious and celebrated Prince Edward Viaduct leaps across the valley, but west on Bloor the bridge over Rosedale Valley Road is nearly as impressive. It's a massive yet often-overlooked piece of infrastructure; from below, the bridge and the nearby subway tube appear triumphant.

Rosedale Valley Road down below is a beautiful, not-so-secret downtown escape route for motorists. People moving more slowly can catch a glimpse of the remains of the old Castle Frank carriage drive carved into the slopes of the ravine if they look closely, especially when the trees are bare. The name Castle Frank was always used tongue-in-cheek, first for the summer home of Upper Canada's first lieutenant-governor, John Graves Simcoe – it was more of a wooden country lodge than a castle, so they went for an over-the-top name, demonstrating that a sense of humour was possible even in the hard days of early Toronto – who named it after his son Francis. The lodge was located south of where the TTC station is now, but it burned down in 1829. Whatever archaeological traces still exist are likely buried in the garden of one of the homes on Castle Frank Crescent. Down in the valley, the carriage drive the Simcoes used to get from York to their lodge can be seen at the back of St. James' Cemetery, sloping east toward Bayview, where it once turned north and went up the other side to the erstwhile castle.

To get a sense of this obscured ridge, take a walk around the high school – a modern midcentury gem itself – where it hugs the top of the ravine. At its easternmost point, there's a unique view into the underside of the Prince Edward Viaduct, where the subway trains rumble by, popping out of their underground tunnel and finding themselves suddenly high above the ground. Here, too, there's a long wooden staircase leading down to Bayview Avenue. It's worth the climb down to feel just how big the bridge's arches and concrete anchors are. (They built 'em big back in 1917.) In front of the school, there's a small plaque that tells the story of Castle Frank.

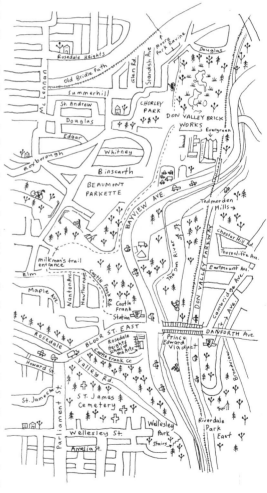

The Rosedale Valley, which runs below and adjacent to Castle Frank (another trail leads down to it from behind the station), was where I learned it's possible to snowshoe in the biggest city in Canada. In the few years prior to his mysterious death in 1917, the Canadian painter Tom Thomson lived and worked out of a tool shed behind the Group of Seven Studio Building on Severn Street at the top of the Rosedale Valley near Yonge. It is the last building southbound subway passengers see before the train enters the tunnel to Bloor-Yonge station. It's also where Thomson started his nocturnal snowshoe adventures down the Rosedale Valley toward the Don River, by what is now Castle Frank station. I knew of the Thomson shack, but it wasn't until I read Kevin

Irie's 2012 collection of poetry, *Viewing Tom Thomson: A Minority Report*, that I learned of Thomson's snowshoeing. The tool shack was moved in 1968, preserved as part of the McMichael gallery's Group of Seven collection in Kleinburg, just north of Toronto, but I wanted to see if it was still possible to follow in what I imagine are Thomson's snowshoe-steps, one hundred years later. So I bought my first pair of snowshoes.

Carrying my new snowshoes, I left home, then on Isabella Street, at around 10:00 p.m. on a Sunday night, just as freezing rain was beginning to fall on top of the thick snow. The quiet man who was always standing outside my building with a cigarette gave me an odd look as I passed him with my odd-looking contraptions (modern snowshoes no longer look like tennis racquets). I walked a few blocks to the dead end of Collier Street, an isolated stretch of Victorian homes off Church Street as it curves by the Rosedale Valley. A gently sloped wooden staircase here meanders down to the valley floor. Snowshoes have metal teeth on the bottom that dig into the crusty snow, so the buried stairs were easy to descend. With snowshoes, there's more freedom to walk away from trails in winter and go places you can't get to in other seasons.

The Studio Building stands about two hundred metres uphill, where Thomson would have begun his trek. This moment was imagined in Irie's poem 'Severn Road, Rosedale Ravine, Toronto': 'Don your snowshoes, / slip out the door past Severn Road / down Rosedale Ravine. Snow / falls, not to plunge into darkness / but to keep the blackness from engulfing / the night.' Irie, third-generation Japanese-Canadian, referred to his poetry collection as a 'minority report' because of, in his words, 'ambivalent feelings toward this iconic painter, not for his brilliant art, but for his status as a representative of what it means to be Canadian.' In the collection, Irie brings Thomson's paintings to life as he sees them, in Toronto and elsewhere. The book also provides another reconciliation, that of the Tom Thomson who has come to symbolize a Canada of vast wilderness and the Thomson who did some of his most well-known work a five-minute walk from Yonge and Bloor. Since Canadians live in and around cities, it's an important urbanization of the Thomson legend, and I followed what I imagined might have been his path, atop the windrows of plowed snow to the Brick Works and back. Though it's the defining landscape characteristic along south Rosedale, the ravine has a way of feeling elusive, sometimes north of Bloor Street East, sometimes south, sometimes not in view at all.

Back at Castle Frank subway station, walk directly up Castle Frank Road until you come to a pedestrian passageway on the right. It leads into Craigleigh Gardens, a fine and nearly secret urban park that was once the grounds of a large estate. It was bequeathed to the City, and today the fancy dogs of the Canadian aristocracy do their business here. Exit the park on its western, South Drive side and find the entrance to Milkman's Lane, a gravel path that continues into the valley (this one following the sometimes-buried Yellow Creek). Stay right at the fork at the bottom (left leads up to Mount Pleasant Road and, eventually, to the Yonge and St. Clair neighbourhood) and pass by the Bayview/DVP off-ramp. You'll surprise motorists not expecting to see a pedestrian at eye level as they round the curve. This was my route back up to 'civilization' on that icy and wet Tom Thomson snowshoe trek.

If you ever find yourself in a class-war shouting match with a Rosedale resident, call their neighbourhood a swamp – you wouldn't exactly be lying. Below the mansions perched on the edge of the Don Valley is the Binscarth Swamp, a hardwood wetland that expands in the spring, sometimes overtaking the trail that leads to the Brick Works. These wetlands were restored in the early 2000s and seem far from Castle Frank station, even though at this point they're only about a fifteen- or twenty-minute walk away.

A little further on, the Don Valley Brick Works will appear through the trees, a thirty-minute walk northeast of Castle Frank station (that is, if you're not slowed by the many distractions along the way). For nearly a century, the Brick Works drove a wide and deep industrial wedge into Rosedale. That sounds dirty and violent, and perhaps it was, but this place built the city. Between 1889 and 1984, the site produced the bricks that built Old City Hall, Casa Loma, Convocation Hall, Queen's Park, and countless homes throughout the city. Extending beneath Rosedale mansions, the quarry is one of the few places in Toronto where we can see our geological history – there have even been fossils of an extinct species of scary-sounding, but possibly adorable, 'giant beaver' found here. A woman who lived above the quarry on Douglas Crescent told me that, before the industrial site was closed, she and her neighbours would have to adjust the pictures in their homes and count the plaster cracks whenever the workers dynamited at the site. Since 1987, millions of dollars have been poured into the Brick Works to restore some of the buildings and create a sprawling wetland in the old quarry, complete with an elegant, zigzag boardwalk.

The old corrugated-metal buildings here sat vacant for nearly two decades. Urban infiltrators found ways inside them, and their pictures are plentiful on the internet, as are stories of the guy who made the site his home. Evergreen, a non-profit environmental organization, converted the site into a $55-million 'global showcase for green design' – a nature-ish version of the Distillery District. Through this plan, they've not only created some of the aforementioned wetlands, but they also restored many of the heritage buildings on the site. Past proposals weren't as kind or public-space-minded: in the 1980s, a developer called Torvalley planned to build 750 houses on the slopes of the quarry, and commercial buildings at the bottom. Rosedalians and an ad hoc group called the Friends of the Valley stopped all that. Located in the former borough of East York, the development would have meant a huge increase in the municipality's tax base, which was relatively small compared to that of its wealthier neighbours. Years later, another ad hoc Rosedale group tried to stop a switchback path from being built, though today it beautifully connects Chorley Park with the valley trails and Brick Works below.

The demise of Torvalley set the stage for a series of events to unfold, events that created the unique industrial-urban-wilderness mash-up we have today. The Brick Works can be visited any time, but they're especially fun to visit at night. When the drive-in crowds have gone and the summer farmers' market has packed up in late afternoon, the site becomes a dreamy place that you might have all to yourself. Late one hot July evening, a friend and I sat on the boardwalk and had a long talk – long talks take on greater importance and come easier in surroundings like this – our feet dangling above the lily pads and frogs, with a view of the St. James Town electric mountain range rising above the trees. In the background, traffic on the DVP hummed at a steady rate. Later, we climbed the circular path to the Governor's Bridge Lookout, high above the Brick Works site, from which you can see a panoramic view of the entire valley. Do the same during winter nights, on skis or snowshoes, for an equally beautiful but quite different experience.

Gerrard Street

 pack a lunch

 dress to impress

 offspring friendly

Connecting walk: Downtown East Side

At the time of Confederation, Toronto was a tight grid of small streets that hugged the lakefront. The Toronto Gaol, or Don Jail, was a severe sight on a hill across the valley. Today, Gerrard Street still crosses the Don River just east of what's now Cabbagetown. The Don is the great psychological divide between downtown and everything east, and at Gerrard it's a straight and shallow ditch of a river. The open space of the valley – which is narrow here too – as seen from the Gerrard Street Bridge, can still evoke what it may have been like to leave the core in the city's early days and travel east on a dirt road, the Don Jail looming on the other side of the river.

Despite its ominous look and the stories of the Victorian atrocities (and more recent ones) that have taken place here, the Don Jail was constructed as a reform jail, where prisoners could work in the fields outside. Stand in front of it, under the dead eyes of the Father Time carving set into the doorway arch, and it's easy to imagine the last moments of the convicted before they were brought inside.

Some of Toronto's worst and most notorious villains have spent time here. The bank-robbing Boyd Gang – described as 'the most desperate criminals ever locked in the Don Jail' by a newspaper of the time – escaped from the jail while awaiting trial for the murder of a police officer in 1952. (It was their second escape from the Don, where the gang members had met in the first place.) Their escape sparked an eight-day manhunt that entranced local news organizations. Two members of the gang were later hanged back-to-back at the jail. And in 1962, the last execution in a Canadian jail took place here, and involved another double hanging, this one of murderers Ronald Turpin and Arthur Lucas. Even former Maple Leafs president Harold Ballard spent time in the Don Jail after he was convicted of fraud and theft in the early 1970s.

Today, the old jail building is part of a new expansion of Bridgepoint Hospital. Michael McClelland of ERA Architects, the firm that restored the building for Bridgepoint, has called it 'one of the most intact British-style prisons left in North America.'

The Don Jail was built between 1859 and 1864 by architect William Thomas, an English transplant responsible for many early Victorian buildings in Toronto. The jail's design was progressive in that it allowed a considerable amount of light into the central atrium and came equipped with a ventilation system that was better than those in most homes at the time. Watch *Cocktail* if you want to see it pretending to be Tom Cruise's 'Cell Block Bar' in the 1988 film.

By 1977, the conditions in the old part of the jail were so bad that there were calls to raze the building. Ontario's correctional services minister at the time called the conditions in the building a 'monument to human degradation and misery,' but then-alderman and soon-to-be-mayor John Sewell, one of those responsible for saving it, rebuked him, saying, 'On that basis, the first thing that should come down is the Legislature Building. More terrible things have happened there than anywhere else.'

Across the street from the jail, in the corner of a parking lot, there is a ceremonial Chinese arch that was erected by the local BIA in 2009 after years of fundraising. The arch marks the entrance to Toronto's East Chinatown, which, while not exactly forgotten, has been struggling for years. With the Spadina Chinatown downtown, the Scarborough Agincourt Chinatown, and the Markham Chinatown (home of the Pacific Mall) to compete with, Gerrard's Chinatown is smaller than the others. Yet, as the strip has gentrified here and there, and though it's adjacent to wealthy Riverdale, some of that old character has managed to survive.

To get a sense of Riverdale, hang a left up Howland Road, which runs north of Gerrard a block east of Broadview Avenue, just as Chinatown begins to fade out. One block up at Simpson Avenue, you'll see the Metropolitan Community Church of Toronto or, as it's better known, the Gay Church. It's here that Canada's first same-sex marriage was

Withrow Park

Bain Co-Op

Bain Ave.

Withrow Ave.

Riverdale Ave.

Langley Ave.

←Cabbagetown

Bridgepoint Health Foundation

Riverdale Library

Metropolitan Community Church of Toronto

Howland Rd.

No Frills

Simpson Ave.

Gerrard/Carlaw (Prospect Park)

Gerrard Square

The Don Jail

Gerrard St East

Chinese Arch

East Chinatown

Creative Works Studio

De Grassi St.

Logan Ave.

Carlaw Ave.

Matty Eckler Recreation Centre

performed in 2001. It's often hailed as a benchmark of Toronto's tolerance and progressive nature, but note that the church's long-time (but now retired) reverend Brent Hawkes performed the ceremony wearing a bullet-proof vest.

Follow Simpson one block east and Logan Avenue five blocks north and find, in the heart of deepest, darkest Riverdale, Canada's first social housing project: the Bain Co-op. Built between 1913 and the mid-1920s by a group of Toronto philanthropists who called themselves the Toronto Housing Authority, the Bain was influenced by the egalitarian Garden City urban-planning movement that started in England in the late nineteenth century. The idea was to have a balance between residences and green space.

The Bain has 260 apartments that range from one- to four-bedroom units, and a population of approximately four hundred, but you would never know it. The first time I stumbled upon the Bain, I was completely surrounded by it before I realized I was in something different, a place a little more planned out and denser than the rest of Riverdale. The Bain is just below a mild escarpment that runs through Riverdale and can turn an alley or quiet street into a San Franciscan slope for a block. The differences in elevation and density of houses and trees give it a *Swiss Family Robinson* feel.

Underneath a canopy of massive London plane trees with bark that looks like desert camouflage, the Bain's grassy courtyards seem too big for such a tightly built community, but they fit in with ease. They give way to footpaths that lead through a jungle of secret tiny patios. Children's toys are left out all night, porches are stuffed with bric-a-brac, and laundry hangs between buildings on those old-fashioned pulley lines. On warm summer nights, you can overhear conversations, televised baseball games, and other, less recognizable sounds of domesticity. Few places are so public and intimate at once.

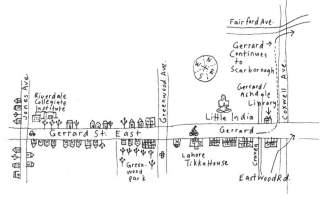

The community here seems to mirror the close-knit architecture. The Bain has had a softball team since the 1990s and holds craft shows and street festivals. And those egalitarian Garden City ideals are expressed in the affordable rents: in the early 2020s, rates ranged from under $1,099 for a one-bedroom to a stunningly low $1,810 for a four-bedroom. There are also subsidies available for co-op members who are in short-term financial difficulty, and around half the members are on RGI (rent geared to income) or other subsidies.

This is social housing with few of the woes postwar developments like Regent Park, Moss Park, and Don Mount Court suffered before complete renovations. Eric Arthur, the late Toronto architect and professor, and the author of the seminal 1964 work *Toronto: No Mean City*, would take his students on walks through the Bain. In the late 1960s, he was already saying it had much to teach about how to make low-income housing livable and built to a high standard.

In 2013, both the Bain and Spruce Court, a somewhat similar housing project in nearby Cabbagetown, celebrated their one hundredth anniversaries, events that really highlighted how, unfortunately, co-ops haven't been built much since the last affordable glory days of the 1990s. Spruce and Bain were originally designed by British-born architect Eden Smith. 'They were built for the working people,' said Paul Mackey, a twenty-year resident of Spruce Court and its resident historian, when we spoke during the anniversary year. 'There was access to the street from all the apartments, lots of cross-ventilation, a new invention called the closet, gas stoves, running water – things not available in tenements.'

'They were both established at a time when Toronto was straining under devastating income and health inequality,' said Michael Shapcott, former director of housing and innovation at the Wellesley Institute, a research and policy organization that looks at health, housing, and equality issues. 'Many of the newcomers (Jewish and Irish, primarily) flooding into the city were being segregated into slums with terrible housing conditions and, as a result, the health outcomes were atrocious.' One hundred years later, the inequality may not be as stark as it was when Toronto had vast slums without plumbing and with dirt floors, but it has become a proper crisis after simmering hotter and hotter for years, seen dramatically in the scarceness of affordable places to live for people of modest or even middle-class means.

The majority of co-ops we have today, some seventeen thousand units throughout Toronto and York Region alone, were created between 1973 and

1995 under federal and provincial funding programs. 'Canada's co-ops were recognized in the 1990s as a "global best practice" by the United Nations because there are no financial barriers to entry,' said Shapcott, noting the irony that the recognition came as we discontinued the programs. Unlike a standard apartment building, co-ops are governed collectively and offer a mix of subsidized and market rents. Not all are in the older style of the Bain or Spruce; there are many varieties across the GTA that appeal to all sensibilities. The modern Hugh Garner co-op east of Parliament Street, on the edge of Cabbagetown, feels like a 1970s Swedish dream. At the foot of Bathurst Street, the Windward, Harbour Channel, and Harbourside co-ops have a mix of apartment-building and cottage styles. Some cater to artists, like Beaver Hall on McCaul just north of Queen, and Arcadia co-op, also at Bathurst Quay. As lots were built in the 1980s and 1990s, there are some excellent postmodern specimens. Many co-ops have emergency funds for tenants who find themselves unable to make rent. Co-op living isn't for everyone – the anonymity that big cities afford decreases – but as decent housing is increasingly out of reach for a growing population in the GTA, co-ops might be a good idea in need of revival. There's hope, though: in early 2024 a massive new co-op was announced for Scarborough by Kennedy station, so a new era may yet begin.

Back out on Gerrard, Riverdale's coziness gives way to Gerrard's continued varied urban state. De Grassi Street is here, a road that competes with Yonge for the status of most famous in Canada, due to the various TV shows that were named after the fictitious Degrassi Junior High and Degrassi High schools. (The series of series actually began with *The Kids of Degrassi Street*, which was filmed using local children as actors in a park on the street a block south of Dundas, just a five-minute walk from here.) For those of us who grew up outside of Toronto, the shows based on De Grassi were a portal into what our teen lives might have been like had we lived in the city: more walking and attached houses and apartments, radical things when seen from suburban Canada.

Just around the corner, there's a storefront that used to be painted with slogans like 'Drunk drivers are lousy lovers' and 'Welcome to Metro, 156 languages spoken, including French,' a rare example of curmudgeon-graffiti. In the 1970s and early 1980s, the shop was called Handy Andy's Dry Cleaners, and the proprietor would regularly change the signs in the window to attack then prime minister Pierre Elliott Trudeau, to proclaim that abortion was murder, and to tease Quebec for its language laws. The signs continued to change long after the owner closed the store itself, until the messages were finally frozen in time. That 1990s axe continued to grind away well into the new millenium. An informal landmark like this can exist for a long time and then suddenly simply disappear, as this one did in the late 2000s, when a new owner renovated it for future retail uses. These days, it's mentioned only in passing now and then when a memory is sparked. 'Hey, wasn't this where … ?' Once something physical disappears in the city, our memory of it no longer has a place to root, and it becomes fleeting, sometimes even forgotten.

The fact that Gerrard could recently support this kind of weirdness makes it more interesting than some more celebrated, gentrified parts of the city. The street is made up of a mix of residential and commercial buildings, and the line between the two is often blurred: storefront windows look into makeshift living rooms lit by harsh fluorescent tubes, while some front porches lead into computer and electronics stores.

Beyond the Carlaw underpass lies Gerrard Square, one of Toronto's not-at-all-fancy neighbourhood malls. (It's nicknamed 'Gerrard Scare' by those unsympathetic to its presence.) The mall underwent a complete renovation in the late 2000s. Before the renovation, a fictionalized version of it was used as the community hub in a short-lived CBC soap called *Riverdale*, an unsuccessful Canadian version of *Coronation Street*. (Though it's unsung in many ways, Gerrard and its environs seem to have found their way into Canadian television mythology.) With the renovation, the square lost its traditional anchors (Sears, BiWay) and then found new ones (Staples, Home Depot), and it's now a stucco fortress with a somewhat antiseptic interior. It's much less interesting now than it would have been if it were populated by the hodgepodge of tenants that make so many past-their-prime, second- and third-tier malls interesting by allowing for informal community hubs to develop (low-rent malls don't want to kick anybody out). It's worth a wander, though, as the change in environment from Gerrard is dramatic. I've found myself in that Home Depot on more than one occasion, somewhat panicked and surrounded by burly contractors, trying to find the one item that would make some problem go away. It makes railing against big-box stores more difficult (though, as you will have seen elsewhere in this book, not impossible), because they have what people need, even if it's hard to find. This particular

Home Depot is about as urban as they get and comes with a parking garage rather than acres of parking lot. The eventual opening of the Ontario Line's Gerrard station here will bring tremendous pressure to build up bigger in this area. There is already a development plan underway at nearby Riverdale Shopping Centre on the other side of the tracks.

Gerrard continues east, becoming mainly residential for a number of blocks until Greenwood, where it becomes a retail strip again, and then India Bazaar, 'North America's Largest South Asian Mainstreet Marketplace,' according to the area BIA's marketing copy. The informal beginning of India Bazaar was dominated by the ever-expanding Lahore Tikka House. The restaurant always had a chaotic campsite look to it, but the two-storey restaurant was one of the first South Asian establishments to build its own new structure. (As of this writing, though, the restaurant was closed after a fire.) The India Bazaar strip was first established in the early 1970s, when the Eastwood Theatre started showing Bollywood films. Institutions such as theatres and places of worship establish beachheads in many ethnic strips, and the community follows. And like many strips, those communities eventually move on, a newer, more mixed population moves in, but the ethnic shopping remains. In the summer, some of the stores expand onto the narrow sidewalk, where they sell cane juice (a year's worth of sugar intake in one cup!) and roasted corn. It probably violates a number of city bylaws, but, as in Chinatown, this appropriation of the sidewalk for public-private uses is a break from the usual boring and orderly way of doing things in Toronto. Like the East Chinatown we passed through just a few blocks back, this South Asian area now competes with suburban clusters in places such as Brampton.

Before you catch the Gerrard streetcar north on Coxwell, take a walk south down a curious street called Craven. An oddity of planning, the west side of Craven is dominated by a municipally maintained long fence behind which you can see the backyards of homes on the adjacent street. On the east side, a string of homes – some tiny, some tall, some just plain weird – continues down to Queen Street. This oddity was formed when the edge of urban development kept creeping out behind houses on Ashdale, the street to the west, back when zoning and bylaws were looser or nonexistent. Like a lot of places along Gerrard, Craven Road functions differently than the rest of Toronto. Gerrard continues east after a jog up Coxwell, becoming mostly residential again, and later even industrial, and eventually ends quietly in Scarborough, a few kilometres after it loses its streetcar tracks at Main Street.

The Beach

neighbourhood jaunt

bathing suit optional

scenic views

Connecting walks: Dundas, Downtown East Side

As the 501 Queen streetcar heads east past Coxwell, it enters an interzone between neighbourhoods. Here Leslieville fades and the Beach appears. Though hard-liners will always point out where the historic or official boundaries of a neighbourhood are, people have some fuzzy latitude when it comes to identifying the neighbourhood they like. In 2000, when I was moving to Toronto, my future roommate and I drove down Queen East, thinking it would be the same as Queen West. It wasn't – the east side was quieter then, and still is, in comparison, but that's changing too. In the decades that followed, the east has started to look more western. Restaurants, galleries, and the usual shops that mark a neighbourhood with rising property values are plentiful. The end of this line – the Beach – has always been solidly middle-class.

The interzone between Coxwell and Woodbine now includes History, a live concert venue, as well as parkland that leads down to Lake Ontario, ensuring a physical divide between the neighbourhoods. Greenwood Racetrack, which was once on Woodbine, at the foot near Lake Ontario, is one of many horse tracks around Toronto that have disappeared. In the 1990s, there was a debate over what to do with this vast tract of land, as many wanted more parkland and others wanted it developed.

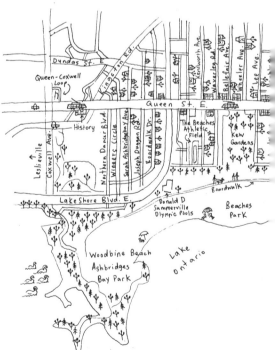

The compromise reached saw some land dedicated to a park and, on the rest, five streets of dense housing built in the New Urbanist style. While the buildings here are single-family homes, they keep their garages in back-facing laneways, and there are no parking pads or driveways out front. When the complex was built, many criticized it for being sterile or banal, but if you look at archival pictures of celebrated Toronto neighbourhoods like the Annex or Little Italy, you'll find that they looked the same when they were built: new, awkward, and treeless. As it ages, trees grow in, and people make changes to their properties, it's begun to blend in with the surrounding neighbourhoods. The mid-rise condos that were built on Queen Street itself will, with the patina of age and a more diverse mixture of tenants, look more like the retail strips of older neighbourhoods too.

In the mid-1980s, Beach residents declared they didn't want to be another Yorkville and fought the high-rise condos and chain restaurants that were trying to move into the neighbourhood. Starbucks eventually moved in, but the neighbourhood's look and feel has largely been preserved, though locals have often complained there aren't enough 'good' restaurants or shops on their Queen Street strip, but those require more people living there to support

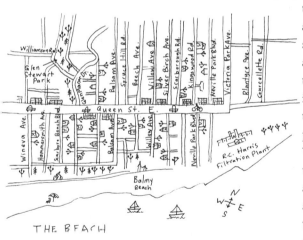

THE BEACH

them. The Beach has always struck me as a shade of what I imagine a small Ontario cottage town may have felt like in the 1920s. It might be the handful of white picket fences just east of Woodbine or the way the residential streets abruptly end at the actual beaches that line the lakeshore. Wander around for a bit and, without any thought or effort, you're suddenly on the sand listening to waves, which is just the way summer holidays are supposed to work. Even the wooden boardwalk itself blends smoothly with the grass next to it.

And though you'll hear Torontonians use both terms, the Beach residents also definitely declared that the area is, in fact, 'the Beach' and not 'the

Beaches.' In the 1980s, the City installed fourteen street signs that said 'the Beaches,' and eventually removed them due to controversy. In 2006, the Beach BIA (then called the Beaches BIA) held a poll, and 58 per cent of those who voted went for 'the Beach.' Both sides claimed their version was historically correct, but the new name is better because it turns this chunk of Toronto into an inhabitable notion: most people only visit the beach, but residents of the Beach get to live there all the time.

The centre of the Beach is Kew Gardens, where an elaborate castle-like children's play area is 'dedicated to all the smiling faces you see around here.' It's reminiscent of the 'innocent amusements' that Joseph Williams advertised in 1879, when Kew Gardens opened on Queen Victoria's sixtieth birthday. Williams had spent thirteen years turning a portion of his land into the park, which was named after his favourite place in England. According to his advertisements, people could dance and 'obtain all temperate drinks, but no spirituous liquors,' which seems about right for uptight old Toronto. Today, you can get spirits without hassle, though lattes appear to be the neighbourhood drink of choice.

The Beach was always a place of amusement for the rest of Toronto. Until 1925, the area between Leuty and McLean was home to the Scarboro Beach Amusement Park, and another park was located at the end of Queen near Victoria Park Avenue, where the R. C. Harris Water Treatment Plant currently resides. Both parks are now gone, but adventure can still be had where the Glen Stewart Ravine gently touches Queen Street. The ravine begins as a civilized dip meandering north from Queen between fine residential streets until, after a few blocks, it goes deep, surrounded by steep walls and covered in a thick forest. You can lose your sense of direction in here: you think you're moving due north, but you veer east and west at times, following the course of an ancient stream. On occasion, you can hear the sound of trickling water. My friends and I walked here in the pitch black of night once, barely able to follow the path, which was lit only by the shafts of light from houses sitting high above at the ravine's edge and by the glow of our cellphone screens. The path eventually leads to a steep staircase that deposits hikers in from vast wilderness onto Kingston Road, the Beach's upper main drag, where civilization comes in the form of flower shops and cute pubs.

Back down on Queen, the end is near. At Neville Park Boulevard – an odd dead-end street that fills up a ravine of its own – is the terminus of the 501 streetcar, a small loop where water trickles onto the tracks, an effort the

TTC makes in some locations to muffle the steel-on-steel squealing of turning streetcars. Next door is the place in Toronto most likely to have people saying, 'They don't build 'em like they used to': the R. C. Harris Filtration Plant, which overlooks Lake Ontario. Dubbed the 'Palace of Purification' by Michael Ondaatje in his novel *In the Skin of a Lion*, the plant has undergone extensive renovations, and the art deco buildings are as beautiful as they were when they were built.

Sadly, we don't get to see 'em like we used to either. Since 9/11, interior tours have been hard to come by, save for special occasions, so many of us will never know just how magnificent this public work really is. The exterior is best visited at night. Follow the service road and staircases around the buildings and down to the tiny beach. Standing here, with the waves crashing and the vastness of Lake Ontario roiling south, it's easy to feel like Jay Gatsby looking out over Long Island Sound on the grounds of his estate, but instead of a personal prewar empire at our backs, we collectively share in the Palace of Purification.

The Port Lands and Leslie Spit

 pack a lunch

 dress to impress

 scenic views

Connecting walks: Downtown East Side

Toronto can be a chameleon, looking and feeling dramatically different depending where your feet are planted. It's why this town, like Los Angeles, can play so many other places in films. The lack of a distinct look – a problem for some – frees up the city to be many things, even fantasylands. Toronto seems like a page out of a graphic novel when viewed from the Port Lands: a stylized city where the cluster of downtown skyscrapers is immediately adjacent to a wide-open landscape of freeway on-ramps, swampy scrubland, and industrial wasteland. Think Gotham City, where the darkness at the edge of town is not so far away from the bright lights of the city centre. With the addition of glass-point towers at the Gooderham & Worts Distillery on the north side of the Gardiner, this view has become even sharper.

The Port Lands is one place to really see how untrustworthy Toronto's landscape is. Not that it's dishonest, but rather that it's hard to tell if the ground itself is natural or human-made. Where the city meets the lake is a great place to see this: the shoreline has been altered by humans along much of its length, especially in the Port Lands. The Don River itself originally meandered down its valley like a minor Mississippi and emptied gently into the marshy delta of Ashbridges Bay, where silt was deposited and there was a gentle and wildlife-filled transition from river to lake. Beginning around 1912, the bay was gradually filled in with material excavated from the foundations of new buildings that were going up in the rest of the city. Natural curves became right angles and the zone between land and lake became formal and abrupt. The Don River was forced to make a hard right turn into Keating Channel after passing under Lake Shore Boulevard and unceremoniously into Toronto's harbour in a post-industrial landscape.

If this is the Port Lands of your memory – and it absolutely is for many, as it was like this for decades – seeing it today is to feel as if you're transported to another dimension. To the south of what was Keating Channel is an absolutely massive earthworks project, one of the biggest of its kind in the world, that has naturalized the mouth of the Don. See it to appreciate the scale of it all: 1.4-million cubic metres of soil was moved and remediated (cleaned up), creating a new 1.5-kilometre river valley for the Don. Redeveloping the Port Lands has been thirty years in the making, eventually led by Waterfront Toronto, the agency overseeing all this, but not without grassroots activist and advocacy groups working years ago to plant the seeds.

It puts a lie to the familiar phrase 'Nothing is happening on the waterfront.' Things take time when they're done right. The new arched pedestrian and transit bridges, floated here on barges from Halifax, with the 'mainland' skyline in the background, will certainly become one of the most photographed scenes in Toronto. Waterfront Toronto worked with the Toronto and Region Conservation Authority on the renaturalization here, and while this will be a beautiful thing, it's ultimately a flood protection project too, recreating the role Ashbridges Marsh once played. Plans for the Port Lands include vast, mixed-use neighbourhoods with thousands of residential units in this area. The conservation authority's work makes all that development here possible and helps prevent nightmare scenarios in the future.

The project will take years to complete, so there's still ample industrial landscape to be found. Beyond the Don Roadway and along Commissioners Street, there are high-voltage towers and, adjacent to them, the giant Pinewood film studios sitting amid other industrial buildings. Things here are airport-scaled, and the size and space tell a silent story of unrealized industrial potential. On late-evening walks here, we've come across film sets that use the roadway as a kind of drag strip where *Mad Max*–style chases play out. It's a surprise this isn't a popular spot for illicit drag races and street racing – the suburban arterials seem to have cornered the market on that kind of activity. A little further east, Commissioners passes the giant turning basin for the port. This unsung body of water is massive and affords back-door views of the mothballed Hearn Generating Station and the newer Portlands Energy Centre, which opened after its builders won a battle with nearby residents opposed to its construction. It's easy to feel sympathy for the residents – nobody wants to live near a power plant – but herein lies the rub of places like Toronto's Port: Should it continue to fulfill our industrial needs or should it completely clean up and become part of the shiny new post-industrial city?

By the drawbridge, alongside Cherry Street and in the turning basin, lake freighters are often docked at the piers here. It's always a surprise to find a working ship here because, though this is Toronto's port, we seldom think of ourselves as a port city, partly because we never really succeeded at being one.

After the St. Lawrence Seaway opened in the 1950s, the Toronto Harbour Commission (precusor to PortsToronto) developed this area to welcome an expected shipping boom. Most of the big ocean-going container ships continued to stop in Halifax and Montreal, however, and, like in many ports in Europe and North America, much of the work here had dried up by the 1970s and 1980s. Other grand plans, including an Olympic bid, came and went.

The Lafarge Canada building and its associated cement-ingredient silos still churn, for now, as does Rebel Nightclub next door and an industrial-sized adult amusement park whose main draws are booze, golf, and beach volleyball. The long driveway to the attractions runs alongside a double-decked driving range that has doubled as a drive-in theatre. Along the fence, there are plastic PVC tubes that suck used golf balls into a central automated machine that makes a musical sound as the balls bounce against the walls of the hollow pipes.

Unlike some of the other older industrial buildings around the port, many of which are solidly built and sometimes have a streamlined modern or art deco flair, these buildings feel temporary, as if they're just keeping the ground warm until something permanent is built in their place. However, when you are standing under the massive cement counterbalances that hang off the drawbridge over the turning-basin channel, it all feels quite real and solid, and you may wonder about your own mortality, and about how such weight could simply hang there in mid-air for so many decades.

Walk south of the bridge, and Cherry Beach comes into view. It's a good view too. With the white beach house at the end of the road, followed by the lake, and the thin and rocky shore of the Leslie Street Spit in the background, it feels very much like you're approaching a Muskoka lodge. For a brief time, the ferry to Rochester, New York, docked nearby, giving this 'end of Toronto' place a bit of international verve, though the now-closed shed-like ferry terminal just looks shed-like, unromantic, and, like the golf and nightclub buildings, quick and temporary. The facilities at Cherry Beach were greatly improved by the city in the 2000s, but there's still much wild territory to explore to the east and west of the beach house. To the west, paths lead through a thicket of trees growing out of the sandy soil – part of the large off-leash dog park here – to the Eastern Gap, where Ward's Island was once attached to the mainland until an 1858 storm broke the passage open. For a time, a group called Promise held weekly Sunday-afternoon dance parties here, but they've since moved to the eastern side of Cherry Beach after coming to something of a truce with the police, who would routinely unplug the generators and shut the party down.

After dark, cars pull in and out of this parking lot late into the night. Few people get out, and the windows steam. Today's secret sex is benign compared to Cherry Beach's past reputation – one that's less *Happy Days* and more *Sopranos*. In the early 1980s, Toronto band Pukka Orchestra wrote 'Cherry Beach Express,' a song that will likely never play at the Policeman's Ball, with lyrics that described riding the Express as being handcuffed to a chair in 52 Division, having a broken face and ribs, and being forced to confess under this kind of duress.

Unwin Avenue leads east parallel to the shore, straight toward the abandoned smokestack of the old Hearn Generating Station – opened in 1951 but shut down in 1983 – which dominates the horizon. It's an impressive piece of industrial heritage and architecture, one that has lured many clandestine urban explorers (one of whom died when he fell through a hole in the floor), and, less tragically, art festivals like Luminato one year, as well as many proposals for its future. Buildings like this are almost 'too big to tear down' – but what to do with them? Some have suggested it should get the Tate Modern treatment and become a second site for the Art Gallery of Ontario, but that kind of money is hard to come by in Canada. For now, it's an impressive backdrop for the still-rough Port Lands.

The staged car collision scene in David Cronenberg's *Crash* was filmed along Unwin (look for the recognizable remnant railway tracks adjacent to the road). A number of small, long-established sailing clubs, like Water Rat, line the shore. These clubs are a cheaper version of the Royal Canadian Yacht Club, providing access to the lake for people who can't afford to moor or tow a boat but want to get out on the water in their kayak or tiny catamaran.

The Day-Glo artificial turf of the new soccer fields that are also along Unwin replaced a yard of massive, rusting oil drums. Friends and I explored here once, squeezing our bodies through narrow passages and into huge metal rooms where our voices reverberated. I watched from the ground as the braver among us climbed the rickety staircase that snaked around the side of the largest drum to what I was told was a magnificent view of the skyline. Rusty and full of broken glass, it was the kind of ruin rare in Toronto, a city that, though it's almost in the Midwest, and though it suffered its share of industrial exodus after the Free Trade Agreement was signed in the late 1980s, tends not to let its abandoned areas stay abandoned for too long.

As Unwin passes the Hearn plant and crosses a small bridge, the industrial wilds begin to give way to natural ones. A road to the right passes through a prairie-like grassland to the Outer Harbour Marina, home to larger crafts than places like Water Rat can welcome. The marina sits at the head of the Leslie Street Spit, a wild piece of artificial land that sticks out of the eastern Port Lands five kilometres into Lake Ontario. There is a small trail that leads off the marina road to the Spit Road (really an extension of Leslie Street), but the main entrance to the Spit can be found further down Unwin, where it meets the official end of Leslie Street proper. Until recently, the park was closed on weekdays, as it was being continually expanded by trucks full of debris rumbling up the Spit Road. The road seems like a country highway, complete with yellow line down the middle. Today the entrance has been improved with a fabulous new pavilion that includes washrooms designed by architect Megan Torza of the firm DTAH.

I've been out on the Spit in a variety of circumstances. I often come alone, on a bike ride, as there are no stop signs or traffic lights to interrupt my momentum. It's remote yet urban enough for some strange sights, like the fire I saw burning out of control in a pile of rubble one evening that looked like movie-set fires from *Full Metal Jacket*, or the man I saw once who squatted suddenly in the middle of the road, pulled down his pants to take a crap, and then quickly hiked up his pants and walked away, waving at unseen spectres in the air.

Whenever I think I know the Leslie Street Spit, it reveals another part of itself to me. One reason for that is it's still growing and changing, as it receives the refuse of Toronto's razed buildings, sidewalks, and concrete utility poles. While most sections are 'done,' there are still a few raw edges, growing like the molten coastline of Iceland or Hawaii, inching out into the lake. One season, the old, tile-covered concrete TTC waste bins that were replaced by terrorism-proof, see-through bags, ended up in a pile on the Spit, though they seem to have either been buried by more refuse or spirited away by muscle-bound collectors of civic memorabilia.

I've mostly seen the Spit – or Tommy Thompson Park, as it's officially known – by bicycle, which is a very particular way to experience it. At around five kilometres from gate to tip, it's a daunting walk, so a speedier bike ride is the usual choice, though I salute all those who ride the bikeshare tanks out this far. The tip was always the destination, the reward, while the parts in between seemed boring in comparison. This is a false perception, but a consequence of having a tip to get to. The problem with cycling is it's too fast, and the details blur by. During the first pandemic summer, the Spit became a refuge. The first time cycling out, in the first weeks of a slightly loosened lockdown, when the relative safety of outdoor activity was becoming apparent, the ride was a bit fraught. Closer to the mainland, the path seemed too crowded with everyone passing too close, but those five kilometres do ultimately afford room to spread out. Things also chilled out as weeks passed.

One warm mid-June day during a particularly socially distanced period, we cycled to Cherry Beach with the intention of swimming, but it was too crowded, so we continued on and out to the Spit. Standing at the tip, I noticed somebody swimming. It had never occurred to me to swim off it, despite the tip being named Vicki Keith Point, as it's where at least one of her marathon swims across Lake Ontario ended. Since we were outfitted with bathing suits, we waded in where a beach had formed in recent years. It's rocky, jagged, and there is some rebar to watch for, but it was some of the best water I've ever swum in off Toronto. Clean, sometimes cold, sometimes warm (as is Lake Ontario's mercurial way), it reminded me of rocky Mediterranean swims in Malta, in particular getting out of the water and not having to deal with sandy feet. More friends came on subsequent trips, and we would swim a few hundred metres up and down the shoreline, looking over toward the impossible Toronto skyline. It was, as pandemic summers go, heaven.

More beaches have formed down the outer, southeast-facing shore, as waves eat away at the once harsher, more abrupt, shoreline. It's clear that, with some work, the Spit could become a swimming destination, though for now it's definitely 'wild swimming,' as beaches are forming naturally amid the unnatural materials. They're reminiscent, in reverse, of the beaches that were part of Ontario Place's original design. It's ironic, though, as one reason the beach at Hanlan's Point on Toronto Island has diminished so much in recent years is because the Spit blocks the replenishing sands that once came from the Scarborough Bluffs.

One bright Sunday in winter, I skied to the tip. Slower than cycling, faster than walking, it's a good pace. The roadway was packed flat with snow, so it was like a groomed trail. For the first kilometre or so, I passed other skiers and hikers, but as I got further out I had it to myself, the upside of double digits below zero. Skirting the rugged outer coastline – rebar and concrete chunks being the definitive kind of rugged, perhaps – I noticed that the spray from the crashing waves coats everything in a thick sarcophagus of ice, making the most fantastic sculptures that also catch the light. Another night I went out with a group on an evening ski. No need for lamps in the winter, as the ambient glow of the city, reflected and amplified by the snow, is like a bright twilight. In the super-cold, the city makes a humming sound in the distance – perhaps from cars or rooftop HVAC units singing in unison – but it's as if it's vibrating there across the harbour, trying to keep warm.

Cormorant

Walking the Spit has afforded even more discovery, as the smaller, side paths become the routes taken, always another one to discover and follow. Some non-official trails are lined with bricks, a kind of DIY landscape design by Spit visitors, along with the well-photographed rebar and brick sculptures. I've now made it by foot to the tip, but the diversions from the main road are numerous, and the less-explored coves and rubble beaches each have their own character, depending on the type of refuse dumped there. Further out, on the newer sections, there's more chunks of granite countertops, as those became in fashion, and in other places there's more midcentury tile work. Refuse can tell a story, of course.

Slow walks have also revealed the thoughtfulness that has gone into the sanctioned landscape design of the Spit. Though the naturalization has been, well, natural, it's also been guided by the Toronto and Region Conservation Authority and advocated for by groups of enthusiasts, like the Friends of the Spit. Reading _Accidental Wilderness: The Origins and Ecology of Toronto's Tommy Thompson Park_ by landscape architect Walter H. Kehm, with photographs by Robert Burley, added an additional layer to my understanding of this aspect of the guided nature here: earthworks that can't be fully appreciated at first glance and ponds that do more than just provide a home for birds. Oh, but there are birds, especially cormorants.

About halfway out along the Spit is the cormorant habitat. You can hear and smell them from the main road long before you can see them. During nesting season, this area is off-limits but it can be walked at other times, just heed the signage. It's a Hitchcockian sound, thousands of cawing buzzards, but with added smell-o-vision: the fishy stink is worthy of the Digby, Nova Scotia, scallop fleet, though here the expanse of the Bay of Fundy is replaced by a Toronto skyline obscured by the silhouettes of circling birds, vegetation that has become stunted and trees leafless, victims of a fowl strain of herbicide that endlessly drops from their bird bums. It's as if Edward Gorey were a landscape designer.

One summer evening, I was with a group that kayaked over from Cherry Beach. As we entered the lagoon, surrounded by the denuded trees, the birds weren't cawing, but there was still lots to hear. As our kayaks silently slid through the water, there was the sound of thousands of birds eating, a constant crunching of endless beaks along with the odd sound of rain, but it was not rain, it was the birds pooping away. No soundscape in Toronto has ever come close to matching how incredible this was, but I only need to hear it once.

This wilderness was unplanned, but it was man-made, as were the rest of the Port Lands. The Toronto Harbour Commission began building the Spit in the 1950s to serve as a breakwater for expanded port activity. Though the steamers didn't come, Toronto kept growing, and all the rubble and waste of our city-building was dumped here. As it grew, the Spit was colonized by cottonwood and poplar forests that include some four hundred plant species. Those cormorants are joined by gulls and some three hundred other species of birds, migratory and resident.

In 1976, a plan was floated to build a $26-million aquatic park with marinas, an amphitheatre, and even a waterskiing centre. Soon after, the Friends of the Spit was formed, and they lobbied the City to keep the space public and turn it into the nature preserve it has become.

It was named Tommy Thompson Park, after the former Toronto Parks and Recreation commissioner responsible for those great 'Please walk on the grass' signs. It's a jagged place littered with twisted metal and chunks of Toronto's buildings, around which wander coyotes, foxes, and snakes – the kind of place you could hurt yourself, the kind adventurous kids (and adults) find so magical. It's amazing it's all just across the water from downtown Toronto.

Back out at the entrance to the Spit, it's a short walk up Leslie to Lake Shore Boulevard, past a collection of community gardens. To the east, another stack rises on the horizon, this one part of the Ashbridges Bay Wastewater Treatment Plant, perhaps as impressive an industrial operation as the Hearn plant but, being a sewage plant, somewhere further down the list of infrastructure we like to celebrate. In contrast, the new streetcar barns nearby, with landscaped edges and windows in the sound barrier wall that allow for peeks at operations, is the kind of nerdy infrastructure that we prefer to think about, and reminds us we're in a proper big city. The connection to the city along Leslie is as strange as the Cherry Street one, but instead of a comic-book landscape looking over to the skyline and a recreated river mouth, it feels like you've been transported to a suburban arterial on the periphery of the city, or somewhere along the 401 or QEW. Twinned Tim Hortons and Wendy's restaurants sit across from a Starbucks with a drive-through, and both structures are located in big supermarket parking lots across from a Canadian Tire. This landscape comes into view slowly, like a mirage, causing some cognitive dissonance: we're getting closer to the city, but it looks like we're further away from it than ever.

Perhaps after so much post-industrial and natural wilderness, the re-entrance to the city needs to be slow, tempered by these big-box comfort stations, just as divers require decompression after scuba diving to avoid getting the bends. Pass through this interzone territory and soon, just a few more blocks up Leslie, you'll find Queen Street and the cozy streetcar city we expect to find in old Toronto.

Acknowledgements

Early and substantially shorter versions and portions of the essays in this book have appeared in a few places. Many originally started out in EYE WEEKLY, Toronto's late, great alt-weekly (RIP), first as general city pieces, then as a column (which was first called 'Stroll' and, later, 'Psychogeography'). Special thanks to Edward Keenan for editing those two columns, as well as the first edition of this book. Parts of this book also appeared in the *Toronto Star*, first in the 'Insight' section (previously called 'Ideas'). That section's editor at the time, Alfred Holden, was tireless in his pursuit of ideas and novel angles, and often a brief email exchange or conversation about something random would become the basis for a new article. His own Toronto writing in *Taddle Creek* magazine was an early inspiration as well, and email exchanges with him still generate writing ideas.

Since 2012 I've been writing a weekly column in the *Star*, which has allowed me the time to explore more of Toronto and has contributed a great deal to this updated and expanded edition. My many editors over the years at the *Star* have been generous and helpful; the paper is a humane place that still requires opinion columns to be fact-based. My colleagues at *Spacing* magazine have been the finest people I could have hoped to work with over the twenty years since we launched it, and some of those pieces, particularly my long-running 'Toronto Flâneur' column, have made their way into this book as well. Other publications, like *The Local*, led by editor Nick Hune Brown, provided the resources to explore Toronto even deeper.

Thanks to the *Toronto Star* and its image archive, and to that paper's past and present staff photographers for the use of some of the photos that appear in these pages. The complete list of photographers appears on page 324, and I extend personal gratitude to each one.

Though I fell in love with Toronto long before I moved here, the people I've met here – the human infrastructure of my city – have made life in Toronto exceed all expectations. This book is a collaborative effort, and the brains of many folks around the city have been picked over the past quarter century, as various people contributed thoughts and direction to this long exploration of Toronto, or simply came along for the walk.

At Coach House Books, Alana Wilcox, Crystal Sikma, James Lindsay, Stuart Ross, Phil Bardach, Sasha Tate-Howarth, and Lindsay Yates have made this new edition possible, with Crystal bearing the enormous burden of editing hundreds of updates and additions, big and small, keeping the details straight, and being gently encouraging while doing so. The original edition was the work of Alana Wilcox, Christina Palassio, Evan Munday, Kira Dreimanis, and Stan Bevington.

Endless thanks to Marlena Zuber, for coming on that second walk long ago and thinking it would be a good idea to make psychogeographic paintings and maps, many of which are scattered throughout this book. Her maps tell stories too, and she enthusiastically updated them to reflect a changed Toronto, no small effort on her part.

It's good to walk alone sometimes, but lots of friends came on walks that contributed to this book. Sebastian, a.k.a. 'The Young Citizen,' was a four-footed furry flâneur companion who led me around the city with a psycho-geographic method of his own, taking me to places I might not have sniffed out myself. His contribution to this book can't be overlooked. Early on, Anna Bowness and Jessica Duffin Wolfe were very helpful in figuring out how a contemporary flâneur identity might work in literary form. My agent, Samantha Haywood, has been wonderful, smart, and patient. Elizabeth Bowie produces writing ideas regularly. 'The Thread' members have bounced ideas around and absorbed writing laments: Todd Irvine, Dale Duncan, Simon Reader, Lisan Jutras, Ivor Tossell, and Kelli Korducki. My parents gave in long ago to this strange career of mine and thankfully have been supportive.

Robert Ruggiero has been a mostly willing, long-suffering spousal companion on, and sometimes-instigator of, walks that contributed to this new edition. With its publication, our hundreds of kilometres of seemingly endless pandemic walks can now be considered productive time and critical research outings, but even without writing a book, walking is always an ideal use of time. Now there's young Augustine, who may or may not want to go on excessive city walks, but we'll give it a shot.

Credits

The passage on page 8 is taken from Walter Benjamin's *The Arcades Project* (Cambridge: Harvard University Press, 1999). Page 11 quotes Rebecca Solnit's *Wanderlust: A History of Walking* (New York: Penguin, 2000). Page 15 includes quotes from Pier Giorgio Di Cicco's *Municipal Mind: Manifestos for the Creative City* (Mansfield Press, 2007). An excerpt from Russell Smith's novel *How Insensitive* (Porcupine's Quill, 1994) appears on page 38. A passage from the Amy Lavender Harris book *Imagining Toronto* (Mansfield Press, 2010) appears on page 66. John Bentley Mays's *Emerald City: Toronto Visited* is quoted on page 78 (Toronto: Viking, 1994). Elamin Abdelmahmoud's description of Highway 401 from his book *Son of Elsewhere* (Penguin Random House Canada, 2022) appears on pages 150–151. The description of the Ontario Legislature on page 86 is from Charles Dickens's *American Notes for General Circulation* (London: Chapman & Hall, 1842). A passage from Alfred Holden's essay 'Dupont at Zenith' appears on page 156 (Toronto: *Taddle Creek Magazine*, 1998). Page 157 quotes Dionne Brand's novel *Love Enough* (Penguin Random House Canada, 2014). A passage from Walter Benjamin's *Moscow Diary* (Cambridge: Harvard University Press, 1986) is used on page 163. An excerpt from an essay by Veronica Madonna published in *Concrete Toronto: A Guidebook to Concrete Architecture from the Fifties to the Seventies* (Toronto: Coach House Books, 2007) appears on page 197. Lines from Robert Frost's 'Stopping by Woods on a Snowy Evening,' originally published in New Hampshire, appear on page 218 (New York: Henry Holt and Co., 1923). An excerpt from a Kevin Irie poem, from his book *Viewing Tom Thomson, A Minority Report* (Frontenac House, 2012) appears on page 296. Michael Ondaatje's description of the Prince Edward Viaduct from *In the Skin of a Lion* (Toronto: McClelland and Stewart, 1987) appears on page 264, and his description of the R. C. Harris Water Treatment Plant from the same book is on page 309. Jane Pitfield's description of Thorncliffe Park in her book *Leaside* (Toronto: Dundurn, 2008) is quoted on page 252. Hugh Garner's description of Cabbagetown, from his novel *Cabbagetown* (Whitby: Ryerson Press, 1968) appears on page 289.

Photos and Illustrations

Coach House Books appreciates the generous support of the *Toronto Star* in providing archival photos.

All maps and illustrations by **Marlena Zuber**. Marlena has been an illustrator for over twenty years and has received various awards in Canada and the U.S. for her illustrations. In addition to making maps and illustrating books and magazines, she has fifteen years of experience in Toronto and eight years experience in North Hastings County as an arts program coordinator, facilitator, educator, and creative community builder with adults and youth from various backgrounds and abilities. Marlena lives in the beautiful town of Maynooth.

Index

Shawn Micallef is the author of *Frontier City: Toronto on the Verge of Greatness,*
Full Frontal TO: Exploring Toronto's Vernacular Architecture, and *The Trouble With*
Brunch: Work, Class, and the Pursuit of Leisure. He's a weekly columnist at the
Toronto Star, instructor at University of Toronto, a senior fellow at Massey
College, and a co-founder and senior editor of the magazine *Spacing.*

Typeset in Albertina and Neautraface 2.

Printed at the Coach House on bpNichol Lane in Toronto, Ontario, on Rolland paper, which was manufactured in Saint-Jérôme, Quebec. This book was printed with vegetable-based ink on a 1973 Heidelberg KORD offset litho press. Its pages were folded on a Baumfolder, gathered by hand, bound on a Sulby Auto-Minabinda, and trimmed on a Polar single-knife cutter.

Coach House is located in Toronto, which is on the traditional territory of many nations, including the Mississaugas of the Credit, the Anishnabeg, the Chippewa, the Haudenosaunee, and the Wendat peoples, and is now home to many diverse First Nations, Inuit, and Métis peoples. We acknowledge that Toronto is covered by Treaty 13 with the Mississaugas of the Credit. We are grateful to live and work on this land.

First edition edited by Edward Keenan
New edition edited by Crystal Sikma
Cover by David Gee, with maps by Marlena Zuber
Interior design by Crystal Sikma, with maps and illustrations by Marlena Zuber
Author photo by Dewey Chang

Coach House Books
80 bpNichol Lane
Toronto ON M5S 3J4
Canada

mail@chbooks.com
www.chbooks.com